Lecture Notes in Computer S

T0230545

Commenced Publication in 1973
Founding and Former Series Editors:
Gerhard Goos, Juris Hartmanis, and Jan van Leeuwen

Editorial Board

Martin Steffen   Gianluigi Zavattaro (Eds.)

Formal Methods for Open Object-Based Distributed Systems

7th IFIP WG 6.1 International Conference, FMOODS 2005
Athens, Greece, June 15-17, 2005
Proceedings

 Springer

Volume Editors

Martin Steffen
Christian-Albrechts-Universität zu Kiel
Institut für Informatik und Praktische Mathematik
Hermann-Rodewald-Str. 3, 24118 Kiel, Germany
E-mail: ms@informatik.uni-kiel.de

Gianluigi Zavattaro
Dipartimento di Scienze dell'Informazione
Università degli Studi di Bologna
Mura A. Zamboni, 7, 40127 Bologna, Italy
E-mail: zavattar@cs.unibo.it

Library of Congress Control Number: 2005926702

CR Subject Classification (1998): C.2.4, D.1.3, D.2, D.3, F.3, D.4

ISSN   0302-9743
ISBN-10   3-540-26181-8 Springer Berlin Heidelberg New York
ISBN-13   978-3-540-26181-0 Springer Berlin Heidelberg New York

Springer is a part of Springer Science+Business Media

springeronline.com

© IFIP International Federation for Information Processing, Hofstrasse 3, A-2361 Laxenburg, Austria 2005
Printed in Germany

Typesetting: Camera-ready by author, data conversion by Olgun Computergrafik
Printed on acid-free paper   SPIN: 11494881   06/3142   5 4 3 2 1 0

Preface

This volume contains the proceedings of FMOODS 2005, the 7th IFIP WG 6.1 International Conference on *Formal Methods for Open Object-Based Distributed Systems*. The conference was held in Athens, Greece on June 15–17, 2005. The event was the seventh meeting of this conference series, which is held roughly every year and a half, with the earlier events held respectively in Paris, Canterbury, Florence, Stanford, Twente, and Paris.

The goal of the FMOODS series of conferences is to bring together researchers whose work encompasses three important and related fields:

- formal methods;
- distributed systems;
- object-based technology.

Such a convergence is representative of recent advances in the field of distributed systems, and provides links between several scientific and technological communities, as represented by the conferences FORTE, CONCUR, and ECOOP.

The objective of FMOODS is to provide an integrated forum for the presentation of research in the above-mentioned fields, and the exchange of ideas and experiences in the topics concerned with the formal methods support for open object-based distributed systems. For the call for papers, aspects of interest included, but were not limited to: formal models; formal techniques for specification, design, or analysis; verification, testing, and validation; component-based design; formal aspects of service-oriented computing; semantics and type systems for programming, coordination, or modelling languages; behavioral typing; multiple viewpoint modelling and consistency between different models; transformations of models; integration of quality-of-service requirements into formal models; formal models for security; formal approaches to distributed component frameworks; and applications and experience, carefully described. Work on these aspects of (official and de facto) standard notation and languages for service oriented design, e.g. web services orchestration languages, was explicitly welcome.

In total 49 abstracts and 42 papers were submitted to this year's conference, covering the full range of topics listed above. Out of the submissions, 19 research papers were selected by the Program Committee for presentation. We would like to express our deepest appreciation to the authors of all submitted papers and to the Program Committee members and external reviewers who did an outstanding job in selecting the best papers for presentation.

For the second time, the FMOODS conference was held as a joint event, this time in federation with the 5th IFIP WG 6.1 International Conference on *Distributed Applications and Interoperable Systems* (DAIS 2005). The co-location of the FMOODS and DAIS conferences provided an excellent opportunity to the participants for a wide and comprehensive exchange of ideas within the domain of distributed systems and applications. Both FMOODS and DAIS address this domain, the former with its emphasis on formal approaches the latter on practical solutions. Their combination in a single event ensured that both theoretical foundations and practical issues were presented and discussed.

Special thanks to Lazaros Merakos, for acting as the General Chair of the joint conferences DAIS and FMOODS 2005; his support made this event happen. We would also like to thank Gordon Blair, Rocco de Nicola, and Andreas Reuter for agreeing to present invited talks at the conference.

We thank Costas Polychronopoulos, for acting as Local Arrangements Chair, and John Derrick for his work as Publicity Chair. We would also like to thank the FMOODS Steering Committee (John Derrick, Roberto Gorrieri, Guy Leduc, and Elie Najm) for their advice. Thanks also to Roberto Lucchi for his valuable help in managing the submission server.

June 2005   Martin Steffen
                                                      Gianluigi Zavattaro

Organization

General Chair	Lazaros Merakos (University of Athens, Greece)
Program Chairs	Martin Steffen (University of Kiel, Germany)
	Gianluigi Zavattaro (University of Bologna, Italy)
Local Arrangements	Costas Polychronopoulos
	(University of Athens, Greece)
Publicity Chair	John Derrick (University of Kent, UK)

Steering Committee

John Derrick
Roberto Gorrieri
Guy Leduc
Elie Najm

Program Committee

Wil van der Aalst (Netherlands)
Lynne Blair (UK)
Frank van Breugel (Canada)
Michele Bugliesi (Italy)
John Derrick (UK)
Sophia Drossopoulou (UK)
Alessandro Fantechi (Italy)
Kokichi Futatsugi (Japan)
Andy Gordon (UK)
Roberto Gorrieri (Italy)
Jan Jürjens (Germany)
Cosimo Laneve (Italy)
Luigi Logrippo (Canada)
Elie Najm (France)
Uwe Nestmann (Switzerland)
Ernesto Pimentel (Spain)
Erik Poll (Netherlands)
Andreas Prinz (Norway)
Arend Rensink (Netherlands)
Bernhard Rumpe (Germany)
Martin Steffen (Germany)
Perdita Stevens (UK)
Carolyn Talcott (USA)
Vasco Thudichum Vasconcelos (Portugal)
Nalini Venkatasubramanian (USA)
Heike Wehrheim (Germany)
Gianluigi Zavattaro (Italy)

Referees

Kamel Adi
Andreas Bauer
Johannes Borgström
Alex Buckley
Luis Caires
Ugo Dal Lago
Ferruccio Damiani
Grit Denker
Susan Eisenbach
Harald Fecher
Rachele Fuzzati
Borislav Gajanovic
Vladimir Gapeyev
Simon Gay
Sebastian Gutierrez-Nolasco
William Heaven
Marcel Kyas

Roberto Lucchi
Francisco Martins
Franco Mazzanti
Masaki Nakamura
Kazuhiro Ogata
Martijn Oostdijk
Liviu Pene
G. Michele Pinna
Andreas Schäfer
Takahiro Seino
Peter Sewell
Matthew Smith
Christoph Sprenger
Emilio Tuosto
Björn Victor
Martijn Warnier
Lucian Wischik

Table of Contents

Invited Talk

Pattern Matching over a Dynamic Network of Tuple Spaces 1
Rocco De Nicola, Daniele Gorla, and Rosario Pugliese

Models and Calculi

A Dynamic Class Construct for Asynchronous Concurrent Objects 15
Einar Broch Johnsen, Olaf Owe, and Isabelle Simplot-Ryl

An Abstract Machine for the Kell Calculus........................... 31
Philippe Bidinger, Alan Schmitt, and Jean-Bernard Stefani

XPi: A Typed Process Calculus for XML Messaging 47
Lucia Acciai and Michele Boreale

UML

Checking the Validity of Scenarios in UML Models 67
Holger Rasch and Heike Wehrheim

An Extended Type System
for OCL Supporting Templates and Transformations 83
Marcel Kyas

A Semantics for UML-RT Active Classes via Mapping into Circus........ 99
Rodrigo Ramos, Augusto Sampaio, and Alexandre Mota

Security

Towards an Integrated Formal Analysis for Security and Trust 115
Fabio Martinelli

A Formal Security Analysis of an OSA/Parlay Authentication Interface ... 131
*Ricardo Corin, Gaetano Di Caprio, Sandro Etalle,
Stefania Gnesi, Gabriele Lenzini, and Corrado Moiso*

Composition and Verification

Tracing Integration Analysis in Component-Based Formal Specifications .. 147
*Martín López-Nores, José J. Pazos-Arias, Jorge García-Duque,
Belén Barragáns-Martínez, Rebeca P. Díaz-Redondo,
Ana Fernández-Vilas, Alberto Gil-Solla, and Manuel Ramos-Cabrer*

CompAr: Ensuring Safe Around Advice Composition 163
    Renaud Pawlak, Laurence Duchien, and Lionel Seinturier

Guaranteeing Resource Bounds for Component Software 179
    Hoang Truong

Analysis of Java Programs

Specification and Verification of Encapsulation in Java Programs 195
    Andreas Roth

Detecting Errors in Multithreaded Programs
by Generalized Predictive Analysis of Executions 211
    Koushik Sen, Grigore Roşu, and Gul Agha

Web Services

Transforming Information in RDF to Rewriting Logic 227
    Alberto Verdejo, Narciso Martí-Oliet, Tomás Robles,
    Joaquín Salvachúa, Luis Llana, and Margarita Bradley

Modeling- and Analysis Techniques
for Web Services and Business Processes 243
    Wolfgang Reisig

A Distributed Implementation of Mobile Nets as Mobile Agents 259
    Nadia Busi and Luca Padovani

Specification and Verification

On Correctness of Dynamic Protocol Update 275
    Paweł T. Wojciechowski and Olivier Rütti

Property-Driven Development of a Coordination Model
for Distributed Simulations 290
    Rolf Hennicker and Matthias Ludwig

A Timing Analysis of AODV 306
    Sibusisiwe Chiyangwa and Marta Kwiatkowska

Author Index 323

Pattern Matching over a Dynamic Network
of Tuple Spaces

Rocco De Nicola[1], Daniele Gorla[2,*], and Rosario Pugliese[1]

[1] Dipartimento di Sistemi e Informatica, Università di Firenze
{denicola,pugliese}@dsi.unifi.it
[2] Dipartimento di Informatica, Università di Roma "La Sapienza"
gorla@di.uniroma1.it

Abstract. In this paper, we present recent work carried on μKLAIM, a core calculus that retains most of the features of KLAIM: explicit process distribution, remote operations, process mobility and asynchronous communication via distributed tuple spaces. Communication in μKLAIM is based on a simple form of pattern matching that enables withdrawal from shared data spaces of matching tuples and binds the matched variables within the continuation process. Pattern matching is orthogonal to the underlying computational paradigm of μKLAIM, but affects its expressive power. After presenting the basic pattern matching mechanism, inherited from KLAIM, we discuss a number of variants that are easy to implement and test, by means of simple examples, the expressive power of the resulting variants of the language.

1 Introduction

In the last decade, programming computational infrastructures available globally for offering uniform services has become one of the main issues in Computer Science. The challenges come from the necessity of dealing at once with issues like communication, co-operation, mobility, resource usage, security, privacy, failures, etc. in a setting where demands and guarantees can be very different for the many different components. KLAIM (*Kernel Language for Agents Interaction and Mobility*, [5]) is a tentative response to the call for innovative theories, computational paradigms, linguistic mechanisms and implementation techniques for the design, realization, deployment and management of global computational environments and their application.

KLAIM is an experimental language specifically designed to program distributed systems made up of several mobile components interacting through multiple distributed tuple spaces. Its communication model builds over, and extends, LINDA's notion of generative communication through a shared tuple space [11]. The LINDA model was originally proposed for parallel programming on isolated machines; multiple, possibly distributed, tuple spaces have been advocated later [12] to improve modularity, scalability and performance, and fit well in a global computing scenario.

---

* Most of the work presented in this paper was carried on while the second author was a PhD student at the University of Florence.

M. Steffen and G. Zavattaro (Eds.): FMOODS 2005, LNCS 3535, pp. 1–14, 2005.

Table 1. μKLAIM Syntax

NETS	COMPONENTS
$N ::= \mathbf{0} \mid l :: C \mid N_1 \parallel N_2 \mid (\nu l)N$	$C ::= \langle t \rangle \mid P \mid C_1 \mid C_2$
TUPLES	TEMPLATES
$t ::= u \mid t_1, t_2$	$T ::= u \mid !x \mid T_1, T_2$
ACTIONS	
$a ::= \mathbf{in}(T)@u \mid \mathbf{read}(T)@u \mid \mathbf{out}(t)@u \mid \mathbf{eval}(P)@u \mid \mathbf{new}(l)$	
PROCESSES	
$P ::= \mathbf{nil} \mid a.P \mid P_1 \mid P_2 \mid *P$	

KLAIM has proved to be suitable for programming a wide range of distributed applications with agents and code mobility [5, 6] and it has originated an actual programming language, X-KLAIM [1], that has been implemented by exploiting Java [2].

The main drawback of KLAIM is that it is not an actual programming language, nor a process calculus. The main aim of some our recent works (grouped together in [13]) has been the definition of a process calculus derived from KLAIM that retains all its distinctive features and expressive power, and develop over it the type theoretic and semantical foundations of the language. The resulting calculus has been called μKLAIM and, in [8], we have proved that it can reasonably encode KLAIM.

In this paper, we first describe μKLAIM (Section 2). Then, in Section 3, we present some recent enhancements of the basic formalism to deal with some low-level features, namely inter-node connections and failures. In Section 4, we argue on alternative forms of pattern matching for retrieving tuples. So far, KLAIM and its variants have used LINDA's original pattern matching, because of its simplicity. Nevertheless, other variants could be adopted without compromising language implementability, actually enhancing the overall expressive power. A novel contribution of this paper is the informal examination of this topic. Section 5 concludes the paper.

2   The Calculus μKLAIM

2.1   Syntax

The syntax of μKLAIM is reported in Table 1. A countable set $\mathcal{L}$ of *names* $l, l', \ldots, u, \ldots, x, y, \ldots$ is assumed. Names provide the abstract counterpart of the set of *communicable objects* and can be used as localities and variables: we do not distinguish between these kinds of objects. Notationally, we prefer letters $l, l', \ldots$ when we want to stress the use of a name as a locality and $x, y, \ldots$ when we want to stress the use of a name as a variable. We will use u for basic variables and localities.

Nets are finite collections of nodes where processes and tuple spaces can be allocated. A *node* is a pair $l :: C$, where locality l is the address of the node and C is the parallel component located at l. *Components* can be processes or (located) tuples. *Located tuples*, $\langle t \rangle$, are inactive components representing tuples in a tuple space (TS, for

Table 2. The Pattern Matching Function

$match(l; l) = \epsilon$	$match(T_1; t_1) = \sigma_1 \quad match(T_2; t_2) = \sigma_2$
$match(!x; l) = [l/x]$	$match(T_1, T_2; t_1, t_2) = \sigma_1 \circ \sigma_2$

short) that have been inserted either in the initial configuration or along a computation by executing an action **out**. The TS located at l results from the parallel composition of all located tuples residing at l. In $(\nu l)N$, name l is private to N; the intended effect is that, if one considers the term $N_1 \parallel (\nu l)N_2$, then locality l of N_2 cannot be referred from within N_1.

Tuples are sequences of names. *Templates* are patterns used to select tuples in a TS. They are sequences of names and formal fields; the latter ones are written $! x$ and are used to bind variables to names.

Processes are the μKLAIM active computational units. They are built up from the inert process **nil** and from five basic operations, called *actions*, by using action prefixing, parallel composition and replication. The informal semantics of process actions is as follows. Action **in**$(T)@u$ looks for a matching tuple $\langle t \rangle$ in the TS located at u; intuitively, a template matches against a tuple if both have the same number of fields and corresponding fields match, i.e. they are the same name, or one is a formal while the other one is a name. If $\langle t \rangle$ is found, it is removed from the TS, the formal fields of T are replaced in the continuation process with the corresponding names of t and the operation terminates. If no matching tuple is found, the operation is suspended until one is available. Action **read**$(T)@u$ is similar but it leaves the selected tuple in u's TS. Action **out**$(t)@u$ adds the tuple t to the TS located at u. Action **eval**$(P)@u$ sends process P for execution at u. Action **new**(l) creates a new node in the net at the reserved address l. Notice that **new** is the only action not indexed with an address because it always acts locally; all the other actions explicitly indicate the (possibly remote) locality where they will take place.

Names occurring in terms can be bound by action prefixes or by restriction. More precisely, in processes **in**$(T)@u.P$ and **read**$(T)@u.P$ the prefixes bind the names in the formal fields of T within P; in process **new**$(l).P$, the prefix binds l in P; in $(\nu l)N$, the restriction binds l in N. A name that is not bound is called *free*. The sets $bn(\cdot)$ and $fn(\cdot)$ (of bound and free names, resp., of term $\cdot$) are defined accordingly, and so is *alpha-conversion*. In the sequel, we shall assume that bound names in terms are all distinct and different from the free ones (by possibly applying alpha-conversion, this requirement can always be satisfied).

2.2 Operational Semantics

μKLAIM operational semantics is given in terms of a structural congruence and a reduction relation. The *structural congruence*, $\equiv$, identifies nets which intuitively represent the same net. It is inspired to π-calculus' structural congruence (see, e.g., [16]) and states that '$\parallel$' is a monoidal operator with **0** as identity, that **nil** is the identity for $|$', that alpha-equivalent nets do coincide, and that the order of restrictions in a net is irrelevant.

Table 3. μKLAIM Reduction Relation

(R-Out)	(R-New)
$l :: \mathbf{out}(t)@l'.P \parallel l' :: \mathbf{nil} \longmapsto l :: P \parallel l' :: \langle t \rangle$	$l :: \mathbf{new}(l').P \longmapsto (\nu l')(l :: P \parallel l' :: \mathbf{nil})$
(R-Eval)	(R-Res) $\dfrac{N \longmapsto N'}{(\nu l)N \longmapsto (\nu l)N'}$
$l :: \mathbf{eval}(P_2)@l'.P_1 \parallel l' :: \mathbf{nil} \longmapsto l :: P_1 \parallel l' :: P_2$	
(R-In) $\dfrac{match(T;t) = \sigma}{l :: \mathbf{in}(T)@l'.P \parallel l' :: \langle t \rangle \longmapsto l :: P\sigma \parallel l' :: \mathbf{nil}}$	(R-Par) $\dfrac{N_1 \longmapsto N_1'}{N_1 \parallel N_2 \longmapsto N_1' \parallel N_2}$
(R-Read) $\dfrac{match(T;t) = \sigma}{l :: \mathbf{read}(T)@l'.P \parallel l' :: \langle t \rangle \longmapsto l :: P\sigma \parallel l' :: \langle t \rangle}$	(R-Struct) $\dfrac{N \equiv N_1 \quad N_1 \longmapsto N_2 \quad N_2 \equiv N'}{N \longmapsto N'}$

Moreover, the following laws are crucial to our setting:

$$
\begin{aligned}
\text{(Clone)} &\quad l :: C_1|C_2 \equiv l :: C_1 \parallel l :: C_2 \\
\text{(Repl)} &\quad l :: *P \equiv l :: P \mid *P \\
\text{(RepNil)} &\quad l :: *\mathbf{nil} \equiv l :: \mathbf{nil} \\
\text{(Ext)} &\quad N_1 \parallel (\nu l)N_2 \equiv (\nu l)(N_1 \parallel N_2) \quad \text{if } l \notin fn(N_1)
\end{aligned}
$$

Law (Clone) turns a parallel between co-located components into a parallel between nodes (by relying on this law, commutativity and associativity of '|' follows). Law (Repl) unfolds a replicated process; however, when the replicated process is **nil**, the unfolding is useless (see rule (RepNil)). Finally, law (Ext) is the standard π-calculus' rule for scope extension; it states that the scope of a restricted name can be extended, provided that no free name is captured.

The reduction relation is given in Table 3. It relies on the *pattern matching* function $match(\_;\_)$ that verifies the compliance of a tuple w.r.t. a template and associates values to variables bound in the template. Intuitively, a tuple matches a template if they have the same number of fields, and corresponding fields match. Formally, function *match* is defined in Table 2 where we let 'ϵ' be the empty substitution and '$\circ$' denote substitutions composition. Here, a substitution σ is a mapping of names for names; $P\sigma$ denotes the (capture avoiding) application of σ to P.

The operational rules of μKLAIM can be briefly motivated as follows. Rule (R-Out) states that execution of an output sends the tuple argument of the action to the target node. However, this is possible only if the target node does exist in the net. Rule (R-Eval) is similar, but deals with process spawning. Rules (R-In) and (R-Read) require existence of a matching datum in the target node. The tuple is then used to replace the free occurrences of the variables bound by the template in the continuation of the process performing the actions. With action **in** the matched datum is consumed while with action **read** it is not. Rule (R-NEW) states that action **new**(l') creates a new node at a reserved address l'. Rules (R-PAR), (R-RES) and (R-STRUCT) are standard.

μKLAIM adopts a LINDA-like [11] communication mechanism: data are anonymous and associatively accessed via pattern matching, and communication is asynchronous. Indeed, even if there exist action prefixes for placing data to (possibly remote) nodes, no synchronization takes place between (sending and receiving) processes, because their interactions are mediated by nodes, that act as data repositories.

2.3 Observational Semantics

We now present a preorder on μKLAIM nets yielding sensible semantic theories. We follow the approach put forward in [10] and use *may testing* equivalence. Intuitively, two nets are may testing equivalent if they cannot be distinguished by any external observer taking note of the data offered by the observed net. More precisely, an *observer O* is a net containing a node whose address is a reserved locality name test. A computation reports *success* if, along its execution, a datum at node test appears; this is written $\overset{OK}{\Longrightarrow}$.

Definition 1 (May Testing Equivalence). May testing, $\sqsubseteq$, *is the least equivalence on* μKLAIM *nets such that, for every* $N \sqsubseteq M$, *it holds that* $N \parallel O \overset{OK}{\Longrightarrow}$ *if and only if* $M \parallel O \overset{OK}{\Longrightarrow}$, *for any observer O.*

The problem underneath the definition of may testing we have just presented is the universal quantification over observers. This makes it hard to prove equivalences in practice. In [13], we have developed an alternative characterisations of $\simeq$ as a trace-based equivalence and a co-inductive proof technique as a bisimulation-based equivalence. However, these definitions have been omitted from this paper: here, it suffices to have a sensible notion of equivalence to equate nets.

3 Node Connections and Failures

In this section we present two enhancements of the basic framework presented so far. Such enhancements allow us to better model some global computing phenomena.

3.1 Modelling Connections

In [7], we developed the behavioural theory of a language derived from μKLAIM by introducing explicit inter-node connections and process actions to dynamically change them. The syntax of the resulting calculus, that is called τKLAIM (*topological* KLAIM), can be obtained by adding the following productions to those in Table 1:

$$N ::= \cdots \mid \{l_1 \rightarrow l_2\} \qquad a ::= \cdots \mid \textbf{conn}(u) \mid \textbf{disc}(u)$$

A *connection* (or *link*) is a pair of node addresses $\{l_1 \rightarrow l_2\}$ stating that the nodes at addresses l_1 and l_2 are directly linked. Actions **conn**(l_2) and **disc**(l_2) aim at changing the network topology: once executed at l_1 they create/remove a link $\{l_1 \rightarrow l_2\}$ from the net.

The operational semantics of TKLAIM is obtained by modifying that of μKLAIM to take into account information on existing connections. First, the following structural rules are added

$$l :: \mathbf{nil} \equiv \{l \rightarrow l\} \qquad \{l_1 \rightarrow l_2\} \equiv \{l_1 \rightarrow l_2\} \parallel l_1 :: \mathbf{nil} \parallel l_2 :: \mathbf{nil}$$

They state that nodes are self-connected and that connections are established only between actual nodes. Second, the reduction relation of Table 3 is modified so that axioms check existence of proper connections enabling process actions. For example, rule (R-OUT) now becomes

$$l :: \mathbf{out}(t)@l'.P \parallel \{l \rightarrow l'\} \longmapsto l :: P \parallel \{l \rightarrow l'\} \parallel l' :: \langle t \rangle$$

Thus, the sending operation is enabled only if the source and the target nodes are directly connected. Analogous modifications are needed for rules (R-EVAL), (R-IN) and (R-READ). Of course, we also need two new axioms for the two new primitives

$$(\text{R-CONN}) \quad l :: \mathbf{conn}(l').P \parallel l' :: \mathbf{nil} \longmapsto l :: P \parallel \{l \rightarrow l'\}$$

$$(\text{R-DISC}) \quad l :: \mathbf{disc}(l').P \parallel \{l \rightarrow l'\} \longmapsto l :: P \parallel l' :: \mathbf{nil}$$

The behavioural theory of TKLAIM presented in Section 2.3, and modified to take connections into account, has been used in [9] to state and prove the properties of a well-known routing protocol for mobile systems, namely the *handover protocol* [15] proposed by the European Telecommunication Standards Institute (ETSI) for the GSM Public Land Mobile Network.

TKLAIM can be easily accommodated to model a finer scenario where connections must be activated by a handshaking between the nodes involved (this feature is similar to the so-called *co-capabilities* of Safe Ambients [14]). This mechanism can be implemented by introducing a new action **acpt** that, by synchronizing with an action **conn**, authorises the creation of a new connection either from a specific node or from any node. An enabling action corresponding to **disc** seems to be less reasonable, but could be handled similarly.

Action **acpt**(l) by a process located at l' means that l' is ready to activate a connection with l; thus, the operational rule for activating a connection now becomes

$$(\text{R-CONN}_1) \quad l :: \mathbf{conn}(l').P \parallel l' :: \mathbf{acpt}(l).Q \longmapsto l :: P \parallel \{l \rightarrow l'\} \parallel l' :: Q$$

Similarly, action **acpt**($!x$) by a process located at l' means that l' is ready to activate a connection with any node, whose address will be bound to x in the continuation. In this case, the operational rule for activating a connection is

$$(\text{R-CONN}_2) \quad l :: \mathbf{conn}(l').P \parallel l' :: \mathbf{acpt}(!x).Q \longmapsto l :: P \parallel \{l \rightarrow l'\} \parallel l' :: Q[^l/x]$$

3.2   Modelling Failures

In [9], we enriched TKLAIM with some simple but realistic ways to model failures in global computing systems. We model failures of nodes and of node components by adding the annihilating rule

$$(\text{R-FailN}) \qquad l :: C \longmapsto \mathbf{0}$$

to τKLAIM's operational rules that serves different purposes. Indeed, axiom (R-FAILN) models one of the following:

- *message omission*, if C represents a part of the tuple space at l (i.e. C is of the form $\langle t_1 \rangle | \ldots | \langle t_n \rangle$);
- node *fail-silent* failure, if, in the overall net, l occurs as address only in $l :: C$;
- *abnormal termination* of some processes running at l, if in the overall net there are other nodes with address l.

Modelling failures as disappearance of a resource (a datum, a process or a whole node) is a simple, but realistic, way of representing failures in a global computing scenario [3]. Indeed, while the presence of data/nodes can be ascertained, their absence cannot because there is no practical upper bound to communication delays. Thus, failures cannot be distinguished from long delays and should be modelled as totally asynchronous and undetectable events.

Clearly, our failure model can be easily adapted to deal with link failures too. To this aim, we only need to add the operational rule

$$(\text{R-FailC}) \qquad \{l_1 \rightarrow l_2\} \longmapsto \mathbf{0}$$

that models the (asynchronous and undetectable) failure of the link between nodes l_1 and l_2.

The behavioural theory of τKLAIM presented in Section 2.3 can be adapted to cope with failures. In [9], we used some resulting equational laws to prove the properties of a well-known distributed fault-tolerant protocol, namely the *k–set agreement* [4], and of a simplified routing task, namely discovering the neighbours of a given node.

4 Experimenting with Pattern Matching

The pattern matching function adopted by KLAIM and its variants is essentially that of LINDA, that was introduced by Gelernter in its seminal paper [11]. It enables withdrawal from the shared data space of matching tuples and binds the matched variables within the continuation process. This choice was driven both by historical and simplicity reasons. To be precise, KLAIM's pattern matching differs from LINDA's original one in that it does not allows tuples to contain formal fields. This feature, called *inverse structured naming*, was introduced for widening matching possibilities (tuples' formal fields can be matched by any value of the same type), rather than for communication purposes (indeed, tuples' formal fields are never replaced by corresponding values).

Several other alternatives could be considered that simplify the task of programming. In the rest of this section, we will present a number of variants and briefly discuss, by means of simple examples, the expressive power of the resulting variants of the language. We shall limit our interest to variants of the matching function of Table 2 that can be 'easily' implemented also in a distributed setting.

For each variant, we shall present a simple motivating example and show that the suggested modification simplifies programming when compared with the same task written in μKLAIM. In the examples, wherever we find it convenient, we shall use basic data values (e.g. strings) to improve readability.

4.1 Enforcing Name Difference

KLAIM's pattern matching permits selecting a tuple that contains a specific value (name), say l, in a specific field, say the i-th one: it suffices to use a template containing l in its i-th field. But one could be, instead, interested in selecting those tuples that have a precise structure but do not contain a l in their i-th field. To this aim, we extend the syntax of templates as

$$T \quad ::= \quad \cdots \quad \Big| \quad \neg u\,!x$$

and, correspondingly, we extend the pattern matching function of Table 2 by adding the axiom

$$match(\neg\, l\,!x; l') = [l'/x] \qquad \text{if } l' \neq l \tag{1}$$

Clearly, this extension of the pattern matching function does not compromise implementability.

Let μKLAIM$^{\neq}$ be μKLAIM with the two modifications just presented. Then, we can easily implement in μKLAIM$^{\neq}$ a standard if-then-else construct, as follows

$$\textbf{if } l_1 = l_2 \textbf{ then } P_1 \textbf{ else } P_2 \quad \triangleq \quad \textbf{new}(l').\textbf{out}(l_1)@l'.(\textbf{in}(l_2)@l'.P_1 \mid \textbf{in}(\neg\, l_2\,!x)@l'.P_2)$$

with $l' \notin fn(l_1, l_2, P_1, P_2)$ and $x \notin fn(P_2)$. By relying on may-testing, we can easily state and prove the soundness of this implementation as follows:

$$l_1 = l_2 \quad \text{implies that} \quad l :: \textbf{if } l_1 = l_2 \textbf{ then } P_1 \textbf{ else } P_2 \; \simeq \; l :: P_1$$
$$l_1 \neq l_2 \quad \text{implies that} \quad l :: \textbf{if } l_1 = l_2 \textbf{ then } P_1 \textbf{ else } P_2 \; \simeq \; l :: P_2$$

In μKLAIM such a construct is not finitary implementable, assuming (as usual) that the set of names is infinite. At most, we can use process

$$\textbf{new}(l').\textbf{out}(l_1)@l'.(\textbf{in}(l_2)@l'.P_1 \mid \textbf{in}(!x)@l'.P_2)$$

where, however, P_2 could also be executed whenever $l_1 = l_2$.

Notice that the implementation in μKLAIM$^{\neq}$ of the if-then-else we have just presented can be achieved with a simpler formulation of templates and pattern matching. Indeed, it suffices to add fields of the form $\neg u$, with rule (1) replaced by

$$match(\neg l; l') = \epsilon \qquad \text{if } l' \neq l$$

However, the general formulation exploiting fields of the form $\neg u\,!x$ enables us to program more sophisticated applications. As an example, we consider a 'fair server', that never serves the same client two consecutive times. The code required for this task is the following:

$$P \triangleq \textbf{in}(!x)@l.\textbf{new}(l').\textbf{out}(x)@l'.(<\textit{Serve client } x > \; \mid \; *Q)$$

$$Q \triangleq \textbf{in}(!y)@l'.\textbf{in}(\neg\, y\,!z)@l.\textbf{out}(z)@l'. <\textit{Serve client } z >$$

The fair server is located at l and it runs process P. Client processes invoke the service by sending to l the address of the node where they run. Then, process P retrieves the first service request (coming from x), creates a new node l' to store the currently served client, serves x and then activates the replicated process Q. The latter one retrieves from l' the last served client y and waits for a new request coming from a client z different from y; it then stores z in l' and serves z.

The application we have just presented can be useful in a distributed system to avoid starvation of client processes. If we want to extend it to the case where n client processes must be regularly alternated, we need a more general form of pattern matching. This can be obtained by defining a small language for name expressions like

$$\xi \ ::= \ u \ \mid \ \neg u \ \mid \ \xi_1 \vee \xi_2 \ \mid \ \xi_1 \wedge \xi_2$$

where the only operations on names are tests for equality and difference combined by logical connectors and/or. Now, templates are defined as

$$T \ ::= \ \xi\,!x \ \mid \ T_1, T_2$$

Notice that the old field $!x$ would be an abbreviation for $(l \vee \neg l)!x$ (for a generic l) and the old field u would be an abbreviation for $u!x$ (for an unused variable x). The pattern matching rule (1) is now replaced by rule

$$match(\xi\,!x; l) = [l/x] \qquad \text{if } l \models \xi$$

where the compatibility check $l \models \xi$ is defined as expected

$$l \models l \qquad\qquad\qquad l \models \xi_1 \vee \xi_2 \quad \text{if } l \models \xi_1 \text{ or } l \models \xi_2$$

$$l \models \neg l' \quad \text{if } l \neq l' \qquad l \models \xi_1 \wedge \xi_2 \quad \text{if } l \models \xi_1 \text{ and } l \models \xi_2$$

4.2   Scope of Name Binders

In the previous sections, we have assumed that the scope of name binders contained within templates is the process following the action that has the template as argument. However, it is possible to consider as part of the scope of a name also those template fields that syntactically follow the binder of the name. This feature could be exploited for retrieving tuples that contain multiple occurrences of the same name (value), whatever it is.

For example, consider the data base of a travel agency storing information about clients. This can be modelled by associating to the agency a locality l whose TS hosts the data base as tuples of the form

$$\langle\, Name\,,\ TripID\,,\ Departure\_Date\,,\ Return\_Date\,,\ Destination\,\rangle$$

Consider now a query for the record of a client that has planned with the agency a one-day trip to Rome (e.g., this could be needed to perform a market research). In the new formulation of the calculus, this can be very easily implemented by action

$$\mathbf{read}(!x_n, !x_i, !x, x, \text{``Rome''})@l$$

To extend the scope of a name binder to the remaining part of the template where it occurs, the pattern matching function in Table 2 has to be modified. We must reformulate function *match* in order to apply the partial substitution calculated after the analysis of the first i fields to the analysis of the $(i+1)$-th field. To formalise this idea, let p range over template fields, i.e.

$$p \; ::= \; u \; \mid \; !x$$

Then, the pattern matching rules of Table 2 now become

$$\frac{match_\sigma(T;t) = \sigma_1 \quad match_{\sigma_1}(p;l) = \sigma_2}{match_\sigma(T,p;t,l) = \sigma_2} \qquad \begin{array}{l} match_\sigma(u;l) = \epsilon \quad \text{if } u = l \text{ or } \sigma(u) = l \\[4pt] match_\sigma(!x;l) = \sigma \circ [l/x] \end{array}$$

Function $match$ is invoked in rules (R-In) and (R-Read) as $match_\epsilon(T;t)$.

It should be apparent that the effect of the matching mechanism above, that permits enforcing selection of tuples where the very same field occurs repeatedly, cannot be achieved in its full generality in μKlaim. At the best, it could be somehow simulated under the (restrictive) assumption that the duplicated values are known in advance or can be guessed. Coming back to the travel agency example, we could write, e.g.,

$$\textbf{read}(!x_n, !x_i, 1/1/05, 1/1/05, \text{``Rome''})@l$$

but in this way we would only select those clients that went to Rome on January the 1st, 2005.

Also in a language with the full power of the if-then-else, like μKlaim$^{\neq}$, achieving the effect of the pattern matching above poses some problems. Indeed, consider the process

$$A \triangleq \textbf{in}(!x, !y)@l.\textbf{if } x = y \textbf{ then } P \textbf{ else out}(x, y)@l.A$$

where, for simplicity, we have used recursive process definitions (that can be simulated by relying on replication, see e.g. [16]). This encoding of action $\textbf{in}(!x, x)@l.P$ is not fully satisfactory because it introduces divergence: process A can repeatedly access at l a tuple of the form $\langle l_1, l_2 \rangle$, with $l_1 \neq l_2$.

4.3   Exact Matching

Linda's pattern matching enables the consumer of a datum to specify some constraints over the accessed tuple (i.e., the values occurring at some precise positions of the tuple). A symmetric capability is not available for the producer of a tuple, i.e. it cannot specify any constraint over the template used for retrieving the tuple. This fact forbids the storing of reserved data at public tuple spaces. For example, let d be a reserved datum stored at l, e.g.

$$l :: \langle d \rangle$$

Then, any process knowing l can easily retrieve d with action $\textbf{in}(!x)@l$.

To provide data producers with the capability of controlling data retrievals, we slightly extend the syntax of tuples from Table 1 to become

$$t \; ::= \; \cdots \; \mid \; u!$$

Intuitively, a name marked with a '!' occurring within a tuple can only be matched by the very same name occurring at the corresponding position within a template and not by a formal field. Hence, the pattern matching function of Table 2 must also include the axiom

$$match(l; l!) = \epsilon$$

In particular, both $match(!x; l!)$ and $match(l'; l!)$, with $l' \neq l$, will fail. Let μKLAIM$^!$ be the variant of μKLAIM with exact name matching.

In μKLAIM$^!$, tuple fields marked with a ' !' act as passwords (of a symmetric cryptographic system) that retrievers must exhibit in order to access the tuple. In this way, secret data can be freely stored at public TSs; for example, the node

$$(\nu n)(l :: \langle n!, d \rangle \mid P)$$

is safe in that no other process than P can (immediately) access d, whatever be the rest of the net.

4.4 Nested Tuples

In KLAIM and all its variants tuples and templates are plain sequences of fields; roughly speaking, they are *lists* of fields. A straightforward generalisation of this definition is allowing *nested* tuples/templates, i.e. lists of fields that can contain other lists.

To model nested tuples/templates, we overload notation $\langle \cdot \rangle$ and modify the syntax of tuples and templates from Table 1 to become

$$t ::= \cdots \mid \langle t \rangle \qquad\qquad T ::= \cdots \mid \langle T \rangle$$

The pattern matching function is smoothly adapted to deal with nested arguments. We just need to add such rules as the following ones

$$\frac{match(T; t) = \sigma}{match(\langle T \rangle; \langle t \rangle) = \sigma} \qquad match(!x; t) = [t/x]$$

to the definition of function *match* given in Table 2. The first rule extends pattern matching by still requiring that matching templates and tuples have the same structure. The second rule allows to match entire tuples with a single variable; in such a setting, it should also be possible to assign entire tuples to variables and to use projection operators for retrieving each tuple field.

Notice that the two rules must not be necessarily used both at the same time. For instance, let μKLAIM^{nt} be the variant of μKLAIM with nested tuples and pattern matching extended using the first rule above. A simple application is the modelling of tree-like structures, similar to XML documents. For example, binary trees can be easily obtained by restricting the syntax of nested tuples as follows

$$t ::= u \mid \langle t_1 \rangle, u, \langle t_2 \rangle$$

Clearly, trees can be somehow modelled in μKLAIM by using tuples corresponding to a preorder visit of the tree. To univocally identify the tree

$$\langle a \rangle, b, \langle c \rangle$$

in μKLAIM we could use the tuple

$$b, \textbf{left}, a, \textbf{right}, c$$

where **left** and **right** are a reserved names used to delimit the two subtrees. However, the exact name matching of μKLAIM$^!$ is needed in order to faithfully simulate the pattern matching function of μKLAIM^{nt}. Thus, μKLAIM^{nt} can be encoded in μKLAIM$^!$, but the ease of programming makes μKLAIM^{nt} a valid proposal as well.

4.5   Collecting Multisets of Tuples

We conclude this section with another variant of the matching function, called *matchAll*, that permits matching a template T and a multiset of tuples $\mathcal{M}$, and returning the multiset of substitutions induced by all matchings. Notationally, given a component C of the form $\langle t_1 \rangle \mid \cdots \mid \langle t_n \rangle$, we shall use $\mathcal{M}(C)$ to denote the multiset of tuples $\{\langle t_1 \rangle, \cdots, \langle t_n \rangle\}$; we will use $\uplus$ to denote multiset union.

Function *matchAll*$(T; \mathcal{M})$ returns a pair consisting of:

1. the multiset Σ of substitutions, containing the elements $\sigma_1, \ldots \sigma_n$ (corresponding to the single tuples t_i in $\mathcal{M}$ that match template T), and
2. the multiset $\mathcal{M}'$ of the tuples t_j in $\mathcal{M}$ that do not match T.

Function *matchAll*$(T; \mathcal{M})$ can be defined in terms of function *match* given in Table 2 as follows:

$$matchAll(T; \{\!\{\}\!\}) = \langle \{\!\{\}\!\}, \{\!\{\}\!\} \rangle \qquad \frac{matchAll(T; \mathcal{M}) = \langle \Sigma, \mathcal{M}' \rangle}{matchAll(T; \mathcal{M} \uplus \{\!\{t\}\!\}) = \begin{cases} \langle \Sigma \uplus \{\!\{\sigma\}\!\}, \mathcal{M}' \rangle & \text{if } match(T; t) = \sigma \\ \langle \Sigma, \mathcal{M}' \uplus \{\!\{t\}\!\} \rangle & \text{otherwise} \end{cases}}$$

To show its usefulness, we use function *matchAll* to model the semantics of the construct **forall** used in the programming language X-KLAIM [1]. Intuitively, process

$$\textbf{forall in}(T)@l \textbf{ do } P$$

retrieves all the tuples $t_1, \ldots t_n$ located at l that match T, then uses the substitutions $\sigma_i = match(T, t_i)$ to execute n instances of P with the different substitutions (i.e., $P\sigma_1, \ldots P\sigma_n$). To formalize the semantics of **forall**, we find it convenient to make use of a construct for sequential composition of processes, that we shall write $P_1; P_2$. The operational semantics of sequential composition is modelled by the following rules where, to avoid name capture, we assume that $bn(P_1) \cap fn(P_2) = \emptyset$:

$$\frac{l :: P_1 \equiv l :: \textbf{nil}}{l :: P_1; P_2 \equiv l :: P_2} \qquad\qquad \frac{l :: P_1 \parallel N \longmapsto l :: P_1' \parallel N'}{l :: P_1; P_2 \parallel N \longmapsto l :: P_1'; P_2 \parallel N}$$

Now, the semantics of **forall** can be modelled as follows:

$$\frac{matchAll(T; \mathcal{M}(\langle t_1 \rangle \mid \cdots \mid \langle t_n \rangle)) = \langle \{\!\{\sigma_{i_1}, \cdots, \sigma_{i_k}\}\!\}, \mathcal{M}(C') \rangle}{l :: \textbf{forall in}(T)@l \textbf{ do } P \parallel l' :: \langle t_1 \rangle \mid \cdots \mid \langle t_n \rangle \longmapsto_{l'} l :: P\sigma_{i_1}; \cdots; P\sigma_{i_k} \parallel l' :: C'}$$

$$\frac{N_1 \longmapsto_l N_1'}{N_1 \parallel N_2 \longmapsto_l N_1' \parallel N_2} \quad N_2 \text{ does not contain tuples located at } l$$

The two rules above define a new transition relation $\longmapsto_l$ that is parameterized with respect to the address l of the node where the tuple space is located. This parametrization is necessary for ensuring that the entire tuple space at l is used as a parameter of *matchAll*. The operational semantics of the resulting language is given by the union of relations $\longmapsto$ (defined in Table 3) and $\longmapsto_l$, for any l.

5 Conclusions

We have briefly presented μKLAIM, a simple calculus that retains the main features of KLAIM, and have summarised some recent linguistic extensions that permit the explicit modelling of inter-node connections and of nodes and links failures. We have then sketched a research that we are currently pursuing that aims at assessing the impact of plugging into the calculus more powerful pattern matching mechanisms. By means of simple examples, we have shown how flexible (but still implementable) pattern matching policies can ease the task of programming global computing application. Clearly, the study of relative expressiveness, possible encodings and minimality deserves a deeper attention and will be the subject of future investigations.

References

1. L. Bettini, R. De Nicola, G. Ferrari, and R. Pugliese. Interactive Mobile Agents in X-KLAIM. In P. Ciancarini and R. Tolksdorf, editors, *Proc. of the 7th Int. IEEE Workshops on Enabling Technologies: Infrastructure for Collaborative Enterprises*, pages 110–115. IEEE Computer Society Press, 1998.
2. L. Bettini, R. De Nicola, and R. Pugliese. KLAVA: a Java Package for Distributed and Mobile Applications. *Software – Practice and Experience*, 32:1365–1394, 2002.
3. L. Cardelli. Abstractions for mobile computation. In J. Vitek and C. Jensen, editors, *Secure Internet Programming: Security Issues for Mobile and Distributed Objects*, number 1603 in LNCS, pages 51–94. Springer, 1999.
4. S. Chaudhuri. More Choices Allow More Faults: Set Consensus Problems in Totally Asynchronous Systems. *Information and Computation*, 105(1):132-158, 1993.
5. R. De Nicola, G. Ferrari, and R. Pugliese. KLAIM: a Kernel Language for Agents Interaction and Mobility. *IEEE Transactions on Software Engineering*, 24(5):315–330, 1998.
6. R. De Nicola, G. Ferrari, and R. Pugliese. Programming Access Control: The KLAIM Experience. In C. Palamidessi, editor, *Proc. of the 11th International Conference on Concurrency Theory (CONCUR'00)*, volume 1877 of *LNCS*, pages 48–65. Springer-Verlag, 2000.
7. R. De Nicola, D. Gorla, and R. Pugliese. Basic observables for a calculus for global computing. Research Report 07/2004, Dipartimento di Informatica, Università di Roma "La Sapienza". Available at http://www.dsi.uniroma1.it/~gorla/publications.htm.
8. R. De Nicola, D. Gorla, and R. Pugliese. On the expressive power of KLAIM-based calculi. Research Report 09/2004, Dipartimento di Informatica, Università di Roma "La Sapienza". Available at http://www.dsi.uniroma1.it/~gorla/ publications.htm. An extended abstract appeared in *Proc. of EXPRESS'04*, ENTCS.
9. R. De Nicola, D. Gorla, and R. Pugliese. Global computing in a dynamic network of tuple spaces. In J. Jacquet and G. Picco, editors, *Proc. of COORDINATION'05*, number 3454 in LNCS, pages 157–172. Springer, 2005.

10. R. De Nicola and M. Hennessy. Testing equivalence for processes. *Theoretical Computer Science*, 34:83–133, 1984.
11. D. Gelernter. Generative Communication in Linda. *ACM Transactions on Programming Languages and Systems*, 7(1):80–112, 1985.
12. D. Gelernter. Multiple Tuple Spaces in Linda. In J. G. Goos, editor, *Proceedings, PARLE '89*, volume 365 of *LNCS*, pages 20–27, 1989.
13. D. Gorla. *Semantic Approaches to Global Computing Systems*. PhD thesis, Dip. Sistemi ed Informatica, Univ. di Firenze, 2004.
14. F. Levi and D. Sangiorgi. Controlling interference in ambients. In *Proceedings of POPL '00*, pages 352–364. ACM, 2000.
15. F. Orava and J. Parrow. An algebraic verification of a mobile network. *Journal of Formal Aspects of Computing*, 4:497–543, 1992.
16. J. Parrow. An introduction to the pi-calculus. In J. Bergstra, A. Ponse, and S. Smolka, editors, *Handbook of Process Algebra*, pages 479–543. Elsevier Science, 2001.

A Dynamic Class Construct
for Asynchronous Concurrent Objects

Einar Broch Johnsen[1], Olaf Owe[1], and Isabelle Simplot-Ryl[2]

[1] Department of Informatics, University of Oslo, Norway
{einarj,olaf}@ifi.uio.no
[2] LIFL, CNRS-UMR 8022, University of Lille I, France
ryl@lifl.fr

Abstract. Modern applications distributed across networks such as the Internet may need to evolve without compromising application availability. Object systems are well suited for runtime upgrade, as encapsulation clearly separates internal structure and external services. This paper considers a mechanism for dynamic class upgrade, allowing class hierarchies to be upgraded in such a way that the existing objects of the upgraded class and of its subclasses gradually evolve at runtime. The mechanism is integrated in Creol, a high-level language which targets distributed applications by means of concurrent objects communicating by asynchronous method calls. The dynamic class construct is given a formal semantics in rewriting logic, extending the semantics of the Creol language.

1 Introduction

For critical distributed applications, which are long lived and have high availability requirements, it is important that system components can be upgraded in response to new requirements that arise over time without compromising application availability. Requirements that necessitate component upgrade may be additional features and improved performance, as well as bugfixes. Examples of such applications are found in banks, air traffic control systems, aeronautics, financial transaction processes, and mobile and Internet applications. For these systems, manual reconfiguration and recompilation of components are both impractical, due to component distribution, and unsatisfactory, due to the high availability requirements. Instead, upgrades and patches should be applicable at runtime. Early approaches to software distribution and upgrading [2, 4, 6, 14, 16, 21, 26] do not address the need for continuous availability during upgrades. More recently, the issue of runtime reconfiguration and upgrade has attracted attention [1, 3, 5, 7, 11, 13, 15, 22, 25, 27]. For large distributed systems, it seems desirable to perform upgrades in an asynchronous and modular way, such that upgrades propagate automatically through the distributed system. An automatic upgrade system should [1, 27]: propagate upgrades automatically, provide a means to control *when* components may be upgraded, and ensure the availability of system services even in the course of an upgrade process, when components of different versions coexist.

In this paper, we propose and formalize a solution to these issues, taking an object-oriented approach. Our solution is based on a dynamic class construct, allowing class definitions to be upgraded at runtime. Upgrading a class affects all future instances of

M. Steffen and G. Zavattaro (Eds.): FMOODS 2005, LNCS 3535, pp. 15–30, 2005.

the redefined class and of its subclasses. Further, all *existing* object instances of the class and its subclasses are upgraded. In contrast to e.g. [1], our approach is completely distributed, and no centralized versioning repository is required. No specific measures are needed by the programmer to anticipate and prepare for future upgrades, as the upgrade process itself is handled transparently by the runtime system. Whereas [5, 9, 10, 29] present formal systems for upgrades of sequential languages or modifications to single objects, we are not aware of any formalization of modular upgrades for concurrent object systems. In contrast to all the cited works, our approach addresses and exploits *inheritance*, supports synchronous as well as *asynchronous* communication, and allows both *nonterminating, active*, and reactive processes in objects to be upgraded.

This paper considers dynamic class upgrades in the Creol language [17–19], which specifically targets open distributed systems with concurrent objects, has multiple inheritance, and supports both asynchronous and synchronous invocation of object methods. Creol has an operational semantics defined in rewriting logic [23] and an interpreter running on the Maude platform [8, 23]. In this paper, a dynamic class construct is proposed and formalized in rewriting logic through integration in Creol's operational semantics.

Paper overview. Sect. 2 summarizes the Creol language and presents the dynamic class construct, Sect. 3 provides two examples, Sect. 4 presents the operational semantics, Sect. 5 discusses related work, and Sect. 6 concludes the paper.

2   A Language for Asynchronously Communicating Objects

This section briefly reviews the basic features of Creol [17–19], a high-level language for distributed concurrent objects. We distinguish data, typed by data types, and objects, typed by interfaces. The language allows both synchronous and asynchronous invocation of methods, based on a uniform semantics. Attributes (object variables) and method declarations are organized in classes, which may have data and object parameters. Concurrent objects have their own processor which evaluates local processes, i.e. program code with *processor release points*. Processes may be *active*, reflecting autonomous behavior initiated at creation time by the *run* method, or *reactive*, i.e. in response to method invocations. Due to processor release points, the evaluation of processes may be interleaved. The values of an object's program variables may depend on the non-deterministic interleaving of processes. Therefore a method instance may have local variables supplementing the object variables, in particular the values of formal parameters are stored locally. An object may contain several (pending) instances of the same method, possibly with different values for local variables.

2.1   Asynchronous and Synchronous Method Invocations

All object interaction happens through method calls. A method may be invoked either synchronously or asynchronously [17]. When a process invokes a method asynchronously, the process may continue its activity until it requests a reply to the call or it is suspended by arriving at a processor release point in its code. In the asynchronous setting method calls can always be emitted, as a receiving object cannot block communication. *Method overtaking* is allowed: if methods offered by an object are invoked in one order, the object may start evaluation of the method instances in another order.

An asynchronous method call is made with the statement $t!x.m(\text{E})$, where $t \in \text{Label}$ provides a locally unique reference to the call, x is an object expression, m a method name, and E an expression list with the actual parameters supplied to the method. Labels identify invocations and may be omitted if a reply is not explicitly requested. Return values from the call are explicitly fetched, say in a variable list V, by the statement $t?(\text{V})$. This statement treats V as a list of future variables [30]: If a reply has arrived, return values are assigned to V and evaluation continues. In the case of a local call, i.e. when the value of x is the same as *this* object, the processor is released to start evaluation of the call. Otherwise, process evaluation is blocked. In order to avoid blocking in the asynchronous case, *processor release points* are introduced for reply requests (Sect. 2.2): If no reply has arrived, evaluation is *suspended* rather than blocked.

Synchronous (RPC) method calls, immediately blocking the processor while waiting for a reply, are written $p(\text{E};\text{V})$; this is shorthand for $t!p(\text{E});t?(\text{V})$, where t is a fresh label variable. The language does not support monitor reentrance (except for local calls), mutual synchronous calls may therefore lead to deadlock. In order to evaluate local calls, the invoking process must eventually suspend its own evaluation. In particular, the evaluation of synchronous local calls will precede the active process. Local calls need not be prefixed by an object identifier, in which case they may be identified syntactically as internal. The keyword *this* is used for self reference in the language.

2.2 Processor Release Points

Guards g in statements **await** g explicitly declare potential processor release points. When a guard which evaluates to false is encountered during process evaluation, the process is suspended and the processor released. After processor release, any pending process may be selected for evaluation. The type Guard is defined inductively:

- $wait \in \text{Guard}$ (explicit release),
- $t? \in \text{Guard}$, where $t \in \text{Label}$,
- $b \in \text{Guard}$, where b is a boolean expression over local and object state,
- $g_1 \wedge g_2$ and $g_1 \vee g_2$, where $g_1, g_2 \in \text{Guard}$.

Use of *wait* will always release the processor. The reply guard $t?$ is enabled if a reply to the call with label t has arrived. Evaluation of guard statements is atomic. We let **await** $g \wedge t?(\text{V})$ abbreviate **await** $g \wedge t?; t?(\text{V})$ and we let **await** $p(\text{E};\text{V})$, where p is a method call (external or internal), abbreviate $t!p(\text{E});$ **await** $t?(\text{V})$ for some fresh label t.

Statements can be composed to reflect requirements to the internal object control flow. Let S_1 and S_2 denote statement lists. An unguarded statement list is always enabled. Sequential composition may introduce guards: **await** g is a potential release point in $S_1;$ **await** $g; S_2$. Nondeterministic choice $S_1 \square S_2$ may select S_1 once S_1 is enabled or S_2 once S_2 is enabled, and suspends if neither branch is enabled. Nondeterministic merge $S_1 \| S_2$ evaluates the statements S_1 and S_2 in some interleaved and enabled order. In addition there are standard constructs for if-statements and internal method calls, including recursive calls. Note that for the purposes of dynamic upgrades, recursive calls replace while-loops in the language. Assignment to local and object variables is expressed as $\text{V} := \text{E}$ for a disjoint list of program variables V and an expression list E, of matching types. In-parameters as well as *this*, *label*, and *caller* are read-only variables.

Syntactic categories.	Definitions.
g in Guard	$g ::= wait \mid b \mid t? \mid g_1 \wedge g_2 \mid g_1 \vee g_2$
p in MtdCall	$p ::= x.m \mid m@classname \mid m$
s in Stm	$\text{S} ::= s \mid s; \text{S}$
t in Label	$s ::= \textbf{skip} \mid (\text{S}) \mid \text{S}_1 \square \text{S}_2 \mid \text{S}_1 \| \text{S}_2$
v in Var	$\mid \text{V} := \text{E} \mid v := \textbf{new } classname(\text{E})$
e in Expr	$\mid \textbf{if } b \textbf{ then } \text{S}_1 \textbf{ else } \text{S}_2 \textbf{ fi}$
x in ObjExpr	$\mid t!p(\text{E}) \mid !p(\text{E}) \mid p(\text{E}; \text{V}) \mid t?(\text{V})$
b in Bool	$\mid \textbf{await } g \mid \textbf{await } g \wedge t?(\text{V}) \mid \textbf{await } p(\text{E}; \text{V})$
m in Mtd	

Fig. 1. An outline of the language syntax for method definitions, with typical terms for each category. Capitalized terms such as S, V, and E denote lists, sets, or multisets of the given syntactic categories, depending on the context.

With release points, the object need not block while waiting for replies. This approach is more flexible than future variables: suspended processes or new method calls may be evaluated while waiting. If the called object never replies, deadlock is avoided as other activity in the object is possible. However, when the reply arrives, the *continuation* of the process must compete with other pending and enabled processes.

2.3 Multiple Inheritance and Virtual Binding

The Creol language provides a mechanism for multiple inheritance [18] where all attributes and methods of a superclass are inherited by the subclass, and where superclass methods may be redefined. Class inheritance is declared by a keyword **inherits** which takes as argument an *inheritance list*; i.e., a list of class names $C(\text{E})$ where E provides the actual class parameters. We say that a method or attribute is defined *above* a class C if it is declared in C or in at least one of the classes inherited by C. Internal calls are executed on the caller and may therefore take advantage of the statically known class structure to invoke specific method declarations. We introduce the syntax $t!m@C(\text{E})$ for asynchronous and $m@C(\text{E}; \text{V})$ for synchronous internal invocation of a method above C in the inheritance graph from C or a subclass of C. These calls may be bound without knowing the exact class of *this* object , so they are called *static*. In contrast calls without @, called *virtual*, need to identify the actual class of the callee at runtime in order to bind the call. We assume that attributes have unique names in the inheritance graph; this may easily be enforced at compile time and implies that attributes are bound statically. Consequently, a method declared in a class C may only access attributes declared above C. In a subclass, an attribute x of a superclass C is accessed by the qualified reference $x@C$. The language syntax is given in Fig. 1.

Virtual binding. When a method is virtually invoked in an object o of class C, a method declaration is identified in the inheritance graph of C and bound to the call. For simplicity, the call is bound to the first matching method definition above C in the inheritance graph, in a left-first depth-first order. Assume given a nominal subtype relation as a reflexive partial ordering $\prec$ on types, including interfaces. A data type may only be a subtype of a data type and an interface may only be a subtype of an interface. If $T \prec T'$ then any value of T may masquerade as a value of T'. Subtyping for type tuples is the pointwise extension of the subtype relation: $T \prec T'$ if the tuples T and T' have the same length l and $T_i \prec T_i'$ for every i ($0 \le i \le l$) and types T_i and T_i' in position i in T and T'. To explain the typing and binding of methods, subtyping is extended to function spaces $A \to B$, where A and B are (possibly zero-length) type tuples:

$$A \to B \prec A' \to B' = A \prec A' \wedge B' \prec B.$$

The static analysis of an internal call $m(\text{E}; \text{V})$ will assign unique types to the in- and out-parameter depending on the textual context. Say that the actual parameters are textually declared as $\text{E} : T_\text{E}$ and $\text{V} : T_\text{V}$. The call is *type correct* if there is a method declaration $m : A \to B$ above the class C such that $T_\text{E} \to T_\text{V} \prec A \to B$. The binding of an asynchronous call $t!m(\text{E})$ with a reply $t?(\text{V})$ or **await** $t?(\text{V})$, is handled as the corresponding synchronous call $m(\text{E}; \text{V})$.

At runtime the object making the internal call $m : T_\text{E} \to T_\text{V}$ will be of a subclass C' of C and the virtual binding mechanism will bind to a declaration of $m : A' \to B'$ such that $T_\text{E} \to T_\text{V} \prec A' \to B'$, taking the first such m above C'. Because C is inherited by C', the virtual binding is guaranteed to succeed. External calls $t!o.m(\text{E})$ are virtually bound in the graph above the dynamically identified class of o. Provided that the declared interface of o supports the method signature, successful binding is guaranteed for any instance of a type-correct class implementing the interface.

2.4   System Evolution Through Class Upgrade

System change is addressed through a mechanism for class upgrade, which allows existing and future objects of the upgraded class and of its subclasses to evolve. A class may be subjected to a number of upgrades. In an upgrade, new attributes, methods, and superclasses may be added to a class definition, and old methods may be modified. In order to allow old method instances to evaluate safely and avoid runtime type errors, no attributes, methods, or inherited classes may be removed as part of a class upgrade. Although more restrictive, empirical studies suggest that addition and redefinition of services are far more common forms of software evolution than removal [29].

Attributes may be added. New attributes may be added to a class. The addition of a new attribute with the same name as another attribute already defined in the class is not allowed. The addition of an attribute having the same name as an inherited attribute is allowed. The instance of the class will then have both attributes, which are accessed by qualified names (see Sect. 2.3). As attribute names are statically expanded into qualified names, old code will continue to use the same attributes as before the upgrade.

Methods may be added or redefined. We consider the effect of adding or redefining a method in a class C with respect to the sub- and superclasses of C. If a method is *redefined* in C, the method's code is replaced in all instances of C and the old method definition is no longer available. This leads to a *subtyping discipline* for method redefinitions in order to ensure that virtual binding succeeds. Consequently, we allow a method's internal data structures to be replaced, but for redefinition covariance and contravariance is required for the method's in- and out-parameters, respectively.

If a method is *added* to a class, virtual binding guarantees that old calls are type correct without placing any restrictions on the new method. All kinds of overloading of inherited methods are allowed, including overloading with respect to the number of in- or out-parameters. For method declarations with the same number of in- and out-parameters overloading may be with respect to parameter types, possibly only for out-parameters. If a method m is added to C and m is previously defined in a superclass C' of C, the new definition in C will override (and hide) the inherited method m of C' in the sense that a call which matches both definitions will be bound differently after the upgrade. The superclass method is still available by the static call $m@C'$. Virtual binding ensures that calls that were type correct before the class upgrade remain type correct. If a method m is added to C and m is previously defined in a subclass C'' of C, a new override relationship will be introduced. However, virtual binding preserves the type correctness of old calls as well as the virtually bound calls of the upgraded class. The addition of a method to a class C does not need to be restricted by definitions in the sub- or superclasses of C.

Superclasses may be added. If a class C is added as a superclass during a class upgrade, the attributes and methods defined in C and its superclasses become available. The binding mechanism works in a left-first depth-first order, so the order of the list of inherited classes is crucial: to minimize the effect of new superclasses on the virtual binding mechanism, the new superclasses are added at the end of the inheritance list.

In order to avoid runtime errors in the case when old code contains calls to the *new* method with the old parameter list, we do not allow the formal parameter list of a class to be extended. (It is straightforward to avoid this restriction using default values.) In addition we do not allow the types of formal parameters to change; wider types could create errors for old code operating on new objects whereas narrower types could create errors for new code operating on old objects. Consequently, the actual parameters to the new superclasses must be expressed by means of the old class parameters and attributes.

3   Examples

Two examples of dynamic upgrade are considered. Upgrade is used to add a new service to an existing class, with visible effects to users of this class, and to change a communication protocol at runtime, to increase the system performance in a transparent manner.

3.1   Example: A Bank Account

Consider a bank account of interface *Account*, with methods for deposit and transfer of funds, such that a transfer must wait until the account has sufficient funds.

```
class BankAccount implements Account                              --- Version 1
begin var bal : Int = 0
with Any
    op deposit (in sum : Nat) == bal := bal+sum
    op transfer (in sum : Nat, acc : Account) ==
        await bal ≥ sum ; bal := bal−sum; acc.deposit(sum)
end
```

Dynamic class upgrade allows the addition of new services to such an application without stopping the system. Let us consider the addition of overdraft facilities. The upgrade of the *BankAccount* class will add a method *overdraft_open* such that an object supporting the *Banker* interface may set a maximal overdraft amount for the account. The *transfer* method will be upgraded to take this new facility into account.

upgrade class BankAccount --- *Version 2*
begin var overdraft : Nat = 0
with *Any*
   op transfer (**in** sum : Nat, acc : Account) ==
      await bal $\geq$ sum$-$overdraft; bal := bal$-$sum; acc.deposit(sum)
with *Banker*
   op overdraft_open (**in** max : Nat) == overdraft := max
end

An *overdraft* variable is added during upgrade. Pending transfer processes in an object await the old guard, whereas new transfer calls to the object get the new guard.

3.2 Example: Broadcast in Ad Hoc Networks

Consider a wireless broadcast mechanism for ad hoc networks, using the *blind-flooding* protocol: When a node receives a message with a previously unseen sequence number, the message is sent to all neighbors and the sequence number is recorded.

class Node (neighbors : List[Oid]) --- *Version 1*
begin var set : NatSet = emptySet
with *Any*
   op broadcast (**in** msg : Data, seqNbr : Nat) ==
      if seqNbr $\notin$ set **then** !neighbors.broadcast(msg, seqNbr); set := set $\cup$ {seqNbr} **fi**
end

The statement !*neighbors.m*(...) expands to a list of asynchronous calls to all elements in the *neighbors* list.

   This protocol is "localized": a node communicates with its direct neighbors and may ignore the overall network topology. However, there is a significant number of message collisions. Recently the *Neighbor Elimination Scheme* protocol has been introduced, which improves performance by reducing the total number of transmissions [28]. In the new protocol, a node knows both its neighbors and their neighbors. Intuitively, when a node receives a message it observes the communications for a certain time (using a timeout) and then decides not to resend the message if all of its neighbors have already received it. The system will now be upgraded to the new protocol at runtime.

   We introduce a data type *Assoc* for sets of pairs to record the sequence numbers and sets of neighbors for the active broadcasts, with constructors *empty* :$\rightarrow$ *Assoc* and *add* : *Assoc* $\times$ *Nat* $\times$ *NatSet* $\rightarrow$ *Assoc*. Define functions *isEmpty* : *Assoc* $\times$ *Nat* $\rightarrow$ *Bool*, *rem* : *Assoc* $\times$ *Nat* $\times$ *Oid* $\rightarrow$ *Assoc*, and *remAll* : *Assoc* $\times$ *Nat* $\rightarrow$ *Assoc* by the equations

$isEmpty(empty, n)$ $= true$
$isEmpty(add(a, n, s), n')$ $= $ **if** $n = n'$ **then** $s = \emptyset$ **else** $isEmpty(a, n')$ **fi**
$rem(empty, n, o)$ $= empty$
$rem(add(a, n, s), n', o)$ $= $ **if** $n = n'$ **then** $add(a, n, s \setminus \{o\})$ **else** $add(rem(a, n', o), n, s)$**fi**
$remAll(empty, n)$ $= empty$
$remAll(add(a, n, s), n')$ $= $ **if** $n = n'$ **then** $remAll(a, n')$ **else** $add(remAll(a, n'), n, s)$ **fi**

The *Node* class may now be upgraded:

upgrade Node   *--- Version 2*
begin var a : Assoc = empty;
with *Any*
    op broadcast (**in** m : Data, n : Nat) == **if** n $\in$ set **then** rem(a,n,`caller`)
      else set := set $\cup$ {n}; add(a,n,neighbors); rem(a,n,`caller`);
        await wait $\vee$ isEmpty(a,n);
         if $\neg$ isEmpty(a,n) **then** !neighbors.broadcast(m,n) **else** remAll(a,n) **fi fi**
end

Here the *set* and *neighbors* attributes are reused from the previous class version. The *wait* guard is used for delay, suspending the process for some amount of time. After the class upgrade, active *Node* objects are upgraded independently and at different times. There is a transitory period during which system performance gradually improves.

4   An Operational Semantics for Dynamic Class Upgrade

The operational semantics of Creol is defined in rewriting logic (RL) [23]. A rewrite theory is a 4-tuple $\mathcal{R} = (\Sigma, E, L, R)$ where the signature Σ defines the function symbols, E defines equations between terms, L is a set of labels, and R is a set of labeled rewrite rules. Rewrite rules apply to terms of given sorts. Sorts are specified in (membership) equational logic (Σ, E), the functional sublanguage of RL which supports algebraic specification in the OBJ [12] style. When modeling computational systems, different system components are typically modeled by terms of the different sorts defined in the equational logic. The global state configuration is defined as a multiset of these terms.

RL extends algebraic specification techniques with transition rules: The dynamic behavior of a system is captured by rewrite rules supplementing the equations which define the term language. From a computational viewpoint, a rewrite rule $t \longrightarrow t'$ may be interpreted as a *local transition rule* allowing an instance of the pattern t to evolve into the corresponding instance of the pattern t'. When auxiliary functions are needed in the semantics, these are defined in equational logic, and are evaluated in between the state transitions [23]. Rewrite rules apply to local fragments of a state configuration. If rewrite rules may be applied to nonoverlapping subconfigurations, the transitions may be performed in parallel. Consequently, concurrency is implicit in RL. Conditional rewrite rules are allowed, where the condition can be formulated as a conjunction of rewrites and equations which must hold for the main rule to apply:

$$subconfiguration \longrightarrow subconfiguration \textbf{ if } condition$$

A number of concurrency models have been successfully represented in RL [8, 23], including Petri nets, CCS, Actors, and Unity, as well as the ODP computational model [24]. RL also offers its own model of object orientation [8], but inheritance in this model does not easily allow method overloading and redefinition. Rules in RL may be formulated at a high level of abstraction, closely resembling a compositional operational semantics.

System configurations. A Creol method call will be reflected by a pair of messages, and object activity will be organized around a *message queue* which contains incoming messages and a *process queue* which contains pending processes, i.e. remaining parts of method instances. In order to increase parallelism in the RL model, message queues will be external to object bodies. A state configuration is a multiset combining Creol objects, classes, messages, and queues. The associative constructor for lists is represented by ';', and the associative and commutative constructor for multisets by whitespace.

Objects in RL are commonly written as terms $\langle O : C \,|\, a_1 : v_1, \ldots, a_n : v_n \rangle$ where O is the object's identifier, C is its class, the a_i's are the names of the object's attributes, and the v_i's the corresponding values [8]. Adopting this form of presentation, we define Creol objects, classes, and external message queues as RL objects [17]. Omitting RL sorts, a Creol object is represented by an RL object $\langle Ob \,|\, Cl, Pr, PrQ, Lvar, Att, Lab \rangle$, where Ob is the object identifier, Cl the class name and *version number*, Pr the active process code, PrQ a multiset of pending processes with unspecified queue ordering, and $Lvar$ and Att the local and object state, respectively. Let a sort τ be partially ordered by $<$, with least element 1, and let $Next : \tau \to \tau$ be such that $\forall x . x < Next(x)$. Lab is used to generate label values, which are terms of sort τ. Thus, the object identifier Ob and the generated local label value provide a globally unique identifier for each method call. A Creol object's message queue is represented as an RL object $\langle Qu \,|\, Ev \rangle$, where Qu is the queue identifier and Ev a multiset of unprocessed messages. Each message queue is associated with one specific Creol object. The statement *new* $C(\mathrm{E})$ creates a new object (and associated queue) with a unique object identifier, object variables as listed in the class parameter list E and in Att, and places an instance of the *run* method in Pr.

Creol classes are represented by RL objects $\langle Cl \,|\, Inh, Att, Mtds, Tok \rangle$, where Cl is the class name and version number, Inh the inheritance list, Att a list of attributes, $Mtds$ a multiset of methods, and Tok an arbitrary term of sort τ. Version n of a class named C will conventionally be denoted $C \# n$. The rules for the static language constructs may be found in [17, 18]. We shall here focus on the rules for dynamic class constructs.

4.1 Implicit Inheritance Graphs and Virtual Binding

In order to define dynamic reconfiguration mechanisms, the inheritance graph will not be statically given. Rather, the binding mechanism dynamically inspects the class hierarchy as present in the global state configuration. A *bind* message is sent from a class to its superclasses, resulting in a *bound* message returned to the object generating the *bind* message. This way, the inheritance graph is unfolded dynamically and as far as necessary when needed. This approach is used for virtual binding, and for collecting and instantiating the class variables of an object instance. We here present the virtual binding mechanism (see [18] for attribute collection). When the invocation

$invoc(o, m, Sig, In)$ of a method m is found in the message queue of an object o of class C, a message $bind(o, m, Sig, In, C)$ is generated where Sig is the method signature as provided by the caller and In is the list of actual in-parameters. Virtual calls are handled by the following rule:

$$\langle o: Ob \,|\, Cl: C \# n \rangle \; \langle o: Qu \,|\, Ev: Q \; invoc(o, m, Sig, In) \rangle$$
$$\longrightarrow \langle o: Ob \,|\, Cl: C \# n \rangle \; \langle o: Qu \,|\, Ev: Q \rangle \; bind(o, m, Sig, In, C \# n)$$

Static method calls are generated by means of the same mechanism but without inspecting the *actual* class of the callee, thus surpassing local definitions:

$$\langle o: Qu \,|\, Ev: Q \; invoc(o, m@C, Sig, In) \rangle \longrightarrow \langle o: Qu \,|\, Ev: Q \rangle \; bind(o, m, Sig, In, C \# 0)$$

If m is defined locally in a class C with a matching signature, a process with the declared method code and local state is returned in a *bound* message. The object state is not upgraded at this point, so a match between the version numbers of C is not required for method binding. Otherwise, the *bind* message is retransmitted to the superclasses of C in a left-first depth-first order:

$$bind(o, m, Sig, In, \varepsilon) \longrightarrow bound(o, none)$$
$$bind(o, m, Sig, In, (C \# n); I') \; \langle C \# n': Cl \,|\, Inh: I, Mtds: M \rangle$$
$$\longrightarrow \textbf{if } match(m, Sig, M) \textbf{ then } bound(o, get(m, M, In)) \textbf{ else } bind(o, m, Sig, In, I; I') \textbf{ fi}$$
$$\langle C \# n: Cl \,|\, Inh: I, Mtds: M \rangle$$

The auxiliary predicate $match(m, Sig, M)$ is true if m is declared in M with a signature Sig' such that $Sig \prec Sig'$, and the function get fetches method m in the method multiset M of the class, and returns a process with the method's code and local state. Values of the actual in-parameters In, the caller o' and the label value n are stored in the local state. The resulting process w is loaded into the internal process queue of the callee, as defined by the rule:

$$bound(o, w) \; \langle o: Ob \,|\, PrQ: W \rangle \longrightarrow \langle o: Ob \,|\, PrQ: w; W \rangle$$

4.2   Upgrading Class Definitions

In order to control the upgrade propagation, class representations include a version number; i.e., a counter which records the number of times the class has been upgraded. Class upgrade may be direct or indirect through the upgrade of one of the superclasses. When a class is upgraded, its version number is incremented. Each time a (direct) superclass of a class C is upgraded, the version number of the class is incremented: although the definition of C itself has not changed, the class may have more attributes or methods by the way of inheritance. To propagate the upgrades properly, each class will record the version number of each of its inherited classes. Therefore the inherited classes are represented as a list of class names and version numbers:

$$\langle C \# n: Cl \,|\, Inh: (C_1 \# n_1); (C_2 \# n_2); \ldots, Att: \_, Mtds: \_, Tok: \_ \rangle$$

Semantically a class upgrade is realized through the insertion of a new RL object $upgrade(C, I, A, M)$ in the global state configuration at runtime, where C is the identifier of the class to be upgraded, I is an inheritance list, A is a state, and M is a multiset of method definitions. The effect of the upgrade is that new inherited classes and attributes are added. Likewise new methods are added, but redefined methods must be treated differently: when a redefined method is added, the old version of the method must be removed. After the upgrade, the version number of the class is incremented. Let $\langle m, Sig, Body \rangle \in$ M denote that a method m with signature Sig and body $Body$ is defined in a method multiset M. Define M $\oplus$ M$'$ as M$' \cup \{ \langle m, Sig, Body \rangle \mid \langle m, Sig, Body \rangle \in$ M $\wedge$ $\neg \exists Body'.\langle m, Sig, Body' \rangle \in$ M$' \}$. The mechanism for *direct class upgrade* is captured in Creol's operational semantics by the following rule, which performs the upgrade using $\oplus$ to overwrite methods:

$$upgrade(C, \text{I}', \text{A}', \text{M}')\langle C \# n : Cl \mid Inh : \text{I}, Att : \text{A}, Mtds : \text{M}, Tok : T \rangle$$
$$\longrightarrow \langle C \# (n+1) : Cl \mid Inh : \text{I}; \text{I}', Att : \text{A}; \text{A}', Mtds : \text{M} \oplus \text{M}', Tok : T \rangle$$

When a class is upgraded by addition of some elements, its subclasses are also upgraded: although the definitions of the subclasses do not change, these classes indirectly acquire new attributes or methods by the way of inheritance. It is therefore necessary to propagate upgrade information to subclasses. The mechanism for *indirect class upgrade* is captured by the following equation:

$$\langle C \# n : Cl \mid Inh : \text{I}; (C' \# n'); \text{I}' \rangle \langle C' \# n'' : Cl \mid \rangle$$
$$= \langle C \# (n+1) : Cl \mid Inh : \text{I}; (C' \# n''); \text{I}' \rangle \langle C' \# n'' : Cl \mid \rangle \text{ if } n'' > n'$$

Note that the use of equations enables the version number update to execute in zero rewrite steps, which corresponds to locking the upgraded class object.

An example illustrates the effect of class upgrades at the semantic level. Let $\langle C \# 1 : Cl \mid Inh : (C_1 \# 1), Att : x; y; \text{A}, \ldots \rangle$ be the RL representation of a class C with parameters x and y, and attributes A. Let ε denote the empty list. The class will be upgraded with an additional ancestor class C_2 with an actual parameter x, by inserting the term $upgrade(C, (C_2(x) \# 1), \varepsilon, \varepsilon)$ into the global state of the running system. Later, the upgrade rule applies, resulting in the modified class representation $\langle C \# 2 : Cl \mid Inh : (C_1 \# 1); (C_2(x) \# 1), Att : x; y; \text{A}, \ldots \rangle$. If the class C_2 has been upgraded from its initial version, the equation reapplies, upgrading the version number of C_2 to the current version and incrementing the version number of the class C.

The example shows that we do not need knowledge of the actual version number of a class in the running system to add it as a superclass to the class we are upgrading, it suffices to use the initial version number. Consequently multiple upgrades do not cause upgrades to be forgotten, although the results of multiple (simultaneous) upgrades may vary due to the distributed topology reflected by the asynchronous upgrade rule.

The proposed class upgrade mechanism has some advantages. First, upgrade propagations are locally managed and classes need not know about their instances. Moreover, the version number recalls the number of changes applied to a class but old versions of a class are removed. Finally, there are no upgrade conflicts: one upgrade is performed at a time. If several upgrades redefine the same method the result may depend on the order in which the upgrades are performed, but the final result is stable. In order to enforce this discipline in a distributed setting where multiple copies of the class exist on different physical sites, there would typically be one master copy from which upgrades propagate to the other copies (the issue of duplicate classes is not treated here).

4.3   Upgrading Object Instances

In order to control the upgrades of object instances of an upgraded class, an object will include information about its current class version in its class attribute *Cl*. At initialization, the class attribute will store the name and current version of its class. When a class has been upgraded new object instances automatically get the new class attributes, due to the dynamic mechanism for collecting class variables (Sect. 4.1). However the upgrade of existing object instances of the class must be closely controlled.

Recall that the binding mechanism is dynamic: each time an object needs to evaluate a method, it requests the code associated with this method name. The code of suspended methods has already been loaded, and will be able to complete their evaluation. Problems may arise when calling new methods or new versions of methods using new attributes that are not presently available in the object. *The upgrade of an object has to be performed after the upgrade of its class and before new code which may rely on new class attributes is evaluated.* As processes may be recursive and even nonterminating, objects cannot generally be expected to reach a state without pending processes, even if the loading of processes corresponding to new method calls from the environment is postponed as in [1, 9]. Consequently, it is too restrictive to wait for the completion of all pending methods before applying an upgrade. However, Creol objects may reach *quiescent* states when the processor has been released and before a pending process has been activated. In the case of process termination or an inner suspension point, *Pr* is empty. Any object which does not deadlock is guaranteed to eventually reach a quiescent state. In particular nonterminating activity is implemented by means of recursion, which ensures at least one quiescent state in each cycle. The mechanism for *object upgrade*, applied to quiescent states, is captured by the following equation:

$$\langle o : Ob \,|\, Cl : C \,\#\, n, Pr : \varepsilon \rangle \langle C \,\#\, n' : Cl \,|\, Att : \mathrm{A} \rangle$$
$$= \langle o : Ob \,|\, Cl : C \,\#\, n', Pr : \varepsilon \rangle \, \langle C \,\#\, n' : Cl \,|\, Att : \mathrm{A} \rangle \, getAttr(o, C, \mathrm{A}) \ \textbf{if } n' > n$$

A similar equation handles local synchronous calls.

Due to the implicit inheritance graph, upgrade of attributes is handled as standard object instantiation; this is given by the equations for *getAttr*, which recursively compute an object state from provided values for class parameters. For object upgrade the present object state A replaces the initial values, thus only new attributes get values computed while inspecting the inheritance graph starting at class *C*. The use of equations corresponds to locking the object. Evaluation results in a term $gotAttr(o, \mathrm{A}')$ where A' is the resolved attribute list with values. The mechanism for *state upgrade*, replacing the old object state by the the new one, is captured by the following equation:

$$gotAttr(o, \mathrm{A}') \, \langle o : Ob \,|\, Att : \mathrm{A} \rangle = \langle o : Ob \,|\, Att : \mathrm{A}' \rangle$$

The described runtime mechanism allows the upgrade of active objects. Attributes are collected at upgrade time while code is loaded "on demand". A class may be upgraded several times before the object reaches a quiescent state, so the object may have missed some upgrades. However a single state upgrade suffices to ensure that the object, once upgraded, is a complete instance of the present version of its class. The upgrade mechanism ensures that an object upgrade has occurred before new code is evaluated.

After an upgrade the object is in a transitional mode, where its attributes are new but old code may still occur in the process queue. This explains why attributes may neither be removed nor change types during class upgrade. With this restriction, the evaluation of old code can be completed without errors. Notice that if a call to a redefined method *m* appears in remaining old code, the call will nevertheless be bound to the new version of *m*. This does not cause difficulties provided that the restrictions to covariance for in-parameters and contravariance for out-parameters are respected. This way, the use of recursion rather than while-loops allows a smooth upgrade of nonterminating activity.

4.4 Example: Analysis of a Bank Account Upgrade

The bank account example of Sect. 3.1 is now reconsidered to illustrate the operational semantics and its executable aspect, in order to provide some insight into the behavior of the asynchronous update mechanism. We define an initial configuration consisting of the original bank class and two new bank accounts *b* and *c* together with a deposit invocation, say !*b.deposit*(100), followed by a transfer !*b.transfer*(200, *c*). The transfer will be suspended since the balance is not large enough. We then augment the initial configuration with the class upgrade

> upgrade(BankAccount, ε, overdraft : Nat =100,
> **op** transfer (**in** sum : Nat, acc : Account) ==
> **await** bal ≥ sum−overdraft; bal := bal−sum; acc.deposit(sum))

In order to see the effect of executing the operational semantics, we use Maude's search facilities to search for all possible final states. The search results in two solutions: Both have succeeded in upgrading the bank account objects. In one solution the *b* account has a final balance of 100 and a pending transfer invocation which cannot be completed, whereas the other solution has a final balance of -100 and no pending code. In the the first solution the transfer invocation is bound before bank account *b* is upgraded, with the result that the transfer is suspended and cannot be completed (since it awaits *bal* ≥ *sum*). In the second solution, the bank account is upgraded before the transfer invocation is bound, with the result that the transfer is completed (since the upgraded transfer awaits *bal* ≥ *sum* − *overdraft*).

Can we guarantee that an upgrade will succeed? In order to illustrate this problem, we introduce a nonterminating activity: Let an object recursively make asynchronous calls !*b.deposit*(0) (which have no effect on the state of *b*). In this case a search for final states does not succeed, but we can search for all solutions for *N* deposit calls. Ignoring pending calls, there are two solutions for every fixed *N*: one solution has an upgraded class and the other does not. The analysis suggests that there is a race condition between the evaluation of *bind* and *update* messages with regard to the class representation in the global configuration. As the update rule is continuously enabled, weak fairness is needed to guarantee that the update will succeed. For simulation Maude's predefined fair rewrite strategy ensures that class updates will eventually be applied. In contrast the update rule for the object state is only enabled in quiescent states. Unless the object deadlocks quiescent states occur regularly, which suggests that strong fairness is needed to ensure that the update is applied. This problem is circumvented by using equations in RL; state updates have priority and will always be selected if enabled.

5   Related Work

Although many approaches to reconfigurable distributed systems [2, 4, 6, 14, 16, 21, 26] do not address availability requirements during reconfiguration, availability is an essential feature of many modern distributed applications. Dynamic or online system upgrade considers how running systems may evolve. Recently, several authors have investigated type-safe mechanisms for runtime upgrade of imperative [29], functional [5], and object-oriented [10] languages. The latter paper considers object instance evolution (reclassification) in Fickle, based on a type system which guarantees type safety when an object changes its class. These approaches consider the upgrade of single type declarations, procedures, objects, or components in the sequential setting. Fickle has been extended to multithreading [9], but restrictions to runtime reclassification are needed; e.g., an object with a nonterminating (recursive) method will not be reclassified.

Work on version control for modular systems aims at more generic upgrade support. Some approaches allow multiple versions of a module to coexist after an upgrade [3, 5, 11, 13, 15], while others keep only the latest version by performing a global update or "hot-swapping" [1, 7, 22, 25]. Another important distinction between different approaches is their treatment of active behavior. Upgrade of active behavior may be disallowed [7, 13, 22, 25], delayed [1, 9], or supported [15, 29]. Most approaches favoring global updates do not support the upgrade of an active module running the old version. A system which addresses the upgrade of active code is proposed in [29] for the setting of type declarations and procedures in (sequential) C. However, the approach is synchronous in the sense that upgrades which cannot be applied immediately will fail.

Dynamic class constructs may be considered as a form of version upgrade. Hjálmtýsson and Gray [15] propose an approach for C++ based on proxy classes through which the actual class is linked (reference indirection). Their approach supports multiple versions of each class. Because existing objects of the class are not upgraded, activity in existing objects is uninterrupted. Dynamic class upgrade in Java has been proposed using proxy classes [25] and by modifying the Java virtual machine [22]. Both approaches are based on global upgrade, but the approaches are not applicable to active objects.

Automatic upgrade based on lazy global update is addressed in [1] for distributed objects and in [7] for persistent object stores. Although the object instances of upgraded classes are upgraded in these works, inheritance is not addressed which limits the effect of class upgrade. Further, these approaches cannot handle (nonterminating) active code. Our approach supports multiple inheritance, but restricts upgrades to addition and redefinition and may therefore avoid these limitations. Only one version of an upgraded class is kept in the system but active objects may still be upgraded. Upgrade is asynchronous and distributed, and may therefore be temporarily delayed.

6   Conclusion

Many critical distributed systems need to be modified without compromising availability requirements. This paper exploits the class structure of object-oriented programs to introduce evolution of the inheritance graph at runtime. We have presented a novel construct for dynamic class upgrade in distributed object-oriented systems and formalized its operational semantics in rewriting logic. Upgrading a class has an effect on all its subclasses and all object instances of these classes. The construct allows classes to be extended with new attributes, new methods, and new ancestor classes, while existing methods may be redefined. A subtype relationship is needed for the redefinition of methods, while extension is not restricted. Active and nonterminating code may be upgraded. The mechanism ensures that virtual binding will still succeed after an upgrade.

Our formalization uses equations to update class version numbers for indirect class upgrade and to upgrade individual objects. This seems natural at a high level of abstraction. At a lower level of abstraction this semantics may lead to temporary locks on objects, since equations apply between rewrite steps. It is therefore of interest to investigate how these equations may be replaced by rules. In particular the equations for object upgrade could be reformulated as rules. However this would require the messages controlling method binding and attribute updating to include version number information, using conditional rules to ensure consistent version numbering.

In future work, we plan to study how dynamic class constructs as proposed in this paper may be improved through type analysis and provide formal proof that such upgrade mechanisms preserve strong typing. Furthermore it is interesting to consider upgrade mechanisms addressing several (hierarchies of) classes simultaneously. Such mechanisms could probably allow a more flexible notion of upgrade. In particular mutual and cyclic dependencies between objects could be addressed directly in the same upgrade. It seems probable that such package upgrades may require a more synchronized upgrade mechanism than the mechanism proposed here, resulting in considerably more overhead in the distributed concurrent setting.

References

1. S. Ajmani, B. Liskov, and L. Shrira. Scheduling and simulation: How to upgrade distributed systems. In *9th Workshop on Hot Topics in Operating Systems (HotOS-IX)*, pages 43–48. USENIX, May 2003.
2. J. P. A. Almeida, M. Wegdam, M. van Sinderen, and L. Nieuwenhuis. Transparent dynamic reconfiguration for CORBA, *Proc. 3rd Intl. Symp. on Distributed Objects and Applications (DOA)*, pages 197–207. IEEE CS Press, Sep. 2001.
3. J. L. Armstrong and S. R. Virding. Erlang - an experimental telephony programming language. In *XIII Intl. Switching Symposium*, June 1990.
4. C. Bidan, V. Issarny, T. Saridakis, and A. Zarras. A dynamic reconfiguration service for CORBA. In *4th Intl. Conf. on Configurable Dist. Systems*, pages 35–42. IEEE, May 1998.
5. G. Bierman, M. Hicks, P. Sewell, and G. Stoyle. Formalizing dynamic software updating. In *Proc. of the 2nd Intl. Workshop on Unanticipated Software Evolution (USE)*, Apr. 2003.
6. T. Bloom. *Dynamic Module Replacement in a Distributed Programming System*. PhD thesis, MIT, 1983. Also available as MIT LCS Tech. Report 303.
7. C. Boyapati, B. Liskov, L. Shrira, C.-H. Moh, and S. Richman. Lazy modular upgrades in persistent object stores. In R. Crocker and G. L. S. Jr., editors, *Proc. ACM Conf. on Object-Oriented Programming Systems, Languages and Applications (OOPSLA'03)*, pages 403–417. ACM Press, 2003.
8. M. Clavel, F. Durán, S. Eker, P. Lincoln, N. Martí-Oliet, J. Meseguer, and J. F. Quesada. Maude: Specification and programming in rewriting logic. *Theoretical Computer Science*, 285:187–243, Aug. 2002.
9. F. Damiani, M. Dezani-Ciancaglini, and P. Giannini. Re-classification and multithreading: Fickle$_{MT}$. In *Proc. Symp. on Applied Computing (SAC'04)*, pages 1297–1304. ACM, 2004.

10. S. Drossopoulou, F. Damiani, M. Dezani-Ciancaglini, and P. Giannini. More dynamic object re-classification: Fickle$_{II}$. *ACM Trans. on Prog. Lang. and Systems*, 24(2):153–191, 2002.
11. D. Duggan. Type-Based hot swapping of running modules. In C. Norris and J. J. B. Fenwick, editors, *Proc. of the 6th Intl. Conf. on Functional Programming(ICFP 01)*, volume 36, 10 of *ACM SIGPLAN notices*, pages 62–73, New York, Sept. 2001. ACM Press.
12. J. A. Goguen, T. Winkler, J. Meseguer, K. Futatsugi, and J.-P. Jouannaud. Introducing OBJ. In J. A. Goguen and G. Malcolm, editors, *Software Engineering with OBJ: Algebraic Specification in Action*, Advances in Formal Methods, chapter 1, pages 3–167. Klüwer, 2000.
13. D. Gupta, P. Jalote, and G. Barua. A formal framework for on-line software version change. *IEEE Trans. Software Eng.*, 22(2):120–131, 1996.
14. R. S. Hall, D. Heimbigner, A. van der Hoek, and A. L. Wolf. An architecture for post-development configuration management in a wide-area network. In *Intl. Conf. on Dist. Computing Systems*, pages 269–279. IEEE CS Press, May 1997.
15. G. Hjálmtýsson and R. S. Gray. Dynamic C++ classes: A lightweight mechanism to update code in a running program. In *Proc. 1998 USENIX Technical Conf.* USENIX, May 1998.
16. C. R. Hofmeister and J. M. Purtilo. A framework for dynamic reconfiguration of distributed programs. Technical Report CS-TR-3119, University of Maryland, College Park, 1993.
17. E. B. Johnsen and O. Owe. An asynchronous communication model for distributed concurrent objects. In *Proc. 2nd IEEE Intl. Conf. on Software Engineering and Formal Methods (SEFM'04)*, pages 188–197. IEEE CS Press, Sept. 2004.
18. E. B. Johnsen and O. Owe. Inheritance in the presence of asynchronous method calls. In *Proc. 38th Hawaii Intl. Conf. on System Sciences (HICSS'05)*. IEEE CS Press, Jan. 2005.
19. E. B. Johnsen, O. Owe, and E. W. Axelsen. A run-time environment for concurrent objects with asynchronous methods calls. In *Proc. 5th Intl. Workshop on Rewriting Logic and its Applications (WRLA'04)*, Electr. Notes Theor. Comput. Sci. 117: 375–392, Jan. 2005.
20. A. Ketfi and N. Belkhatir. A metamodel-based approach for the dynamic reconfiguration of component-based software. In J. Bosch and C. Krueger, editors, *Proc. Intl. Conf. on Software Reuse 2004*, LNCS 3107, pages 264–273. Springer, 2004.
21. J. Kramer and J. Magee. The Evolving Philosophers Problem: Dynamic change management. *IEEE Trans. Software Eng.*, 16(11):1293–1306, Nov. 1990.
22. S. Malabarba, R. Pandey, J. Gragg, E. Barr, and J. F. Barnes. Runtime support for type-safe dynamic Java classes. In E. Bertino, editor, *14th European Conf. on Object-Oriented Programming (ECOOP'00)*, LNCS 1850, pages 337–361. Springer, June 2000.
23. J. Meseguer. Conditional rewriting logic as a unified model of concurrency. *Theoretical Computer Science*, 96:73–155, 1992.
24. E. Najm and J.-B. Stefani. A formal semantics for the ODP computational model. *Computer Networks and ISDN Systems*, 27:1305–1329, 1995.
25. A. Orso, A. Rao, and M. J. Harrold. A technique for dynamic updating of Java software. In *Proc. Intl. Conf. on Software Maintenance (ICSM 2002)*, pages 649–658. IEEE CS Press, Oct. 2002.
26. T. Ritzau and J. Andersson. Dynamic deployment of Java applications. In *Java for Embedded Systems Workshop*, London, May 2000.
27. C. A. N. Soules, *et al.* System support for online reconfiguration. In *Proc. 2003 USENIX Technical Conf.*, pages 141–154. USENIX, 2003.
28. I. Stojmenović, M. Seddigh, and J. Zunic. Dominating sets and neighbor elimination based broadcasting algorithms in wireless networks. *IEEE Trans. on Parallel and Distributed Systems*, 13:14–25, 2002.
29. G. Stoyle, M. Hicks, G. Bierman, P. Sewell, and I. Neamtiu. *Mutatis Mutandis*: Safe and flexible dynamic software updating. In *Proc. of the Conf. on Principles of Programming Languages (POPL'05)*, pages 183–194. ACM Press, Jan. 2005.
30. A. Yonezawa. *ABCL: An Object-Oriented Concurrent System*. The MIT Press, 1990.

An Abstract Machine for the Kell Calculus*

Philippe Bidinger**, Alan Schmitt, and Jean-Bernard Stefani

INRIA Rhône-Alpes, 38334 St Ismier, France
{Philippe.Bidinger,Alan.Schmitt,Jean-Bernard Stefani}
@inrialpes.fr

Abstract. The Kell Calculus is a family of process calculi intended as a basis for studying distributed component-based programming. This paper presents an abstract machine for an instance of this calculus, a proof of its correctness, and a prototype OCaml implementation. The main originality of our abstract machine is that it does not mandate a particular physical configuration (e.g. mapping of localities to physical sites), and it is independent of any supporting network services. This allows to separate the proof of correctness of the abstract machine per se, from the proof of correctness of higher-level communication and migration protocols which can be implemented on the machine.

1 Introduction

The Kell calculus [18, 17] is a family of higher-order process calculi with hierarchical localities and locality passivation, which is indexed by the pattern language used in input constructs. It has been introduced to study programming models for wide-area distributed systems and component-based systems. A major assumption in a wide-area environment is the need for modular dynamicity, *i.e.* the ability to modify a running system by replacing some of its components, or by introducing new components (*e.g.* plug-ins). The Kell calculus can be seen as an attempt to understand the operational basis of *modular dynamicity*: localities in the Kell calculus model named components, and locality passivation provides the basis for dynamic reconfiguration operations.

Two of the main design principles for the calculus are to keep all the actions "local" in order to facilitate its distributed implementation, and to allow different forms of localities to coexist. A consequence of the locality principle is that the calculus allows different forms of networks to be modeled (by different processes). Thus, on the one hand, an implementation of the calculus should not need to consider atomic actions occurring across wide-area networks. On the other hand, an implementation of the calculus should not imply the use of purely asynchronous communications between localities: one can have legitimate implementations of the calculus that exploit and rely on the synchronous or quasi-synchronous properties of specific environments (e.g. a local machine with different processes, a high-performance, low-latency local area network for homogeneous PC clusters).

---

* This work has been supported by EU project MIKADO IST-2001-32222.
** Partly supported by EU IHP Marie Curie Training Site 'DisCo: Semantic Foundations of Distributed Computation', contract HPMT-CT-2001-00290.

M. Steffen and G. Zavattaro (Eds.): FMOODS 2005, LNCS 3535, pp. 31–46, 2005.
© IFIP International Federation for Information Processing 2005

We present in this paper a distributed abstract machine for an instance of the Kell calculus, and its implementation in OCaml. The original feature of our abstract machine is that, in contrast to other works on abstract machines for distributed process calculi, it does not depend on a given network model, and can be used to implement the calculus in different physical configurations. Let us explain in more detail what this means. An implementation of our abstract machine typically comprises two distinct parts:

- An implementation of the abstract machine specification per se, that conforms to the reduction rules given in section 3 below.
- Libraries, in the chosen implementation language, that provides access to network services, and that conform to a Kell calculus model of these services (i.e. a Kell calculus process).

For instance, assume that one wants to realize a physical configuration consisting of a network N, that interconnects two computers m_1 and m_2, that each run an implementation of the Kell calculus abstract machine, and a Kell calculus program (P_1 and P_2, respectively). This configuration would be modelled in the Kell calculus by the process

$$C \triangleq N[\texttt{Net} \mid m_1[\texttt{NetLib} \mid P_1] \mid m_2[\texttt{NetLib} \mid P_2]]$$

where the process Net models the behavior of network N, and where the process NetLib models the presence, at each site, of a library providing access to the network services modeled by Net. From the point of view of the Kell calculus abstract machine, the library NetLib is just a standard Kell calculus process, but whose communications will have side-effects (i.e. accessing the actual network services modelled by Net) outside the abstract machine implementation.

The interesting aspect of our approach is the fact that we can thus provide implementations for different environments which all rely on the same abstract machine description and implementation. Consider for instance the physical configuration consisting of a network N, that interconnects two computers m_1 and m_2, that each run two separate processes, p_i^1 and p_i^2 ($i = 1, 2$). Each process p_i^j runs an implementation of the abstract machine, with a program Q_i^j. This configuration can be modelled by

$$C' \triangleq N[\texttt{Net} \mid M_1 \mid M_2]$$

$$M_1 \triangleq m_1[\texttt{NetOS} \mid \texttt{Ipc} \mid p_1^1[\texttt{NetLib} \mid \texttt{IpcLib} \mid Q_1^1] \mid p_1^2[\texttt{NetLib} \mid \texttt{IpcLib} \mid Q_1^2]]$$

$$M_2 \triangleq m_2[\texttt{NetOS} \mid \texttt{Ipc} \mid p_2^1[\texttt{NetLib} \mid \texttt{IpcLib} \mid Q_2^1] \mid p_2^2[\texttt{NetLib} \mid \texttt{IpcLib} \mid Q_2^2]]$$

where the process NetOS models the presence, at each site m_i, of some means (e.g. an operating system library) to access the network services modeled by Net, where the process Ipc models the presence, at each site, of a local communication library (e.g. an interprocess communication library provided by the local operating system), and where the processes NetLib and IpcLib model the presence, at each process p_i^j, of interfaces for accessing the different communication services provided, respectively, by the combination Net and NetOS, and by Ipc. Again, NetLib and IpcLib both appear as standard Kell calculus processes from the point of view of the abstract machine (i.e. they communicate with other processes by message exchange and can become passivated with their enclosing locality). However, the communication services they give access to can have very different semantics, if only in terms of reliability, latency, or security. The important point to note is that different communication services can coexist in the same implementation, and can be used selectively by application processes.

An important benefit of the independence of our abstract machine specification from any supporting network services, made possible by the local character of primitives in the Kell calculus, is the simplification of its proof of correctness. Indeed, the proof of correctness of our abstract machine does not involve the proof of a non-trivial distributed migration protocol, as is the case, for instance, with the JoCaml implementation of the distributed Join calculus [5], or with various abstract machines for ambient calculi [7, 10, 5, 14] [1]. Furthermore, the correctness of the machine is ensured, regardless of the network services used for the actual implementation.

The abstract machine described in this paper constitutes a first step in a potential series of more and more refined abstract machines, getting us closer to a provably correct implementation of the calculus. Such a progressive approach aims at breaking up the proof of correctness of an abstract machine close to implementation into more tractable steps. For this reason, our abstract machine remains non-deterministic, and still has a number of high-level constructs such as variable substitution. Compared to the calculus, the abstract machine realizes three important functions: (1) it handles names and name restriction; (2) it "flattens" a Kell calculus process with nested localities into a configuration of non-nested localities with dependency pointers; (3) it makes explicit high-level process marshalling and unmarshalling functions which are involved in the implementation of the locality passivation construct of the Kell calculus.

The correctness of the abstract machine is stated, following [14], as barbed bisimilarity between a process of the calculus and its abstract machine interpretation. However, the results we obtain are in fact stronger than pure barbed bisimilarity as they involve some form of contextual equivalence. The results are stated using a strong form of bisimilarity, for we use a notion of sub-reduction to abstract away purely administrative reductions. Proofs can be found in the long version of this paper, available at [11].

The paper is organized as follows. Section 2 presents the instance of the Kell calculus we use in this paper. Section 3 specifies our abstract machine for the calculus. In Section 4 we give a correctness result for the abstract machine. In Section 5, we discuss an Ocaml prototype implementation of our abstract machine. In Section 6, we discuss related works. Section 7 concludes the paper with a discussion of future work.

2   The Kell Calculus: Syntax and Operational Semantics

2.1   Syntax

We now define the instance of the kell calculus we use in this paper. We allow five kinds of input patterns: *kell patterns*, that match a subkell, *local patterns*, that match a local message, *up patterns*, that match a message in the parent kell, and two kinds of *down patterns*, that match a message from a subkell. The syntax of the Kell calculus, together with the syntax of evaluation contexts, is given below:

---

[1] Note that the Channel Ambient abstract machine presented in [13] assumes that ambients may synchronize, for instance to run an **in** primitive. This assumption might be difficult to implement in an asynchronous distributed setting.

$$P ::= \mathbf{0} \mid x \mid \xi \triangleright P \mid \nu a.P \mid P \mid P \mid a[P] \mid a\langle \widetilde{P} \rangle$$

$$P_* ::= \mathbf{0} \mid x \mid \xi \triangleright P \mid P_* \mid P_* \mid a[P_*] \mid a\langle \widetilde{P} \rangle$$

$$\xi ::= a\langle \widetilde{u} \rangle \mid a\langle \widetilde{u} \rangle^{\downarrow} \mid a\langle \widetilde{u} \rangle^{\downarrow^a} \mid a\langle \widetilde{u} \rangle^{\uparrow} \mid a[x]$$

$$u ::= x \mid (x)$$

$$\mathbf{E} ::= \cdot \mid \nu a.\mathbf{E} \mid a[\mathbf{E}] \mid P \mid \mathbf{E}$$

Filling the hole $\cdot$ in an evaluation context $\mathbf{E}$ with a Kell calculus term Q results in a Kell calculus term noted $\mathbf{E}\{Q\}$.

We assume an infinite set N of *names*. We let a, b, x, y and their decorated variants range over N. Note that names in the kell calculus act both as name constants and as (name or process) variables. We use $\widetilde{V}$ to denote finite vectors $(V_1, \ldots, V_q)$. Abusing notation, we equate $\widetilde{V}$ with the word $V_1 \ldots V_n$ and the set $\{V_1, \ldots, V_n\}$.

Terms in the Kell calculus grammar are called *processes*. We note K the set of Kell calculus processes. We let P, Q, R and their decorated variants range over processes. We say that a process is in *normal form* when it does not contain any name restriction operator. We use P_*, Q_*, R_* and their decorated variants to denote these processes. We call *message* a process of the form $a\langle \widetilde{P} \rangle$. We call *kell* [2] a process of the form $a[P]$, with a called the name of the kell. In a kell of the form $a[\ldots \mid a_j[P_j] \mid \ldots \mid Q_k \mid \ldots]$ we call *subkells* the processes $a_j[P_j]$. We call *trigger* a process of the form $\xi \triangleright P$, where ξ is a *receipt pattern* (or *pattern*, for short). A pattern can be an *up pattern* $a\langle \widetilde{u} \rangle^{\uparrow}$, a *down pattern* $a\langle \widetilde{u} \rangle^{\downarrow^b}$ or $a\langle \widetilde{u} \rangle^{\downarrow}$, a *local pattern* $a\langle \widetilde{u} \rangle$, or a *control pattern* $a[x]$. A down pattern $a\langle \widetilde{u} \rangle^{\downarrow^b}$ matches a message on channel a coming from a subkell named b. A down pattern $a\langle \widetilde{u} \rangle^{\downarrow}$ matches a message on channel a coming from any subkell.

In a term $\nu a.P$, the scope extends as far to the right as possible. In a term $\xi \triangleright P$, the scope of $\triangleright$ extends as far to the right as possible. Thus, $a\langle c \rangle \triangleright P \mid Q$ stands for $a\langle c \rangle \triangleright (P \mid Q)$. We use standard abbreviations from the the π-calculus: $\nu a_1 \ldots a_q.P$ for $\nu a_1. \ldots \nu a_q.P$, or $\nu \widetilde{a}.P$ if $\widetilde{a} = (a_1 \ldots a_q)$. By convention, if the name vector $\widetilde{a}$ is empty, then $\nu \widetilde{a}.P \triangleq P$. We also note $\prod_{i \in I} P_i$, $I = \{1, \ldots, n\}$ the parallel composition $(P_1 \mid (\ldots (P_{n-1} \mid P_n) \ldots))$. By convention, if $I = \emptyset$, then $\prod_{i \in I} P_i \triangleq \mathbf{0}$.

A pattern ξ acts as a binder in the calculus. All names x that do not occur within parenthesis () in a pattern ξ are bound by the pattern. We call *pattern variables* (or *variables*, for short) such bound names in a pattern. Variables occurring in a pattern are supposed to be linear, i.e. there is only one occurrence of each variable in a given pattern. Names occurring in a pattern ξ under parenthesis (i.e. occurrences of the form (x) in ξ) are *not* bound in the pattern. We call them free pattern names (or free names, for short). We assumes that bound names of a pattern are disjoint from free names. The other binder in the calculus is the ν operator, which corresponds to the restriction operator of the π-calculus. Free names (fn), bound names (bn), free pattern variables (fpn), and bound pattern names (bpn) are defined as usual. We just point out the handling of free pattern names:

$$\mathtt{fpn}(a\langle \widetilde{u} \rangle) = \{a\} \cup \{x \in \mathsf{N} \mid (x) \in \widetilde{u}\} \qquad \mathtt{bpn}(a\langle \widetilde{u} \rangle) = \{x \in \mathsf{N} \mid x \in \widetilde{u}\}$$

---

[2] The work "kell" is intended to remind the word "cell", in a loose analogy with biological cells.

$$\nu a.\mathbf{0} \equiv \mathbf{0} \ [\text{S.Nu.Nil}] \qquad\qquad \nu a.\nu b.P \equiv \nu b.\nu a.P \ [\text{S.Nu.Comm}]$$

$$\frac{a \notin \text{fn}(Q)}{(\nu a.P) \mid Q \equiv \nu a.P \mid Q} \ [\text{S.Nu.Par}] \qquad \frac{P =_\alpha Q}{P \equiv Q} \ [\text{S.}\alpha] \qquad \frac{P \equiv Q}{\mathbf{E}\{P\} \equiv \mathbf{E}\{Q\}} \ [\text{S.Context}]$$

Fig. 1. Structural equivalence

$$\frac{a \neq b}{a[\nu b.P] \overset{\equiv}{\to} \nu b.a[P]} \ [\text{SR.New}] \qquad\qquad \frac{P \overset{\equiv}{\to} P'}{E[P] \overset{\equiv}{\to} E[P']} \ [\text{SR.Context}]$$

$$\frac{P' \equiv P \quad P \overset{\equiv}{\to} Q \quad Q \equiv Q'}{P' \overset{\equiv}{\to} Q'} \ [\text{SR.Struct}]$$

$$\frac{\tilde{v} = \tilde{u}\varphi}{c\langle\tilde{v}\rangle \mid b[R \mid (c\langle\tilde{u}\rangle^\uparrow \rhd Q)] \to b[R \mid Q\varphi]} \ [\text{R.In}] \qquad \frac{\tilde{v} = \tilde{u}\varphi}{c\langle\tilde{v}\rangle \mid (c\langle\tilde{u}\rangle \rhd Q) \to Q\varphi} \ [\text{R.Local}]$$

$$\frac{\tilde{v} = \tilde{u}\varphi \quad \downarrow^\bullet = \downarrow^b \wedge \downarrow^\bullet = \downarrow}{b[c\langle\tilde{v}\rangle \mid R] \mid (c\langle\tilde{u}\rangle^{\downarrow^\bullet} \rhd Q) \to b[R] \mid Q\varphi} \ [\text{R.Out}]$$

$$\frac{}{a[P_*] \mid (a[x] \rhd Q) \to Q\{P_*/x\}} \ [\text{R.Pass}] \qquad \frac{P \to Q}{\mathbf{E}\{P\} \to \mathbf{E}\{Q\}} \ [\text{R.Context}]$$

$$\frac{P' \equiv P \quad P \to Q \quad Q \equiv Q'}{P' \to Q'} \ [\text{R.Struct}] \qquad \frac{P' \overset{\equiv^*}{\to} P \quad P \to Q}{P' \to Q} \ [\text{R.Struct.Extr}]$$

Fig. 2. Reduction Relation

We call *substitution* a function $\phi : \mathsf{N} \to \mathsf{N} \uplus \mathsf{K}$ from names to names and Kell calculus processes that is the identity except on a finite set of names. We note supp the support of a substitution (*i.e.* $\text{supp}(\phi) = \{i \in \mathsf{N} \mid \phi(i) \neq i\}$). We assume when writing $\xi\phi$ that $\text{fpn}(\xi) \cap \text{supp}(\phi) = \emptyset$ and that $\text{supp}(\phi) \subseteq \text{bpn}(\xi)$.

We note $P =_\alpha Q$ when two terms P and Q are α-convertible.

Formally, the reduction rules in section 2.2 could yield terms of the form $P[Q]$, which are not legal Kell calculus terms (i.e. the syntax does not distinguish between names playing the role of name variables, and names playing the role of process variables). However, a simple type system can be used to rule out such illegal terms.

2.2 Reduction Semantics

The operational semantics of the Kell calculus is defined in the CHAM style [1], via a structural equivalence relation and a reduction relation. The structural equivalence $\equiv$ is the smallest equivalence relation that verifies the rules in Figure 1 and that makes the parallel operator $\mid$ associative and commutative, with $\mathbf{0}$ as a neutral element.

The reduction relation $\to$ is the smallest binary relation on K that satisfies the rules given in Figure 2.

Notice that we do not have structural equivalence rules that deal with scope extrusion beyond a kell boundary (i.e we do not have the Mobile Ambient rule $a[\nu b.P] \equiv \nu b.a[P]$, provided $b \neq a$). This is to avoid phenomena as illustrated below:

$$(a[x] \rhd x \mid x) \mid a[\nu b.P] \; \to \; (\nu b.P) \mid (\nu b.P) \qquad (a[x] \rhd x \mid x) \mid \nu b.a[P] \; \to \; \nu b.P \mid P$$

However, such name extrusion is still needed to allow communication across kell boundaries. The solution adopted here is to allow only scope *extrusion* across kell boundaries and to restrict passivation to processes without name restriction in evaluation context. Formally, this is achieved by requiring a process to be in normal form (P_*) in rule R.PASS and by adding a scope extrusion sub-reduction relation $\overset{\equiv}{\to}$.

Rules R.IN and R.OUT govern the crossing of kell boundaries. Only messages may cross a kell boundary. In rule R.IN, a trigger receives a message from the outside of the enclosing kell. In rule R.OUT, a trigger receives a message from a subkell.

3   Abstract Machine

3.1   Syntax

Following [14], our abstract machine is specified in the form of a process calculus whose terms, called *machine terms*, correspond to abstract machine states. Intuitively, a machine term consists in a set of localities, each executing a different program, organized in a tree by means of pointers between localities.

The syntax of the abstract machine calculus is given below:

$$M ::= \mathbf{0} \quad | \quad L \quad | \quad M \mid M \qquad\qquad M_* ::= \mathbf{0} \quad | \quad L_* \quad | \quad M_* \mid M_*$$
$$L ::= h : m[P]_{k,S} \qquad\qquad\qquad L_* ::= h : m[P_*]_{k,S}$$
$$S ::= \emptyset \quad | \quad h \quad | \quad S, S$$

$$P ::= \mathbf{0} \quad | \quad x \quad | \quad \xi \rhd P \quad | \quad \nu a.P \quad | \quad P \mid P \quad | \quad a[P] \quad | \quad a\langle \widetilde{P} \rangle \quad | \quad \mathbf{reify}(k, M_*)$$
$$P_* ::= \mathbf{0} \quad | \quad x \quad | \quad \xi \rhd P \quad | \quad P_* \mid P_* \quad | \quad a\langle \widetilde{P} \rangle$$
$$\xi ::= a\langle \widetilde{u} \rangle \quad | \quad a\langle \widetilde{u} \rangle^{\downarrow} \quad | \quad a\langle \widetilde{u} \rangle^{\downarrow^a} \quad | \quad a\langle \widetilde{u} \rangle^{\uparrow} \quad | \quad a[x]$$
$$u ::= x \quad | \quad (x) \qquad x \in \mathsf{N} \qquad h,k,l \in \mathsf{MN} \qquad a,m \in \mathsf{N} \cup \mathsf{MN}$$

Terms generated by the productions M, M_* in the abstract machine grammar are called *machine terms* (or *machines* for short, when no ambiguity arises), and are ranged over by M, N and their decorated variants. We designate their set by M. Machine terms make use of two sorts of names: the set N and a disjoint infinite set MN whose elements are called *machine names*. We call *locality* a machine term of the form $h : m[P]_{k,S}$. In a locality $h : m[P]_{k,S}$, m is the name of the kell the locality represents, h is the machine name of the locality, k is the machine name of its parent locality, S is the set of the machine names of its sublocalities, and P is the *machine process* being run at locality h. We use three particular machine names: $\mathbf{r}$, $\mathbf{rn}$ and $\mathbf{rp}$, which denote, respectively, the machine name of the root locality, the name of the root kell (associated with the root locality), and the machine name of the (virtual) root parent locality. Machine names appearing in a machine term are all unique (in contrast to kell names).

$$\frac{M =_\alpha N}{M \equiv N} \ [\text{M.SE.}\alpha] \qquad\qquad \frac{P \equiv P' \qquad S \equiv S'}{l : h[P]_{k,S} \equiv l : h[P']_{k,S'}} \ [\text{M.SE.CTX}]$$

Fig. 3. Structural equivalence for machines

We call MK the set of machine processes (i.e. terms generated via the productions P, P_* in the abstract machine grammar), and we have $\mathsf{K} \subseteq \mathsf{MK}$. The machine processes are slightly different from Kell calculus processes. First a new term $\mathbf{reify}(k, M_*)$ is introduced to represent a passivated machine. The term M_* is a tree of machines encoded as a parallel composition of localities and k is the machine name of the root of this tree. Secondly, the names that can be used by a machine process belong to $\mathsf{N} \cup \mathsf{MN}$. This point will be made clear in the next subsection. A machine process is in normal form, written P_*, when it has no name restriction operator nor kells in evaluation context. A machine is in normal form when all machine processes in its localities are in normal form. We use the $._*$ suffix to denote machines and processes in normal form. The definitions and conventions given in section 2 extend to machine processes. Note that we use the same meta-variables to denote processes and machine processes. When it is not clear from the context, we will precise whether a variable denote a process or a machine process.

3.2 Reduction Semantics

The reduction relation is defined as for the calculus via a structural congruence relation and a reduction relation.

First, we define two equivalence relations (both denoted by $\equiv$), on machine processes and sets of localities, respectively, as the smallest relations that make the parallel operator $|$ (resp. the , operator) associative and commutative with $\mathbf{0}$ (resp. $\emptyset$) as a neutral element. Then, we define the structural congruence $\equiv$ on machines as the smallest equivalence relation that verifies the rules in figure 3 and that makes the parallel operator $|$ associative and commutative with $\mathbf{0}$ as a neutral element.

This structural equivalence, together with the rules M.S.CTX and M.S.STR, allows us to view machines as sets of localities and terms S as sets of machine names. Note that the equivalence relation on machine processes is different from the one on kell calculus processes as it does not contain rules dealing with restriction. This is because restriction is handled by the abstract machine as a name creation operator (rule M.S.NEW).

The reduction relation is defined as the smallest relation that satisfies the rules in Figures 4 and 5. It uses a subreduction relation $\overset{\equiv}{\rightarrow}$. The first subreduction rule, M.S.NEW, deals with restriction, which is interpreted as name creation. The reason the rule imposes the newly created name to be a machine name is related to the correctness proof, where we need to distinguish between restricted and free Kell names. Rule M.S.CELL creates a new locality when a kell is in the locality process. Rule M.S.ACT activates a passivated machine. Activation involves releasing the process held in the root locality of the passivated machine in the current locality, and releasing the sublocalities of the passivated machine as new sublocalities of the current locality.

$$\frac{l\ fresh \in \mathsf{MN}}{h : n[(\nu a.P) \mid Q]_{k,S} \overset{\equiv}{\to} h : n[P\{l/a\} \mid Q]_{k,S}} \quad [\text{M.S.New}]$$

$$\frac{h'\ fresh \in \mathsf{MN}}{h : n[m[P] \mid Q]_{k,S} \overset{\equiv}{\to} h : n[Q]_{k,(S,h')} \mid h' : m[P]_{h,\emptyset}} \quad [\text{M.S.Cell}]$$

$$\frac{\begin{array}{c} M_* = l : n[R_*]_{l',S'} \mid M'_* \\ \mathbf{locnames}(M'_*) = \{l_i/i \in I\} \quad k_i\ fresh \in \mathsf{MN},\ i \in I \end{array}}{h : m[\mathbf{reify}(l, M_*) \mid P]_{k,S} \overset{\equiv}{\to} h : m[R_* \mid P]_{k,(S,S'\{k_i/l_i\}_{i \in I}} \mid M'_*\{h/l\}\{k_i/l_i\}_{i \in I}} \quad [\text{M.S.Act}]$$

$$\frac{M \overset{\equiv}{\to} M'}{M \mid N \overset{\equiv}{\to} M' \mid N} \ [\text{M.S.Ctx}] \qquad \frac{M \equiv M' \quad M' \overset{\equiv}{\to} M'' \quad M'' \equiv M'''}{M \overset{\equiv}{\to} M'''} \ [\text{M.S.Str}]$$

Fig. 4. Sub-reduction for machines

The reduction rules M.IN, M.OUT, M.LOCAL, and M.PASS are the direct equivalent of the Kell calculus rules R.IN, R.OUT, R.LOCAL, and R.PASS, respectively. In rule M.PASS, the localities passivated are in normal form.

The reduction rules use the auxiliary function **locnames**, the predicate **tree**, and the notion of well-formed machine, which we now define.

The predicate $\mathbf{tree}(M, l, a, p)$ is defined as follows (where S may be empty):

$$\mathbf{tree}(M, l, a, p) = (M \equiv l : a[P]_{p,S} \mid \prod_{j \in S} M_j) \wedge_{j \in S} \mathbf{tree}(M_i, l_j, a_j, p_j)$$

with the additional condition that l, p, l_j, p_j are all distinct.

The function $\mathbf{locnames}(M)$ designates the set of locality names of all localities present in a machine M.

We say that a machine M is *well-formed* if we have $\mathbf{tree}(M, \mathbf{r}, \mathbf{rn}, \mathbf{rp})$. The set of well-formed machines is noted WFM. Finally, we will need the relation $\cong$ defined as follows: $M \cong N$ if and only if $\mathbf{tree}(M, l, m, p)$ and $M\sigma \equiv N\sigma'$ where σ and σ' are injective renaming of machine names such that $\sigma(l) = \sigma'(l) = l$ and $\sigma(p) = \sigma'(p) = p$ and if $m \in \mathsf{MN}$, $\sigma(m) = \sigma'(m) = m$.

4 Correctness

We establish the correctness of our abstract machine by establishing a strong bisimilarity result between Kell calculus processes and their interpretation by the abstract machine. The notion of equivalence we adopt is strong barbed bisimulation [15], which we denote by $\sim$. This notion of bisimulation can be used to compare different transition systems, provided that they are equipped with observability predicates and a reduction relation. An originality of our correctness result is that it relies on a strong form of barbed bisimilarity, instead of a weak one. This is possible because we abstract away administrative reduction rules through the subreduction relations in both the calculus and the abstract machine semantics. Our main result is the following:

Theorem 1 (Correctness). *For any Kell calculus process P, we have* $[\![P]\!] \sim P$.

$$\frac{P \to P'}{P \mid Q \to P' \mid Q} \; [\text{M.PAR}] \qquad\qquad \frac{\xi = c\langle\widetilde{u}\rangle}{\xi\varphi \mid (\xi \triangleright Q) \to Q\varphi} \; [\text{M.LOCAL}]$$

$$\frac{\xi = c\langle\widetilde{u}\rangle^{\uparrow}}{h : a[\xi\varphi \mid P]_{k,S} \mid h' : b[(\xi \triangleright Q) \mid R]_{h,S'} \mapsto h : a[P]_{k,S} \mid h' : b[Q\varphi \mid R]_{h,S'}} \; [\text{M.IN}]$$

$$\frac{\xi = c\langle\widetilde{u}\rangle^{\downarrow} \; \vee \; \xi = c\langle\widetilde{u}\rangle^{\downarrow^a}}{h : a[\xi\varphi \mid P]_{h',S} \mid h' : b[(\xi \triangleright Q) \mid R]_{k',S'} \mapsto h : a[P]_{h',S} \mid h' : b[Q\varphi \mid R]_{k',S'}} \; [\text{M.OUT}]$$

$$\frac{M_* = l : a[R_*]_{h,S'} \mid M'_* \qquad \mathbf{tree}(M_*, l, a, h)}{h : m[(a[x] \triangleright P) \mid Q]_{k,S} \mid M_* \mapsto h : m[P\{\mathbf{reify}(l, M_*)/x\} \mid Q]_{k,S\setminus l}} \; [\text{M.PASS}]$$

$$\frac{M \mapsto M'}{M \mid N \mapsto M' \mid N} \; [\text{M.CTX}] \qquad \frac{M \equiv M' \qquad M' \mapsto M'' \qquad M'' \equiv M'''}{M \mapsto M'''} \; [\text{M.STR}]$$

$$\frac{P \to P'}{h : m[P]_{k,S} \mapsto h : m[P']_{k,S}} \; [\text{M.RED}] \qquad \frac{M \overset{\equiv}{\to}^* M' \qquad M' \mapsto M''}{M \to M''} \; [\text{M.NORM}]$$

Fig. 5. Reduction for machines

This theorem asserts the equivalence of any Kell calculus process P with its translation in the abstract machine calculus. In the rest of this section we give the main definitions and intermediate results that intervene in the proof of Theorem 1.

We first define the translation of a Kell calculus process in the abstract machine calculus.

Definition 1. $[\![P]\!] = \mathbf{r} : \mathbf{rn}[P]_{\mathbf{rp},\emptyset}$

A first important property of our model is to ensure that the tree structure of the machine is preserved through reduction.

Proposition 1 (Well-Formedness). *If* $\mathbf{tree}(M, l, a, p)$ *and* $M \cong M'$, $M \overset{\equiv}{\to} M'$, $M \mapsto M'$, *or* $M \to M'$, *then* $\mathbf{tree}(M', l, a, p)$. *In particular, well-formedness is preserved by reduction. Moreover, for any process* P, $[\![P]\!]$ *is well-formed.*

From now on, unless otherwise stated, we only consider machine terms M such that $\mathbf{tree}(M, l, a, p)$ for some names l, a, p. The definitions of strong barbed bisimulation and strong barbed bisimilarity are classical [15]. We reproduce them below.

Definition 2 (Strong barbed bisimulation). *Let* TS_1 *and* TS_2 *be two sets of transition systems equipped with the same observability predicates* $\downarrow_a$, $a \in \mathbb{N}$. *A relation* $R \subseteq TS_1 \times TS_2$ *is a* strong barbed simulation *if whenever* $(A, B) \in R$, *we have*

- *If* $A \downarrow_a$ *then* $B \downarrow_a$
- *If* $A \to A'$ *then there exists* B' *such that* $B \to B'$ *and* $(A', B') \in R'$

A relation R *is a* strong barbed bisimulation *if* R *and* R^{-1} *are both strong barbed simulations.*

Definition 3 (Strong barbed bisimilarity). *Two transition systems A and B are said to be* strongly barbed bisimilar, *noted $A \sim B$, if there exists a strong barbed bisimulation R such that $(A, B) \in R$.*

To define strong bisimilarity for Kell calculus processes and machines we rely on the following observability predicates.

Definition 4 (Observability predicate for processes). *If P is a Kell calculus process, $P \downarrow_a$ holds if one of the following cases holds:*

1. $P \equiv \overset{\equiv}{\rightarrow}^* \nu\widetilde{c}.a\langle\widetilde{P}\rangle \mid R \mid P'$, *with $a \notin \widetilde{c}$*
2. $P \equiv \overset{\equiv}{\rightarrow}^* \nu\widetilde{c}.m[a\langle\widetilde{P}\rangle \mid R] \mid P'$, *with $a \notin \widetilde{c}$*
3. $P \equiv \overset{\equiv}{\rightarrow}^* \nu\widetilde{c}.a[P] \mid P'$, *with $a \notin \widetilde{c}$*

Definition 5 (Observability predicate for machines). *If M is a well-formed machine and $a \in N$, $M \downarrow_a$ holds if one of the following cases holds:*

1. $M \equiv \overset{\equiv}{\rightarrow}^* \mathbf{r} : \mathbf{rn}[a\langle\widetilde{P}\rangle \mid R]_{\mathbf{rp},S} \mid M'$
2. $M \equiv \overset{\equiv}{\rightarrow}^* h : m[a\langle\widetilde{P}\rangle \mid R]_{\mathbf{r},S} \mid M'$
3. $M \equiv \overset{\equiv}{\rightarrow}^* h : a[P]_{\mathbf{r},S} \mid M'$

Intuitively , a barb on a means that after an arbitrary number of administrative reductions, a process P (or machine M) can exhibit a local message (clause 1), a up message (clause 2), or a kell message (clause 3). These observations are similar to those find *e.g.* in Ambient calculi.

We now define two equivalence relations over machines that we use to state correctness properties. The first one identifies two machines that have the same normal form. The second one corresponds to a form of strong barbed congruence. Note that the second one is defined on well-formed machine only.

Lemma 1 (Normal form). *If M is a machine term, then there exists M'_* such that $M \overset{\equiv}{\rightarrow}^* M'_*$. Moreover, if $M \equiv \overset{\equiv}{\rightarrow}^* M''_*$ then $M'_* \cong M''_*$. Besides, $M \not\rightarrow$ if and only if $M = M'_*$ for some M'_*.*

Definition 6 (Equivalence). *Two machines M and N are said to be* equivalent, *noted $M \doteq N$, if they have the same normal form (up to $\cong$).*

From now on, we will use the same notation M_* for a normal form of M (*i.e.* $M \overset{\equiv}{\rightarrow}^* M_* \not\rightarrow$), and for an arbitrary term in normal form.

Definition 7. *Let $M = l : n[P]_{p,S} \mid M'$ be a machine such that $\mathbf{tree}(M, l, n, p)$ and h a fresh machine name. We define:*

$$M \mid Q = l : n[P \mid Q]_{p,S} \mid M'$$
$$a[M] = l : n[\mathbf{0}]_{p,h} \mid h : a[P]_{l,S} \mid M'\{h/l\}$$
$$\nu a.M = M\{h/a\}$$

We extend these definitions to any contexts of the following form:

$$\mathbf{E} ::= . \quad \mid \quad (R \mid \mathbf{E}) \quad \mid \quad a[\mathbf{E}] \quad \mid \quad \nu a.\mathbf{E}$$

Definition 8 (Contextual equivalence for machines). *Two well-formed machines M and N are contextually equivalent ($M \sim_c N$) if and only if $\forall \mathbf{E}, \mathbf{E}[M] \sim \mathbf{E}[N]$.*

We check easily that $\sim_c$ is the largest relation over machines included in strong barbed bisimilarity that is a preserved by $a[.]$, $\nu a..$ and $. \mid R$.

Lemma 2. *$\sim_c$, $\doteq$, $\cong$ and $\equiv$ are equivalence relations.*

Lemma 3. *We have $\equiv \subseteq \cong \subseteq \doteq$ and if we consider the restrictions of these relations to well-formed machines, they are all strong barbed bisimulation and $\doteq \subseteq \sim_c$.*

We now state two properties that relate machine reductions to process reductions (soundness), and process reductions to machine reductions (completeness).

Proposition 2 (Soundness). $[\![P]\!] \to M \implies P \to P'$ *with* $[\![P']\!] \sim_c M$.

Proof. For lack of space, we only give here a sketch of the proof. We first define by induction an inverse translation function $[\![.]\!]^{mac}$ from machines to processes. This function has three roles: to expand the "reified" processes, to rebuild the tree structure of the term, and to recreate restricted names from machine names.

The soundness proposition results from the following lemmas:

Lemma 4. *If M is well-formed and $M \overset{\equiv}{\to} N$ then $[\![M]\!]^{mac} \equiv \overset{*}{\to} [\![N]\!]^{mac}$.*

Lemma 5. *If M is well-formed and $M \mapsto N$ then $[\![M]\!]^{mac} \mapsto [\![N]\!]^{mac}$.*

Lemma 6. *If M is a well-formed machine, then $[\![[\![M]\!]^{mac}]\!] \sim_c M$. If P is a process, then $[\![[\![P]\!]]\!]^{mac} \equiv P$.*

Proposition 3 (Completeness). $P \to P' \implies [\![P]\!] \to \sim_c [\![P']\!]$

Proof (Sketch).
The proof of this proposition is on induction on the derivation of $P \to P'$ and need the two following lemmas:

Lemma 7. *If $P \equiv P'$ then $[\![P]\!] \doteq [\![P']\!]$. If $P \overset{\equiv}{\to} P'$ then $[\![P]\!] \doteq [\![P']\!]$.*

Lemma 8. *Let P_* be a process and M_* a machine such that $\mathbf{tree}(M_*, p, a, r)$. If we have $p : a[P_*]_{p',\emptyset} \overset{\equiv}{\to}^* \cong M_*$ then for any machine N we have $N\{\mathbf{reify}(p, M_*)/x\} \sim_c N\{P_*/x\}$.*

The proof of Theorem 1 then results immediately from Propositions 2 and 3 by showing that the relation $\{\langle [\![P]\!], P \rangle \mid P \in \mathsf{K}\}$ is a strong barbed bisimulation up to $\sim_c$.

5   Implementation

We have implemented a prototype of our abstract machine in OCaml, which realizes a Kell calculus interpreter, and is available at [11]. The source language for the interpreter (called `kcl`) is essentially a typed extension of the calculus presented in this paper, with values. Values are either basic (integers, lists, strings), higher-order (process abstractions, passivated processes) or expressions built upon classical operators such as arithmetic operators or marshalling/unmarshalling primitives.

User programs are first parsed and typed-checked using a simple type inference algorithm. Then, they are executed by a runtime that follows closely the reductions of the abstract machine. Unlike the abstract machine, the runtime is deterministic (we do not detail here the particular reduction strategy we use). Moreover, we use environments in order to avoid the use of substitutions. The freshness conditions in the rules M.S.CELL, M.S.ACT and M.S.NEW are implemented either through the use of runtime pointers for locality names, or by a global fresh identifier generator for names created by a *new* instruction.

An independent part of the interpreter allows user programs to access various services as library functions, which may also be modeled as Kell Calculus processes. More precisely, we can see an interpreter as a context $\text{vmid}[\text{Lib} \mid u[\cdot]]$ executing a user program P (filling the hole) according to the rules of the abstract machine. The program P can use services specified in Lib that correspond to OCaml functions, but are accessed transparently from P like any other receiver. Similarly, these functions can generate messages in the vmid locality that can be received by P. In the implementation, messages sent from the top level of P are treated differently whether they are addressed to a receiver in Lib or not. A very simple library could be $\text{Lib} = (\text{echo}^{\downarrow}\langle x \rangle \diamond Q)$, where Q specifies the output of the string x on the standard output, and where $\diamond$ denotes to a replicated input construct (which can be encoded in the Kell calculus as shown in [17]).

A distributed configuration of interpreters can be specified as follows. If we run the programs $P_0, \ldots, P_n$ on different interpreters, the resulting behavior is specified by the following term

$$\text{Net} \mid \text{vmid}_0[\text{Lib}(\text{vmid}_0) \mid u[P_0]] \mid \ldots \mid \text{vmid}_n[\text{Lib}(\text{vmid}_n) \mid u[P_n]]$$

where we assume vmid names to be distinct. The processes Lib model the local libraries and Net the network. In our implementation they are mainly defined as follows (omitting the type annotations):

$$\text{Lib}(\text{vmid}) = (\text{send}^{\downarrow}\langle x, y \rangle \diamond \text{send}\langle x, y \rangle \mid (\text{recv}^{\uparrow}\langle(\text{vmid}), y\rangle \diamond \text{msg}\langle x \rangle \mid (\text{echo}^{\downarrow}\langle x \rangle \diamond Q)$$

$$\text{Net} = \text{send}^{\downarrow}\langle x, y \rangle \diamond \text{rcv}\langle x, y \rangle$$

These processes specify an environment allowing the exchange of asynchronous messages between interpreters, and providing some output capability. The vmid name allows to send messages to uniquely deignated kells. In addition, marshalling and unmarshalling functions allow to send arbitrary values over the network.

We give in Figure 6 the code of a distributed application consisting of a client and a server that simply executes the code that it receives. vm is a constructor that builds an identifier for a virtual machine (typically to locate a name server) from an address and a port. thisloc is bound to the identifier of the machine in which it is evaluated. The construct def in corresponds to an input $(\xi \triangleright P)$ and rdef to a replicated input. We use marshalling and unmarshalling functions that convert arbitrary values to string and conversely.

The execution of the server and the client on two different machines gives the following result.

```
client.kcl
new a in new b in new c in
let serverid = vm ("plutonium.inrialpes.fr", 6000) in
let myid = thisloc in
  ( def a [ X ] in send < serverid, marshall(X) > )
| ( def b [ X ] in X )
| ( def c [ X ] in X | X)
| a [ send < myid, marshall ( echo <"good">
      | b[c[echo <"bye">]] ) >
      | echo < "hello" > ]
| rdef msg up < X > in unmarshall(X) as proc
```

```
server.kcl
rdef msg up < X > in X
```

Fig. 6. kcl example

```
plutonium:~/kcl-0.1/bidinger$ kcl server.kcl -p 6000
hello

californium:~/kcl-0.1/bidinger$ kcl client.kcl -p 7000
good
bye
bye
```

6   Related Work

There has been a number of recent papers devoted to the description and implementation of abstract machines for distributed process calculi. One can cite notably the Jocaml distributed implementation of the Join calculus [6, 5], the Join calculus implementation of Mobile Ambients [7], Nomadic Pict [21, 19], the abstract machine for the M-calculus [9], the Fusion Machine [8], the PAN and GCPAN abstract machines for Safe Ambients [14, 10], the CAM abstract machine for Channel Ambients [13]. In addition, there have been also implementations of distributed calculi such as the Seal calculus [20], Klaim [2], or DiTyCO [12].

Our abstract machine specification has been designed to be independent from the actual implementation environment and the network services it provides. It thus can be used in widely different configurations. For instance, one is not limited to mapping top-level localities to physical sites as in [7, 5, 9], or does not need to introduce physical sites as a different locality abstractions than that of the supported calculus as in [10, 14]. This separation between abstract machine behavior and network semantics is not present in other abstract machines for distributed process calculi.

The Seal calculus [4] and the M-calculus [16] are the only calculi that share with the Kell calculus a combination of local actions and hierarchical localities, and could thus achieve a similar independence between abstract machine and network services. No abstract machine is described for the Seal calculus, however (only an implementation is mentioned in [20]), and the M-calculus abstract machine described in [9] relies on a fixed network model and a mapping of top-level localities to physical sites. Calculi which rely on an explicit flat network model such as Nomadic Pict, DiTyCO, Klaim have abstract machines and implementations which presuppose a given physical configuration and its supporting network model.

The Fusion Machine implements the general fusion calculus, where no localities are present, but the abstract machine itself is based on a fixed asynchronous network model. Furthermore, because of the nature of communications in Fusion, the Fusion machine relies on a non-trivial migration protocol for achieving synchronization in presence of multiple sites. In contrast to our calculus and abstract machine, this prevents distributed Fusion programs to directly, and at no cost, exploit low-level network services such as a basic datagram service.

Abstract machines and implementations for distributed process calculi with hierarchical localities other than the Seal calculus and the M-calculus, namely the Join calculus and Ambient calculi, must implement migration primitives, which forces a dependence on a given network model. For instance, the JoCaml abstract machine for the distributed join calculus [5] depends on an asynchronous message passing network model and on a specific interpretation of the locality hierarchy (top level localities are interpreted as physical sites). The PAN [14] and GCPAN [10] abstract machines for Safe Mobile Ambients depend as well on an asynchronous message passing network model for specifying the migration of ambients between sites (corresponding to the interpretation of the Ambient primitive open), and on the introduction of a notion of execution site, not related to ambients. The Channel Ambient abstract machine [13] leaves in fact the realization of its in and out migration primitives unspecified.

7   Conclusion

We have presented an abstract machine for an instance of the Kell calculus, and discussed briefly its OCaml implementation. The originality of our abstract machine lies in the fact that it is independent from any network services that could be used for a distributed implementation. Indeed, as our simple OCaml implementation illustrates, we can isolate network services provided by a given environment in language libraries that can be reified as standard Kell calculus processes for use by Kell calculus programs. While this means that our abstract machine, just as the Kell calculus, does not embody any sophisticated abstraction for distributed programming, it demonstrates that the calculus and its associated machine provide a very flexible basis for developing these abstractions. Furthermore, this independence has the advantage of simplifying the proof of correctness of our abstract machine, as it does not depend on the correctness proof of a sophisticated distributed protocol.

Much work remains of course towards a provably correct implementation of the calculus. Our non-deterministic abstract machine remains too abstract in a number of dimensions to be the basis for an efficient implementation of the calculus. First, truly local actions can only be realized, and efficiency obtained, if there is some determinacy in routing messages to triggers (as it is enforced in our OCaml implementation). One can think of applying a type system similar to that reported in [3], which guarantees the unicity of kell names, to obtain linearity conditions ensuring the unicity of message destinations. Secondly, an efficient machine would require a more deterministic behavior. Here we face the prospect of a more difficult proof of correctness, and more difficulty in stating the correctness conditions, which must probably relate the non-determinism at the calculus level with the determinism of the abstract machine through some sort of fairness condition.

References

1. G. Berry and G. Boudol. The chemical abstract machine. *Theoretical Computer Science, vol. 96*, 1992.
2. L. Bettini, M. Loreti, and R. Pugliese. Srtuctured nets in klaim. In *Proceedings of the 2000 ACM Symposium on Applied Computing, ACM Press*, 2000.
3. P. Bidinger and J.B. Stefani. The Kell Calculus: Operational Semantics and Type System. In *Proc. 6th IFIP FMOODS International Conference*, volume 2884 of *LNCS*. Springer, 2003.
4. G. Castagna and F. Zappa. The Seal Calculus Revisited. In *In Proceedings 22th FST-TCS*, number 2556 in LNCS. Springer, 2002.
5. Fabrice Le Fessant. *JoCaml: Conception et Implantation d'un Langage à Agents Mobiles.* PhD thesis, Ecole Polytechnique, 2001.
6. C. Fournet, G. Gonthier, J.J. Levy, L. Maranget, and D. Remy. A calculus of mobile agents. In *In Proceedings 7th International Conference on Concurrency Theory (CONCUR '96), Lecture Notes in Computer Science 1119.* Springer Verlag, 1996.
7. C. Fournet, J.J. Levy, and A. Schmitt. An asynchronous distributed implementation of mobile ambients. In *Proceedings of the International IFIP Conference TCS 2000, Sendai, Japan, Lecture Notes in Computer Science 1872.* Springer, 2000.
8. Philippa Gardner, Cosimo Laneve, and Lucian Wischik. The fusion machine. In *CONCUR 2002*, volume 2421 of *LNCS*. Springer-Verlag, 2002.
9. F. Germain, M. Lacoste, and J.B. Stefani. An abstract machine for a higher-order distributed process calculus. In *Proceedings of the EACTS Workshop on Foundations of Wide Area Network Computing (F-WAN)*, July 2002.
10. D. Hirschkoff, D. Pous, and D. Sangiorgi. An Efficient Abstract Machine for Safe Ambients, 2004. Unpublished. Available at: http://www.cs.unibo.it/~sangio/DOC_public/gcpan.ps.gz.
11. The Kell calculus page. http://sardes.inrialpes.fr/kells/.
12. L. Lopes, F. Silva, A. Figueira, and V. Vasconcelos. DiTyCO: An Experiment in Code Mobility from the Realm of Process Calculi. In *Proceedings 5th Mobile Object Systems Workshop (MOS'99)*, 1999.
13. A. Phillips, N. Yoshida, and S. Eisenbach. A distributed abstract machine for boxed ambient calculi. In *Proceedings of ESOP 2004*, LNCS. Springer-Verlag, April 2004.
14. D. Sangiorgi and A. Valente. A Distributed Abstract Machine for Safe Ambients. In *Proceedings of the 28th ICALP*, volume 2076 of *LNCS*. Springer-Verlag, 2001.
15. D. Sangiorgi and S. Walker. *The π-calculus: A Theory of Mobile Processes.* Cambridge University Press, 2001.
16. A. Schmitt and J.B. Stefani. The M-calculus: A Higher-Order Distributed Process Calculus. In *Proceedings 30th Annual ACM Symposium on Principles of Programming Languages (POPL)*, 2003.
17. A. Schmitt and J.B. Stefani. The Kell Calculus: A Family of Higher-Order Distributed Process Calculi. In P. Quaglia, editor, *Global Computing*, volume 3267 of *LNCS*. Springer, 2004.
18. J.B. Stefani. A Calculus of Kells. In *Proceedings 2nd International Workshop on Foundations of Global Computing*, 2003.

19. A. Unyapoth and P. Sewell. Nomadic Pict: Correct Communication Infrastructures for Mobile Computation. In *Proceedings ACM Int. Conf. on Principles of Programming Languages (POPL)*, 2001.
20. J. Vitek and G. Castagna. Towards a calculus of secure mobile computations. In *Proceedings Workshop on Internet Programming Languages, Chicago, Illinois, USA, Lecture Notes in Computer Science 1686, Springer*, 1998.
21. P. Wojciechowski and P. Sewell. Nomadic Pict: Language and Infrastructure. *IEEE Concurrency, vol. 8, no 2*, 2000.

XPi: A Typed Process Calculus for XML Messaging*

Lucia Acciai[1] and Michele Boreale[2]

[1] Laboratoire d'Informatique Fondamentale de Marseille, Université de Provence
lucia.acciai@lif.univ-mrs.fr
[2] Dipartimento di Sistemi e Informatica, Università di Firenze
boreale@dsi.unifi.it

Abstract. We present XPi, a core calculus for XML messaging. XPi features asynchronous communications, pattern matching, name and code mobility, integration of static and dynamic typing. Flexibility and expressiveness of this calculus are illustrated by a few examples, some concerning description and discovery of web services. In XPi, a type system disciplines XML message handling at the level of channels, patterns, and processes. A run-time safety theorem ensures that in well-typed systems no service will ever receive documents it cannot understand, and that the offered services, even if re-defined, will be consistent with the declared channel capacities.

1 Introduction

The design of globally distributed systems, like Web Services (WS, [23]) or business-to-business applications [5], is more and more centered around passing of messages in the form of XML documents. Major reasons for the emergence of message-passing are its conceptual simplicity, its minimal infrastructural requirements, and its neutrality with respect to back-ends and platforms of services [6]. These features greatly ease interoperability and integration.

It is generally recognized that some of the proposed languages and standards for WS draw their inspiration from the π-calculus [19]. The latter conveys the message-passing paradigm in a distilled form. In practice, at one extreme we find languages like WSDL [12], useful to describe service interfaces, but saying very little about behaviour. At the other extreme, we find proposed standards like BPEL4WS [2], oriented to detailed descriptions of services, but hardly amenable to formal analysis. In other words, we are experiencing a significant gap between theory (formal models and analysis techniques) and practice (programming) in the field of distributed applications.

As a first step toward filling this gap, we aim at giving a concise semantic account of XML messaging and of the related typing issues. To this purpose, we present *XPi*, a process language based on the asynchronous π-calculus. Prominent features of XPi are: patterns generalizing ordinary inputs, ML-like pattern

---

* This work has been partially supported by EU within the IST FET - Global Computing initiative, projects MIKADO and PROFUNDIS.

M. Steffen and G. Zavattaro (Eds.): FMOODS 2005, LNCS 3535, pp. 47–66, 2005.

matching, and integration of static and dynamic typing. Our objective is to study issues raised by these features in connection with name and code mobility. A more precise account of our work and contributions follows.

For the sake of simplicity, syntax and reduction semantics of untyped XPi are first introduced (Section 2). In XPi, resource addresses on the net are represented as *names*, which can be generally understood as channels at which services are listening. *Messages* passed around are XML documents, represented as tagged/nested lists, in the vein of XDuce [15, 16]. Services and their clients are *processes*, that may send messages to channels, or query channels to retrieve messages obeying given patterns. Messages may contain names, which are passed around with only the *output capability* [20]. Practically, this means that a client receiving a service address cannot use this address to re-define the service. This assumption is perfectly sensible, simplifies typing issues, and does not affect expressive power (see e.g. [7, 17]). Messages may also contain mobile code in the form of *abstractions*, roughly, functions that take some argument and yield a process as a result. More precisely, abstractions can consume messages through pattern matching, thus supplying actual parameters to the contained code and starting its execution. This mechanism allows for considerable expressiveness. For example, we show that it permits a clean encoding of encryption primitives, hence of the spi-calculus [1], into XPi.

Types (Section 3) discipline processing of messages at the level of channels, patterns, and processes. At the time of its creation, each channel is given a *capacity*, i.e. a type specifying the format of messages that can travel on that channel. *Subtyping* arises from the presence of star types (arbitrary length lists) and union types, and by lifting at the level of messages a subtyping relation existing on basic values. The presence of a top type $\mathbf{T}$ enhances flexibility, allowing for such types as "all documents with an external tag f, containing a tag g and something else", written $\mathsf{T} = f[g[\mathbf{T}], \mathbf{T}]$. Subtyping is contravariant on channels: this is natural if one thinks of services, roughly, as functions receiving their arguments through channels. Contravariance calls for a bottom type $\bot$, which allows one to express such sets of values as "all channels that can transport documents of some type $\mathsf{S} < \mathsf{T}$", written $ch(f[g[\bot], \bot])$. Abstractions that can safely consume messages of type T are given type $(\mathsf{T})\mathsf{Abs}$. Interplay between pattern matching, types, and capacities raises a few interesting issues concerning *type safety* (Section 4). Stated in terms of services accessible at given channels, our run-time safety theorem ensures that in well-typed systems, first, no service will ever receive documents it cannot understand, and second, that the offered service, even when re-defined, will comply with the statically declared capacities. The first property simply means that no process will ever output messages violating channel capacities. The second property means that no service will hang due to a input pattern that is not consistent with the channel's capacity (a form of "pattern consistency"). Type checking is entirely static, in the sense that no run-time type check is required.

Our type system is partially inspired by XSD [13], but is less rich than, say, the language of [9]. In particular, we have preferred to omit recursive types. While certainly useful in a full blown language, recursion would raise technicalities that hinder issues concerning name and code mobility. Also, our pattern language is quite basic, partly for the similar reasons of simplicity, partly because more sophisticated patterns can be easily simulated.

The calculus described so far enforces a strictly static typing discipline. We also consider an extension of this calculus with *dynamic abstractions* (Section 5), which are useful when little or nothing is known about the actual types of incoming messages. Run-time type checks ensure that substitutions arising from pattern matching respect the types statically assigned to variables. Run time safety carries over. We shall argue that dynamic abstractions, combined with code mobility and subtyping, can provide linguistic support to such tasks as publishing and querying services.

There have been a number of proposals for integrating XML manipulation primitives into statically typed languages. We conclude (Section 6) with some discussion on recent related work in this field, and with a few directions for future extensions.

2 Untyped XPi

Syntax. We assume a countable set of *variables* $\mathcal{V}$, ranged over by x, y, z, $\ldots$, a set of *tags* $\mathcal{F}$, ranged over $f,g,\ldots$, and a set of *basic values* $\mathcal{BV}$ v, w, $\ldots$. We leave $\mathcal{BV}$ unspecified (it might contain such values as integers, strings, or Java objects), but assume that $\mathcal{BV}$ contains a countable set of *names* $\mathcal{N}$, ranged over by a, b, c, $\ldots$. $\mathcal{N}$ is partitioned into a family of countable sets called *sorts* $S, S', \ldots$. We let u range over $\mathcal{N} \cup \mathcal{V}$ and $\tilde{x}, \ldots$ denote a tuples of variables.

Definition 1 (messages, patterns and processes). *The set $\mathcal{M}$ of XPi messages $M, N, \ldots$, the set Q of XPi patterns $Q, Q', \ldots$ and the set P of XPi processes $P, R, \ldots$ are defined by the syntax in Table 1. In $Q_{\tilde{x}}$, we impose the following linearity condition: $\tilde{x}$ is a tuple of distinct names and each $x_i \in \tilde{x}$ occurs at most once in Q.*

In the style of XDuce [15, 16] and $\mathbb{C}$Duce [3] XML documents are represented in XPi as tagged ordered list that can be arbitrarily nested; these are the messages being exchanged among processes. A message can be either a basic value, a variable, a tagged message, a list of messages, or an abstraction. The latter take the form $(Q_{\tilde{x}})P$, where variables $\tilde{x}$ represent formal parameters, to be replaced by actual parameters at run-time. A pattern is simply an abstraction-free message. For the sake of simplicity, we have ignored tag-variables that could be easily accommodated. Also, note that patterns do not allow for direct decomposition of documents into sublists (akin to the pattern p, p' in XDuce). The latter can be easily encoded though, as we show later in this section.

Process syntax is a variation on the π-calculus. In particular, asynchronous (non blocking) output on a channel u is written $\bar{u}\langle M \rangle$, and u is said to occur in *output subject position*. Nondeterministic guarded summation $\sum_{i \in I} a_i.A_i$ waits for any message matching A_i's pattern at channel a_i, for some $i \in I$, consumes this

Table 1. Syntax of XPi messages, patterns and processes.

Message	$M ::=$	v	*Value*
		$\mid x$	*Var*
		$\mid f(M)$	*Tag*
		$\mid LM$	*List*
		$\mid A$	*Abstraction*
List of messages $LM ::=$		$[]$	*Empty list*
		$\mid x$	*Var*
		$\mid M \cdot LM$	*Concatenation*
Abstraction	$A ::=$	$(Q_{\tilde{x}})P$	*Pattern and Continuation*
		$\mid x$	*Var*
Pattern	$Q ::=$	v	*Value*
		$\mid x$	*Var*
		$\mid f(Q)$	*Tag*
		$\mid LQ$	*List*
List of patterns $LQ ::=$		$[]$	*Empty list*
		$\mid x$	*Var*
		$\mid Q \cdot LQ$	*Concatenation*
Process	$P ::=$	$\bar{u}\langle M \rangle$	*Output*
		$\mid \sum_{i \in I} a_i.A_i$	*Guarded Summation*
		$\mid P$ else R	*Else*
		$\mid P_1 \mid P_2$	*Parallel*
		$\mid !P$	*Replication*
		$\mid (\nu a)P$	*Restriction*

message and continues as prescribed by A_i; names a_i are said to occur in *input subject position*. Note that the syntax forbids variables in input subject position, hence a received name cannot be used as an input channel; in other words, names are passed around with the output capability only. Parallel composition $P_1 \mid P_2$ represents concurrent execution of P_1 and P_2. Process P else R behaves like P, if P can do some internal reduction, otherwise reduces to R. This operator will be useful for coding up, e.g., if-then-else, without the burden of dealing with explicit negation on pattern. Replication $!P$ represents the parallel composition of arbitrarily many copies of P. Restriction $(\nu a)P$ creates a fresh name a, whose initial scope is P. Usual binding conventions and notations (alpha equivalence $=_\alpha$, free and bound names fn$(\cdot)$ and bn$(\cdot)$, free and bound variables fv$(\cdot)$ and bv$(\cdot)$) apply. We let $\mathcal{M}_{cl}$ be the set of closed messages and $\mathcal{P}_{cl}$ be the set of closed processes.

Notations. The following abbreviations for messages and patterns are used: $[M_1,M_2,\ldots,M_{k-1},M_k]$ stands for $M_1 \cdot (M_2 \cdot (\ldots (M_{k-1} \cdot (M_k \cdot [])) \ldots))$, while $f[M_1,M_2,\ldots,M_{k-1},M_k]$ stands for $f([M_1,M_2,\ldots,M_{k-1},M_k])$. The following abbreviations for processes are used: $\mathbf{0}$, $a_1.A_1$ and $a_1.A_1 + a_2.A_2 + \cdots + a_n.A_n$ stand for $\sum_{\{i \in I\}} a_i.A_i$ when $|I| = 0$, $|I| = 1$, and $|I| = n$, respectively; $(\nu a_1,\ldots,a_n)P = (\nu \widetilde{a})P$ stands for $(\nu a_1)\ldots(\nu a_n)P$. We sometimes save on subscripts by marking binding occurrences of variables in abstractions by a '?' symbol, or by replacing a binding occurrence of a variable by a don't care symbol, '_', if that variable does not occur in the continuation process. E.g. $([f[?x],g[\_]])P$ stands for $([f[x],g[y]]_{\{x,y\}})P$ where $y \notin$ fv(P).

Our list representation of XML ignores algebraic properties of concatenation (such as associativity, see [16]). We simply take for granted some translation from actual XML documents to our syntax. The following example illustrates informally what this translation might look like.

Example 1. An XML document encoding an address book (on the left) and its representation in XPi (on the right)[1]:

```
<addrbook>                          addrbook[ person[ name("John Smith"),
    <person>                                          tel(12345),
        <name>John Smith</name>                       emailaddrs[email("john@smith"),
        <tel>12345</tel>                                        email("smith@john")]
        <emailaddrs>                          ],
            <email>john@smith</email>         person[ name("Eric Brown"),
            <email>smith@john</email>                 tel(678910),
        </emailaddrs>                                 emailaddrs[]
    </person>                                 ]
    <person>                          ]
        <name>Eric Brown</name>
        <tel>678910</tel>
        <emailaddrs></emailaddrs>
    </person>
</addrbook>.
```

Note that a sequence of tagged documents such as `<tag1>M</tag1>` `<tag2>N</tag2>`$\cdots$ is rendered as an ordered list `[tag1(M), tag2(N),`$\cdots$`]`. A pattern that extracts name and telephone number of the first person of the address book above is: $\texttt{Q}_{xy} = \texttt{addrbook[person[name(?x),tel(?y),\_],\_]}$.

Reduction semantics. A *reduction relation* describes system evolution via internal communications. Following [18], XPi reduction semantics is based on *structural congruence* $\equiv$, defined as the least congruence on processes satisfying the laws in Table 2. The latter permit certain rearrangements of parallel composition, replication, and restriction. The relation $\equiv$ extends to abstractions, hence

---

[1] We shall prefer the typewriter font whenever useful to improve on readability.

Table 2. Structural congruence.

$$
\begin{array}{c}
P =_\alpha R \Rightarrow P \equiv R \\[4pt]
P|R \equiv R|P \\[4pt]
(P|R_1)|R_2 \equiv P|(R_1|R_2) \\[4pt]
P|\mathbf{0} \equiv P \\[4pt]
!P \equiv P|!P \\[4pt]
(\nu a)(P|R) \equiv P|(\nu a)R \quad \text{if} \quad a \notin \mathrm{fn}(P) \\[4pt]
(\nu a)\mathbf{0} \equiv \mathbf{0} \\[4pt]
(\nu a)(\nu b)P \equiv (\nu b)(\nu a)P
\end{array}
$$

Table 3. Reduction semantics.

$$
(\textsc{com}) \quad \frac{j \in I \quad a_j = a, \quad A_j = (Q_{\tilde{x}})P, \quad \mathrm{match}(M,Q,\sigma)}{\overline{a}\langle M \rangle \mid \sum_{i \in I} a_i.A_i \to P\sigma}
$$

$$
(\textsc{struct}) \; \frac{P \equiv P', \quad P' \to Q', \quad Q' \equiv Q}{P \to Q} \qquad (\textsc{ctx}) \; \frac{P \to P'}{(\nu \tilde{a})(P|R) \to (\nu \tilde{a})(P'|R)}
$$

$$
(\textsc{else}_1) \; \frac{P \to P'}{P \;\text{else}\; Q \to P'} \qquad\qquad (\textsc{else}_2) \; \frac{P \nrightarrow}{P \;\text{else}\; Q \to Q}
$$

to messages, in the expected manner. The reduction semantics also relies on a standard matching predicate, that matches a (linear) pattern against a closed message and yields a substitution.

Definition 2 (substitutions and matching). *Substitutions $\sigma, \sigma', \ldots$ are finite partial maps from the set $\mathcal{V}$ of variables to the set $\mathcal{M}_{cl}$ of closed messages. We denote by ε the empty substitution. For any term t, $t\sigma$ denotes the result of applying σ onto t (with alpha-renaming of bound names and variables if needed). Let M be a closed message and Q be a linear pattern:* $\mathrm{match}(M,Q,\sigma)$ *holds true if and only if* $\mathrm{dom}(\sigma) = \mathrm{fv}(Q)$ *and* $Q\sigma = M$; *in this case, we also say that M matches Q.*

Definition 3 (reduction). *The reduction relation, $\to \,\subseteq\, \mathcal{P}_{cl} \times \mathcal{P}_{cl}$, is the least binary relation on closed processes satisfying the rules in Table 3.*

Derived constructs and examples. XPi allows for straightforward definition of a few powerful constructs, that will be used in later examples. In the following, we shall freely use recursive definitions of processes, that can be coded up using replication [18].

- *Application.* A functional-like application for abstractions, $A \bullet M$, can be defined as $(\nu c)(\overline{c}\langle M \rangle | c.A)$, for any $c \notin \mathrm{fn}(M,A)$.

– *Case.* A pattern matching construct relying on a *first match* policy, written

$$\text{Case } M \text{ of } \quad (Q_1)_{\tilde{x}_1} \Rightarrow P_1, \ (Q_2)_{\tilde{x}_2} \Rightarrow P_2, \cdots, (Q_k)_{\tilde{x}_k} \Rightarrow P_k$$

evolves into P_1 if M matches Q_1 (with substitutions involved), otherwise evolves into P_2 if M matches Q_2, and so on; if there is no match, the process is stuck. This construct can be defined in XPi as follows (assuming precedence of • on else and right-associativity for else):

$$(Q_1)_{\tilde{x}_1} P_1 \bullet M \quad \text{else} \quad (Q_2)_{\tilde{x}_2} P_2 \bullet M \quad \text{else} \quad \cdots \quad \text{else} \quad (Q_k)_{\tilde{x}_k} P_k \bullet M.$$

– *Decomposition.* A process that attempts to *decompose* a message M into two sublists that satisfy the patterns $Q_{\tilde{x}}$ and $Q'_{\tilde{y}}$ and proceeds like P (with substitutions for $\tilde{x}$ and $\tilde{y}$ involved), if possible, otherwise is stuck, written: M as $Q_{\tilde{x}}, Q'_{\tilde{y}} \Rightarrow P$, can be defined as the recursive process $R([[], M])$, where:

$$R([l, x]) = \text{Case } x \text{ of } ?y \cdot ?w \Rightarrow (\text{Case } l@y \text{ of } Q_{\tilde{x}} \Rightarrow (\text{Case } w \text{ of } \quad Q'_{\tilde{y}} \Rightarrow P,$$
$$\_ \Rightarrow R([l@y, w])),$$
$$\_ \Rightarrow R([l@y, w])).$$

Here we have used a list-append function @, which can be easily defined via a call to a suitable recursive process. Most common list manipulation constructs can be easily coded up in this style. We shall not pursue this direction any further.

Example 2 (a web service). Consider a web service WS that offers two different services: an audio streaming service, offered at channel *stream*, and a download service, offered at channel *download*. Clients that request the first kind of service must specify a streaming channel and its bandwidth ("high" or "low"), so that WS can stream one of two mp3 files (v_{low} or v_{high}), as appropriate. Clients that request download must specify a channel at which the player will be received. A client can run the downloaded player locally, supplying it appropriate parameters (a local streaming channel and its bandwidth). We represent streaming on a channel simply as an output action along that channel:

$$WS \overset{\triangle}{=} !(\quad stream.(\texttt{req\_stream[bandwidth("low"),channel(?x)]})\bar{x}\langle v_{low}\rangle$$
$$+ \ stream.(\texttt{req\_stream[bandwidth("high"),channel(?y)]})\bar{y}\langle v_{high}\rangle$$
$$+ \ download.(\texttt{req\_down(?z)})\bar{z}\langle Player\rangle \quad).$$

Player is an abstraction:

$$Player \overset{\triangle}{=} (\texttt{req\_stream[bandwidth(?y),channel(?z)]})(\text{ Case } y \text{ of } \texttt{"low"} \Rightarrow \bar{z}\langle v_{low}\rangle$$
$$\texttt{"high"} \Rightarrow \bar{z}\langle v_{high}\rangle \quad).$$

Note that the first two summands of WS are equivalent to *stream.Player*. However, the extended form written above makes it possible a static optmization of channels (see Example 5).

A client that asks for low bandwidth streaming, listens at s and then proceeds like C is:

$$C_1 \stackrel{\triangle}{=} (\nu s)(\overline{stream}\langle \texttt{req\_stream[bandwidth("low"),channel}(s)\texttt{]}\rangle \mid s.(?v)C).$$

Another client that asks for download, then runs the player locally, listening at a local high bandwidth channel s is C_2 defined as:

$$(\nu d, s)(\quad \overline{download}\langle \texttt{req\_down}(d)\rangle \mid d.(?x_p)(x_p \bullet$$
$$\texttt{req\_stream[bandwidth("high"),channel}(s)\texttt{]} \mid s.(?v)C) \quad).$$

Encryption and decryption. Cryptographic primitives are sometimes used in distributed applications to guarantee secrecy and authentication of transmitted data. As a testbed for expressiveness, we show how to encode shared-key encryption and decryption primitives à la spi-calculus [1] into XPi. We shall see an example of application of these encodings in Section 5. We first introduce XPi^{cr}, a cryptographic extension of XPi that subsumes shared-key spi-calculus, and then show how to encode XPi^{cr} into XPi. Message syntax is extended with the following clause, that represents encryption of M using N as a key:

$$M \quad ::= \quad \cdots \mid \{M\}_N \qquad (encryption)$$

where N does contain neither abstractions nor encryptions. Process syntax is extended with a case operator, that attempts decryption of M using N as a key and if successful binds the result to a variable x :

$$P \quad ::= \quad \cdots \mid \mathrm{case}\, M \,\mathrm{of}\, \{x\}_N \,\mathrm{in}\, P \qquad (decryption)$$

where N does contain neither abstractions nor encryptions, M is a variable or a message of the form $\{M'\}_{N'}$ and x binds in P. Patterns remain unchanged, in particular they may not contain encryptions or abstractions. The additional reduction rule is:

$$(\textsc{Dec}) \quad \mathrm{case}\, \{M\}_N \,\mathrm{of}\, \{x\}_N \,\mathrm{in}\, P \to P[M/x].$$

Next, two translation functions, one for messages ($[\![\cdot]\!]$) and one for processes ($(\!|\cdot|\!)$), are defined from XPi^{cr} to XPi. The translations of messages follow a familiar continuation-passing style. The relevant clauses of the definition, by structural induction, are as follows (on the others the functions just go through the structure of terms):

$$[\![u]\!] = u$$
$$[\![\{M\}_N]\!] = ([N, ?x])\overline{x}\langle[\![M]\!]\rangle$$

$$(\!|\overline{u}\langle M\rangle|\!) = \overline{u}\langle[\![M]\!]\rangle$$
$$(\!|\mathrm{case}\, M \,\mathrm{of}\, \{x\}_N \,\mathrm{in}\, P|\!) = (\nu r)\,([\![M]\!] \bullet [N, r] \mid r.(?x)\,(\!|P|\!)).$$

Following [22], let us define the barb predicate $P \Downarrow a$ as follows: there is P' s.t. $P \to^* P'$ and P' has either an input summand $a.A$ or an output $\overline{a}\langle M\rangle$ which are not in the scope of a (νa), an else or guarded summation. The encoding defined above is correct, in the sense that it preserves reductions and barbs in both directions, as stated by the proposition below. Note that, by compositionality, this implies the encoding is fully abstract w.r.t. barbed equivalence (see e.g. [7]).

Table 4. Syntax of types.

Types	T ::=	bt	*Basic type* (bt $\in \mathcal{BT}$)
		| **T**	*Top*
		| **⊥**	*Bottom*
		| $f(\mathsf{T})$	*Tag* ($f \in \mathcal{F}$)
		| LT	*List*
		| T+T	*Union*
		| (T)Abs	*Abstraction*
List types	LT ::=	[]	*Empty*
		| *T	*Star*
		| T·LT	*Concatenation*

Proposition 1. *Let P be a closed process in XPi^{cr}.*

1. *if $P \to P'$ then $\langle P \rangle \to^* \langle P' \rangle$;*
2. *if $\langle P \rangle \to P'$ then $\exists P'' \in XP i^{\mathrm{cr}}$ s.t. $P' \to^* \langle P'' \rangle$;*
3. *$P \Downarrow a$ if and only if $\langle P \rangle \Downarrow a$.*

3   A Type System

In this section, we define a type system for XPi that disciplines messaging at the level of channels, patterns and processes. The system guarantees that well-typed processes respect channels capacities at runtime. In other words, services are guaranteed to receive only requests they can understand, and conversely, services offered at a given channel will be consistent with the type declared for that channel. XPi's type system draws its inspiration from, but is less rich than, XML-Schema [13]. Our system permits to specify types for basic values (such as string or int) and provides tuple types (fixed-length lists) and star types (arbitrary-length lists); moreover, it provides abstraction types for code mobility. For the sake of simplicity, we have omitted attributes and recursive types.

Message types and subtyping. We assume an unspecified set of *basic types* $\mathcal{BT}$ bt, bt',... that might include int, string, boolean, or even Java classes. We assume that $\mathcal{BT}$ contains a countable set of *sort names* in one-to-one correspondence with the sorts $\mathcal{S}, \mathcal{S}',...$ of $\mathcal{N}$; by slight abuse of notation, we denote sort names by the corresponding sorts.

Definition 4 (types). *The set $\mathcal{T}$ of types, ranged over by T, S, ..., is defined by the syntax in Table 4.*

Note the presence of the union type T+T', that is the type of all messages of type T or T', and of the star type *T, that is the type of all lists of elements of type T. (T)Abs is the type of all abtractions that can consume messages of type T. Finally, note the presence of **T** and **L** types. **T** is simply the type of all messages. On the contrary, no message has type **L**, but this type is extremely useful for the purpose of defining channel types, as we shall see below.

Notation. The following abbreviations for types are used: $[T_1, T_2, \ldots, T_{k-1}, T_k]$ stands for $T_1 \cdot (T_2 \cdot (\ldots (T_{k-1} \cdot (T_k \cdot [])) \ldots))$, while $f[T_1, T_2, \ldots, T_{k-1}, T_k]$ stands for $f([T_1, T_2, \ldots, T_{k-1}, T_k])$.

Example 3. A type for address books, on the left (see message M in Example 1), and a type for all SOAP messages, consisting of an *optional* header and a body, enclosed in an envelope, on the right:

```
addrbook[ *person[ name(string),              envelope[ [] + header(T),
                   tel(int),                                   body(T)
                   emailaddrs(*email(string))]]        ].
```

Next, we associate types with channels, or more precisely with sorts. This is done by introducing a "capacity" function.

Definition 5. *A capacity function is a surjective map from the set of sorts to the set of types.*

In the sequel, we fix a generic capacity function. We shall denote by $ch(\mathsf{T})$ a generic sort that is mapped to T. Note that, by surjectivity of the capacity function, for each type T there is a sort $ch(\mathsf{T})$. In particular, $ch(\mathbf{T})$ is the sort of channels that can transport anything. In practice, determining capacity T of a given channel a, i.e. that a belongs to $ch(\mathsf{T})$, might be implemented with a variety of mechanisms, such as attaching to a an explicit reference to T's definition. We abstract away from these details.

List and star types and the presence of **T** and **L** naturally induce a subtyping relation. For example, a service capable of processing messages of type $\mathsf{T} = f(*\ \mathsf{int})$ must be capable of processing messages of type $\mathsf{T}' = f[\mathsf{int}, \mathsf{int}]$, i.e. T' is a subtype of T. Subtyping also serves to lift a generic subtyping preorder on basic types, $\prec$, to all types.

Definition 6 (subtyping). *The subtyping relation $< \subseteq \mathcal{T} \times \mathcal{T}$ is the least reflexive and transitive relation closed under the rules of Table 5.*

Note that we disallow subtyping on abstractions. The reason for this limitation will be discussed shortly after presenting the type checking system (see Remark 1). Also note that subtyping is contravariant on sorts capacities (rule (SUB-SORT)): this is natural if one thinks of a name of capacity T as, roughly, a function that can take arguments of type T. As a consequence of contravariance, for any T, we have $ch(\mathsf{T}) < ch(\mathbf{L})$, that is, $ch(\mathbf{L})$ is the type of all channels.

Type checking. A *basic typing* relation $v : \mathsf{bt}$ on basic values and basic types is presupposed, which is required to respect subtyping, i.e. whenever $\mathsf{bt} \prec \mathsf{bt}'$ and $v : \mathsf{bt}$ then $v : \mathsf{bt}'$. We further require that for each bt there is at least one $v : \mathsf{bt}$,

Table 5. Rules for subtyping.

$$\text{(Sub-Sort)} \quad \frac{T < T'}{ch(T') < ch(T)}$$

$$\text{(Sub-Top)} \quad \frac{}{T < T} \qquad\qquad \text{(Sub-Bottom)} \quad \frac{}{\bot < T}$$

$$\text{(Sub-Basic)} \quad \frac{bt1 \prec bt2}{bt1 < bt2} \qquad\qquad \text{(Sub-Tag)} \quad \frac{T' < T}{f(T') < f(T)}$$

$$\text{(Sub-Star}_1) \quad \frac{}{[\,] < {*}T} \qquad\qquad \text{(Sub-Star}_2) \quad \frac{T' < T, \;\; LT < {*}T}{T'{\cdot}LT < {*}T}$$

$$\text{(Sub-Star}_3) \quad \frac{T' < T}{{*}T' < {*}T} \qquad\qquad \text{(Sub-List)} \quad \frac{T_1 < T'_1, \;\; LT < LT'}{T_1{\cdot}LT < T'_1{\cdot}LT'}$$

$$\text{(Sub-Union}_1) \quad \frac{T < T' \text{ or } T < T''}{T < T'+T''} \qquad \text{(Sub-Union}_2) \quad \frac{T' < T, \;\; T'' < T}{T'+T'' < T}$$

and that for each v the set of bt's s.t. $v : bt$ has a minimal element. On names and sort names the basic typing relation is the following: $a : S$ iff $a \in S'$ for some $S' < S$.

Contexts $\Gamma, \Gamma', \ldots$ are finite partial maps from variables $\mathcal{V}$ to types $\mathcal{T}$, sometimes denoted as sets of variable bindings $\{x_i : T_i\}_{i \in I}$ (x_i's distinct). We denote the empty context by $\emptyset$. Assume $\tilde{x}$ a set of variables; we denote by $\Gamma_{-\tilde{x}}$ the context obtained from Γ by removing the bindings for the variables in $\tilde{x}$, and by $\Gamma_{|\tilde{x}}$ the context obtained by restricting Γ to the bindings for the variables in $\tilde{x}$. The subtyping relation is extended to contexts by letting $\Gamma_1 < \Gamma_2$ iff $\text{dom}(\Gamma_1) = \text{dom}(\Gamma_2)$ and $\forall x \in \text{dom}(\Gamma_1)$ it holds that $\Gamma_1(x) < \Gamma_2(x)$. Union of contexts Γ_1 and Γ_2 having disjoint domains is written as $\Gamma_1 \cup \Gamma_2$ or as Γ_1, Γ_2 if no ambiguity arises. Sum of contexts Γ_1 and Γ_2 is written as $\Gamma_1 + \Gamma_2$ and is defined as $(\Gamma_1 + \Gamma_2)(x) = \Gamma_1(x) + \Gamma_2(x)$ if $x \in \text{dom}(\Gamma_1) \cap \text{dom}(\Gamma_2)$, otherwise $(\Gamma_1 + \Gamma_2)(x) = \Gamma_i(x)$ if $x \in \text{dom}(\Gamma_i)$ for $i = 1, 2$.

Type checking relies on a type-pattern matching predicate, $\text{tpm}(T, Q, \Gamma)$, whose role is twofold: (1) it extracts from T the types expected for variables in Q after matching against messages of type T, yielding the context Γ, (2) it checks that Q is consistent with type T, i.e. that the type of Q is of a subtype of T under Γ.

Definition 7 (type-pattern match). *The predicate* $\text{tpm}(T, Q, \Gamma)$ *is defined by the rules in Table 6.*

As expected, type checking works on an *annotated syntax*, where each $Q_{\tilde{x}}$ is decorated by a context Γ for its binding variables $\tilde{x}$, written $Q_{\tilde{x}} : \Gamma$, with $\tilde{x} = \text{dom}(\Gamma)$, or simply $Q : \Gamma$, where it is understood that the binding variables of Q are $\text{dom}(\Gamma)$. For notational simplicity, we shall use such abbreviations as $a.(f[?x : T, ?y : T'])P$ instead of $a.(f[x, y] : \{x : T, y : T'\})P$, and assume don't care variables '_' are always annotated with $\mathbf{T}$. Reduction semantics carries over to annotated closed processes formally unchanged.

Table 6. Matching types and patterns.

$$(\text{TPM-TOP}) \quad \frac{Q \neq x}{\text{tpm}(\mathbf{T}, Q, \Gamma)}, \; \forall x \in \text{fv}(Q) : \Gamma(x) = \mathbf{T}$$

$$(\text{TPM-EMPTY}) \; \frac{}{\text{tpm}([\,],[\,],\emptyset)} \quad (\text{TPM-VAR}) \quad \frac{}{\text{tpm}(\mathsf{T}, x, \{x : \mathsf{T}\})}$$

$$(\text{TPM-VALUE}) \; \frac{v : \text{bt}}{\text{tpm}(\text{bt}, v, \emptyset)} \quad (\text{TPM-TAG}) \quad \frac{\text{tpm}(\mathsf{T}, Q, \Gamma)}{\text{tpm}(f(\mathsf{T}), f(Q), \Gamma)}$$

$$(\text{TPM-STAR}_1) \; \frac{}{\text{tpm}(*\mathsf{T}, [\,], \emptyset)} \quad (\text{TPM-STAR}_2) \; \frac{\text{tpm}(\mathsf{T}, Q, \Gamma_1), \; \text{tpm}(*\mathsf{T}, LQ, \Gamma_2)}{\text{tpm}(*\mathsf{T}, Q \cdot LQ, \Gamma_1 \cup \Gamma_2)}$$

$$(\text{TPM-LIST}) \; \frac{\text{tpm}(\mathsf{T}, Q, \Gamma_1), \; \text{tpm}(L\mathsf{T}, LQ, \Gamma_2)}{\text{tpm}(\mathsf{T} \cdot L\mathsf{T}, Q \cdot LQ, \Gamma_1 \cup \Gamma_2)}$$

$$(\text{TPM-UNION}) \; \frac{\text{tpm}(\mathsf{T}_0, Q, \Gamma_0) \quad \text{or} \quad \text{tpm}(\mathsf{T}_1, Q, \Gamma_1)}{\text{tpm}(\mathsf{T}_0 + \mathsf{T}_1, Q, \Gamma)}, \quad \text{where:}$$

$$\Gamma = \begin{cases} \Gamma_0 + \Gamma_1 & \text{if } \text{tpm}(\mathsf{T}_0, Q, \Gamma_0) \text{ and } \text{tpm}(\mathsf{T}_1, Q, \Gamma_1) \\ \Gamma_i & \text{if } \text{tpm}(\mathsf{T}_i, Q, \Gamma_i) \text{ and for no } \Gamma' \; \text{tpm}(\mathsf{T}_{i+1 \bmod 2}, Q, \Gamma'), \; i = 0, 1 \end{cases}$$

In what follows, we shall use the following additional notation and terminology. We say that a type T is *abstraction-free* if T contains no subterms of the form $(\mathsf{T}')\text{Abs}$. A context Γ is abstraction-free if for each $x \in \text{dom}(\Gamma)$, $\Gamma(x)$ is abstraction-free. We use $\Gamma \vdash u \in ch(\mathsf{T})$ as an abbreviation for: either $u = a \in ch(\mathsf{T})$ or $u = x \in \mathcal{V}$ and $\Gamma(x) = ch(\mathsf{T})$.

The type checking system, defined on open terms, consists of two sets of inference rules, one for messages and one for processes, displayed in Table 7 and 8, respectively. These two systems are mutually dependent, since abstractions may contain processes, and processes may contain abstractions. Note that the system is entirely syntax driven, i.e. the process P (resp. the pair (M, T)) determines the rule that should be applied to check $\Gamma \vdash P$ (resp. $\Gamma \vdash M : \mathsf{T}$).

The most interesting of these rules is (TM-ABS). Informally, $\Gamma \vdash A : (\mathsf{T})\text{Abs}$ ensures that under Γ the following is true: (1) abstraction $A = (Q_{\tilde{x}} : \Gamma_Q)P$ behaves safely upon consuming messages of type T (because the type at which the actual parameters will be received is a subtype of the type declared for formal parameters, $(\Gamma_1)_{|\tilde{x}} < \Gamma_Q$, and because of $\Gamma, \Gamma_Q \vdash P : ok$); (2) the pattern Q is consistent with type T, i.e. essentially the run-time type of Q is a subtype of T (because of type-pattern match and of $\Gamma_{|\tilde{y}} < (\Gamma_1)_{|\tilde{y}}$). This guarantees existence of a message of type T that matches the pattern. Moreover, no ill-formed pattern will arise from Q (abstraction-freeness).

Rule (T-IN) checks that an abstraction A residing at channel $a \in ch(\mathsf{T})$ can safely consume messages of type T, and that there do exist messages of type T that match the pattern of A. Conversely (T-OUT) checks that messages sent at u be of type T. Input and summation (rule (T-SUM)) are dealt with separately only for notational convenience. Finally, it is worth to notice that, by definition

Table 7. Type system for messages.

(TM-EMPTY) $\dfrac{}{\Gamma \vdash []:[]}$		(TM-TOP) $\dfrac{}{\Gamma \vdash M : \mathsf{T}}$	
(TM-VALUE) $\dfrac{v : \mathsf{bt}}{\Gamma \vdash v : \mathsf{bt}}$		(TM-VAR) $\dfrac{\Gamma(x) < \mathsf{T}}{\Gamma \vdash x : \mathsf{T}}$	
(TM-TAG) $\dfrac{\Gamma \vdash M : \mathsf{T}}{\Gamma \vdash f(M) : f(\mathsf{T})}$		(TM-LIST) $\dfrac{\Gamma \vdash M : \mathsf{T}, \quad \Gamma \vdash LM : \mathsf{LT}}{\Gamma \vdash (M \cdot LM) \ : \ (\mathsf{T} \cdot \mathsf{LT})}$	
(TM-STAR$_1$) $\dfrac{}{\Gamma \vdash []:*\mathsf{T}}$		(TM-STAR$_2$) $\dfrac{\Gamma \vdash M : \mathsf{T}, \quad \Gamma \vdash LM : *\mathsf{T}}{\Gamma \vdash (M \cdot LM) \ : \ *\mathsf{T}}$	

$$(\text{TM-UNION}) \quad \frac{\Gamma \vdash M : \mathsf{T} \quad \text{or} \quad \Gamma \vdash M : \mathsf{T}'}{\Gamma \vdash M : \mathsf{T} + \mathsf{T}'}$$

$$(\text{TM-ABS}) \quad \frac{\mathrm{tpm}(\mathsf{T}, Q, \Gamma_1), \quad (\Gamma_1)_{|\tilde{x}} < \Gamma_Q, \quad (\Gamma_1)_{|\tilde{y}} > \Gamma_{|\tilde{y}}, \quad \Gamma, \Gamma_Q \vdash P : ok}{\Gamma \vdash (Q : \Gamma_Q)P : (\mathsf{T})\mathrm{Abs}}$$

where $\tilde{x} = \mathrm{dom}(\Gamma_Q)$, $\tilde{y} = \mathrm{fv}(Q) \setminus \tilde{x}$ and $(\Gamma_1)_{|\tilde{y}}$ is abstraction-free

Table 8. Type system for processes.

$$(\text{T-IN}) \quad \frac{a \in ch(\mathsf{T}), \quad \Gamma \vdash A : (\mathsf{T})\mathrm{Abs}}{\Gamma \vdash a.A : ok}$$

$$(\text{T-OUT}) \ \frac{\Gamma \vdash u \in ch(\mathsf{T}), \quad \Gamma \vdash M : \mathsf{T}}{\Gamma \vdash \overline{u}\langle M \rangle : ok} \qquad (\text{T-SUM}) \ \frac{\forall i \in I, \quad \Gamma \vdash a_i.A_i : ok \quad |I| \neq 1}{\Gamma \vdash \sum_{i \in I} a_i.A_i : ok}$$

$$(\text{T-REP}) \ \frac{\Gamma \vdash P : ok}{\Gamma \vdash !P : ok} \qquad (\text{T-PAR}) \ \frac{\Gamma \vdash P : ok, \quad \Gamma \vdash R : ok}{\Gamma \vdash (P|R) : ok}$$

$$(\text{T-RES}) \ \frac{\Gamma \vdash P : ok}{\Gamma \vdash (va)P : ok} \qquad (\text{T-ELSE}) \ \frac{\Gamma \vdash P : ok, \quad \Gamma \vdash R : ok}{\Gamma \vdash P \ \mathrm{else}\ R : ok}$$

of $a : S$, rule (TM-VALUE) entails subsumption on channels (i.e. $\Gamma \vdash a : S$ and $S < S'$ implies $\Gamma \vdash a : S'$). The remaining rules should be self-explanatory.

In the sequel, for closed annotated processes P, we shall write $P : ok$ for $\emptyset \vdash P : ok$, and say that P is well-typed. Similarly for $M : \mathsf{T}$, for closed annotated M.

Example 4. Assume $a \in ch(*\mathrm{int})$ and $b \in ch(f[\mathrm{int}, *\mathrm{int}])$. Then $P : ok$, where:

$$P = a.(?y : *\mathrm{int})b.(f[?x : \mathrm{int}, y])\overline{a}\langle x \cdot y \rangle \mid \overline{a}\langle [4,5] \rangle \mid \overline{a}\langle [4,5,6] \rangle.$$

Note that, if we change the sort of b into $ch(f[\mathrm{int}, [\mathrm{int},\mathrm{int}]])$, then P is not well-typed, as rule (TM-ABS) fails on $A = (f[?x : \mathrm{int}, y])\overline{a}\langle x \cdot y \rangle$. This is intuitively correct, because a possible run-time type of A is $(f[\mathrm{int}, [\mathrm{int},\mathrm{int},\mathrm{int}]])\mathrm{Abs}$, which is not consistent with the capacity associated to b, that is $f[\mathrm{int}, [\mathrm{int},\mathrm{int}]]$.

To illustrate the use of $ch(\mathsf{T})$ and $ch(\mathbf{L})$, and contravariance on sort names, consider a "link process" ([7]) that constantly receives any *name* on a and sends it along b. This can be written as $!a.(?x : ch(\mathbf{L}))\overline{b}\langle x \rangle$. This process is well-typed provided $a \in ch(ch(\mathsf{T}))$, for some T, and that $b \in ch(ch(\mathbf{L}))$.

Remark 1 (on abstractions and subtyping). To see why we disallow subtyping on abstractions, consider the types $\mathsf{T} = [f(\mathsf{int}), f(\mathsf{int})]$ and $*f(\mathsf{int}) = \mathsf{T}'$. Clearly $\mathsf{T} < \mathsf{T}'$. Assume we had defined subtyping *covariant* on abstractions, so that $(\mathsf{T})\mathsf{Abs} < (\mathsf{T}')\mathsf{Abs}$. Now, clearly $A = (?x : \mathsf{T})\mathbf{0} : (\mathsf{T})\mathsf{Abs}$, but *not* $A : (\mathsf{T}')\mathsf{Abs}$ (the condition $(\Gamma_1)_{|\bar{x}} < \Gamma_Q$ of (TM-ABS) fails). In other words, a crucial subtyping property would be violated.

On the other hand, assume we had defined subtyping *contravariant* on abstractions, so that $(\mathsf{T}')\mathsf{Abs} < (\mathsf{T})\mathsf{Abs}$. Consider $A' = (Q : \Gamma_Q)\mathbf{0}$, where $Q : \Gamma_Q = [f(?x : \mathsf{int}), f(?y : \mathsf{int}), f(?z : \mathsf{int})]$; clearly $A' : (\mathsf{T}')\mathsf{Abs}$, but *not* $A' : (\mathsf{T})\mathsf{Abs}$ (simply because there is no type-pattern match between T and Q). This would violate again the subtyping property.

Typing rules for application and case. The rules below can be easily derived from the translation of derived constructs application and case to the base syntax. In the following, we let $\mathsf{T}_{M,\Gamma}$ denote the *exact type* of M under Γ, obtained from M by replacing each x by $\Gamma(x)$, each name $a \in ch(\mathsf{T})$ by $ch(\mathsf{T})$, each other v by the least type bt s.t. $v : \mathsf{bt}$, and, recursively, each abstraction subterm $(Q : \Gamma_Q)P$ by $(\mathsf{T}_Q, \Gamma \cup \Gamma_Q)\mathsf{Abs}$. The rule for application is:

$$(\text{T-APPL}) \quad \frac{\Gamma \vdash A : (\mathsf{T}_{M,\Gamma})\mathsf{Abs}}{\Gamma \vdash A \bullet M : ok}.$$

that is easily proven sound recalling that $A \bullet M = (\nu c)(c.A|\bar{c}\langle M \rangle)$ (c fresh), and assuming that c is chosen s.t. $c \in ch(\mathsf{T}_{M,\Gamma})$.

Concerning Case, first note that the typed version of this construct contemplates annotated patterns, thus: Case M of $Q_1 : \Gamma_{Q_1} \Rightarrow P_1, \ldots, Q_k : \Gamma_{Q_k} \Rightarrow P_k : ok$. Then, relying on the rule for application, the typing rule for case can be written as:

$$(\text{T-CASE}) \quad \frac{\forall i = 1, \ldots, k : \ \Gamma \vdash (Q_i : \Gamma_{Q_i})P_i \bullet M : ok}{\Gamma \vdash \text{Case } M \text{ of } Q_1 : \Gamma_{Q_1} \Rightarrow P_1, \ldots, Q_k : \Gamma_{Q_k} \Rightarrow P_k : ok}.$$

Example 5 (a web service, continued). Consider the service defined in Example 2. Assume a basic type mp3 of all mp3 files, such that $v_{low}, v_{high} : \mathsf{mp3}$, and a basic type l-mp3 of low quality mp3 files, s.t. $v_{low} : \mathsf{l\text{-}mp3}$, but *not* $v_{high} : \mathsf{l\text{-}mp3}$. Assume $\mathsf{l\text{-}mp3} < \mathsf{mp3}$; note that this implies that $ch(\mathsf{mp3}) < ch(\mathsf{l\text{-}mp3})$, i.e. if a channel can be used for streaming generic files, it can also be used for streaming low-quality files, which fits intuition. Let T be `req_stream[bandwidth(string),channel(`$ch(\mathsf{mp3})$`)]` and fix the following capacities for channels *stream* and *download*: $stream \in ch(\mathsf{T})$ and $download \in ch(\texttt{req\_down}(ch((\mathsf{T})\mathsf{Abs})))$. An annotated version of WS, which permits in principle a static optimization of channels (assuming allocation of low-quality channels is less expensive than generic channels'):

$WS =!(\quad stream.(\texttt{req\_stream[bandwidth("low"),channel(}?x : ch(\mathsf{l\text{-}mp3})\texttt{)])}\bar{x}\langle v_{low} \rangle$

$\qquad + stream.(\texttt{req\_stream[bandwidth("high"),channel(}?y : ch(\mathsf{mp3})\texttt{)])}\bar{y}\langle v_{high} \rangle$

$\qquad + download.(\texttt{req\_down[}?z : ch((\mathsf{T})\mathsf{Abs})\texttt{])}\bar{z}\langle Player \rangle \quad)$

where *Player* is the obvious annotated version of the player of Example 2. It is easy to check that $Player : (\mathsf{T})\mathsf{Abs}$ and that $WS : ok$.

4   Run-Time Safety

The safety property of our interest can be defined in terms of channel capacities, message types, and consistency. First, a formal definition of pattern consistency.

Definition 8 (T-consistency). *A type* T *is consistent if* $\mathbf{L}$ *does not occur in* T. *A pattern* Q *is* T-*consistent if there is a message* $M : T$ *that matches* Q.

Note that all sort names, including $ch(\mathbf{L})$, are consistent types by definition. A safe process is one whose output and input actions are in agreement with channel capacities, as stated by the definition below. Of course, for input actions it makes sense to require consistency (condition 2) only if the input channel has in turn a consistent capacity.

Definition 9 (safety). *Let* P *be an annotated closed process.* P *is safe if and only if for each name* $a \in ch(T)$:

1. *whenever* $P \equiv (\nu \tilde{h})(\overline{a}\langle M \rangle \,|\, R)$ *then* $M : T$;
2. *suppose* T *is consistent. Whenever* $P \equiv (\nu \tilde{h})(S \,|\, R)$, *where* S *is a guarded summation, a.A a summand of* S *and* Q *is* A's *pattern, then* Q *is* T-*consistent.*

Theorem 1 (run-time safety). *Let* P *be a closed annotated process. If* $P : ok$ *and* $P \rightarrow^* P'$ *then* P' *is safe.*

5   Dynamic Abstractions

Although satisfactory in most situations, a static typing scenario does not seem appropriate in those cases where little is known in advance on actual types of data that will be received from the network.

Example 6 (a directory of services). Suppose one has to program an online directory of (references to) services. Upon request of a service of type T, for *any* T, the directory should lookup its catalog and respond by sending a channel of type $ch(T)$ along a reply channel. If the reply channel is fixed statically, it must be given capacity $ch(\mathbf{L})$, that is, any channel. Then, a client that receives a name at this channel must have some mechanism to cast at runtime this generic type to the subtype $ch(T)$, which means going beyond static typing. If the reply channel is provided by clients the situation does not get any better. E.g. consider the following service (here we use some syntactic sugar for the sake of readability):

$$!request.(\texttt{req}[?t : \mathsf{T}\mathsf{d}, ?x_{rep} : ch(\mathsf{T}\mathsf{r})]) \,\texttt{let}\, y = lookup(t) \,\texttt{in}\, \overline{x_{rep}}\langle y \rangle$$

where *lookup* is a function from some type $\mathsf{T}\mathsf{d}$ of type-descriptors to the type of *all* channels, $ch(\mathbf{L})$. It is not clear what capacity $\mathsf{T}\mathsf{r}$ the return channel variable x_{rep} should be assigned. The only choice that makes the above process well typed is to set $\mathsf{T}\mathsf{r} = ch(\mathbf{L})$, that is, x_{rep} can transport any channel. But then, a client's call to this service like $\overline{request}\langle \texttt{req}[v_{td},r]\rangle$, where r has capacity $ch(\mathsf{T})$, is not well typed (because $r \in ch(ch(\mathsf{T}))$ and $ch(ch(\mathsf{T}))$ is not a subtype of $ch(\mathsf{T}\mathsf{r}) = ch(ch(\mathbf{L}))$).

Even ignoring the static vs. dynamic issue, the schemas sketched above would imply some form encoding of type and subtyping into XML, which is undesirable if one wishes to reason at an abstract level. As we shall see below, dynamic abstractions can solve these difficulties.

The scenario illustrated in the above example motivates the extension of the calculus presented in the preceding sections with a form of dynamic abstraction. The main difference from ordinary abstractions is that type checking for pattern variables is moved to run-time. This is reflected into an additional communication rule, that explicitly invokes type checking. We describe below the necessary extensions to syntax and semantics. We extend the syntactic category of Abstractions thus:

$$A ::= \cdots \mid (\!(Q_{\tilde{x}} : \Gamma)\!)P \; \textit{Dynamic abstraction}$$

with $\tilde{x} = \text{dom}(\Gamma)$. We let D range over dynamic abstractions and A over all abstractions. We add a new reduction rule:

$$(\text{COM-D}) \quad \frac{j \in I, \; a_j = a, \quad A_j = (\!(Q_{\tilde{x}} : \Gamma)\!)P, \quad \text{match}(M, Q, \sigma), \quad \forall y \in \text{dom}(\sigma) : \sigma(y) : \Gamma(y)}{\overline{a}\langle M \rangle \mid \sum_{i \in I} a_i.A_i \to P\sigma}.$$

We finally add a new type checking rule. For this, we need the following additional notation. Given Γ_1 and Γ_2, we write $\Gamma_1 \lesseqgtr \Gamma_2$ if $\text{dom}(\Gamma_1) = \text{dom}(\Gamma_2)$ and $\forall x \in \text{dom}(\Gamma_1)$ there is a consistent type T s.t. $\mathsf{T} < \Gamma_1(x)$ and $\mathsf{T} < \Gamma_2(x)$.

$$(\text{TM-ABS-D}) \quad \frac{\text{tpm}(\mathsf{T}, Q, \Gamma_1), \quad (\Gamma_1)_{|\tilde{x}} \lesseqgtr \Gamma_Q, \quad (\Gamma_1)_{|\tilde{y}} > \Gamma_{|\tilde{y}}, \quad \Gamma, \Gamma_Q \vdash P : ok}{\Gamma \vdash (\!(Q_{\tilde{x}} : \Gamma_Q)\!)P : (\mathsf{T})\text{Abs}}$$

where $\tilde{y} = \text{fv}(Q) \setminus \tilde{x}$ and $(\Gamma_1)_{|\tilde{y}}$ is abstraction free. The existence of a common consistent subtype for Γ_Q and $(\Gamma_1)_{|\tilde{x}}$ ensures a form of dynamic consistency for Q, detailed below.

We discuss now the extension of run-time safety. The safety property needs to be extended to inputs formed with dynamic abstractions. A stronger form of pattern consistency is needed.

Definition 10 (dynamic T-consistency). *An annotated pattern* $Q : \Gamma$ *($\text{fv}(Q) = \text{dom}(\Gamma)$) is dynamically T-consistent if there is a message $M : \mathsf{T}$ s.t.* $\text{match}(Q, M, \sigma)$ *and* $\forall x \in \text{dom}(\sigma)$ *we have* $\sigma(x) : \Gamma(x)$.

Definition 11 (dynamic safety). *Let P an annotated closed process. P is dynamically safe if for each name $a \in \text{ch}(\mathsf{T})$ conditions 1 and 2 of Definition 9 hold, and moreover the following condition is true: Suppose T is consistent. Whenever $P \equiv (\nu\tilde{h})(S \mid R)$, where S is a guarded summation, $a.D$ is a summand of S and $Q : \Gamma$ is D's annotated pattern, then $Q : \Gamma$ is dynamically T-consistent.*

Theorem 2 (run-time dynamic safety). *Let P be an annotated closed process in the extended language. If $P : ok$ and $P \to^* P'$ then P' is dynamically safe.*

Example 7 (a directory of services, continued). Consider again the directory of services. Clients can either request a (reference to a) service of a given type, by sending a message to channel *discovery*, or request the directory to update its catalog with a new service, using the channel *publish*. Each request to *discovery* should contain some type information, which would allow the directory to select a (reference to a) service of that type, taking subtyping into account. Types cannot be passed around explicitly. However one can pass a dynamic abstraction that will do the selection on behalf of the client and return the result back to the client at a private channel. The catalog is maintained on a channel *cat* local to the directory. Thus the directory process can be defined as follows, where $\prod_{i\in I}!\overline{cat}\langle c_i\rangle$ stands for $!\overline{cat}\langle c_1\rangle\,|\cdots|\,!\overline{cat}\langle c_n\rangle$ (for $I = 1,\ldots,n$) and the following capacities are assumed: $discovery \in ch((ch(\mathbf{L}))\mathsf{Abs}$, $publish, cat \in ch(ch(\mathbf{L}))$.

$$Directory \overset{\triangle}{=} (\mathsf{v}\,cat)(\prod_{i\in I}!\overline{cat}\langle c_i\rangle\,|\,!\,publish.(?y : ch(\mathbf{L}))!\overline{cat}\langle y\rangle$$
$$|\,!\,discovery.(?x : (ch(\mathbf{L}))\mathsf{Abs})\,cat.x\,)$$

Note that $(ch(\mathbf{L}))\mathsf{Abs}$ is the type of all abstractions that can consume some channel. A client that wants to publish a new service S that accepts messages of some type T at a new channel $a \in ch(\mathsf{T})$ is:

$$C_1 \overset{\triangle}{=} (\mathsf{v}\,a)(\overline{publish}\langle a\rangle\,|\,S).$$

A client that wants to retrieve a reference to a service of type T, or any subtype of it, is:

$$C_2 \overset{\triangle}{=} (\mathsf{v}\,r)(\overline{discovery}\langle\langle?z : ch(\mathsf{T})\rangle\!\rangle\bar{r}\langle z\rangle\rangle\,|\,r.(?y : ch(\mathsf{T}))C'\,).$$

Suppose $r \in ch(ch(\mathsf{T}))$. Assuming S and C' are well typed (the latter under $\{y : ch(\mathsf{T})\}$), it is easily checked that the global system

$$P \overset{\triangle}{=} Directory\,|\,C_1\,|\,C_2$$

is well typed too.

In reality, the above solution would run into security problems, as the directory executes blindly any abstraction received from clients ($cat.x$). Moreover, services originating from unauthorized clients should not be published. We can avoid these problems using encryption so to authenticate both abstractions and published services. We rely on the encoding of encryption primitives[2] described in Section 2. Assume that every client C_j shares a secret key k_j with the directory. A table associating clients identifiers and keys is maintained on a channel *table* local to the directory (hence secure). Assume that identifiers $id_j,\ldots$ are of a basic type identifier, that keys $k_j,\ldots$ are names of a sort Key and let $\mathsf{enc}(\mathsf{T})$ be the type of messages $\{M\}_k$ where $M : \mathsf{T}$. Fix the following capacities: $cat \in ch(ch(\mathbf{L}))$, $table \in ch(\mathtt{[id(identifier),key(Key)]})$, $publish \in ch(\mathtt{service\_p[id(identifier),channel(enc}(ch(\mathbf{L})))\mathtt{]})$, and $discovery \in ch(\mathtt{service\_d[id(identifier),abstr(enc}((ch(\mathbf{L}))\mathsf{Abs}))\mathtt{]})$. The process $Directory_s$ is:

---

[2] For the purpose of the present example, we extend the encoding to the typed calculus by $[\![\{M\}_k]\!] \overset{\triangle}{=} ([k, ?x : ch(\mathbf{T})])\bar{x}\langle[\![M]\!]\rangle$, and $\langle\!$case M of $\{x : \mathsf{T}\}_k$ in $P\rangle \overset{\triangle}{=} (\mathsf{v}\,r)([\![M]\!] \bullet [k,r]\,|\,r.(?x : \mathsf{T})\langle\!\langle P\rangle\!\rangle)$, with $r \in ch(\mathbf{T})$.

$Directory_s \stackrel{\triangle}{=} (\nu cat, table)\Big(\prod_{i \in I}!\,\overline{cat}\langle c_i \rangle \mid \prod_{j \in J}!\,\overline{table}\langle [\mathtt{id}(id_j),\mathtt{key}(k_j)] \rangle$

$\qquad \mid !\,publish.(\mathtt{service\_p}[\mathtt{id}(?x:\mathsf{identifier}),\mathtt{channel}(?z_c:\mathsf{enc}(ch(\mathbf{L})))])$

$\qquad\qquad table.([\mathtt{id}(x),\mathtt{key}(?x_k:\mathsf{Key})])\,\mathsf{case}\ z_c\ \mathsf{of}\ \{y:ch(\mathbf{L})\}_{x_k}\ \mathsf{in}\ !\overline{cat}\langle y \rangle$

$\qquad \mid !\,discovery.(\mathtt{service\_d}[\mathtt{id}(?x:\mathsf{identifier}),\mathtt{abstr}(?z_a:\mathsf{enc}((ch(\mathbf{L}))\mathsf{Abs}))])$

$\qquad\qquad table.([\mathtt{id}(x),\mathtt{key}(?x_k:\mathsf{Key})])\,\mathsf{case}\ z_a\ \mathsf{of}\ \{y:(ch(\mathbf{L}))\mathsf{Abs}\}_{x_k}\ \mathsf{in}\ cat.y \Big)$

The client C_1 may be rewritten as:

$$C_1' \stackrel{\triangle}{=} (\nu a)(\overline{publish}\langle\mathtt{service\_p}[\mathtt{id}(id_1),\mathtt{channel}(\{a\}_{k_1})]\rangle \mid S)$$

and C_2 as:

$$C_2' \stackrel{\triangle}{=} (\nu r)(\overline{discovery}\langle\mathtt{service\_d}[\mathtt{id}(id_2),\mathtt{abstr}(\{(\!|?z:ch(\mathsf{T})|\!)\overline{r}\langle z \rangle\}_{k_2})]\rangle \mid r.(?y:ch(\mathsf{T}))C').$$

Suppose $a \in ch(\mathsf{T}')$, $r \in ch(ch(\mathsf{T}))$ and assume S and C' are well typed under the appropriate contexts. The global system

$$P_s \stackrel{\triangle}{=} (\nu k_1, k_2)(Directory_s \mid C_1' \mid C_2')$$

is well typed too. An attacker may intercept messages on *publish* or *discovery* and may learn the identifiers of the clients, but not the secret shared keys. As a consequence, it cannot have *Directory_s* publish unauthorized services or run unauthorized abstractions.

6   Conclusions and Related Work

XPi's type system can be extended into several directions. We are presently considering types that would guarantee "responsiveness" of services. A responsive service would be one that, when invoked at a given a, eventually responds at a given return address r, possibly after collaborating with other services that are equally responsive. This extension would be along the lines of Sangiorgi's *uniform receptiveness* [21]. Such a system might be augmented with primitives for managing quality of service in terms of response time.

A number of proposals aim at integrating XML processing primitives in the context of traditional, statically typed languages and logics. The most related to our work are XDuce [16] and CDuce, [3], two typed (functional) languages for XML document processing. XPi's list-like representation of documents draws its inspiration from them. TQL [9] is both a logic and a query language for XML, based on a spatial logic for the Ambient calculus [10]. All these languages support query primitives more sophisticated than XPi's patterns, but issues raised by communication and code/name mobility, which are our main focus, are of course absent.

Early works aiming at integration of XML into process calculi, or vice-versa, are [14] and [4]. Xdπ [14] is a calculus for describing interaction between data and processes across distributed locations; it is focused on process migration rather than communication. A type system is not provided. Iota [4] is a concurrent XML scripting language for home-area networking. It relies on syntactic subtyping, like

XPi, but is characterized by a different approach to XML typing. In particular, Iota's type system just ensures well-formedness of XML documents, rather than the stronger validity, which we consider here.

Roughly contemporary to ours, and with similar goals, are [8] and [11]. The language πDuce of [8] features asynchronous communication and code/name mobility. Similarly to XDuce's, πDuce's pattern matching embodies built-in type checks, which may be expensive at run-time. The language in [11] is basically a π-calculus enriched with a rich form of "semantic" subtyping and pattern matching. Code mobility is not addressed. Pattern matching, similarly to πDuce's, performs type checks on messages. By contrast, in XPi static type checks and plain pattern matching suffice, as types of pattern variables are checked statically against channel capacities. We confine dynamic type checking to dynamic abstractions, which can be used whenever no refined typing information on incoming messages is available (e.g. at channels of capacity **T**). Both [11] and [8] type systems also guarantee a form of absence of deadlock, which however presupposes that basic values do not appear in patterns. In XPi, we thought it was important to allow basic values in patterns for expressiveness reasons (e.g., they are crucial in the encoding of the spi-calculus presented in Section 2).

References

1. M. Abadi and A.D. Gordon. A Calculus for Cryptographic Protocols: The Spi Calculus. *Information and Computation*, 148(1):1-70, Academic Press, 1999.
2. T. Andrews, F. Curbera, and S. Thatte. Business Process Execution Language for Web Wervices, v1.1, 2003. http://ifr.sap.com/bpel4ws.
3. V. Benzaken, G. Castagna, and A. Frisch. Cduce: An XML-Centric General-Purpose Language. In *Proceedings of the ACM International Conference on Functional Programming*, 2003.
4. G.M. Bierman and P. Sewell. Iota: A concurrent XML scripting language with applications to Home Area Networking. Technical Report 577, University of Cambridge Computer Laboratory, 2003.
5. Biztalk Server Home. http://www.microsoft.com/biztalk/.
6. S. Bjorg and L.G. Meredith. Contracts and Types. *Communication of the ACM*, 46(10), October 2003.
7. M. Boreale. On the Expressiveness of Internal Mobility in Name-Passing Calculi. *Theoretical Computer Science*, 195, 1998.
8. A. Brown, C. Laneve, and L.G. Meredith. πDuce: A process calculus with native XML datatypes. Manuscript. 2004.
9. L. Cardelli and G. Ghelli. TQL: A Query Language Semistruictured Data Based on the Ambient Logic. *Mathematical Structures in Computer Science*, 14:285–327, 2004.
10. L. Cardelli and A.D. Gordon. Mobile ambients. *Theoretical Computer Science*, 240(1), 2000.
11. G. Castagna, R. De Nicola, and D. Varacca. Semantic subtyping for the π-calculus. To appaear in *Proc. of LICS'05*.
12. E. Christensen, F. Curbera, G. Meredith, and S. Weerawarana. Web Services Description Language 1.1. W3C Note, 2001.
http://www.w3.org/TR/2001/NOTE-wsdl-20010315.

13. D.C. Fallside. XML Schema Part 0: Primer. W3C Recommendation, 2001.
    http://www.w3.org/TR/2001/REC-xmlschema-0-20010502.
14. P. Gardner and S. Maffeis. Modeling Dynamic Web Data. In *Proceedings of DBPL 2003*, volume 2921 of *LNCS*. Springer, 2003.
15. H. Hosoya and B. Pierce. Regular Expression Pattern Matching for XML. *Journal of Functional Programming*, 2002.
16. H. Hosoya and B. Pierce. Xduce: A Statically Typed XML Processing Language. In *Proceedings of ACM Transaction on Internet Technology*, 2003.
17. M. Merro. Locality and polyadicity in asynchronous name-passing calculi. In *Proceedings of FoSSaCS 2000*, volume 1784 of *LNCS*, pages 238–251. Springer, 2000.
18. R. Milner. The Polyadic π-Calculus: a Tutorial. Technical Report ECS-LFCS-91-180, LFCS, Dept. of Computer Science, Edinburgh University, 1991.
19. R. Milner, J. Parrow, and D. Walker. A calculus of Mobile Processes, part I and II. *Information and Computation*, 100:1–41 and 42–78, 1992.
20. B. Pierce and D. Sangiorgi. Typing and Subtyping for Mobile Process. *Mathematical Structures in Computer Science*, 6(5), 1996.
21. D. Sangiorgi. The name discipline of uniform receptiveness. *Theoretical Computer Science*, 221, 1999.
22. D. Sangiorgi and R. Milner. Barbed bisimulation. *Proc. of Concur'92*, LNCS, Springer, 1992.
23. Web services activity web site, 2002. http://www.w3.org/2002/ws.

Checking the Validity of Scenarios in UML Models*

Holger Rasch and Heike Wehrheim

Department of Computer Science
University of Paderborn
33098 Paderborn, Germany
{hrasch,wehrheim}@uni-paderborn.de

Abstract. In the UML, sequence diagrams are used to state scenarios, i.e., examples of interactions between objects. As such, sequence diagrams are being developed in the early design phases where requirements on the system are being captured. Their intuitively appealing character and conceptual simplicity makes them an ideal tool for formulating simple properties on a system, even for non-experts. Besides guiding the development of a UML model, sequence diagrams can thus furthermore be used as a starting point for the *verification* of the UML model.

In this paper, we show how the requirements on the system as stated in sequence diagrams can be (semi-automatically) validated for UML models consisting of class diagrams, state machines and structure diagrams. The sequence diagrams that we consider can be universally or existentially quantified or negated, i.e., state scenarios that should always, sometimes or never occur. For validating them in a UML model, we translate both model and sequence diagrams into a formal specification language (the process algebra CSP), and develop procedures for employing the standard CSP model checker (FDR) for checking their validity.

1 Introduction

The complexity of software is steadily increasing. Models of software systems have to reflect this complexity in that they precisely describe all different aspects making up the functionality of a complex system. The UML is a modelling language which supports modelling with different views. Its various diagram types allow for the description of different though not necessarily disjoint aspects of a system: Class diagrams model the static behaviour (data and operations), state machines the dynamic behaviour (protocols), structure diagrams the architectural composition and sequence diagrams typical application scenarios (plus possibly further diagrams for other aspects). Together they model the system to be built. Such a complex model composition immediately poses the question of consistency: is the architectural composition consistent with the

* This research was partially supported by the DFG project ForMooS (grants OL98/3-2 and WE2290/5-1)

M. Steffen and G. Zavattaro (Eds.): FMOODS 2005, LNCS 3535, pp. 67–82, 2005.

interface description of the components, are static and dynamic behaviour non-contradictory, is the scenario as stated in the sequence diagrams actually allowed in the model, etc. In this paper, we develop techniques which can be used for answering the latter question.

The starting point for our study are UML 1.5 sequence diagrams [25] which we extend with features for stating *negation* and *universal* and *existential* quantification (partially coming from UML 2.0 sequence diagrams[1]). These facilities allow to distinguish between different types of scenarios: those never occurring, sometimes occurring (i.e., in at least one run) or always occurring (in all runs). The remaining part of the UML models will consist of class diagrams, state machines and structure diagrams. To achieve the necessary precision in the model (which is mandatory for a verification) we additionally use the Z notation [14, 22] for writing attributes and methods in class diagrams. The question is then whether the sequence diagrams are consistent with the UML model in that the restrictions on the overall behaviour (as laid down in the diagrams) do not prevent desired or allow forbidden scenarios. We develop a technique which allows to automatically check for this kind of consistency. To this end, we translate both sequence diagrams and the rest of the UML model into a formal specification language. The translation of class diagrams, state machines and structure diagrams follows a technique proposed in [17], the translation of the sequence diagrams is inspired by [11] and given in this paper. Since the properties stated in the sequence diagrams all refer to orderings in the communication between objects we have chosen the process algebra CSP for this purpose. CSP [13, 19] has been developed to model and analyse systems exhibiting a large degree of parallelism and communication. Moreover, there is a model checker for CSP (FDR [10]) which can be used for automatically analysing CSP processes. The translation provides us with a semantics of UML model and sequence diagrams in terms of the semantic model of CSP. On this semantic model we formally define validity of a sequence diagram (in the UML model) with respect to existential and universal quantification; negation is obtained by negating the definition of existential quantification. For these validity definitions we develop procedures for automatic checks using the FDR model checker: the validity checks have to be formulated as *refinement checks* between CSP processes which is the type of analysis supported by FDR. To this end we develop testers out of the CSP semantics of sequence diagrams which are then checked against the CSP semantics of the UML model.

The paper is structured as follows: The next section will present an example of a UML model together with a number of allowed or forbidden scenarios stated by sequence diagrams. Section 3 describes the translation of model and sequence diagram to CSP. Section 4 formally defines validity and develops procedures for checking validity via the FDR model checker. The last section concludes.

---

[1] We do not treat other new features of UML 2.0 sequence diagrams here (like combined fragments) since our main interest is in checking validity not in developing a semantics for UML 2.0.

2   Example

In this section we start with introducing the example which will be used for illustrating our technique for checking the validity of scenarios. The example concerns the modelling of cash machines and banks. For the modelling we use a UML profile for reactive systems proposed in [17] and inspired by the ROOM method [20]. This profile allows to describe reactive systems as being built out of processes (active objects) working concurrently and communicating with each other. Each process has an associated interface which describes its communication capabilities. An interface description contains both the methods callable on the active object/process as well as those called by the object.

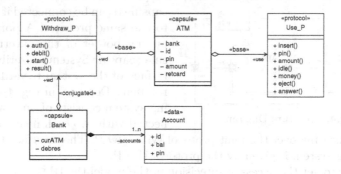

Fig. 1. Class Diagram for capsules Bank and ATM

In the UML profile these active objects or processes are modelled by special *capsule* classes and their interfaces by *protocol* classes. Capsules which share a common protocol can be connected to each other. The dynamic behaviour of the processes, viz. capsules, are given by UML state machines. Figure 1 gives the class diagram for capsules ATM (the cash machine) and Bank. Capsule Bank has one protocol which describes its interface, namely the methods *auth*, *debit*, *start* and *result* that it offers to other processes. Class Account is a passive component which is associated to Bank (every bank has a number of accounts). Capsule ATM has two protocols, one for communication with the Bank and the second one for communication with users. The stereotypes «base» and «conjugated» describe the direction of communication for the protocols.

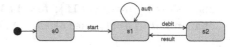

Fig.2. State Machine for Capsule Bank

Figures 2 and 3 depict the protocol state machines for ATM and Bank. They model the allowed ordering of method invocation for objects of class Bank and ATM, respectively.

The reactive system itself is modelled by a structure diagram. Structure diagrams describe the architecture of systems, i.e., their components and their

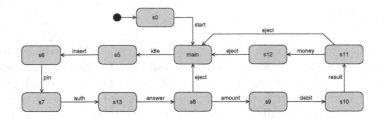

Fig. 3. State Machine for Capsule ATM

interconnection. A capsule in a structure diagram is drawn as a rectangle with ports (white or black boxes) indicating their protocols. Two ports (and thus two capsules) can be connected if they refer to the same protocol. A port residing on the border of the outermost capsule (capsule System) describes the interface of the system towards its environment. Depicted in Fig. 4, our banking system consists of one bank b connected with two cash machines a_1 and a_2 communicating over the joint protocol Withdraw_P. The interface to users of the banking system is given by the protocol Use_P.

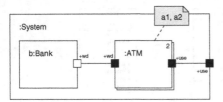

Fig.4. Structure Diagram

In order to get the necessary precision in the model the UML profile furthermore allows to formally specify the signatures of methods in interfaces, and the attributes and methods in classes (both for capsules and passive classes). For this purpose the specification formalism Z [14, 22] is employed. If such a specification is supplied for all methods and attributes a precise and unambiguous meaning can be given to the UML model. This is the prerequisite for formally checking the validity of scenarios. For our example, we only show the *signatures* of methods in interface since we will refer to them when translating sequence diagrams. For the Bank the interface specification in Z is (assuming given types *ID* and *PIN*):

> **method** $auth : \lbrack from : ATM;\ to : \{\texttt{self}\};\ id? : ID;\ pin? : PIN;\ ok! : \mathbb{B}\rbrack$
> **method** $debit : \lbrack from : ATM;\ to : \{\texttt{self}\};\ id? : ID;\ amt? : \mathbb{N}\rbrack$
> **chan** $start : \lbrack from : \{\texttt{self}\};\ to : ATM\rbrack$
> **chan** $result : \lbrack from : \{\texttt{self}\};\ to : ATM;\ ok! : \mathbb{B}\rbrack$

There are two types of operations in the interface: those being declared as **method** are methods of the Bank itself and can be called by other objects; those declared by **chan** are methods that Bank calls on other objects. The parameters of these operations can be divided into *input* (marked with ?), *output* (!) or *simple* parameters. The latter one are used for addressing particular objects. Every method must have two simple parameters specifying the caller (parameter *from*) and callee (parameter *to*) of the method. The value **self** refers to the object itself.

If a parameter has type {self} then the only possible value that the parameter can take is self.

The interface of ATM towards Bank is specified in a complementary way (channels and methods, and input and output reversed). Additionally the interface contains operations for interaction with a user. We always assume to have one class (here called *User*) which models the environment of our system. The interface of this class can be determined from the structure diagram: all protocols of ports residing on the borders of the outermost capsule System are also protocols of the environment class (complementing methods and channels, inputs and outputs). The behaviour of the environment remains unspecified, thus we assume it to behave chaotically (all behaviour allowed). Thus for our interface of ATM towards a user we assume a class User to be given. The interface is

> **method** *insert* : $[$ *from* : *User*; *to* : {self}; *id?* : *ID* $]$
> **method** *pin* : $[$ *from* : *User*; *to* : {self}; *pin?* : *PIN* $]$
> **method** *amount* : $[$ *from* : *User*; *to* : {self}; *amt?* : $\mathbb{N}]$

(plus channels *answer*, *idle*, *money*, *eject*).

This completes the UML model. The development of the model might have been preceded by the modelling of typical (allowed or forbidden) scenarios of the system to be modelled. Such scenarios can be described by sequence diagrams. Here, we use a very simple form of sequence diagrams since our main focus is not on giving a semantics but on checking their validity (for semantics for message sequence charts, the precursors of sequence diagrams, see for instance [11, 15, 16]; for a semantics for UML 2.0 interactions diagrams see [23]). For the banking system we might for instance like to specify that a user never gets money when the ATMs question for enough credit is answered with 'no'. Thus the scenario in Figure 5 is forbidden for our system[2].

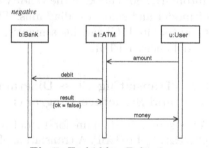

Fig.5. Forbidden Behaviour

In general, sequence diagrams consist of a number of lifelines for objects. These lines are connected by arrows labelled with methods. The sequence diagram thus models orderings for interactions between objects. We use particular objects here (although the scenario should be forbidden for all banks, ATMs and users) since we need to refer to specific objects in our addressing parameters. In principle object names could be left out first and later be instantiated when the validity of scenarios is checked.

Figure 6 shows a possible scenario between bank, ATM and user: when the answer of the bank following the request for an authentication of a pin is not ok then the card should be ejected.

---

[2] Only visible behaviour is of interest here; invisible (τ) steps are ignored.

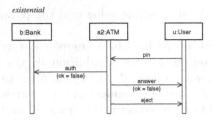

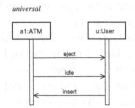

Fig.6. Possible Behaviour   **Fig.7.** Required Behaviour

Figure 7 depicts a scenario which is required to occur in every behaviour *at least once*[3]: after ejecting and idling for a while an insert of another card should be possible.

3   Translating the UML Model to CSP

Given a UML model of a system and a number of sequence diagrams specifying allowed or forbidden scenarios we are interested in knowing whether these scenarios are actually possible (or not possible) in the model. We refer to this as the *validity* of the scenario in the model. Checking the validity of scenarios should at the best be fully automatic; here we propose a technique which is partially automatic. For checking the validity we first of all have to compute the semantics of model and sequence diagrams. This so far has to be done by hand, but can be automated. Given this semantics the check can be carried out with the CSP model checker FDR.

3.1   Translating Class Diagrams, State Machines and Structure Diagrams

As a semantic domain for model and sequence diagrams we have chosen the process algebra CSP. A translation of models, written in our specific UML profile, to CSP can be found in [17]. Roughly, the translation proceeds as follows: The class diagram together with the Z formalisation of interfaces, attributes and methods is translated to Object-Z [21]. The Object-Z classes of capsules are then augmented with CSP process descriptions which are derived from the state machines. A specific CSP process is computed for the outermost capsule *System*. This process describes the architecture of the system and consists of the parallel composition of the capsules in the system. Together, these classes form a CSP-OZ [9] specification. CSP-OZ is a combination of Object-Z and CSP and has a semantics in terms of the semantic model of CSP. Thus we hereby end with a CSP semantics for our UML model. To show at least a small part of the resulting CSP process:

$$\mathbf{main} = Bank[b] \;\|_{\{|\; auth, debit, result, start \;|\}}\; Clients$$
$$Clients = ATM[a1] \;|||\; ATM[a2]$$

---

[3] We currently do not handle conditional cases, i.e., 'whenever some prefix has occurred, *then* the rest of the sequence must follow.'

is the CSP process of class *System* (derived from the structure diagram). It describes the behaviour of the overall system. The operator ||| is the interleaving operator of CSP (parallel composition with no synchronisation) whereas $||_A$ (A being a set of methods) is a parallel composition which requires joint execution of methods in A. This synchronisation set is derived from the joint protocol (Withdraw_P) of Bank and ATM.

3.2 Translating Sequence Diagrams

In the next step we equip the sequence diagrams with a CSP semantics as well. To this end, we first formalise sequence diagrams, i.e., give description of their syntax. This will be the basis for the translation to CSP. As a language for formalising the diagrams we again employ Z. We start with the definition of some basic data types (in particular for the names appearing in the diagrams).

$[Name, Param, Object$ [channel names, parameters, object names]
  $D, UID]$ [data values for parameters, unique identifier for arrows]

The sets which can actually be used here depend on the UML model and can be derived from it. In the banking example, we for instance would have $auth \in Name$, $amt \in Param$, $a1 \in Objects$ etc. The set D is the basic type of values for parameters. As we have already explained, all channels must have two special parameters which are used for addressing the partners in a communication. These are declared | $to, from : Param$
in the axiomatic definition on the right:

Communication channels between components are described by *protocols* in the UML model. A protocol describes the interface of a class, i.e. the methods it provides (with their signature) and the methods it requires. Components that are to be connected with each other in the structure diagram share one (or more) protocols. From this interface information in the protocols we just need the names of channels and their parameters here. They are described in a Z *schema* consisting of a declaration of variables plus predicates giving constraints on the variables (see [22] for an introduction to Z).

$$\begin{array}{l} \underline{\quad Channel\quad\qquad\qquad} \\ name : Name \\ params : \mathbb{P}\, Param \\ \overline{\{to, from\} \subseteq params} \end{array}$$

CSP processes are built over *events*. An event consists of a channel name together with values for parameters, e.g. $answer.b.a1.true$ is an event consisting of the name *answer* plus values b (for parameter *from*), $a1$ (for *to*) and *true* (for *ok*). The notation $?\_$ denotes that any value can be accepted for a parameter. A *partial event* is one in which some of the values for parameters are missing, e.g. $answer.b.a1$ is only a partial event. Given a set of partial events Ev we use the CSP notation $\{| Ev |\}$ to denote the set of completions of Ev. Formalised in Z events are as follows.

$$\begin{array}{l} \underline{\quad Event\quad\qquad\qquad} \\ ch : Channel \\ val : Param \nrightarrow D \cup \{?\_\} \\ \overline{\mathrm{dom}\, val = ch.params} \end{array}$$

In sequence diagrams events will appear as labels of arrows between objects. Whenever values for parameters are left out (which is most often the case) we assume the value to be $?\_$.

Arrows in sequence diagrams are connecting the lifelines of two objects and are labelled with events. To distinguish two arrows with the same label connecting the same lines we attach a unique identifier to each arrow. The values for parameters *to* and *from* of an event attached to an arrow have to agree with the objects connected by the arrow.

Arrow _____

   from, to : *Object*; *event* : *Event*; *uid* : *UID*

   to $\neq$ *from* $\wedge$ *event.to* = *to* $\wedge$ *event.from* = *from*

These definitions form the basis for formalising sequence diagrams. A sequence diagram simply consists of a set of arrows and lifelines. Each line belongs to an object and has a number of arrows going out of it or coming in. On one line arrows are always ordered (hence we describe them as a sequence). A number of additional conditions ensure well-formedness of sequence diagrams. Additionally, every sequence diagram is equipped with an occurrence condition stating whether the specified scenario should never/sometimes or always happen.

   Condition ::= *negative* | *existential* | *universal*

SQ _____

   c : *Condition*

   arrows : $\mathbb{F}$ *Arrow*

   lines : *Object* $\nrightarrow$ iseq *Arrow*

   arrows = *ran* $\bigcup$ ran *lines*

                      [the set *arrows* contains exactly those appearing on lifelines]

   $\forall$ *a* : *arrows* •

      $\#(\{a.from, a.to\} \cap \mathrm{dom}\ lines) = 2\ \wedge$

                      [an arrow belongs to exactly 2 different lifelines]

      $a \in \mathrm{ran}(lines\ a.from) \cap \mathrm{ran}(lines\ a.to)\ \wedge$

                      [*to* and *from* are set to the correct lifelines]

      $a \notin \mathrm{ran} \bigcup \mathrm{ran}(\{a.from, a.to\} \vartriangleleft lines)$

                      [an arrow cannot belong to a wrong lifeline]

   $\exists R : Arrow \leftrightarrow Arrow$ •

      $\forall a_1, a_2 : arrows \mid a_1 \neq a_2$ • $\neg(a_1\ \underline{R}^+\ a_1)\ \wedge$

      $(a_1\ \underline{R}\ a_2 \Leftrightarrow \exists s : \mathrm{ran}\ lines$ • $s \upharpoonright \{a_1, a_2\} = \langle a_1, a_2 \rangle)$

                      [arrows cannot go back in time]

This formalisation of sequence diagrams is the basis for our translation to CSP. Next we define a function from sequence diagrams to CSP processes which defines the translation. The range of the function is the set of CSP processes defined by the following given type:

   [*CSP*]   The precise syntax of processes will not be defined here, for an introduction to CSP see [19]. In the translation we use two operators of CSP: $\rightarrow$ is the *prefix* operator for modelling sequencing and $\parallel$ is the parallel composition. Here we employ *alphabetised* parallel composition: for every process in a parallel composition its alphabet of events is given, and synchronisation has to take place on events in the intersection of alphabets. Syntactically this takes the form $\| (P_i, \alpha_i)$ where i ranges over some index set and the P_i are CSP processes with alphabets α_i. When there are just two processes we write $P_A\|_B Q$. In contrast to ordinary parallel composition alphabetised parallel composition is associative which is convenient here.

The translation proceeds in two steps. The CSP process of the sequence diagram is the parallel composition of the CSP processes belonging to every lifeline of an object. These processes synchronise on shared events. Due to the parameters *to* and *from* in events, an event belongs to the alphabet of exactly two objects (and thus to exactly two CSP processes).

> $trans : SQ \rightarrow CSP$
> ___
> $\forall sq : SQ \bullet trans\ sq = \| \{o : \text{dom } lines \bullet (transLine\ o, alpha\ (o, sq))\}$

The alphabet of an object in a sequence diagram consists of the events over channels appearing on arrows of the object's lifeline with values for parameters *to* and *from* properly filled in.

> $alpha : Object \times SQ \rightarrow \mathbb{P}\ Event$
> ___
> $\forall o : Object, sq : SQ \bullet$
> $\quad alpha(o, sq) = \{| a : \text{ran}(sq.lines\ o) \bullet$
> $\qquad\qquad (a.event.ch)_\bullet(a.event.val)(from)_\bullet(a.event.val)(to) |\}$

Note that the bold dots are those used for separating values of parameters in CSP events. We cannot just plainly use *a.event* here since FDR is not accepting the notation ?_ in sets of events, only in process expressions.

The CSP processes of the lifelines are simply the sequential composition of the events on their arrows.

> $transLine : \text{iseq}\ Arrow \rightarrow CSP$
> ___
> $transLine\langle\rangle = SKIP$
> $\forall sa : \text{iseq}\ Arrow, a : Arrow \bullet transLine\langle a\rangle \frown sa = a.event \rightarrow transLine\ sa$

The occurrence condition plays no role in the translation to CSP. It will be used for defining validity. As an example for the translation consider the sequence diagram in Figure 5 (here u is the identity of the user):

$\| \{$
$(debit.a1.b?\_?\_ \rightarrow result.b.a1.false \rightarrow SKIP,$
$\qquad\qquad \{| debit.a1.b, result.b.a1\}),$
$(amount.u.a1?\_ \rightarrow debit.a1.b?\_?\_ \rightarrow result.b.a1.false \rightarrow money.a1.u?\_ \rightarrow SKIP,$
$\qquad\qquad \{| amount.u.a1, debit.a1.b, results.b.a1, money.a1.u |\}),$
$(amount.u.a1?\_ \rightarrow money.a1.u?\_ \rightarrow SKIP,$
$\qquad\qquad \{| amount.u.a1, money.a1.u |\})\}$

4   Checking Validity

Having defined the CSP semantics of simple sequence diagrams and UML models, it is now possible to check the validity of the scenario in the UML model. For the check we employ the CSP model checker FDR [10]. FDR performs checks for deadlock- and divergence-freedom as well as *refinement* checks between processes. It is based on the semantic models of CSP. To see how we can use FDR for checking validity of sequence diagrams we first give a short summary of CSP's semantic models.

We assume Σ to be a global set of events (of type *Event*). The traces model $\mathcal{T}$ identifies a process P with the (prefix closed) set $traces(P) \subseteq \Sigma^*$ of sequences of events it can perform. Refinement in $\mathcal{T}$ is defined as $P \sqsubseteq_{\mathcal{T}} Q \Leftrightarrow traces(P) \supseteq traces(Q)$. A more powerful model is the stable failures model $\mathcal{F}$, which, in addition to $traces(P)$, records for any trace t of P the set of events R that P can stably refuse after performing t. The set of all these pairs $(t, R) \in \Sigma^* \times \mathbb{P}\,\Sigma$ is called $failures(P)$. A pair (t, Σ) identifies deadlock in $\mathcal{F}$, i.e., a trace after which P refuses all events[4]. The standard model for CSP is the failures-divergences model $\mathcal{N}$. Besides deadlock this model can deal with divergence. The (extension closed) set $divergences(P) \subseteq \Sigma^*$ contains all traces after which P can diverge. The failures in $\mathcal{N}$ differ slightly from those in $\mathcal{F}$; $failures_\perp(P)$ includes all (t, X), $X \subseteq \Sigma$, for any $t \in divergences(P)$ in addition to the stable failures. All three models are supported by the FDR model checker, and refinement checks in these models all amount to checking inclusion between the semantics of processes[5]. Finally, we need the set $infinites(P)$, which belongs to the infinite traces models of CSP. It contains all infinite traces of P including the infinite extensions of divergent traces. It is not supported by FDR, but this does not concern our use of the set.

As a first step in the validation, we are interested in the language of a sequence diagram $sq : SQ$: $\mathcal{L}(sq) = runs(trans\ sq)$, where for a CSP process P $runs(P)$ is used for 'all runs of P'. With 'run' we denote only those finite traces which cannot be extended (apart from termination) and the infinite traces, i.e,

$$runs(P) = \{t : \text{seq}\,\Sigma \mid (t, \Sigma) \in failures_\perp(P)\} \cup infinites(P)$$

Note that this differs from $traces(P)$ since the latter set also contains all prefixes. For the simple sequence diagrams defined in this paper, there are of course only finite runs; in fact, all of the examples here define exactly one sequence of events, i.e., a singleton set as their respective language. The focus in this section is therefore on validating an occurrence condition for a single word; generalisation to a set of words is discussed at the end.

4.1   Occurrence of a Single Word

In the following let P denote the CSP process of the UML model (specified in the class diagram, state machine and structure diagrams) obtained by the translation sketched in Section 3.1. We assume E to be the alphabet of P and let Seq E denote the set of finite and infinite sequences of elements in E.

---

[4] We do not explicitly treat successful termination here.

[5] The more powerful models are needed only for technical reasons; the semantics for sequence diagrams used here does not require them.

Definition 1. Let $sq : SQ$ be a sequence diagram with $\mathcal{L}(sq) = \{s\}$ and P be the CSP process belonging to the UML model. The sequence diagram sq is valid in P iff the following hold:

- $sq.condition = negative \Rightarrow \neg\exists\, t : runs(P);\ u : seq\, E;\ v : Seq\, E \bullet t = u \frown s \frown v,$
- $sq.condition = existential \Rightarrow \exists\, t : runs(P);\ u : seq\, E;\ v : Seq\, E \bullet t = u \frown s \frown v,$
- $sq.condition = universal \Rightarrow \forall\, t : runs(P) \bullet \exists\, u : seq\, E;\ v : Seq\, E \bullet t = u \frown s \frown v.$

To establish these occurrence conditions, it is sufficient to verify the following assertions:

$$\mathbf{A}_\exists : \qquad \exists\, t : traces(P);\ u : seq\, E \bullet t = u \frown s$$

for *negative* and *existential* conditions and

$$\mathbf{A}_\forall : \qquad \forall\, t : runs(P) \bullet \exists\, u : seq\, E;\ v : Seq\, E \bullet t = u \frown s \frown v$$

for *universal* conditions[6].

Since this is neither a refinement check in one of CSP's semantic models nor a check for deadlock- or divergence-freedom, we cannot directly use FDR but first have to reformulate the problem in a way tractable by FDR. The general idea is to use an auxiliary process ('tester'), which performs pattern matching for the sequence s on the stream of events it is offered. This process is then put in parallel to the process P for the system to be analysed, synchronising on the whole alphabet of the system.

The pattern matching consists of keeping track of the longest prefix of s already matched, and calculating the resulting longest prefix after performing the next event. For this, a function δ is defined, which, for some alphabet $E : \mathbb{P}\, Event$ and a word $s : seq\, E$, maps an already matched prefix s_1 of s together with an event e to the maximal prefix of s resulting from appending e to s_1, e.g., $\delta(\{a, b, c\}, \langle a, b, a, c\rangle, \langle a, b, a\rangle, b) = \langle a, b\rangle$.

$\delta : (\mathbb{P}\, Event \times seq\, Event \times seq\, Event \times Event) \nrightarrow seq\, Event$

$\forall\, E : \mathbb{P}\, Event;\ s, s_1, s_2 : seq\, E;\ e : E \mid s_1\ \text{prefix}\ s \bullet \delta(E, s, s_1, e) = s_2 \Leftrightarrow$
$s_2\ \text{prefix}\ s \wedge s_2\ \text{suffix}\ s_1 \frown \langle e\rangle \wedge \neg\exists\, x : E \bullet \langle x\rangle \frown s_2\ \text{suffix}\ s_1 \frown \langle e\rangle$

This is basically the transition function of a deterministic finite automaton, where states are represented as sequences of events; s_1 is the current state, s the final state, e the current input and E the alphabet of the automaton.

Checking Assertion $\mathbf{A}_\exists$. In order to perform this check for some specific sequence of events s, a process S_{match} is constructed from s, which always accepts all

---

[6] Although $runs(P)$ contains all possible (infinite) extensions of divergent traces, this is not relevant for $\mathbf{A}_\forall$, since for any infinite trace included in $runs(P)$ due to divergence, the finite prefix leading to divergence is already included. If s is contained in such a prefix, then all extensions contain it, too, and if it is not contained, then this prefix alone suffices as a counterexample, regardless of the extensions.

events in E until it has performed s; in that case it performs an event $match \notin E$ and stops (deadlocks). Define $S_{match} = S_{\langle\rangle}$ with

$$S_s = match \to STOP$$
$$S_{s_1} = \square_{e:E}\, e \to S_{\delta(E,s,s_1,e)}$$

for all true prefixes $s_1 \subset s$. The *traces* model $(\mathcal{T})$ is sufficient for this test, where S_{match} looks like this:

$$traces(S_{match}) = \{t, t_1 : \text{seq } E \mid \neg(s \text{ infix } t) \wedge (t_1 \subseteq t \frown s \frown \langle match\rangle) \bullet t_1\}$$

Example. As an example, S_{match} is now constructed for the sequence diagram of Fig. 5. Using the abbreviations $A \equiv amount.u.a1?\_$, $D \equiv debit.a1.b?\_?\_$, $M \equiv money.a1.u?\_$ and $R \equiv result.b.a1.false$, as well as $E = \{| amount, debit, result, money |\}$, the language defined by that diagram is the set $\{\langle A, D, R, M\rangle\}$ and we therefore only need to check for the single word in that set, i.e., we can use the construction described above, yielding:

$$S_{match} = S_{\langle\rangle}, \qquad S_{\langle\rangle} = A \to S_{\langle A\rangle}\ \square\ \square_{e:E\setminus\{A\}}\, e \to S_{\langle\rangle}$$
$$S_{\langle A\rangle} = D \to S_{\langle A,D\rangle}\ \square\ \square_{e:E\setminus\{D\}}\, e \to S_{\langle\rangle}$$
$$S_{\langle A,D\rangle} = R \to S_{\langle A,D,R\rangle}\ \square\ \square_{e:E\setminus\{R\}}\, e \to S_{\langle\rangle}$$
$$S_{\langle A,D,R\rangle} = M \to S_{\langle A,D,R,M\rangle}\ \square\ \square_{e:E\setminus\{M\}}\, e \to S_{\langle\rangle}$$
$$S_{\langle A,D,R,M\rangle} = match \to STOP$$

Next we put P and S_{match} in parallel, synchronising on the whole alphabet E of P and hide all of E, since we are only interested in the occurrence of $match$. Then we use FDR for a refinement check in the traces model in order to check for said occurrence:

$$(P \parallel_E S_{match}) \setminus E \sqsubseteq_{\mathcal{T}} match \to STOP \qquad\qquad (*)$$

This is correct since the following correspondence holds

$$(P \parallel_E S_{match}) \setminus E \sqsubseteq_{\mathcal{T}} match \to STOP \qquad \Leftrightarrow \qquad \mathbf{A}_\exists$$

because $(P \parallel_E S_{match}) \setminus E$ cannot, due to hiding E, perform any event but $match$ and $match$ can be performed at most once due to the construction of S_{match}; furthermore, the refinement relation holds, if and only if $(P \parallel_E S_{match}) \setminus E$ can perform $match$ at least once, which again means that P must have a trace which contains s.

Thus, for checking validity of sequence diagrams with negative conditions we use FDR to check $(*)$, if this fails the sequence diagram is valid in the UML model; for sequence diagrams with existential conditions we use $(*)$ as well and validity holds if the test is successful.

Checking Assertion $\mathbf{A}_\forall$. This task is a little more complicated, because of the universal quantification. We cannot use the simple traces model here, but need to take deadlock and divergence into account: if s is to occur on all runs of P, then P must neither be able to deadlock nor to diverge until it has performed s. Furthermore, each (non diverging) infinite run of P has to contain s. Therefore we split this task into two checks. For the first one a process S_{div} is constructed from s, which differs from S_{match} only in the definition

$$S_s = \mathbf{div}$$

that is, it diverges immediately after performing s instead of performing an additional event and stopping. The test using this process is carried out in the *stable failures* model ($\mathcal{F}$), where S_{div} is described as

$$traces(S_{div}) = \{t, t_1 : \text{seq } E \mid \neg(s \text{ infix } t) \wedge (t_1 \subseteq t ^\frown s \bullet t_1\}$$
$$failures(S_{div}) = \{t : traces(S_{div}) \bullet (t, \varnothing)\}$$

Proposition 1. $P \parallel_E S_{div}$ *deadlock free* ($\mathcal{F}$) $\Leftrightarrow P$ *cannot deadlock (in a stable state) until it has performed* s.

Proof. Suppose $P \parallel_E S_{div}$ is deadlock free in $\mathcal{F}$. S_{div} is constructed as not to constrain the behaviour of P unless it has performed s, in which case it diverges and thus prevents P from performing any further events without introducing deadlock. Since S_{div} cannot cause deadlock, it follows that P cannot deadlock in a stable state on all behaviours allowed by S_{div}, i.e, until it has performed s. If on the other hand, P cannot deadlock in a stable state until it has performed s, it follows that $P \parallel_E S_{div}$ is deadlock free in $\mathcal{F}$, since S_{div} does not refuse any event until it has performed s, and then stops P by diverging, which (in $\mathcal{F}$) does not introduce deadlock.   □

The second test requires an auxiliary process S_{not}, which always accepts any event in E, except when it has already performed all but the last event of s, in which case S_{not} refuses exactly that event, but no other. Let $s_0 ^\frown \langle f \rangle = s$, then

$$S_{s_0} = \underset{e:E\backslash\{f\}}{\square} e \rightarrow S_{\delta(E,s,s_0,e)}$$
$$S_{s_1} = \underset{e:E}{\square} e \rightarrow S_{\delta(E,s,s_1,e)}$$

for any prefix $s_1 \subset s$ with $\#s_1 \leqslant \#s - 2$. Finally, $S_{not} = S_{\langle \rangle}$. This test is carried out using the *failures-divergences* model ($\mathcal{N}$). In this model S_{not} looks like this:

$$failures_\perp(S_{not}) = \{t, s_1, s_2 : \text{seq } E; \ e : E; \ R : \mathbb{P}\{e\} \mid$$
$$\neg(s \text{ infix } t) \wedge s = s_1 ^\frown s_2 ^\frown \langle e \rangle \bullet$$
$$(t ^\frown s_1, \text{if } s_2 = \langle \rangle \text{ then } R \text{ else } \varnothing)\}$$
$$divergences(S_{not}) = \varnothing.$$

Proposition 2. $(P \parallel_E S_{not}) \setminus E$ *divergence free* $\Leftrightarrow P$ *cannot diverge until it has performed* s *and* P *has no infinite trace (non-diverging), which does not contain* s.

Proof. Suppose $(P \parallel_E S_{not}) \setminus E$ is divergence free. Since S_{not} does not constrain the behaviour of P unless P wants to perform the last event of s, it follows that P cannot diverge unless it has performed s. Furthermore, since the hiding of E

turns any infinite behaviour of $(P \parallel_E S_{not}) \setminus E$ into divergence, it follows that $(P \parallel_E S_{not})$ does not have infinite traces, i.e., any infinite trace of P contains s. On the other hand, if P cannot diverge until it has performed s and does not have an infinite trace which does not contain s, then $(P \parallel_E S_{not})$ is divergence free and has not infinite traces. Thus $(P \parallel_E S_{not}) \setminus E$ divergence free.   □

Summarising, we have

$$P \parallel_E S_{div} \text{ deadlock free } (\mathcal{F}) \; \wedge \; (P \parallel_E S_{not}) \setminus E \text{ divergence free}$$

if and only if

- P cannot deadlock until it has performed s and
- P cannot diverge until it has performed s and
- P has no infinite trace (non-diverging) which does not contain s,

i.e., any finite or (non-diverging) infinite run of P contains s. For the assertion $\mathbf{A_\forall}$ we thus get the following result

$$P \parallel_E S_{div} \text{ deadlock free } (\mathcal{F}) \; \wedge \; (P \parallel_E S_{not}) \setminus E \text{ divergence free} \quad \Leftrightarrow \quad \mathbf{A_\forall}$$

Validity of sequence diagrams with universal condition can hence be checked using the above two tests.

4.2   Occurrence of a Set of Words

Besides single words the language of a sequence diagram can also contain more than one word. This is the case if the sequence diagram specifies certain interactions to be concurrent. The corresponding CSP process will then contain all possible interleavings in its set of runs. Given not just a single word but a (finite) set $L = \mathcal{L}(sq)$ of words from a sequence diagram sq, there are several possible definitions for 'occurrence' both in the existential as well as in the universal case: does 'possible' mean *in some run r some $s \in L$ occurs* $(\exists\, r\, \exists\, s)$, *each $s \in L$ occurs in some run r* $(\forall\, s\, \exists\, r)$ or *in some run r all $s \in L$ occur* $(\exists\, r\, \forall\, s)$? Does 'required' mean *on all runs r some $s \in L$ occurs* $(\forall\, r\, \exists\, s)$, *some $s \in L$ occurs on all runs r* $(\exists\, s\, \forall\, r)$ or *on all runs r all $s \in S$ occur* $(\forall\, r\, \forall\, s)$?

The third version for each case $(\exists\, r\, \forall\, s,\ \forall\, r\, \forall\, s)$ is clearly too strong as a general interpretation, but all other versions can be justified. In our case, though, since L is derived from a sequence diagram, the actual interleaving of events for which no ordering is implied by the lifelines is irrelevant. Therefore, the weakest versions $(\exists\, r\, \exists\, s,\ \forall\, r\, \exists\, s)$ are sufficient here.

The simplest, yet slightly inefficient way to perform the necessary tests for a set L, is to construct the respective processes for all the $s \in L$ and to use them all at once, i.e., to put them in parallel, synchronising on E.

5   Conclusion

In this paper we proposed a method for checking the validity of (simple) sequence diagrams in UML models written in a specific UML profile for reactive systems.

To this end, we supplied both UML model and sequence diagrams with a CSP semantics and developed procedures for employing the CSP model checker FDR for validity checking. The technique can easily be extended to UML 2.0 sequence diagrams by developing a CSP semantics for them or using the semantics of [23] which defines it as a set of (timed) traces over actions. Our approach of developing testers for validity checking can then stay as it is.

Related work. The question of consistency in models with multiple views (of which our issue is one special aspect) is widely studied. A general approach for defining consistency is studied in [3]. In the context of UML an annual workshop with the topic of consistency is carried out [6]. The use of CSP as a common semantic domain for multiple views in the study of consistency is chosen in [2, 8, 18]. While the first two do not consider sequence diagrams the work of Bolton and Davies addresses sequences diagrams and develops tests for checking whether a scenario is possible in a UML model. They do, however, only treat the case that the scenario starts in the *initial* state; their tests do not cover scenarios happening sometime later after initialisation. As a consequence, checking validity simply amounts to checking for trace refinement and thus FDR thus be directly employed. Syntactic checks of consistency between class and sequence diagrams are proposed in [24]. Using labelled transition systems, [5] defines behavioural consistency for combinations of UML behavioural diagrams (including statecharts and sequence diagrams) as deadlock freedom. They use the SPIN model checker for analysis, but do not give a formal translation from UML to SPIN's input language. An automatic translation for systems described by a set of UML statecharts and enhanced by sequence diagrams to state behaviour of interest to generalised stochastic petri nets is proposed in [1].

The work closest to ours is that carried out in the context of life sequence charts (LSCs) [7]. LSCs are an extension of sequence diagrams with special features for modelling liveness requirements. The work [4] proposes validity checking for LSCs by translating them to the temporal logic LTL and checking them against Statemate models. Based on LSCs, the *play in play out* approach [12] uses a collection of 'played in' examples to specify a whole system, instead of using them only as requirements for an explicit model.

References

1. Simona Bernardi, Susanna Donatelli, and José Merseguer. From UML sequence diagrams and statecharts to analysable petri net models. In *WSOP'02*, pages 35–45. ACM Press, 2002.
2. C. Bolton and J. Davies. Using relational and behavioural semantics in the verification of object models. In *FMOODS'00*, pages 163–182. Kluwer, 2000.
3. H. Bowman, M.W.A. Steen, E.A. Boiten, and J. Derrick. A formal framework for viewpoint consistency. *Formal Methods in System Design*, 21:111–166, 2002.
4. M. Brill, R. Buschermöhle, W. Damm, J. Klose, B. Westphal, and H. Wittke. Formal verification of LSCs in the development process. In *Integration of Software Specification Techniques for Applications in Engineering*. Springer, 2004.

5. Y. Choi and C. Bunse. Behavioral consistency checking for component-based software development using the KobrA approach. In *Consistency Problems in UML-based Software Development III*, Lisbon, Portugal, October 2004. revised papers.
6. Consistency problems in UML-based software development III – understanding and usage of dependency relationships, Lisbon, Portugal, October 2004.
7. W. Damm and D. Harel. LSCs: Breathing life into Message Sequence Charts. In P. Ciancarini and R. Gorrieri, editors, *FMOODS'99*. Kluwer, 1999.
8. G. Engels, R. Heckel, and J. Küster. Rule-based Specification of Behavioral Consistency based on the UML Meta-Model. In Martin Gogolla, editor, *UML 2001*. Springer, 2001.
9. C. Fischer. CSP-OZ: A combination of Object-Z and CSP. In H. Bowman and J. Derrick, editors, *FMOODS'97*, volume 2, pages 423–438. Chapman & Hall, 1997.
10. Formal Systems (Europe) Ltd. *Failures-Divergence Refinement – FDR2 User Manual*, 4th edition, August 1998.
11. T. Gehrke, M. Huhn, A. Rensink, and H. Wehrheim. An algebraic semantics for message sequence chart documents. In S. Budkowski, A. Cavalle, and E. Najm, editors, *FORTE/PSTV'98*, pages 3–18. Kluwer, 1998.
12. D. Harel and R. Marelly. Specifying and Executing Behavioral Requirements: The Play In/Play-Out Approach. *Software and System Modeling*, 2:82–107, 2003.
13. C. A. R. Hoare. *Communicating Sequential Processes*. Prentice-Hall International Series in Computer Science. Prentice-Hall International, 1985.
14. International Organisation for Standardization. *Information technology – Z formal specification notation – Syntax, type system and semantics*, 1st edition, July 2002. ISO/IEC 13568:2002 (E) International Standard.
15. P.B. Ladkin and S. Leue. Interpreting message flow graphs. *Formal Aspects of Computing*, 7(5):473–509, 1995.
16. S. Mauw and M.A. Reniers. An Algebraic Semantics of Basic Message Sequence Charts. *The Computer Journal*, 37(4):269–277, 1994.
17. M. Möller, E.-R. Olderog, H. Rasch, and H. Wehrheim. Linking CSP-OZ with UML and Java: A case study. In *IFM'04*, pages 267–286. Springer, 2004.
18. H. Rasch and H. Wehrheim. Checking Consistency in UML Diagrams: Classes and State Machines. In *FMOODS'03*, pages 229–243. Springer, 2003.
19. A. W. Roscoe. *The Theory and Practice of Concurrency*. Prentice Hall Series in Computer Science. Prentice Hall Europe, 1998.
20. B. Selic, G. Gullekson, and P. T. Ward. *Real-Time Object-Oriented Modeling*. John Wiley & Sons, 1994.
21. G. Smith. *The Object-Z Specification Language*. Advances in Formal Methods. Kluwer, 2000.
22. J. M. Spivey. *The Z Notation: A Reference Manual*. Oriel College, Oxford, 2nd edition, 1998.
23. H. Störrle. Semantics of Interactions in UML 2.0. In *Intl. Workshop on Visual Languages and Formal Methods*, 2003. at HCC'03, Auckland, NZ.
24. A. Tsiolakis and H. Ehrig. Consistency Analysis of UML Class and Sequence Diagrams using Attributed Graph Grammars. In H. Ehrig and G. Taentzer, editors, *GRATRA 2000*, pages 77–86, March 2000. TU Berlin, FB Informatik, TR No. 2000-2.
25. OMG Unified Modeling Language specification, version 1.5, March 2003. http://www.omg.org.

An Extended Type System for OCL
Supporting Templates and Transformations*

Marcel Kyas

Christian-Albrechts-Universität zu Kiel, Germany
mky@informatik.uni-kiel.de

Abstract. Based on our experience in implementing a type-checker for
the Object Constraint Language (OCL), we observed that OCL is not
suitable for constraining a system under development, because changes
in the underlying class diagram unnecessarily invalidate the type correctness of constraints, while their semantic value does not change. Furthermore, the type system of OCL does not support templates.
To alleviate these problems, we extended the type system of OCL with intersection and union types and bounded operator abstraction. The main
advantage of our type system is that it allows more changes in the contextual class diagrams without adapting the OCL constraints.

1 Introduction

The Object Constraint Language (OCL) is a formal specification language that
enables a developer to specify class invariants and pre- and postconditions for
operations in UML models. It is designed to be a query language, like SQL, and
specification language, like Z. Its latest version, OCL 2.0, is described in [1],
to which we refer as *OCL 2.0 proposal*. It aims at a tight integration with the
diagrammatic notations of UML 2.0, which are documented in [2] and [3].

In order to be used widely, OCL has to support the following:

1. A precise syntax which allows writing specifications in a concise and readable way, but which is also machine readable, and therefore also machine
   checkable.
2. A precise semantics which allows evaluation or verification of the model.
3. A type system which is compatible with the well-formedness constraints of
   UML 2.0 class diagrams.
4. A type system which is robust with respect to model transformations like
   refactoring or other changes in class diagrams.

Influenced by our experience in implementing a standard-conforming type-
checker for OCL, we have come to the conclusion that OCL does not adequately
implement these requirements so far:

The first item is not satisfied, because in the UML 2.0 and OCL 2.0 standards
OCL constraints in different syntactical styles are used (compare the constraints
in [2] to the ones in [1]).

---

* Part of this work has been financially supported by IST project Omega (IST-2001-
33522) and NWO/DFG project Mobi-J (RO 1122/9-1, RO 1122/9-2)

M. Steffen and G. Zavattaro (Eds.): FMOODS 2005, LNCS 3535, pp. 83–98, 2005.

The second item is not satisfied, because even though the semantics of OCL is precise enough for evaluating constraints [4, 5], it is not convenient for verification purposes, because the semantics of OCL is operational, and not declarative, as argued in [6], which leads, a.o., to the three-valuedness of the logic.

Items three and four represent the main problem of using OCL for writing constraints on models during different stages of design: the type system of OCL appears to be designed for languages which only use single inheritance and no templates (parameterized classes)[1]. UML 2.0 introduces a new model for templates, which allows classifiers to be parameterized with classifier specifications, value specifications, and operation specifications. The OCL 2.0 proposal does not specify how those parameters can be used in constraints, how they can be constrained, or how these parameters are to be used in constraints and what their meaning is supposed to be. Furthermore, OCL constraints are fragile under the operations of refactoring of class diagrams, package inclusion and package merging. These operations, which often do not affect the semantic value of a constraint, can render constraints ill-typed. This essentially limits the use of OCL to a-posteriori specification of class diagrams.

To solve these problems, we have implemented a more expressive type system based on intersection types, union types, and bounded operator abstraction. Such type systems are already well-understood [7] and solve the problems we encountered elegantly. Our type system supports templates and is more robust under refactoring and package merging than the current type system.

The adaption of the type system to OCL was straight forward. The specification of the OCL standard library had to be changed to make use of the new type system. We have implemented this type system in a prototype tool and all constraints of the OCL 2.0 standard library have been shown to be well-typed with respect to our type system.

This paper is organized as follows: In Sect. 2, we survey the current type system for OCL. In Sect. 3, we describe our different extensions to the type system. In Sect. 4, we summarize the most important results. In Sect. 5 we compare our results with other results and draw some conclusions.

2   State of the Art

In this section, we recall the current type system used for OCL, which has been derived from the OCL 2.0 standard. It is similar to the one presented in [8].

We start with a description of abstract OCL, a simple core language, into which almost all OCL expression can be translated. The grammar is defined by

$$t ::= true \mid false \mid \cdots \mid -1 \mid 0 \mid 1 \mid \cdots \mid self \mid v \mid t.a \mid t.m(t_1, \ldots, t_n)$$
$$\mid \; t \rightarrow m(t_1, \ldots, t_n) \mid t \rightarrow iterate(v_0 : T_0, \ldots, v_n : T_n; a = t \mid t_0)$$
$$\mid \; t \rightarrow flatten(t) \mid \textbf{if } t \textbf{ then } t' \textbf{ else } t'' \textbf{ endif}$$
$$\mid \; let \; v_0(v_{0,0}, \ldots, v_{0,m_0}) : T = t_0, \ldots, v_n(v_{n,0}, \ldots, v_{n,m_n}) : T = t_n \; in \; t$$

---

[1] For example Java before version 5.0.

We do not use @*pre* and qualifiers in our language, because these constructs do not add anything to the type system. We define the operation *flatten*, which flattens collections, as a primitive to OCL, like *iterate*. The reasons for this are discussed in Sect. 3.5.

We now define the abstract syntax of OCL types. We have essentially two kinds of types: elementary types and collection types. The elementary types are classifiers from the model and the elementary data types like *Boolean, Integer,* and so on. The collection types are types which are generic, i.e., they construct a type by applying the collection type to any other type[2]. This distinction is formalized with a kinding system (a type system for types). Kinds are defined by the language $K ::= \star \mid K \to K'$. The kind $\star$ denotes any type which does not take an argument. Type constructors have a kind $K \to K'$, which means that such a constructor maps each type of kind K to a type of kind K'. For example, the elementary data type *Integer* is of the kind $\star$. The collection type *Set* is of the kind $\star \to \star$ and the type *Set(Integer)* is of the kind $\star$. The language of types is defined as follows:

$$T ::= type \mid T(T_1) \mid T_0 \times \cdots \times T_n \to T$$

Here, a *type* is any classifier or template appearing in the contextual class diagram or the OCL standard library. The expression $T(T_1)$ expresses the type which results from instantiating a template parameter of the type T with T_1. The type $T_0 \times \cdots \times T_n \to T$ is used to express the type of properties. The type T_0 is the type of the classifier which defines the property, the types $T_1, \ldots, T_n$ are the types of the parameters of the property. We identify attributes with operations that do not define arguments.

Observe that our language of types does not contain constructs for operator abstraction or universal types. The reason for this is, that you cannot define *new* types in OCL. Instead all types are defined in class diagrams and are used like constants in the type system.

The kinding of a type states whether a type is an elementary type or a template and is formally defined by the system shown in Fig. 1. We write the rules in the usual style: a rule consists of an antecedent and a consequence, which are separated by a line. The antecedent contains the properties that need to be proved in order to apply the rule and conclude its consequence. Each rule has a name, which is stated right of the line in small capitals.

It is an important property of the type system for OCL that new types cannot be defined through OCL expressions (except for tuples, which are out

$T : \star$ For any type or property type T K-ELEM

$T : \star \to \star$ For any parameterized class T K-CONS $\dfrac{T : K \qquad S : K \to K'}{S(T) : K'}$ K-INST

Fig. 1. Kinding System

---

[2] In Sect. 4 we discuss the presence of *dependent types* in class diagrams.

of the scope of this paper). This simplifies the type checking rules a lot. OCL expressions are checked in a context, which contains the information on variable bindings, operation declarations, and the subtype relation encoded in a class diagram. A context Γ maps variable names v to their type, or to undefined if that variable is not declared in this context. We write $\Gamma, v : T$ to denote the context extended by binding the variable v to T, provided that v does not occur in Γ. We write $\Gamma(v) = T$ to state that v has type T in context Γ. The context also contains the information on *type conformance*, i.e. clauses of the form $T \leq S$ derived from the generalization hierarchy, where T and S are types and $\leq$ denotes that T is a subtype of S. We write $\Gamma, T \leq S$ to extend a context with a statement that T is a subtype of S. Any context contains $T \leq T$ for every type T occurring in the model, since the conformance relation is reflexive. If the context Γ contains the declaration $T \leq S$ we denote this with $\Gamma \vdash T \leq S$. We write $\Gamma \vdash t : T$ to denote that t is a term of type T in the context Γ. Contexts which only differ in a different order of their declarations are considered equal. If the context is clear, we omit it in the example derivations. Finally, we assume that the context contains all declarations mandated by the OCL standard library. The subtype relation is transitive and function application is covariant in its arguments and contravariant in its result type. These rules are shown in Fig. 2. In rule S-COLL the notation $\Gamma \vdash C \leq Collection$ means that C ranges over every type which is a subtype of *Collection*. OCL defines *Bag*, *Set*, and *Sequence* as subtypes of *Collection*. Note that *Collection* is a parameterized type, but the rule S-COLL-2 is not sound for classes which define operations which change the contents of the collection [9]. In OCL operations defined on collections do not alter the content, but we cannot assume this in general, therefore we defined these particular assumptions. The typing rules for terms are presented in Fig. 3, except for the typing rule for *flatten*. The type of flatten is actually a dependent type, because it depends on the type of its argument. We present the rule in Sect. 3.5.

Rules T-TRUE, T-FALSE, and T-LIT assign to each literal their type. Especially, T-LIT is an axiom scheme assigning, e.g. the literal 1 the type *Integer* and the literal 1.5 the type *Real*. Rule T-COLL defines the type of a collection literal. The type of a collection is determined by the declared name C and the common supertype of all its members. Rule T-CALL states that if the arguments match the types of a method or a function, then the expression is well-typed and the result has the declared type. The antecedent $\Gamma \vdash C \nleq Collection$ denotes that

$$\frac{\Gamma \vdash C \leq Collection}{\Gamma \vdash C(T) \leq Collection(T)} \text{ S-COLL} \qquad \frac{\Gamma \vdash C \leq Collection \quad \Gamma \vdash T \leq T'}{\Gamma \vdash C(T) \leq C(T')} \text{ S-COLL-2}$$

$$\frac{\Gamma \vdash e : S \quad \Gamma \vdash S \leq T}{\Gamma \vdash e : T} \text{ S-SUB} \qquad \frac{\Gamma \vdash S \leq T \quad \Gamma \vdash T \leq U}{\Gamma \vdash S \leq U} \text{ S-TRANS}$$

$$\frac{\Gamma \vdash T_0 \leq S_0, \Gamma \vdash S_1 \leq T_1, \cdots, \Gamma \vdash S_n \leq T_n \quad \Gamma \vdash T \leq S}{\Gamma \vdash T_0 \times T_1 \times \cdots \times T_n \to T \leq S_0 \times S_1 \times \cdots \times S_n \to S} \text{ S-ARROW}$$

Fig. 2. Definition of Type Conformance

$$\Gamma \vdash true : Boolean \quad \text{T-TRUE} \qquad \Gamma \vdash false : Boolean \quad \text{T-FALSE}$$

$$\Gamma \vdash l : T_l \quad \text{T-LIT} \qquad \frac{\Gamma(v) = T}{\Gamma \vdash v : T} \text{T-VAR}$$

$$\frac{\Gamma \vdash e_1 : T \quad \cdots \quad \Gamma \vdash e_n : T}{C\{e_1, \ldots, e_n\} : C(T)} \text{ if } C \in \{Bag, Set, OrderedSet, Sequence\} \ \text{T-COLL}$$

$$\frac{\Gamma \vdash t_0 : S \quad \Gamma \vdash t_1 : S_1, \cdots, \Gamma \vdash t_n : S_n \quad \Gamma \vdash n : S \times S_1 \times \cdots \times S_n \to T \quad \Gamma \vdash S \not\leq Collection}{\Gamma \vdash t_0.n(t_1, \ldots, t_n) : T} \text{T-CALL}$$

$$\frac{\Gamma \vdash t_0 : C(S) \quad \Gamma \vdash t_1 : S_1, \cdots, \Gamma \vdash t_n : S_n \quad \Gamma \vdash n : C(S) \times S_1 \times \cdots \times S_n \to T \quad \Gamma \vdash C \leq Collection}{\Gamma \vdash t_0 \to n(t_1, \ldots, t_n) : T} \text{T-CCALL}$$

$$\frac{\Gamma \vdash e_0 : Boolean \quad \Gamma \vdash e_1 : T \quad \Gamma \vdash e_2 : T}{if \ e_0 \ then \ e_1 \ else \ e_2 \ endif : T} \text{T-COND}$$

$$\frac{\Gamma \vdash t_0 : C(T) \quad \Gamma \vdash t : S \quad \Gamma, v : T, a : S \vdash e : S \quad \Gamma \vdash C \leq Collection}{\Gamma \vdash t_0 \to iterate(v; a = t \mid e) : S} \text{T-ITERATE}$$

$$\frac{\Gamma \vdash t_0 : T_0 \quad \Gamma, v_0 : T_0 \vdash t : T}{\Gamma \vdash let \ v_0 : T_0 = t_0 \ in \ t \ : T} \text{T-LET}$$

$$\Gamma' = \Gamma, v_0 : T_{0,1} \times \cdots \times T_{0,m_0} \to T_1, \ldots, v_n : T_{n,1} \times \cdots \times T_{n,m_n} \to T_n$$
$$\Gamma', v_{0,0} : T_{0,0}, \ldots, v_{0,m_0} : T_{0,m_0} \vdash t_0 : T_0$$
$$\vdots$$
$$\Gamma', v_{n,0} : T_{n,0}, \ldots, v_{n,m_n} : T_{n,m_n} \vdash t_n : T_n$$
$$\frac{\Gamma' \vdash t : T}{\Gamma \vdash let \ v_0(v_{0,0}, \ldots, v_{0,m_0}) : T_0 = t_0, \ldots, v_n(v_{n,0}, \ldots, v_{n,m_n}) : T = t_n \ in \ t \ : T} \text{T-LET}'$$

Fig. 3. Typing rules for OCL

in context Γ type C is not a subtype of *Collection*. A similar rule for collection calls is given by T-CCALL. Recall that the antecedent $\Gamma \vdash C \leq Collection$ states that the type of t_0 has to be a collection type. Rule T-COND defines the typing of a condition. If the condition e_0 has the type *Boolean* and the argument expressions e_1 and e_2 have a common supertype T, then the conditional expression has that type T. Rule T-ITERATE gives the typing rule for an iterate expression. First, the expression we are iterating over has to be a collection. Then the accumulator has to be initialized with an expression of the same type. Finally, the expression we are iterating over has to be an expression of the accumulator variables type in the context which is extended by the iterator variable and the accumulator variable. Rule T-LET defines the rule for a let expression of the OCL 2.0 standard. Rule T-LET' allows a let-expression where the user can define functions and use mutual recursion. There we add all variables declared by the let expression to context Γ in order to obtain context Γ'. Each expression defined has to be well typed in the context extended by the formal parameters of the definition. Finally, the expression in which we use the definitions has to be well-typed in the context Γ'.

This type system is a faithful representation of the type system given in [1], but we have omitted the typing rules for the boolean connectives, as they are given by Cengarle and Knapp in [5], because each expression using a boolean connective can be rewritten to an operation call expression, e.g., *a and b* is equivalent to *a.and(b)*. We do not have a rule for the undefined value, as presented in [5], because the OCL 2.0 proposal does not define a literal for undefined [1, pp. 48–50][3].

Within the UML 2.0 standard [3] and the OCL 2.0 standard [1] methods are redefined covariantly. We assume that some kind of multi-method semantics for calls of these methods is intended. These redefinitions are not explicitly treated in the OCL 2.0 type system, they can, however, be treated as overloading a method, and hence, be modeled with union-types in our system (see Sec. 3.2), as suggested in, e.g., [7, p. 340].

Also note that our type system makes use of the largest common supertype only implicitly, whereas it is explicitly used in other papers. It is hidden in the type conformance rules of Fig. 2. An example of where we use the largest common supertype can be found in Sect. 3.1. The rules presented here are not designed for a type-checking algorithms, but for deriving well-typedness. Therefore, the type system presented here lacks the unique typing property, but it is adequate with respect to the operational semantics defined in [1] and decidable.

Proposition 1. *The type system is* adequate, *i.e. for any OCL expression e if e : T can be derived in the type system, then e is evaluated to a result of a type conforming to T.*

The type system is decidable, *i.e. there exists an algorithm which either derives a type T for any OCL expression e or reports that no type can be derived for e.*

We use the definitions of this section for the discussion of its limitations in the following sections.

3   Extensions

In this section, we propose various extensions to the type system of OCL which help to use OCL earlier in the development of a system and to write more expressive constraints. We introduce intersection types, union types, operator abstraction, and bounded operator abstraction to the type system of OCL. Intersection types, which express that an object is an instance of all components of the intersection type, are more robust w.r.t. transformations of the contextual class diagram. Union types, which express that an object is an instance of at least one component of the union type, admit more constraints that have a

---

[3] Note that *OclUndefined* is the semantic value of any undefined expression and the "only instance of OclVoid", and there not part of the concrete syntax [1, p. 133]. Calling the property *oclIsUndefined()*, defined for any object, is preferred, because any other property call results in OclUndefined.

meaning in OCL to be well-typed. Parametric polymorphism extends OCL to admit constraints on template without requiring that the template parameter is bound. Bounded parametric polymorphism allows one to specify assumptions on a template parameter. Together, our extensions result in a more flexible type system which admits more OCL constraints to be well typed without sacrificing adequacy or decidability.

3.1 Intersection Types

Consider the following constraint of class *Obs* in Fig. 4:

$$\text{context } Obs \; inv : a \rightarrow union(b).m1() \rightarrow forAll(x \mid x > 1)$$

This is a simple constraint which asserts that the value returned by $m1$ for each element in the collection of a and b is always greater than 1. We show that it is well-typed in OCL using the type system of Sect. 2.

$$\frac{\dfrac{a : Bag(D) \quad b : Bag(C)}{a \rightarrow union(b) : Bag(A)}}{\dfrac{a \rightarrow union(b).m1() : Bag(Integer)}{a \rightarrow union(b).m1() \rightarrow forAll(x \mid x > 1) : Boolean}}$$

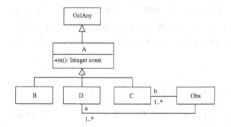
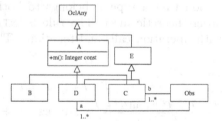

Fig. 4. A simple initial class diagram   **Fig. 5.** The same diagram after a change

Now consider the following question: What happens to the constraint if we change the class diagram to the one in Fig. 5, which introduces a new class E that implements the common functions of classes C and D? The meaning of the constraint is not affected by this change. However, the OCL constraint is not well-typed anymore, as this derivation shows, where the type annotation error is used to state that the type system is not able to derive a type for the expression[4].

$$\frac{\dfrac{a : Bag(D) \quad b : Bag(C)}{a \rightarrow union(b) : Bag(OclAny)}}{a \rightarrow union(b).m1() : \text{error}}$$

---

[4] Recall, that we do not explicitly write the context in examples if it is clear.

The problem is, that the OCL type system chooses the unique and most precise supertype of a and b to type the elements of $a \to union(b)$, which now is $OclAny$, because we now have to choose one of A, E, and $OclAny$, which are the supertypes of C and D. Neither A nor E are feasible, because the type of the expression has to be chosen now. Hence, we are forced to choose $OclAny$. To avoid this problem constraints should be written once the contextual class diagram does not change anymore. Otherwise all constraints have to be updated, which if it is done by hand is a time consuming and error prone task.

The mentioned insufficiency of the type system can be solved in two ways: We can implement a transformation which updates all constraints automatically after such a change, or we introduce a more permissive type system for OCL. Because an automatic update of all constraints entails an analysis of all constraints in *the same way* as performed by the more permissive type system, therefore we extended the type system and leave the constraints unchanged.

The proposed extension is the introduction of intersection types. An intersection type, written $T \wedge T'$ for types T and T' states that an object is of type T and T'. Because $\wedge$ is both an associative and commutative operator, we introduce the generalized intersection $\bigwedge_{T \in \mathcal{T}} T$. In this paper $\mathcal{T}$ is always a *finite* set of types. The empty intersection type $\bigwedge \emptyset$ is the top type, which does not have any instances (and therefore is equivalent to $OclVoid$). Intersection types are useful to explain multiple inheritance [10–12].

We add the rules of Fig. 6 to the type system, which introduces intersection types into the type hierarchy. The rule S-INTERLB and S-INTER formalize the notion that a type T belongs to both types, and that $\wedge$ corresponds to the order-theoretic meet. The rule S-INTERA allows for a convenient interaction with operation calls and functions. This extension of the type system already

$$\Gamma \vdash \bigwedge_{T' \in \mathcal{T}} T' \leq T \text{ for any } T \in \mathcal{T} \quad \text{S-INTERLB}$$

$$\frac{\Gamma \vdash T \leq T' \text{ for all } T' \in \mathcal{T}}{\Gamma \vdash T \leq \bigwedge_{T' \in \mathcal{T}} T'} \quad \text{S-INTER} \qquad \Gamma \vdash \bigwedge_{T' \in \mathcal{T}} (T \to T') \leq T \to \bigwedge_{T' \in \mathcal{T}} T' \quad \text{S-INTERA}$$

Fig. 6. Intersection Types

solves the problem raised for the OCL constraint in the context of Fig. 5, as the derivation in Fig. 7 demonstrates.

The extension of the OCL type system with intersection types is sufficient to deal with transformations which change the class hierarchy by moving common code of a class into a new super-class. This extension is also safe, and does not change the decidability of the type system.

3.2   Union Types

Union types are dual to intersection types. They are not as useful as intersection types, because they do not address a fundamental language concept like multiple

$$\frac{\dfrac{a : Bag(D) \quad D \leq A \quad D \leq E}{a : Bag(A \wedge E)} \qquad \dfrac{b : Bag(C) \quad C \leq A \quad C \leq E}{b : Bag(A \wedge E)}}{\dfrac{\dfrac{\dfrac{a \rightarrow union(b) : Bag(A \wedge E)}{a \rightarrow union(b) : Bag(A)}}{a \rightarrow union(b).m1() : Bag(Integer)}}{a \rightarrow union(b).m1() \rightarrow forAll(x \mid x > 1) : Boolean}}$$

Fig. 7. Type checking with intersection types

Fig. 8. A simple example class diagram

inheritance. They can be used to address overloading of operators, and they do solve type checking problems for collection literals and the union operation of collections in OCL. We explain this by the class diagram in Fig. 8. Consider the expression *context C inv : Set{self.a, self.b}.m(1)* on this class diagram[5]. Assuming that the multiplicities of the associations are 1, we have the derivation

$$\frac{\dfrac{a : A \qquad b : B}{Set\{a, b\} : Set(OclAny)}}{Set\{a, b\}.m(1) : \mathsf{error}}$$

even though both types A and B define the property $m(x : Integer) : Integer$. Here, it is desirable to admit the constraint as well-typed, because it also has a meaning in OCL. Using intersection types does not help here, because stating that a and b have the type $A \wedge B$ is not adequate.

Instead, we want to judge that a and b have the type A *or* B. For this purpose we propose to introduce the union type $A \vee B$. A union type states, that an object is of type A or it is of type B. Again, $\vee$ is associative and commutative, so we introduce the generalized union $\bigvee_{T \in \mathcal{T}} T$. The type $\bigvee \emptyset$ is the universal type, a supertype of *OclAny*, of which any object is an instance. Union types are characterized by the rules in Fig. 9. Rules S-UNIONUB and S-UNION formalize the fact that a union type is the least upper bound of two types. Note that it

$$T \leq \bigvee_{T' \in \mathcal{T}} T' \text{ for any } T \in \mathcal{T}. \quad \text{S-UNIONUB}$$

$$\frac{T' \leq T \text{ for any } T' \in \mathcal{T}}{\bigvee_{T' \in \mathcal{T}} T' \leq T} \quad \text{S-UNION} \quad \bigwedge_{T' \in \mathcal{T}}(T' \rightarrow T) \leq (\bigvee_{T' \in \mathcal{T}} T') \rightarrow T \quad \text{S-UNIONA}$$

Fig. 9. Rules for union types

---

[5] Note that $a : A$ and $b : B$, and both classes define a method $m()$ returning an *Integer*. However, in this case the intended meaning of the constraint is $Set\{self.a.m(1), self.b.m(1)\}$, which is well-defined.

only makes sense to use a property on objects of $A \vee B$ that are defined for A and B. This is stated by the rule S-UNIONA.

Using our extended type system, we can indeed derive that our example has the expected type.

$$\cfrac{\cfrac{a : A \quad b : B}{Set\{a, b\} : Set(A \vee B)} \quad \cfrac{m : A \to Integer \quad m : B \to Integer}{m : A \vee B \to Integer}}{Set\{a, b\} \to collect(m()) : Bag(Integer)}$$

3.3   Parametric Polymorphism

UML 2.0 provides the user with templates[6] (see [3, Sect. 17.5, pp. 541ff.]), which are functions from types or values to types, i.e., they take a type as an argument and return a new type. We first consider the case where the parameter of a class ranges over types. This form of parametric polymorphism is highly useful, as shown, e.g., in [13] and [14]. Adequate support for parametric polymorphism in the specification language is again highly useful, as the proof of a property of a template carries over to all its instantiations [15]. The OCL standard library contains the collection types, which are indeed examples of generic classes.

We have not found yet how the parameter of a template, which is defined in the class diagram, is integrated into OCL's type system. In fact, it is not defined in the proposal how the environment has to be initialized in order to parse expressions according to the rules of Chapter 4 of [1]. For example, consider the following constraint:

(1)
> **context** $Sequence :: excluding(object : T) : Sequence(T)$
> $post : result = self \to iterate(elem; acc : Sequence(T) = Sequence\{\} \mid$
> **if** $elem = object$ **then** acc **else** $acc \to append(object)$ **endif**)

To what does T refer to? Currently, T is not part of the type environment, because it is neither a classifier nor a state but an instance of *TemplateParameter* in the UML metamodel. This constraint is, therefore, not well-typed. But it is worthwhile to admit constraints like (1), because this constraint is valid for any instantiation of the parameter T.

UML 2.0 allows different kinds of template parameters: parameters ranging over classifiers, parameters ranging over value specifications, and parameters ranging over features (properties and operations). In this paper, we only consider parameters ranging over classifiers.

We propose to extend the environment such that Γ contains the kinding judgment $T \in \star$ if T is the parameter of a template. This states that the parameter of a template is a type. Also note that the name of the template classifier alone is not of the kind $\star$ but of some kind $\star \to \cdots \to \star$, depending on the number of type parameters. Additionally, we give the following type checking rules for templates in Fig. 10. These rules generalizes the conforms-to relation previously defined for collection types only. The rule S-INSTSUB states that if a template

---

[6] Also called generics or parameterized classes.

$$\frac{\Gamma \vdash T : K \to K' \quad \Gamma \vdash T' : K \to K' \quad \Gamma \vdash T'' : K \quad \Gamma \vdash T \leq T'}{\Gamma \vdash T(T'') \leq T'(T'')} \text{ S-InstSub}$$

$$\frac{\Gamma \vdash T : K \to K' \quad \Gamma \vdash T' : K \quad \Gamma \vdash T'' : K \quad \Gamma \vdash T' \leq T''}{\Gamma \vdash T(T') \leq T(T'')} \text{ S-InstSub-2}$$

Fig. 10. Subtyping rules for parametric polymorphism

class T is a subtype of another template class T', then T remains a subtype of T' for any class T'' bound to the parameter. This rule is always adequate. The rule T-InstSub-2 states that for any template class T and any types T' and T'' such that T' is a subtype of T'', then binding T' and T'' to the type parameter in T preserves this relation. Note that rule S-InstSub-2 is not always safe. The absence of side-effects in OCL expressions are a fundamental property for the validity of the rule S-Arrow and therefore also for S-InstSub-2. The following counter-example illustrates the importance of the absence of side-effects for the type system. Consider the following fragment of C++ code:

```
class C { public: void m(double *&a) { a[0] = 1.5; } }
void main(void) { int *v = new int[1]; C *c = new C(); c->m(v); }
```

If we allow the S-InstSub-2, then the call c->m(v) is valid, because int is a subtype of double. But within the body of m the assignment a[0] = 1.5 would store a double value into an array of integers, which is not allowed. However, since we assume that each expression is free of side-effects, rule S-InstSub-2 is adequate.

3.4 Bounded Operator Abstraction

While parametric polymorphism in the form of templates is useful in itself, certain properties still cannot be expressed directly as types but have to be expressed in natural language. For example, in the OCL standard the collection property sum() of set has the following specification:

> The addition of all elements in *self*. Elements must be of a type supporting the + operation. The + operation must take one parameter of type T and be both associative: $(a + b) + c = a + (b + c)$, and commutative: $a + b = b + a$. Integer and Real fulfill this condition.

Formally, the post condition of sum does not type check, because a type checker has no means to deduce that T indeed implements the property + as specified. The information can be provided in terms of bounded polymorphism, where the type variable is bounded by a super type. The properties of + can be specified in an abstract class (or interface), say *Sum*, and the following constraints:

(2)
> **context** *Sum*
> *inv* : $self.typeOf().allInstances() \to forAll(a, b, c \mid$
> $a + (b + c) = (a + b) + c)$
> *inv* : $self.typeOf().allInstances() \to forAll(a, b \mid a + b = b + a)$

In Eq. (2) the property *typeOf*() is supposed to return the run-time type of the *self* object. It is important to note that we cannot write *Sum.allInstances*, because the type implementing *Sum* need not provide an implementation of + which work uniformly on all types implementing *Sum*. For example, we can define + on *Real* and on *Vectors* of *Reals*, but it may not make sense to implement an addition operation of vectors to real which returns a real. So we do not want to force the modeler to do this. The purpose of *Sum* is to specify that a classifier provides an addition which is both associative and commutative.

When *Sum* is a base class of a classifier T, and we have a collection of instances of T, then we also know that the property *sum* is defined for this classifier. So *Sum* is a lower bound of the types of T. Indeed, the signature of *Collection* :: *sum* can be specified by $Collection(T \le Sum) :: sum() : T$, which expresses the requirements on T.

Syntactically, we express the type of a bounded template using the notation $\Lambda\tau.C(\tau \le S)$. For this new type constructor we have to define a new kind $\Pi\tau \le S \rightarrow \star$, where S is of kind $\star$. This new kind $\Pi\tau \le S$ states that τ has to be a subtype of S to construct a new type, otherwise the type is not well-kinded.

Observe that type operators are not comparable using the subtype relation. Therefore, bounded operator abstraction does not introduce new rules into the typing system.

3.5 Flattening and Accessing the Run-Time Type of Objects

Quite often it is necessary to obtain the type of an object and compare it. OCL provides some functions which allow the inspection and manipulation of the run-time type of objects. To test the type of an object it provides the operations *oclIsTypeOf()* and *oclIsKindOf()*, and to *cast* or coerce an object to another type it provides *oclAsType()*. In OCL, we also have the type *OclType*, of which the values are the names of all classifiers appearing in the contextual class diagrams[7]. The provided mechanisms are not sufficient, as the specification of the *flatten()* operation shows (see [1]):

> **context** *Set* :: *flatten*() : *Set*(*T2*)
> *post* : *result* = **if** *self*.*type*.*elementType*.*oclIsKindOf*(*CollectionType*)
> (3)   **then** *self* → *iterate*(*c*; *acc* : *Set*() = *Set*{} | *acc* → *union*(*c* → *asSet*()))
> **else** *self*
> **endif**

This constraint contains many errors. First, the type variable *T2* is not bound in the model (see Sect. 3.3 for the meaning of binding), so it is ambiguous whether *T2* is a classifier appearing in the model or a type variable. Next, self is an instance of a collection kind, so the meaning of *self.type* is actually a shorthand for *self→collect(type)*, and there is no guarantee that each instance of the collection defines the property *type*. Of course, the intended meaning of this sub-expression is to obtain the element-type of the members of *self*, but

---

[7] The type *OclType* will be removed but still occurs in the proposal.

one cannot access the environment of a variable from OCL. Next, the type of the accumulator in the iterate expression is not valid, *Set* requires an argument, denoting the type of the elements of the accumulator set (one could use *T2* as the argument).

The obvious solution, to allow the type of an expression depending on the type of other expressions, poses a serious danger: If the language or the type system is too permissive in what is allowed as a type, we cannot algorithmically decide, whether a constraint is well-typed or not. But decidability is a desirable property of a type-system. Instead, we propose to treat the *flatten()* operation as a kind of literal, like *iterate* is treated. For *flatten*, we introduce the following two rules:

$$\frac{e : C(T) \qquad C \leq Collection \qquad T \leq Collection(\tau')}{e \to flatten() : C(\tau')} \text{ T-FLAT}$$

$$\frac{e : C(T) \qquad C \leq Collection \qquad T \not\leq Collection(\tau')}{e \to flatten() : C(T)} \text{ T-NFLAT}$$

The rule T-FLAT covers the case where we may flatten a collection, because its element type conforms to a collection type with element type T'. In this case, T' is the new collection type. The rule T-NFLAT covers the case where the collection e does not contain any other collections. In this case, the result type of *flatten* is the type of collection e.

These rules encode the following idea: For each collection type we define an *overloaded* version of flatten. As written in Sec. 3.2, we are able to define the type of any overloaded operation using a union type. However, using this scheme directly yields infinitary union types, because the number of types for which we have to define a flatten operation is not bounded. The price for this extension is decidability [16].

The drawback of this extension is that the meaning of the collection cannot be expressed in OCL, because we have no way to define T' in OCL. The advantage is, that the decidability of the type system extended in this way is not affected.

4   Adequacy and Decidability

In this section, we summarize the most important results concerning the extended type system. This means that if the type system concludes that an OCL-expression has type T, then the result of evaluating the expression yields a value of a type that conforms to T. The type system is adequate and decidable. For the (operational) semantics of OCL we use the one defined in [1, 4].

Theorem 1. *Let Γ be a context, e an OCL expression, and T a type such that $\Gamma \vdash e : T$. Then the value of e conforms to T.*

Proof. Similar to the one presented in [5] and in [17].   □

Theorem 2. *Let Γ be a context and e be an OCL expression. Then there exists an algorithm which computes a type T such that $\Gamma \vdash e : T$ or returns an error if no such type can be found by the type system.*

Proof. Follows from [17] and [9], since our type system is a special case of the type systems used there.   □

Our type-checking algorithm is based on [17] and [9] but handles union types. It is simpler than the cited ones, because we only have a form of bounded operator abstraction, where type abstractions are not comparable, except for collection types, which is crucial in the proof of decidability. Furthermore, the kind of polymorphism in our type system is ML-like, where type variables (the template parameters) are universally quantified.

However, the type system is incomplete. By this we mean that if *e* is an OCL expression the type system will not compute the most precise type of *e*, but one of its supertypes. One reason for incompleteness is the following: If *e* is a constraint whose evaluation does not terminate, its most specific type is *OclVoid*. But we cannot decide whether the evaluation of a constraint will always terminate.

Indeed, the type system presented in this paper covers a usable set of features and it is still decidable. If we, e.g., also add checking for value specifications of method specifications of templates to the type system, it would become undecidable [18]. Such type systems indeed form the theoretical foundation of interactive theorem provers.

5   Related Work and Conclusions

A type system for OCL has been presented by Clark in [8], by Richter and Gogolla in [19], and by Cengarle and Knapp in [5]. In Sect. 2 we summarized these results and give a formal basis for our proposal.

A. Schürr has described an extension to the type system of OCL [20], where the type system is based on set approximations of types. These approximations are indeed another encoding of intersection and union types. His algorithm does not work with parameterized types and bounded polymorphism, because the normal forms of types required for the proof of Theorem 2 cannot be expressed as finite set approximations. We extended OCL's type system to also include polymorphic specifications for OCL constraints, which is not done by Schürr.

Our type system is a special case of the calculus $F_\wedge^\omega$. This system is analyzed in [17], where a type checking algorithm is given. This calculus is a conservative extension of $F_\le^\omega$. M. Steffen has described a type checking algorithm for $F_\le^\omega$ with polarity information [9]. Our type system does not allow type abstractions in expressions and assumes that all type variables are universally quantified in prenex form.

We have presented extensions to the type system for OCL, which admits a larger class of OCL constraints to be well-typed. Furthermore, we have introduced extensions to OCL, which allow to write polymorphic constraints.

The use of intersection types simplifies the treatment of multiple inheritance. This extension makes OCL constraints robust to changes in the underlying class diagram, e.g., refactoring by moving common code into a superclass. Intersection types are therefore very useful for type-checking algorithms for OCL. Union types simplify the treatment of collection literals, model operator overloading elegantly, and provides unnamed supertypes for collections and objects. Parametric polymorphism as introduced by UML 2.0's templates is useful for modeling. We described how polymorphism may be integrated into OCL's type system and provided a formal basis in type checking algorithms. Bounded parametric polymorphism is even more useful, because it provides the linguistic means to specify assumptions on the type of the type parameters.

We have proposed typing rules for certain functions which can not be formally expressed in OCL. We have shown that this type system is sound, adequate, and decidable.

References

1. Boldsoft and Rational Software Corporation and IONA and Adaptive Ltd.: UML 2.0 OCL Specification. (2003)
   http://www.omg.org/cgi-bin/doc?ptc/2003-10-14.
2. Object Management Group: UML 2.0 Infrastructure Specification. (2003)
   http://www.omg.org/cgi-bin/doc?ptc/2003-09-15.
3. Object Management Group: UML 2.0 Superstructure Specification. (2004)
   http://www.omg.org/cgi-bin/doc?ptc/2004-10-02.
4. Richters, M.: A Precise Approach to Validating UML Models and OCL Constraints. PhD thesis, Universtät Bremen (2002) Logos Verlag, Berlin, BISS Monographs, No. 14.
5. Cengarle, M.V., Knapp, A.: OCL 1.4/5 vs. 2.0 expressions: Formal semantics and expressiveness. Software and Systems Modeling (2003)
6. Kyas, M., Fecher, H., de Boer, F.S., van der Zwaag, M., Hooman, J., Arons, T., Kugler, H.: Formalizing UML models and OCL constraints in PVS. In Lüttgen, G., Madrid, N.M., Mendler, M., eds.: Proc. SFEDL 2004. Volume 115 of ENTCS., Elsevier (2005) 39–47
7. Pierce, B.C.: Types and Programming Languages. MIT Press (2002)
8. Clark, A.: Typechecking UML static models. In France, R.B., Rumpe, B., eds.: Proc. UML'99. Number 1723 in LNCS, Springer-Verlag (1999) 503–517
9. Steffen, M.: Polarized Higher-Order Subtyping. PhD thesis, Technische Fakutät, Friedrich-Alexander-Universität Erlangen-Nürnberg (1997)
10. Cardelli, L., Wegener, P.: On understanding types, data abstraction, and polymorphism. ACM Computing Surveys **17**(4) (1985) 471–522
11. Pierce, B.C.: Programming with Intersection Types and Bounded Polymorphism. PhD thesis, School of Computer Science, Carnegie Mellon University, Pittsburgh, PA 15213 (1991)
12. Compagnoni, A.B., Pierce, B.C.: Intersection types and multiple inheritance. Mathematical Structures in Computer Science **6**(5) (1996) 469–501
13. Meyer, B.: Eiffel: The Language. Prentice Hall (1992)
14. Meyer, B.: Object-Oriented Software Construction. 2nd edn. Prentice Hall (1997)
15. Wadler, P.L.: Theorems for free! In: Fourth International Conference on Functional Programming Languages and Computer Architecture, ACM Press (1989) 347–359
16. Bonsangue, M.M., Kok, J.N.: Infinite intersection types. Information and Computation **186**(2) (2003) 285–318
17. Compagnoni, A.B.: Higher-order subtyping and its decidability. Information and Computation **191**(1) (2004) 41–113

18. Coquand, T., Huet, G.: The calculus of constructions. Information and Computation **76**(2/3) (1988) 95–120
19. Richters, M., Gogolla, M.: OCL: Syntax, semantics, and tools. [21] 42–68
20. Schürr, A.: A new type checking approach for OCL 2.0? [21] 21–40
21. Clark, T., Warmer, J., eds.: Object Modelling with the OCL. In Clark, T., Warmer, J., eds.: Object Modelling with the OCL. Number 2263 in LNCS, Springer-Verlag (2002)

A Semantics for UML-RT Active Classes via Mapping into Circus

Rodrigo Ramos, Augusto Sampaio, and Alexandre Mota

Informatics Center, Federal University of Pernambuco
P.O.Box 7851 - 50.740-540, Recife-PE, Brazil
{rtr,acas,acm}@cin.ufpe.br

Abstract. The lack of a formal semantics for UML-RT makes it inadequate for rigourous system development, especially if the preservation of behaviour is a major concern when applying well-known model transformations, like refactorings and refinements. In this paper, we propose a semantics for UML-RT active classes through a mapping into *Circus*, a specification language that combines CSP, Z and specification statements. As a consequence of the translation, we are able to prove that model transformations preserve both static and dynamic behaviour, using refinement laws and a relational semantics of *Circus*, based on the Unifying Theories of Programming.

Keywords: UML-RT, *Circus*, method integration, model transformations

1 Introduction

As other object-oriented (OO) methods, UML [1] has tremendously influenced the software engineering modeling practice with rich structuring mechanisms. Despite its strengths, the rigorous development of non-trivial applications does not seem feasible without a formal semantics. The reason is that well-known model transformations might not preserve behaviour. This problem is even more serious in a model driven development, where transformations are as important as models, and involve different model views.

In the literature, several efforts address the problem through the integration of UML models with formal languages; there are some approaches to specification [2, 3], like combinations of UML with Z [4] or with CSP [5]. A formalisation of class diagrams using the state-based Z notation is presented in [2]; a detailed comparison of general integration approaches involving Z and Object-oriented extensions of Z is discussed in [6]. Concerning formal semantics of state diagrams, a mapping into CSP processes is presented in [3]; typically, each contribution to formalise UML tends to concentrate on a single view (like state or class diagrams). Although some works like, for instance, [7], use a uniform notation to describe a mapping that considers both structure and behaviour, the presentation is informal, based on examples.

Similar limitations can be found in works [8, 9] that formalise UML-RT [10] (a conservative UML profile that includes active objects to describe concurrent

M. Steffen and G. Zavattaro (Eds.): FMOODS 2005, LNCS 3535, pp. 99–114, 2005.

and distributed applications) using CSP. They focus on the translation of the
UML-RT structural view into CSP [8], and consider the behavioural representation of active objects [9] only partially. For example, statecharts of capules
and protocols, and their relationship with the structure diagrams are not addressed. Also, model transformations are usually neglected or, when considered,
the presentation is informal [11] and does not encompass all the model views.

In this paper, we propose a semantics for UML-RT via mapping into *Circus* [12], a language that combines CSP, Z and specification statements. We
focus on mapping the new elements (active classes and other related constructs)
that UML-RT adds to UML. We consider the following views of a UML-RT
model in an integrated way: class, state and structure diagrams. We propose
and prove a decomposition law for active classes, as an illustration of a sound
model transformation; the law and its proof consider the views mentioned above.

One reason for using *Circus* is that its semantics is defined in the setting
of the Unifying Theories of Programming [13]; this relational model has proved
convenient for reasoning. Another advantage is that *Circus* includes the main
design concepts of UML-RT. Unlike, for instance, CSP-OZ [14], *Circus* decou-
ples event occurrences from state operations (like in UML-RT), and it has been
designed to support a refinement calculus [15]; the decoupling seems crucial for
addressing refinement. The laws of *Circus* have been inspiring both to propose
laws for UML-RT ([16]) and to prove such laws as illustrated in this paper.

The next section gives an overview of UML-RT, and Section 3 introduces
Circus. Section 4 presents a mapping from UML-RT into *Circus*. Soundness of
model transformations is addressed in Section 5, where we propose and prove a
transformation law. Finally, we summarise our results and topics for future work
in Section 6.

2   UML-RT

The specification and design of a distributed system is a complex task involving
data, behaviour, intercommunication and architectural aspects of the model.
In order to fulfill these requirements, UML and ROOM (Real-Time Object-
Oriented Modeling language) have been combined into UML for Real-Time
(UML-RT) [10]. Some of the ROOM techniques also motivated extensions in
the UML 2.0 [17] version. Here we use UML-RT because we consider that the
proposed model for active objects is more consolidated than that proposed for
UML 2.0. Furthermore, UML-RT counts with commercial tool support.

Using stereotype mechanisms, UML-RT introduces four new constructors:
capsule, protocol, port and connector. Capsules (active classes) describe, potentially concurrent, architectural components that may interact with their environment only through signal-based objects called ports. Ports realise protocols,
which define a set of signals that a capsule can receive or send. A protocol
also defines the valid flow of information (signals) between connected ports of
capsules. Connectors act as a physical communication channel between ports.

A UML-RT model of the system is formed of a set of diagrams and system
properties. We choose diagrams that mainly represent the following architec-

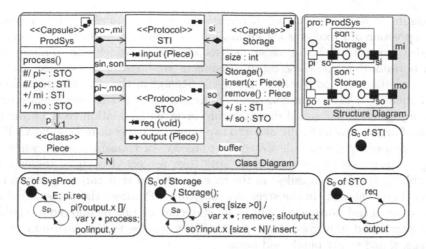

Fig. 1. Class, Structure and State Diagrams of a Manufacturing System

tural views: static data, dynamic behaviour, and dynamic object relationships; these are expressed, respectively, by class, state and structure diagrams. We directly express the system properties by invariants, pre- and post-conditions in *Circus*; they could alternatively be expressed in OCL [18], but an OCL to *Circus* mapping is out of the scope of this work.

In order to illustrate the notation, an example of a simplified manufacturing system is used. In Figure 1 (top left rectangle) a class diagram is presented. Capsules and protocols are graphically represented in the diagram by a box with a stereotype Capsule and Protocol, respectively; a symbol at the top right is also used to characterise their representations. The diagram emphasises the relationships between the ProdSys and Storage capsules. The capsule Storage is a bounded, reactive, *FIFO* buffer that is used to store objects of class Piece, and ProdSys is used to process these objects. These capsules have an association to the protocols, which are used to govern the communication among capsules. The protocol STO declares the input signal req (used to communicate the request of a work piece) and the output signal output (which communicates the delivery of a work piece). The protocol STI declares a signal input to store a piece.

By their own nature, capsules provide a high degree of information hiding. As the communication mechanism is via message passing, all capsule elements are hidden, including not only attributes, but also methods. The capsule Storage has a set of Pieces, represented by the association buffer, and methods to threat this set. The only visible elements in the capsule are ports, which can be connected to other capsule ports to establish communication; here, we assume that this communication is synchronous. This decoupling makes capsules highly reusable. In addition, a capsule can also be defined hierarchically, in terms of subcapsules, each with a state-machine and possibly a hierarchy of compound capsules.

A structure diagram, a kind of collaboration diagram, describes a capsule structural decomposition, showing the capsule interaction through connections among its ports and permitting hierarchically composed models. The structural decomposition of ProdSys is shown in Figure 1 (top right rectangle). It is composed by the capsule instances sin and son of Storage, which also communicate with ports of ProdSys; these capsule instances are created as a consequence of the association of ProdSys with the capsule Storage in the class diagram. Block filled squares in the capsule instances represent their ports, where white ones are conjugated (their signal directions are inverted in relation to the ordinary ports). Ports are basically divided into two types: relay ports and end ports. End ports are used by the capsule statechart to receive or transmit signals, while relay ports are used to connect other ports (like protected ports of the capsule or public ports of subcapsules) in the capsule internal structure diagram to the external environment. In the structure diagram of ProdSys, the ports pi and po are protected end ports used only by its statechart, while mi and mo are public relay ports used only to connect ports of subcapsules to the environment. In Storage, si and so are public end ports.

The capsule behaviour is described in terms of UML-RT statecharts, which extend the ROOMCharts concept [19] and differ from the standard UML statecharts [1] including some adaptations to better describe active objects (for instance, UML-RT statechart do not have final states). A statechart is composed by transitions and states; in general, a transition has the form p.e[g]/a, where e is an input signal, p is the port through which the signal arrives, g is a guard and a is an action. Input signals and a true guard trigger the transition. As a result, the corresponding action is executed.

We assume that events, guards and actions are expressed using the *Circus* notation. For example, in the statechart of Storage, there are two transitions from state Sa. The one on the right triggers if the req signal arrives through port si and the buffer is non-empty. The corresponding action declares a variable x to capture return of the method remove. This is the way it is done in *Circus*, since remove is actually interpreted as a Z-Schema, as explained in the next section. The value od x is then through channel si. The syntax for writing these actions related to communication are also as in *Circus*. In this work we do not consider capsule inheritance, mainly because its semantics in UML-RT is not yet well-defined; according to the ROOMCharts definitions [19], inherited capsule is able to arbitrarily change the behaviour defined in its super capsule.

In UML-RT, states are classified as initial, choice, composite or simple. Initial states are transient states that mark the starting point of a state-machine. A composite state groups other states, whereas a simple one has no other state inside. Choice states are those that involve a decision of which path to take according to its guard; there exist only two outgoing transitions: one is triggered when the guard is true; otherwise the second is triggered. Composite states are divided into two types: Or-States and And-States. An Or-State defines that only one of its substates is active, whereas And-States contain regions that are executed in parallel, and permit each region to have an active state per time. Further details about composite states are presented in Section 4.2.

For a capsule state-machine, we assume that there is a composite state that contains all other states; it is called the top state (S_0) and is implicitly reached when the capsule instance is created. Figure 1 (bottom) presents the statecharts of ProdSys, Storage, STO and STI. Their respective top states (S_0) are Or-States that sequentially execute the inner states. In Storage, for example, the initial state moves to the state Sa. Next it waits the arrival of the input or req signals. The behaviour of Storage is further explained in the next section.

3   Circus

The language *Circus* [12] includes the notion of a process, whose state is defined using a Z schema and behaviour by an action expressed in the CSP notation. Process interaction is defined via channels to communicate values or just synchronise events. Therefore, the specification of a *Circus* program is defined by a sequence of paragraphs, which can include: Z paragraphs, process definitions, and channel declarations. As a simple example, consider the capsule Storate of Figure 1. It can be specified in *Circus* as the following process.

$$| \; N : \mathbb{N}$$

$T_{\text{STI}} ::= \text{input} \ll \text{Piece} \gg$
channel si : T_{STI}
$T_{\text{STO}} ::= \text{req} \mid \text{output} \ll \text{Piece} \gg$
channel so : T_{STO}
process Storage $\mathrel{\widehat{=}}$ **begin**
    state *StorageState* $\mathrel{\widehat{=}}$ [buff : seq Piece; size : $0..N$ | size $= \#$buff $\leq N$]
    initial *StorageInit* $\mathrel{\widehat{=}}$ [*StorageState'* | buff' $= \langle \rangle \wedge$ size' $= 0$]
    insert $\mathrel{\widehat{=}}$ [$\Delta StorageState$; $x?$: Piece | size $< N \wedge$
        buff' $=$ buff $^\frown \langle x? \rangle \wedge$ size' $=$ size $+ 1$]
    remove $\mathrel{\widehat{=}}$ [$\Delta StorageState$; $x!$: Piece | size $> 0 \wedge x! = head$ buff $\wedge$
        buff' $= tail$ buff $\wedge$ size' $=$ size $- 1$]
    Sa $\mathrel{\widehat{=}}$ (size $< N$ & si?input.x $\rightarrow$ insert; Sa)
        $\Box$ (size > 0 & so.req $\rightarrow$ (**var** x : Piece • remove; so!output.x); Sa)
  • *StorageInit*; *Sa*
end

The maximum size of this buffer is a strictly positive constant N. The buffer program takes its inputs and supplies its outputs through the channels si and so, respectively. The free types T_{STI} and T_{STO} categorise the values communicated by these channels. In T_{STO}, req and output are constructors of the free type, used to communicate the request and delivery of objects, respectively. Similarly, in T_{STI}, input is used to represent the storage of objects of type Piece.

In *Circus* the body of a declaration of a process is delimited by the **begin** and **end** keywords; it is composed by a sequence of paragraphs and a main action (after the • symbol), which defines the process behaviour. One of these paragraphs is used to describe the state of the process (identified by the keyword **state**), which encapsulates its data components. Furthermore, the other paragraphs describe process operations and actions, that are used to structure the process specification and the main action.

In our example, the process Storage encapsulates two state components in the Z schema *BufferState*: an ordered list buffer of contents and the size of this list, represented by size. Initially, the buffer is empty and, therefore, its size is zero; this is specified as a state initialisation action *StorageInit*.

The main action initialises the buffer and repeatedly offers the choice of input and req. The signal input is guarded by size $< N$. The process accepts an input whenever there is space to store the new value; in this case, the piece is appended to the bounded sequence and the size incremented. The effect on the state is described by a schema as usual, using the operator insert. The action si?input.$x \rightarrow$ put is a prefixing in the style of CSP. A new input variable x is introduced, and a value input through the channel si is assigned to it. Afterwards, the action insert is executed. The req signal is enabled providing that the buffer contains something (size > 0). Afterwards, the Buffer offers output to deliver a piece. The associated state modification is defined by the remove schema action, which removes the head of buffer and updates the size accordingly.

The example has shown how processes are constructed from actions, but processes may themselves be combined with CSP operators, such as parallel composition $(A_1 \llbracket cs \rrbracket A_2)$. The meaning of a new process constructed in this way is obtained from the conjunction of the constituent states of the processes in composition (A_1 and A_2) and the parallel combination of their main actions, synchronising on the set of channels (cs).

At the level of actions, the Circus parallel operator is actually slightly different from that of CSP. To resolve conflicts in the access to the variables in scope, it requires a synchronisation set and two sets that partition those variables. In the parallelism $A_1 \llbracket ns_1 \mid cs \mid ns_2 \rrbracket A_2$, the actions A_1 and A_2 synchronise on the channels in set cs. Although both A_1 and A_2 have access to all variables, they can only modify the values of the variables in ns_1 and ns_2, respectively.

Further explanation of the *Circus* notation used in this work is introduced as the need arises, in the next section. A more detailed presentation of *Circus*, including its complete grammar and formal semantics, can be found in [20].

4   Semantic Mapping

This section gives meaning to UML-RT elements through a mapping into *Circus*. This translation provides a mapping of structural and behaviour UML-RT elements into *Circus*.

In our approach, UML-RT classifiers with an associated behaviour (capsules and protocols) are mapped into processes, and ports into channels. The mapping of classes has been addressed by several authors, and is out of the scope of our work. For example, in [2] classes are mapped directly into Z paragraphs. In this sense, our work complements those approaches.

In our strategy the target of the translation is a *Circus* specification that is itself the meaning of the original model. Concerning the structure diagrams, we consider that they implicitly define an extensional view of the system; they contain the set of capsule instances. To deal with hierarchical structures, we assume that all capsule instances, ports and connections have distinct names.

When mapping elements declared as a list (such as attributes and methods of a capsule, or signals of a protocol), by convention we single out one of its elements, present its mapping , and invoke a meta function ($\mathcal{TL}()$) to translate the remaining elements. We assume that there are overloaded definitions of $\mathcal{TL}()$ for each kind of list. In practice such lists can obviously be empty, but we avoid this trivial case assuming that they have at least one element.

4.1   UML-RT Structural Elements

A protocol declaration in UML-RT encapsulates both the communication elements and the behaviour. In *Circus*, this gives rise to two major elements: a stateless process that captures this behaviour and a channel to represent the communication elements. Regarding the signals, a possible mapping would be to introduce a channel associated with each signal. Rather, we use a single channel to communicate all signals of a protocol. This channel communicates values of a free type, with each constructor representing a signal. Using a single channel facilitates the mapping of capsules presented next. For instance, it is more convenient to use a single channel in contexts involving synchronisation or renaming.

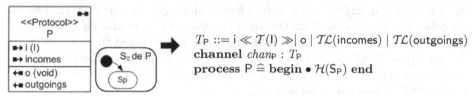

$$T_P ::= i \ll \mathcal{T}(I) \gg| \, o \mid \mathcal{TL}(\text{incomes}) \mid \mathcal{TL}(\text{outgoings})$$
channel $chan_P : T_P$
process $P \cong$ **begin** $\bullet \, \mathcal{H}(S_P)$ **end**

In names like $chan_P$ above, we assume that P is a placeholder for the actual protocol name. In this way, the mapping of protocol STO in the example (Figure 1) generates a corresponding channel $chan_{STO}$. The channel $chan_P$ communicates values of the free type T_P; each value represents a signal. Parameterless signals, like the outgoing signal o above, are translated into constants; parameterised signals are mapped into data type constructors (like i). The type of the parameter is translated into a corresponding *Circus* type by function $\mathcal{T}()$. The remaining signals (incomes and outgoings) are mapped by the function $\mathcal{TL}()$.

The behaviour of the protocol P is represented by $\mathcal{H}(S_P)$, where S_P stands for a state that encloses all other states of its statechart. The function $\mathcal{H}()$, which translates a statechart into a *Circus* action, is explained in Section 4.2.

Capsules are also defined as processes, with methods defined as schema operations, and attributes mapped into a Z state schema (the process state). Each port generates a channel with the same type of the corresponding channel of the protocol, and has its behaviour described by the process obtained from the mapping of its protocol synchronised with that obtained from the capsule statechart. Observe that in UML-RT the type of a port is the protocol itself. In *Circus* the type of the channel originated from the port is the free type that represents the signals (as explained in the mapping of a protocol).

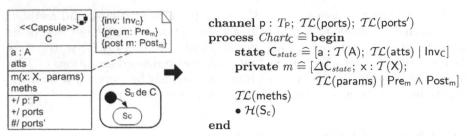

channel p : T_P; $\mathcal{TL}(ports)$; $\mathcal{TL}(ports')$
process $Chart_C \;\hat{=}\;$ **begin**
    state $C_{state} \;\hat{=}\; [a : \mathcal{T}(A);\; \mathcal{TL}(atts) \mid Inv_C]$
    private $m \;\hat{=}\; [\Delta C_{state};\; x : \mathcal{T}(X);$
                       $\mathcal{TL}(params) \mid Pre_m \wedge Post_m]$
    $\mathcal{TL}(meths)$
    $\bullet \; \mathcal{H}(S_c)$
end

In the above mapping, the process $Chart_C$ deals with the views represented by class and state diagrams. It encapsulates all actions that manipulate the private attributes of the capsule C. In the capsule C above, the compartments correspond to attributes, methods and ports. Therefore, a, m and p are those that we single out. The attribute a is mapped to an attribute in the state of $Chart_C$ with its corresponding type in **Circus**, given by $\mathcal{T}(A)$; the other attributes atts are mapped by the function $\mathcal{TL}()$, as previously explained. The invariant Inv_C cames from the UML-RT note element on the left, and it is assumed to be already described in **Circus**. The method m() is mapped to an operator that could change any state attribute and whose parameters are mapped into schema attributes, just like a has been included in the state schema; similarly the function $\mathcal{TL}()$ maps the other methods meths. Like the invariant Inv_C, the pre- and post-conditions Pre_m land $Post_m$ are written in **Circus**. The port p is mapped to a channel with the same type T_P of the channel $Chan_P$ used by the protocol P. The main action of $Chart_C$ is expressed by $\mathcal{H}(S_C)$, which represents the mapping of the statechart of capsule C, explained in Section 4.2.

We need also consider structure diagrams, dealt with by the mapping below. The process that deals with this view represents the observational behaviour of capsule C after considering the restrictions imposed by its ports to the corresponding communication channels used by the process, and considering the parallelism of all its connected subcapsules.

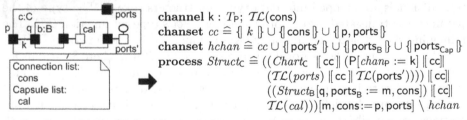

channel k : T_P; $\mathcal{TL}(cons)$
chanset $cc \;\hat{=}\; \{\!| k |\!\} \cup \{\!| cons |\!\} \cup \{\!| p, ports |\!\}$
chanset $hchan \;\hat{=}\; cc \cup \{\!| ports' |\!\} \cup \{\!| ports_B |\!\} \cup \{\!| ports_{Cap} |\!\}$
process $Struct_C \;\hat{=}\; ((Chart_C \;[\![\, cc \,]\!]\; (P[chan_P := k] \;[\![\, cc \,]\!]$
                  $(\mathcal{TL}(ports) \;[\![\, cc \,]\!]\; \mathcal{TL}(ports')))) \;[\![\, cc \,]\!]$
                  $((Struct_B[q, ports_B := m, cons]) \;[\![\, cc \,]\!]$
                  $\mathcal{TL}(cal)))[m, cons := p, ports] \setminus hchan$

In the process ($Struct_C$), the behaviour of $Chart_C$ is synchronised with the behaviour of all ports in capsule C; we single out here the port p, whose behaviour is represented by process P. The channel $chan_P$ used by P has to be renamed with the name of the connector (k) that links the port p to another port in the system. The other ports are similarly mapped by the function $\mathcal{TL}()$. We single out the subcapsule B from the subcapsule list cal, which has all public ports q and $ports_B$ renamed to their associated connections k and cons; $ports_B$ stands for the public port list of B. After parallelising all capsules in the structure diagram of C, an injective function is needed to rename ($[m, cons := p, ports]$) connections to associated public ports, and hide ($\setminus$ *hchan*) connections protected port (and subcapsule port) channels.

Because we represent port connections through renaming and synchronisation, we need to assume that ports are connected in the lower structure level in which they are present; actually this is a good design practice.

4.2   UML-RT Behavioural Elements

Our mapping of capsule and protocol statecharts into **Circus** is based on the work reported in [3], which presents the formalisation of UML statecharts in CSP. Nevertheless, we extend [3] in order to consider **Circus** actions, deal with parallelism (And-States) and composite states with multiple initial points.

Let M be a state-machine, and S_M be the set of states of M. The set of events of M is denoted by E_M, and its actions and boolean guards by A_M and G_M, respectively. Furthermore, let SI_M be the set of all initial states, SCh_M the set of all choice states, SS_M the set of all simple states and SCo_M the set of all composite states of S_M.

As a statechart can be identified by the topmost state that contains inner states, mapping a statechart reduces to mapping a state. Thus, let $\mathcal{H}$ be a function that takes a state and yields its **Circus** representation.

$$\mathcal{H} : S_M \rightarrow CSPAction$$

We assume that an action in A_M is expressed as a method call and, therefore, does not need be translated. Like other predicates, guards in A_M are written using the **Circus** syntax. As ports have an associated channel in **Circus**, with the same name, and signals are expressed as values of this channel type, a signal e of a port p can be directly written as an event pattern matching in **Circus**.

Every pattern to which the mapping function $\mathcal{H}()$ is applied gives rise to a separate mapping rule. On the left of each rule, we illustrate the pattern as a template statechart.

The first pattern address initial states, which have only one outgoing transition, and no entry nor exit actions (actions executed before the state becomes active and inactive, respectively). Let Ai be an initial state, with Ai $\in SI_M$, act() the action of its outgoing transition, and A_1 the target of this transition, then:

Ai ⬤ / act();
  (A_1)   ➡ $\mathcal{H}(Ai) = act(); \; \mathcal{H}(A_1)$

For a choice state, its translation is as follows. Let Ac by a choice state in SCh_M, which has only two outgoing transitions and one guard **g** (these transitions have no events and are triggered depending on the evaluation of **g**), then:

[g] / act$_1$(); (A_1)
  Ac ©   ➡ $\mathcal{H}(Ac) = (g \; \& \; act_1(); \; \mathcal{H}(A_1)) \; \square \; (\neg \, g \; \& \; act_2(); \; \mathcal{H}(A_2))$
[¬g] / act$_2$(); (A_2)

Now suppose the translation of a simple state. Let As by a simple state in SS_M, AC the composite state in SCO_M that encloses it and tls the outgoing transitions of As (where p.e[g]/act is singled out), then:

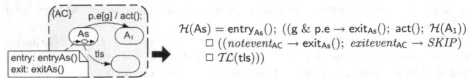

$$\mathcal{H}(\mathsf{As}) = \mathsf{entry}_{\mathsf{As}}(); \ ((\mathsf{g} \ \& \ \mathsf{p.e} \rightarrow \mathsf{exit}_{\mathsf{As}}(); \ \mathsf{act}(); \ \mathcal{H}(\mathsf{A}_1))$$
$$\square \ ((\mathit{notevent}_{\mathsf{AC}} \rightarrow \mathsf{exit}_{\mathsf{As}}(); \ \mathit{exitevent}_{\mathsf{AC}} \rightarrow SKIP)$$
$$\square \ \mathcal{TL}(\mathsf{tls})))$$

When the state As is active, it executes the entry action $\mathsf{entry}_{\mathsf{As}}()$. Then, it waits for a new signal to be communicated by the environment (the external choice captures this decision). Such an event p.e can only be performed if its guard g is satisfied. Finally the exit action $\mathsf{exit}_{\mathsf{As}}()$ and the action $\mathsf{act}()$ associated to the trigged transition are executed. The remaining transitions in tls are mapped by the function $\mathcal{TL}()$, as previously explained. Further the simple state As can exit if an outgoing (group) transition of its enclosing state AC is triggered; in this case, a notify event $\mathit{notevent}_{\mathsf{AC}}$ is sent by AC to ensure that the exit action of As is executed before its exit action. After the execution of the As exit action, an event $\mathit{exitevent}_{\mathsf{AC}}$ is launched to allow the execution of the exit action of AC.

To formalise composite states, we present the translation of a composite And-State with its concurrent regions formed by Or-States. In this scenario, the translation of a composite Or-State is given by an And-State with a unique region. Let AC and EAC be composite states in SCO_M (where EAC encloses AC), Ai_1 and Ai_2 the initial states in SI_M of the regions of AC, tls the outgoing transitions of AC (where $\mathsf{p}_1.\mathsf{e}_1[\mathsf{g}_1]/\mathsf{act}_1$ and $\mathsf{p}_2.\mathsf{e}_2[\mathsf{g}_2]/\mathsf{act}_2$ are singled out) and $[R]$ a renaming function that replaces channels associated to connected ports for the respective channels associated to their connections (see Section 4.1), then:

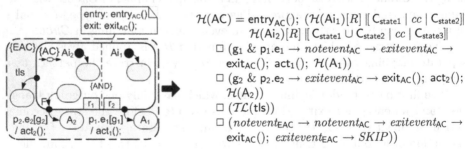

$$\mathcal{H}(\mathsf{AC}) = \mathsf{entry}_{\mathsf{AC}}(); \ (\mathcal{H}(\mathsf{Ai}_1)[R] \ [\![\ C_{\mathsf{state1}} \ | \ cc \ | \ C_{\mathsf{state2}}]\!]$$
$$\mathcal{H}(\mathsf{Ai}_2)[R] \ [\![\ C_{\mathsf{state1}} \cup C_{\mathsf{state2}} \ | \ cc \ | \ C_{\mathsf{state3}}]\!]$$
$$\square \ (\mathsf{g}_1 \ \& \ \mathsf{p}_1.\mathsf{e}_1 \rightarrow \mathit{notevent}_{\mathsf{AC}} \rightarrow \mathit{exitevent}_{\mathsf{AC}} \rightarrow$$
$$\mathsf{exit}_{\mathsf{AC}}(); \ \mathsf{act}_1(); \ \mathcal{H}(\mathsf{A}_1))$$
$$\square \ (\mathsf{g}_2 \ \& \ \mathsf{p}_2.\mathsf{e}_2 \rightarrow \mathit{exitevent}_{\mathsf{AC}} \rightarrow \mathsf{exit}_{\mathsf{AC}}(); \ \mathsf{act}_2();$$
$$\mathcal{H}(\mathsf{A}_2))$$
$$\square \ (\mathcal{TL}(\mathsf{tls}))$$
$$\square \ (\mathit{notevent}_{\mathsf{EAC}} \rightarrow \mathit{notevent}_{\mathsf{AC}} \rightarrow \mathit{exitevent}_{\mathsf{AC}} \rightarrow$$
$$\mathsf{exit}_{\mathsf{AC}}(); \ \mathit{exitevent}_{\mathsf{EAC}} \rightarrow SKIP))$$

When the And-State AC is active, it executes the entry action $\mathit{entry}_{\mathsf{AC}}()$. Then, it executes the initial states of each region. These regions can synchronise their events through the channel set cc, which are the internal connections of the capsule that own the statechart. Each region r_1 and r_2 can only modify the values of the variables in C_{state1} and C_{state2}, respectively; the exit action of AC and the action of its transitions can only modify the values in C_{state3}. The capsule state contains the union of C_{state1}, C_{state2} and C_{state3}. The enclosed states in each region of AC are sequentially reached. At any moment, the state AC can receive an event $\mathsf{p}_1.\mathsf{e}_1$ that triggers a group transition (a transition that emanates directly from the border of the composite state and interrupts the state and substates in any situation, however allowing that they normally finish the execution of their exit-actions). When a group transition is triggered, the event $\mathit{notevent}_{\mathsf{AC}}$ occurs, and

AC waits for the active inner state to execute its exit action. When a notification $exitevent_{AC}$ arrives, the state AC is able to execute its exit action $exit_{AC}$ and the transition action act_1; then it moves to the next state. Transitions that emanate from an enclosed state through a junction point, like the one triggered by $p_2.e_2$, behave similarly, but do not send a $notevent_{AC}$ event. This type of junction is mapped to a transient inner state of AC; for a junction point F, its translation corresponds to $\mathcal{H}(F) = exitevent_{AC} \rightarrow SKIP$. The other outgoing transitions tls of AC can be similarly translated by the function $\mathcal{TL}()$.

As simple states, a composite state AC can be enclosed by another composite state EAC. In this situation, AC receives the notification $notevent_{EAC}$ to indicate the arrival of an event in EAC. When this happens, AC must send $notevent_{AC}$ to its immediate active inner state to ensure that all active enclosed states execute their exit action before the AC exit action. After AC executes $exit_{AC}()$, $exitevent_{EAC}$ is sent to allow EAC to execute its exit action.

For simplicity, we do not consider here history states.

5   Model Transformations and Soundness

Translating UML-RT models into *Circus* can then benefit from the formal semantics as well as the refinement notions and laws of *Circus*. For example, the meaning of capsule refinement is interpreted as process refinement in *Circus*. Similarly, action refinement can be used to capture statechart transformations.

As illustration, we present one transformation law that involves the three most important diagrams of UML-RT: state, class and structure diagrams. As previously mentioned, we consider structure diagrams because they represent some relations between capsules that are not expressed in class diagrams; so they must be taken into account to preserve the model behaviour.

Law 1 decomposes a capsule A into parallel component capsules (B and C) in order to tackle design complexity and to potentially improve reuse. The side condition requires that A must be partitioned, a concept that is explained next.

On the left-hand side of Law 1 the state machine of A is an And-State composed of two states (Sb and Sc), which may interact (internal communication) through the conjugated ports b_2 and c_1 (as captured by the structure diagram on the left-hand side). The other two ports (b_1 and c_2) are used for external communication by states Sb and Sc, respectively. Furthermore, in transitions on Sb, only the attributes batts and the methods bmeths (that may reference only the attributes batts) are used; analogously, transitions of Sc use only the attributes catts and the methods cmeths (that may reference only the attributes catts). Finally, the invariant of A is the conjunction $Inv_B \wedge Inv_C$, where Inv_B involves only batts as free variables, and Inv_C only catts. When a capsule obeys such conditions, we say that it is partitioned. In this case, there are two partitions: one is $\langle batts, Inv_B, bmeths, (b_1, b_2), Sb \rangle$ and the other is $\langle catts, Inv_C, cmeths, (c_1, c_2), Sc \rangle$.

Law 1. *Capsule Decomposition*

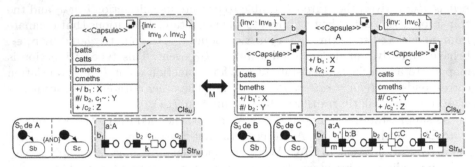

provided $\langle$batts, Inv_B, bmeths, (b_1, b_2), Sb$\rangle$ and $\langle$catts, Inv_C, cmeths, (c_1, c_2), Sc$\rangle$ *partition* A; *The statecharts of the protocol* X *and* Z *are deterministic.*

The effect of the decomposition is to create two new component capsules, B and C, one for each partition, and redesign the original capsule A to act as a mediator. In general, the new behaviour of A might depend on the particular form of decomposition. Law 1 captures a parallel decomposition. On the right-hand side of the law, A has no state machine. It completely delegates its original behaviour to B and C through the structure diagram.

Concerning the structure diagram on the right-hand side of the law, it shows how A encapsulates B and C. When A is created, it automatically creates the instances of B and C, which execute concurrently. The public ports b_1 and c_2 are preserved in A. Capsule B has as its public port an image of b_1, called b_1'. Although this port is public in B, it is only visible inside the structure diagram of A. The role of this port is to allow B to receive the external signals received from A through port b_1, as captured by the connection between b_1' and b_1 in the structure diagram of A. Analogously, c_2 and b_2' have the same relationship, concerning capsules A and C. The internal ports b_2 and c_1 are moved to capsules B and C, respectively, and play the same role as before.

5.1   Soundness

Based on the semantic mapping presented in Section 4, we can translate the two sides of Law 1 and check its validity. Instead of appealing directly to the semantics of *Circus* we can use its refinement laws [12] to carry out the proof. Actually, Law 1 has been inspired by the following law presented for *Circus*. Obviously, when there are no corresponding laws in *Circus*, it might be necessary to carry out the proof directly in the *Circus* UTP semantics. Even when there is a corresponding law in *Circus*, we will see that the proof is more elaborate than using just this law, since we consider structure diagrams.

Law 2. *Process splitting*

Let qd and rd stand for the declarations of the processes Q and R, determined by $Q.st$, $Q.pps$, and $Q.act$, and $R.st$, $R.pps$, and $R.act$, respectively; let F stand for a context which must also make sense as a function on processes. Then

$$\textbf{process } P \; \widehat{=} \; \textbf{begin} \qquad\qquad = \qquad (qd \; rd \; \textbf{process}\, P \; \widehat{=} \; F(Q, R))$$

> **state** *State* $\widehat{=}$ $Q.st \wedge R.st$
> $Q.pps \uparrow R.st$
> $R.pps \uparrow Q.st$
> $\bullet \; F(Q.act, R.act) \; \textbf{end}$

provided $Q.pps$ and $R.pps$ are disjoint with respect to $R.st$ and $Q.st$. $\qquad\square$

In Law 2, the state of P is defined as the conjunction of two other state schemas: $Q.st$ and $R.st$. The actions of P are $Q.pps \uparrow R.st$ and $R.pps \uparrow Q.st$, which handle the partitions of the state separately. In $Q.pps \uparrow R.st$, each schema expression of $Q.pps$ is conjoined with $\Xi R.st$; this means that the state components of $R.st$ do not change (similarly for $R.pps \uparrow Q.st$). Two sets of process paragraphs pps_1 and pps_2 are disjoint with respect to states s_1 and s_2 if, and only if, no command nor CSP action expression in pps_1 refers to components of s_2 or to paragraph names in pps_2; similarly, for pps_2 and components of s_2.

Proof of Law 1. First we deal with the class and the state diagrams. The mapping of these views of capsule A as a *Circus* process is obtained by using the second mapping rule presented in Section 4.1 and the last rule of Section 4.2. We write two partitions using the operator $\uparrow$, as in Law 2. Strictly, the attributes and methods *batts*, *catts*, *bmeths* and *cmeths* must be mapped using the function $\mathcal{TL}()$; here we omit its application for a matter of readability.

> **process** $Chart_A \; \widehat{=} \; \textbf{begin}$
> > **state** $State \; \widehat{=} \; [\text{batts} \wedge \text{catts} \mid \text{Inv}_B \wedge \text{Inv}_C]$
> > bmeths $\uparrow$ catts
> > cmeths $\uparrow$ batts
> > $\bullet \; \mathcal{H}(S_B)[b_2 := k] \; [\![\text{batts} \mid \{\!| k, b_1, c_2 |\!\} \mid \text{catts}]\!]) \mathcal{H}(S_C)[c_1 := k]$
>
> **end**

From Law 2, the following equality holds:

$$Chart_A = Chart_B[b_2 := k] \; [\![\{\!| k, b_1, c_2 |\!\}]\!] \; Chart_C[c_1 := k]$$

where $Chart_B$ and $Chart_B$ are declared as:

> **process** $Chart_B \; \widehat{=} \; \textbf{begin state } State \; \widehat{=} \; [\text{batts} \mid \text{Inv}_B] \; \text{bmeths} \; \bullet \; \mathcal{H}(S_B) \; \textbf{end}$
> **process** $Chart_C \; \widehat{=} \; \textbf{begin state } State \; \widehat{=} \; [\text{catts} \mid \text{Inv}_C] \; \text{cmeths} \; \bullet \; \mathcal{H}(S_C) \; \textbf{end}$

Now we consider the structural part of capsule A. This is mapped into the *Circus* process $Struct_A$, presented below.

$$Structs_A \; \widehat{=} \; (Chart_A[b_2, c_1 := k, k] \; [\![\{\!| k, b_1, c_2 |\!\}]\!] \; X[chan_X := b_1] \; [\![\{\!| k, b_1, c_2 |\!\}]\!]$$
$$Y[chan_Y := k] \; [\![\{\!| k, b_1, c_2 |\!\}]\!] \; Y[chan_Y := k] \; [\![\{\!| k, b_1, c_2 |\!\}]\!] \; Z[chan_Z := c_2]) \setminus \{\!| k |\!\}$$

The structure diagrams of B and C, as well as that of A on the right-hand side of Law 1, are mapped similarly. To avoid confusion between the two occurrences of A in the law, we refer to the occurrence on the left simply as A, and that on the right as A'. Therefore, we want to prove that $Structs_A$ has the same behaviour as $Structs_{A'}$, where the latter is composed of the processes $Structs_B$ and $Structs_C$:

$$Structs'_A \; \widehat{=} \; ((Struct_B[b'_1, b_2 := m, k] \; [\![\{\!| k |\!\}]\!] \; Struct_C[c'_2, c_1 := n, k]) \; [\![\{\!| k |\!\}]\!]$$
$$(X[chan_X := m] \; [\![\{\!| k |\!\}]\!] \; Z[chan_Z := n]))[m, n := b_1, c_2] \setminus \{\!| k |\!\}$$

The proof uses basic laws of CSP [5], which are also valid for *Circus*. One of the laws is the distribution of injective renaming through parallel composition; this is expressed as $f(P \llbracket cs \rrbracket Q) = (f(P) \llbracket f(cs) \rrbracket f(Q))$ and referenced as $f[.] - \llbracket cs \rrbracket -dist$. Two other laws express the associativity $(P \llbracket cs \rrbracket (Q \llbracket cs \rrbracket R) = (P\llbracket cs \rrbracket Q)\llbracket cs \rrbracket R)$ and the symmetry $(P\llbracket cs \rrbracket Q = Q\llbracket cs \rrbracket P)$ of parallel composition. These are referenced bellow as $\llbracket cs \rrbracket -assoc$ and $\llbracket cs \rrbracket -sym$, respectively. Also, we use the fact that unused channels in the synchronism of a parallel operator are redundant, which is expressed as $P \llbracket \alpha P \cup \alpha Q \cup cs \rrbracket Q = P \llbracket \alpha P \cup \alpha Q \rrbracket Q$, where αR is the alphabet of R; we refer this law as $\llbracket cs \rrbracket -null$. Finally, we use the fact that the parallel operator is idempotent under certain restrictions [21]: if P is a deterministic process, then $P \llbracket \alpha P \rrbracket P$; we will refer to this law as $\llbracket cs \rrbracket -idem$.

$Structs_A$

$= [1.\ Expanding\ Chart_A\ in\ Structs_A]$

$(Chart_B [b_2 := k] \ \llbracket \{ k,b_1,c_2 \} \rrbracket Chart_C [c_1 := k] \ \llbracket \{ k,b_1,c_2 \} \rrbracket X[chan_X := b_1] \ \llbracket \{ k,b_1,c_2 \} \rrbracket$
$Y[chan_Y := k] \ \llbracket \{ k,b_1,c_2 \} \rrbracket Y[chan_Y := k] \ \llbracket \{ k,b_1,c_2 \} \rrbracket Z[chan_Z := c_2]) \setminus \{ k \}$

$= [2.\ Applying\ Law\ \llbracket cs \rrbracket -idem\ for\ X[chan_X := b_1]\ and\ Z[chan_Z := c_2],\ and$
$rearranging\ the\ processes\ using\ Laws\ \llbracket cs \rrbracket -assoc\ and\ \llbracket cs \rrbracket -sym]$

$(Chart_B [b_2 := k] \ \llbracket \{ k,b_1,c_2 \} \rrbracket X[chan_X := b_1] \ \llbracket \{ k,b_1,c_2 \} \rrbracket Y[chan_Y := k] \ \llbracket \{ k,b_1,c_2 \} \rrbracket$
$X[chan_X := b_1] \ \llbracket \{ k,b_1,c_2 \} \rrbracket Chart_C [c_1 := k] \ \llbracket \{ k,b_1,c_2 \} \rrbracket Y[chan_Y := k] \ \llbracket \{ k,b_1,c_2 \} \rrbracket$
$Z[chan_Z := c_2] \ \llbracket \{ k,b_1,c_2 \} \rrbracket Z[chan_Z := c_2]) \setminus \{ k \}$

$= [3.\ Applying\ renamings\ [b'_1,b_2 := m,k],\ [c'_1,c_1 := n,k]\ and\ [n,m := c_2,b_1],\ and$
$Law\ f[.] - \llbracket cs \rrbracket -dist]]$

$(((Chart_B \ \llbracket \{ b_2,b'_1,n \} \rrbracket X[chan_X := b'_1] \ \llbracket \{ b_2,b'_1,n \} \rrbracket Y[chan_Y := b_2])[b'_1,b_2 := m,k]$
$\llbracket \{ k,m,n \} \rrbracket X[chan_X := m]) \ \llbracket \{ k,m,n \} \rrbracket$
$((Chart_C \ \llbracket \{ c_1,m,c'_2 \} \rrbracket Y[chan_Y := c_1] \ \llbracket \{ c_1,m,c'_2 \} \rrbracket Z[chan_Z := c'_2])[c'_2,c_1 := n,k]$
$\llbracket \{ k,m,n \} \rrbracket Z[chan_Z := n])[m,n := b_1,c_2]) \setminus \{ k \}$

$= [4.\ Using\ the\ Law\ \llbracket cs \rrbracket -null\ and\ rearranging\ the\ processes\ using\ laws]$
$\llbracket cs \rrbracket -assoc\ and\ \llbracket cs \rrbracket -sym$

$(((Chart_B \ \llbracket \{ b_2,b'_1 \} \rrbracket X[chan_X := b'_1] \ \llbracket \{ b_2,b'_1 \} \rrbracket Y[chan_Y := b_2])[b'_1,b_2 := m,k]$
$\llbracket \{ k,m,n \} \rrbracket ((Chart_C \ \llbracket \{ c_1,c'_2 \} \rrbracket Y[chan_Y := c_1] \ \llbracket \{ c_1,c'_2 \} \rrbracket Z[chan_Z := c'_2])[c'_2,c_1 := n,k]$
$\llbracket \{ k,m,n \} \rrbracket X[chan_X := m]) \ \llbracket \{ k,m,n \} \rrbracket Z[chan_Z := n])[m,n := b_1,c_2]) \setminus \{ k \}$

$= [5.\ Using\ the\ definition\ of\ Struct_B\ and\ Struct_C]$

$((Struct_B [b'_1,b_2 := m,k] \ \llbracket \{ k,m,n \} \rrbracket (Struct_C [c'_2,c_1 := n,k] \ \llbracket \{ k,m,n \} \rrbracket$
$X[chan_X := m]) \ \llbracket \{ k,m,n \} \rrbracket Z[chan_Z := n])[m,n := b_1,c_2]) \setminus \{ k \}$

$= Struct_{A'}$

Three conditional CSP laws are used in the above proof. The condition of Law $\llbracket cs \rrbracket -idem$ (Step 2) is clearly satisfied because the processes X and Z are obtained from the protocols X and Z, which, in Law 1, are assumed to be deterministic. The condition of Law $\llbracket cs \rrbracket -null$ (Step 4) is satisfied since the processes $Chart_B$, $X[chan_X := b'_1]$ and $Y[chan_Y := b_2]$ do not use the channel n; similarly, processes $Chart_C$, $Y[chan_Y := c_1]$ and $Z[chan_Z := c'_2]$ do not use m. The condition of Law $f[.] - \llbracket cs \rrbracket -dist$ (Step 3) is satisfied since following renamings used in the distribution are injective: $[b'_1,b_2 := m,k]$, $[c'_2,c_1 := n,k]$ and $[n,m := c_2,b_1]$

6   Conclusions

We have proposed a formal semantics for capsules, protocols, ports and connections in UML-RT, using *Circus* as a semantic domain. We considered an integrated view involving UML-RT class, state and structure diagrams. Also, we presented a transformation law for capsule decomposition that considers the effect on all these diagrams. Based on the semantic mapping, and on the semantics and laws of *Circus*, we have shown that it is relatively simple to prove such laws. As far as we are aware, an entirely formal approach to transformation of UML-RT models is an original contribution.

Although the target of our translation is a specification language (rather than a more standard mathematical model), the notation of *Circus* includes those of CSP and Z. Both are well-known and mature formalisms. Further, their combination into *Circus* is formally characterised with basis on the unifying theories of programming [20].

The basis for the translation given in this paper is a formalisation of the syntax of UML-RT in Z and in CSP. The formalisation of UML-RT structure diagrams is similar to [8], which formalises only this kind of diagram in CSP, and disregards other views and elements of the architecture, as statecharts and protocols. The work reported in [9] briefly presents some notions that could be used as a basis for a mapping from UML-RT into CSP, but based on these notions it seems rather difficult mapping complex systems in all its aspects without additional assumptions on the dynamic semantics. It briefly covers simple capsule statecharts, and does not give any additional contribution on the *capsule-connector-capsule* translation when compared to [8]. An informal translation of UML-RT to CSP-OZ is also reported in [7] through a case study. Despite the benefit of linking UML-RT to CSP-OZ and Java, the work in [7] does note seem concerned with the soundness of transformations for UML-RT, but rather with platform transformations between these languages. A more general contextualisation of our work has already been given in Section 1.

Currently, we are working on a comprehensive set of laws for UML-RT, exploring their use during the development of a more elaborate version of the example presented in Section 2. Our notion of completeness is based on showing that an arbitrary UML-RT model can be reduced to a UML model extended with a single capsule responsible for all the interactions with the environment. This extended UML model can be regarded as a normal form, and therefore relative completeness of our set of laws can be captured by normal form reduction, following an approach similar to [22].

In general, the laws involve classes and relationships between them as well as with capsules. The semantics of *OhCircus* [23] is being defined as a conservative extension of that of *Circus*, to address object-oriented features. We plan to extend our mapping to consider the full UML-RT notation, using *OhCircus* as semantic domain.

References

1. Object Management Group: OMG Unified Modeling Language Specification. (2003) OMG document formal/03-03-01.
2. Bruel, J.M., France, R., Larrondo-Petrie, M.: An integrated object-oriented and formal modeling environment. Journal of Object-Oriented Programming **10** (1997)

3. Ng, M.Y., Butler, M.J.: Towards Formalizing UML State Diagrams in CSP. In: 1st International Conference on Software Engineering and Formal Methods, IEEE Computer Society (2003)
4. Spivey, M.: The Z Notation: A Reference Manual. second edn. Prentice Hall (1992)
5. Roscoe, A.W.: The Theory and Practice of Concurrency. Prentice-Hall (1998)
6. Amalio, N., Polack, F.: Comparison of formalisation approaches of UML class constructs in Z and Object-Z. In: Third International Conference of B and Z. Volume 2651 of LNCS. (2003)
7. Möller, M., Olderog, E.R., Rasch, H., Wehrheim, H.: Linking CSP-OZ with UML and Java: A Case Study. In: 4th International Conference on Integrated Formal Methods. Volume 2999 of LNCS., Springer (2004)
8. Fischer, C., Olderog, E.R., Wehrheim, H.: A CSP View on UML-RT Structure Diagrams. In: Proceedings of the 4th International Conference on Fundamental Approaches to Software Engineering, Springer (2001)
9. Engels, G., Küster, J.M., Heckel, R., Groenewegen, L.: A methodology for specifying and analyzing consistency of object-oriented behavioral models. In: Proceedings of the 8th European Software engineering Conference, ACM Press (2001)
10. Selic, B., Rumbaugh, J.: Using UML for Modeling Complex RealTime Systems. Rational Software Corporation (1998) available at http://www. rational.com.
11. Engels, G., Heckel, R., Küster, J.M., Groenewegen, L.: Consistency-Preserving Model Evolution through Transformations. In: 5th International Conference on the Unified Modeling Language. Volume 2460 of LNCS., Springer (2002)
12. Sampaio, A., Woodcock, J., Cavalcanti, A.: Refinement in *Circus*. In: International Symposium of Formal Methods Europe. Volume 2391 of LNCS., Springer (2002)
13. Hoare, C.A.R., Jifeng, H.: Unifying Theories of Programming. Prentice-Hall (1998)
14. Fischer, C.: Combination and Implementation of Processes and Data: from CSP-OZ to Java. PhD thesis, Fachbereich Informatik Universität Oldenburg (2000)
15. Morgan, C.: Programming from Specifications. second edn. Prentice Hall (1994)
16. Sampaio, A., Mota, A., Ramos, R.: Class and Capsule Refinement in UML for Real Time. In: Proceedings of the Brazilian Workshop on Formal Methods. Volume 95 of ENTCS. (2004)
17. Object Management Group: OMG Adopted Specification. (2003) OMG documents ptc/03-09-15 and ptc/03-08-02.
18. Richters, M., Gogolla, M.: OCL: Syntax, Semantics, and Tools. In: Object Modeling with the OCL: The Rationale behind the Object Constraint Language. Springer (2002)
19. Selic, B.: An Efficient Object-Oriented Variation of the Statecharts Formalism for Distributed Real-Time Systems. In: 11th IFIP WG10.2 International Conference on Computer Hardware Description Languages and their Applications. Volume A-32 of IFIP Transactions. (1993)
20. Woodcock, J., Cavalcanti, A.: The Semantics of *Circus*. In: ZB 2002: Formal Specification and Development in Z and B. Volume 2272 of LNCS., Springer (2002)
21. Hoare, C.A.R.: Communicating Sequential Processes. Prentice-Hall (1985)
22. Borba, P., Sampaio, A., Cavalcanti, A., Cornélio, M.: Algebraic reasoning for object-oriented programming. Science of Computer Programming **52** (2004)
23. Cavalcanti, A., Sampaio, A., Woodcock, J.: A unified language of classes and processes. In: St Eve: State-Oriented vs. Event-Oriented Thinking in Requirements Analysis, Formal Specification and Software Engineering, Satellite Workshop at FM'03 (2003)

Towards an Integrated Formal Analysis for Security and Trust*

Fabio Martinelli

Istituto di Informatica e Telematica - C.N.R., Pisa, Italy
Fabio.Martinelli@iit.cnr.it

Abstract. We aim at defining an integrated framework for the specification and (automated) analysis for security and trust in complex and dynamic scenarios. In particular, we show how the same machinery used for the formal verification of security protocols may be used to analyze access control policies based on trust management.

1 Introduction

Computer security is a research area that is increasingly receiving the attention of researchers. In particular, consider some security issues in ubiquitous computing systems: these consist of different entities that have to cooperate and share resources to achieve a certain goal. Cooperation is often enabled by trust relationships between entities. There is a tight connection between the security mechanisms used to guarantee the confidentiality and integrity of information and mechanisms used to establish, manage and negotiate trust, reputation and recommendation among the different entities.

In this paper we focus on the integrated formal modeling and analysis of security and trust. In particular, we uniformly model security protocols and some form of access control based on trust management.

Formal languages for modeling distributed systems have been applied in the last decade to the analysis of cryptographic protocols. In this framework, cryptography is usually modeled by representing encryptions as terms of an algebra, e.g., $E(m, k)$ may represent the encryption of a message m with a key k. Usually, the so-called perfect encryption abstraction is adopted: encryptions are considered as injective functions which can be inverted only by knowing the correct information, i.e. the decryption key. For instance, common inference rules for modeling the behavior of the encryption and decryption (in a shared-key schema) are the followings:

$$\frac{m \quad k}{E(m, k)} \qquad \frac{E(m, k) \quad k}{m} \tag{1}$$

* Work partially supported by CNR project "Trusted e-services for dynamic coalitions" and by a CREATE-NET grant for the project "Quality of Protection (QoP)". A preliminary version appeared as [18].

M. Steffen and G. Zavattaro (Eds.): FMOODS 2005, LNCS 3535, pp. 115–130, 2005.

which should be read as: from a message m and a key k we can build the encryption $E(m, k)$; from an encryption $E(m, k)$ and a decryption key k we can obtain the encrypted message m.

The long standing tradition of modeling the specific features of cryptographic functions as term-rewriting rules met the powerful verification techniques developed for process algebras. As a matter of fact, several formal languages for describing communication protocols, for instance CSP [17], have been exploited for representing cryptographic protocols without changes in syntax or semantics: the inference rules have been given at the meta-level of the verification. Instead others, like the π–calculus [1] and the CCS [19, 21], have been effectively refined: the π–calculus have been equipped with two pattern matching constructs for modeling message splitting and shared-key decryption, respectively; the CCS has been equipped with an inference construct that permits to infer new messages from others, i.e.:

$$[m_1 \quad m_n \vdash_r x].P$$

which denotes a process that tries to deduce a message m from the messages in $m_1, \ldots, m_n$ and when it succeeds it substitutes this message for x in the process specification P. The language is called CryptoCCS ([19]).

The inference relation could be defined in many ways. Often, we will consider the transitive closure of the entailment relations used in each process. This would give a complex inference system. Such inference systems allow us to cope with the variety of different crypto-systems that can be found in the literature.

However, when one analyzes a security protocol, usually assumes that public keys, digital certificates, and generally speaking credentials are already given, and does not usually check how these are formated, negotiated and managed. Such a limited view seems not completely appropriate for dynamic, fully interconnected systems, where access control policies may change and typically may also depend on credentials presented by users.

Similarly, when one wishes to formally analyze (e.g., see [2]) access control systems, the authentication mechanisms (usually a security protocol) are considered a priori "secure", without further specification.

While separation of concerns is often desirable, this is not always possible. The interplay between security protocols and access control mechanisms/policies is crucial. Moreover, a good specification and analysis framework should take an holistic point of view.

As a matter of fact, we show that the idea proposed by CryptoCCS of using inference constructs is also useful to model access control mechanisms based on credentials in distributed systems.

Example 1. Indeed, consider a set of credentials, i.e. (signed) messages containing information about access rights. Assume that $\{A, ob_1, +\}_{pr(C)}$ means that the user C (via the signature with its private key $pr(C)$) asserts A has the right to access the object ob_1 and may grant this access to other users (this is denoted through the symbol $+$). A rule like:

$$\frac{\{A, ob_1, +\}_{pr(C)} \quad pr(C) \quad \{grant \quad B, ob_1\}_{pr(A)}}{\{B, ob_1, +\}_{pr(C)}} (acc_C)$$

may be used by the controller C to issue other access right credentials, after receiving an indication by A, i.e. the signed message $\{grant \quad B, ob_1\}_{pr(A)}$.

Thus, we may consider the inference rules as an abstract mechanism to express security policies usually defined using other mathematical models and logics (e.g., see [10, 24]).

In this paper, we deal with the RT trust management system [16]. However, our approach is very general. In particular, we will show also how to encode with inference systems the mechanisms for reasoning about trust proposed in [12] and modeled with different approaches.

Having a unique language will allow us to model the interplay between security protocols that use the trust relationships among different users, and the ways in which these relationships are created (that often rely on security/interaction protocols).

The fact that we can both model cryptography and some form of credential/trust management with the inference construct of CryptoCCS allows us to use the software tools and methodologies already developed for security protocols analysis to the more general case where credentials are explicitly managed. In particular, in [22] a software tool for automated security protocols analysis has been defined in [20] has been extended to cope with a huge class of inference systems.

It is worthy noticing that the CryptoCCS has been previously defined to set up a uniform framework for the analysis of security properties and information flow (non-interference) with the same machinery (e.g., see [5–7]). This helped us quite a lot in establishing a precise correspondence of properties of trust negotiation protocols with non-interference ones (as hinted in [28]).

To sum up, the main contribution of this paper is to present an effective framework, based on the flexibility of the CryptoCCS inference construct, for uniformly specifying and analyzing several aspects of network/system security and trust management.

There are few attempts to analyze security protocols and trust management altogether. A notable example is the recent work in [9]. There the trust is expressed at a meta-level by decorating protocol specifications with formulas of a trust logic and by ensuring that such formulas hold at certain points. Our approach is thus different and is based on modeling trust (in different flavors) inside the protocol specifications.

The paper is organized as follows. Section 2 presents the CryptoCCS language and recalls some of its analysis techniques. Section 3 shows how the CryptoCCS may be naturally used to model trust management languages. Section 4 investigates the relationships between notions of safety in Automated Trust Negotiation and non-interference. Section 5 concludes the paper.

2   CryptoCCS

CryptoCCS [19, 21] is a slight modification of CCS process algebra [23], adopted for the description of cryptographic protocols.

The CryptoCCS model consists of a set of sequential agents able to communicate by exchanging messages.

The data handling part of the language consists of a set of inference rules used to deduce messages from other messages. We consider a set of relations among messages as: $\vdash_r \subseteq \mathcal{M}^{i_r+1}$, where r is the name of the rule and i_r the number of premises. For the sake of simplicity, we assume that $\vdash_r$ (for each $r \in \mathcal{R}$) is decidable.

2.1   The Language Syntax

CryptoCCS syntax is based on the following elements:

- A set Ch of channels, partitioned into a set I of input channels (ranged over by c) and a set O of output channels (ranged over by $\bar{c}$, the output corresponding to the input c);
- A set Var of variables, ranged over by x;
- A set $\mathcal{M}$ of messages, defined over a certain signature, ranged over by M, N, m, n ....

The set $\mathcal{L}$ of CryptoCCS terms (or processes) is defined as follows:

$$P, Q ::= \mathbf{0} \mid c(x).P \mid \bar{c}M.P \mid \tau.P \mid P \mid Q \mid P\backslash L \mid$$

$$A(M_1, \ldots, M_n) \mid [\langle M_1, \ldots, M_r \rangle \vdash_{rule} x]P; Q$$

where $M, M', M_1, \ldots, M_r$ are messages or variables and L is a set of channels. Both the operators $c(x).P$ and $[\langle M_1 \ldots M_r \rangle \vdash_{rule} x]P; Q$ bind variable x in P.

We assume the usual conditions about *closed* and *guarded* processes, as in [23]. We call $\mathcal{P}$ the set of all the *CryptoCCS* closed and guarded terms. The set of actions is $Act = \{c(M) \mid c \in I\} \cup \{\bar{c}M \mid \bar{c} \in O\} \cup \{\tau\}$ (τ is the internal, invisible action), ranged over by a. We define $sort(P)$ to be the set of all the channels syntactically occurring in the term P. Moreover, for the sake of readability, we always omit the termination $\mathbf{0}$ at the end of process specifications, e.g. we write a in place of $a.\mathbf{0}$. We give an informal overview of *CryptoCCS* operators:

- $\mathbf{0}$ is a process that does nothing.
- $c(x).P$ represents the process that can get an input M on channel c behaving like $P[M/x]$).
- $\bar{c}M.P$ is the process that can send m on channel c, and then behaves like P.
- $\tau.P$ is the process that executes the invisible τ and then behaves like P.
- $P_1 \mid P_2$ *(parallel)* is the parallel composition of processes that can proceed in an asynchronous way but they must synchronize on complementary actions to make a communication, represented by a τ.
- $P\backslash L$ is the process that cannot send and receive messages on channels in L; for all the other channels, it behaves exactly like P;
- $A(M_1, \ldots, M_n)$ behaves like the respective defining term P where all the variables $x_1, \ldots, x_n$ are replaced by the messages $M_1, \ldots, M_n$;

$$\frac{m \quad m'}{(m,m')}(\vdash_{pair}) \qquad \frac{(m,m')}{m}(\vdash_{fst}) \qquad \frac{(m,m')}{m'}(\vdash_{snd})$$

$$\frac{m \quad k}{\{m\}_k}(\vdash_{enc}) \qquad \frac{\{m\}_k \quad k}{m}(\vdash_{dec})$$

Fig. 1. An example inference system for shared key cryptography.

– $[\langle M_1, \ldots, M_r \rangle \vdash_{rule} x]P; Q$ is the process used to model message manipulation as cryptographic operations. Indeed, the process $[\langle M_1, \ldots, M_r \rangle \vdash_{rule} x]P; Q$ tries to deduce an information z from the tuple $\langle M_1, \ldots, M_r \rangle$ through the application of rule $\vdash_{rule}$; if it succeeds then it behaves like $P[z/x]$, otherwise it behaves as Q. The set of rules that can be applied is defined through an inference system (e.g., see Figure 1 for an instance).

2.2 The Operational Semantics of CryptoCCS

In order to model message handling (and so cryptography in an abstract way) we use a set of inference rules. Note that *CryptoCCS* syntax, its semantics and the results obtained are completely parametric with respect to the inference system used. We present in Figure 1 an instance inference system, with rules: to combine two messages obtaining a pair (rule $\vdash_{pair}$); to extract one message from a pair (rules $\vdash_{fst}$ and $\vdash_{snd}$); to encrypt a message m with a key k obtaining $\{m\}_k$ and, finally, to decrypt a message of the form $\{m\}_k$ only if it has the same key k (rules $\vdash_{enc}$ and $\vdash_{dec}$, respectively).

In a similar way, inference systems can contain rules for handling the basic arithmetic operations and boolean relations among numbers, so that the value-passing CCS **if-then-else** construct can be obtained via the $\vdash_{rule}$ operator.

Example 2. Natural numbers may be encoded by assuming a single value 0 and a function $S(y)$, with the following rule: $\frac{x}{S(x)}$ *inc*. Similarly, we can define summations and other operations on natural numbers.   ∎

Example 3. We do not explicitly define equality check among messages in the syntax. However, this can be implemented through the usage of the inference construct. E.g., consider rule $\frac{x \quad x}{Equal(x,x)}$ *equal*. Then $[m = m']A$ (with the expected semantics) may be equivalently expressed as $[m \quad m' \vdash_{equal} y]A$ where y does not occur in A. Similarly, we can define inequalities, e.g., $\leq$, among natural numbers.   ∎

The operational semantics of a *CryptoCCS* term is described by means of labeled transition relations, $P \xrightarrow{a} P'$, with the informal meaning that the process P may perform an action a evolving in the process P'. More formally, we consider a *labelled transition system* (*lts*, for short) $\langle \mathcal{P}, Act, \{\xrightarrow{a}\}_{a \in Act} \rangle$, where

$$(input)\frac{m \in \mathcal{M}}{c(x).P \xrightarrow{c(m)} P[m/x]} \qquad (output)\frac{}{\overline{c}m.P \xrightarrow{\overline{c}m} P} \qquad (internal)\frac{}{\tau.P \xrightarrow{\tau} P}$$

$$(\backslash L)\frac{P \xrightarrow{c(m)} P' \quad c \notin L}{P\backslash L \xrightarrow{c(m)} P'\backslash L} \qquad (|)_1\frac{P_1 \xrightarrow{a} P_1'}{P_1 \mid P_2 \xrightarrow{a} P_1' \mid P_2} \qquad (|)_2\frac{P_1 \xrightarrow{c(x)} P_1' \quad P_2 \xrightarrow{\overline{c}m} P_2'}{P_1 \mid P_2 \xrightarrow{\tau} P_1' \mid P_2'}$$

$$(Def)\frac{P[m_1/x_1,\ldots,m_n/x_n] \xrightarrow{a} P' \quad A(x_1,\ldots,x_n) \doteq P}{A(m_1,\ldots,m_n) \xrightarrow{a} P'}$$

$$(\mathcal{D})\frac{\langle m_1,\ldots,m_r \rangle \vdash_{rule} m \quad P[m/x] \xrightarrow{a} P'}{[\langle m_1,\ldots,m_r \rangle \vdash_{rule} x]P;Q \xrightarrow{a} P'}$$

$$(\mathcal{D}_1)\frac{\not\exists m \text{ s.t. } \langle m_1,\ldots,m_r \rangle \vdash_{rule} m \quad Q \xrightarrow{a} Q'}{[\langle m_1,\ldots,m_r \rangle \vdash_{rule} x]P;Q \xrightarrow{a} Q'}$$

Fig. 2. Structured Operational Semantics for CryptoCCS (symmetric rules for $|_1, |_2$ and $\backslash L$ are omitted).

$\{\xrightarrow{a}\}_{a \in Act}$ is the least relation between $CryptoCCS$ processes induced by the axioms and inference rules of Figure 2. The expression $P \stackrel{a}{\Rightarrow} P'$ is a shorthand for $P(\xrightarrow{\tau})^* P_1 \xrightarrow{a} P_2(\xrightarrow{\tau})^* P'$ where $(\xrightarrow{\tau})^*$ denotes a (possibly empty) sequence of transitions labeled τ. The expression $P \Rightarrow P'$ is a shorthand for $P(\xrightarrow{\tau})^* P'$.

2.3   Security Protocol Analysis

The security protocol analysis proposed in [19, 21] is based on the checking of following property:

$$\forall X \text{ s.t. } S \mid X \text{ satisfies } F$$

where F is a logical formula expressing the desired property. Often, when secrecy properties are considered, F models the fact that a given message, i.e. the secret to be verified, is not deducible from a given set of messages, i.e. the knowledge of the intruder X acquired during the computation with S. The verification of such property requires the ability of computing the closure of a inference systems, i.e. the possibility to iteratively apply the inference rules. Given a set $\mathcal{R}$ of inference rules, we consider the deduction relation $\mathcal{D}^{\mathcal{R}} \subseteq \mathcal{P}^{fin}(\mathcal{M}) \times \mathcal{M}$. Given a finite set of closed messages, say ϕ, then $(\phi, M) \in \mathcal{D}^{\mathcal{R}}$ if M can be derived by iteratively applying the rules in $\mathcal{R}$. Under certain sets of assumptions on the form of the rules, we may have that $\mathcal{D}^{\mathcal{R}}(\phi)$ is decidable. Below, we present an example useful in our case (e.g., see also [20]).

2.4   Some Assumptions on the Inference System

Given a well-founded measure on messages, we say that a rule

$$r \doteq \frac{m_1 \quad \cdots \quad m_n}{m_0}$$

is a S-rule (*shrinking* rule), whenever the conclusion is a proper subterm of one of the premises (call such premise *main*). The rule r is a G-rule (*growing* rule) whenever the conclusion is strictly larger than each of the premises, and all the variables in the conclusion must be in the premises.

Definition 1. *We say that an inference system enjoys a G/S property if it consists only of G-rules and S-rules, moreover whenever a message can be deduced through a S-rule, where one of the main premises is derived by means of a G-rule, then the same message may be deduced from the premises of the G-rule, by using only G-rules.*

Several of the inference systems used in the literature for describing cryptographic systems enjoy this restriction[1].

Indeed, using G-rules for inferring the main premises of an S-rules, is unuseful. Thus, shrinking rules may be significantly applied only to messages in ϕ and to messages obtained by S-rules. However, since the measure for classifying the S-rules is well-founded then such a shrinking phase would eventually terminate when applied to a closed set of messages ϕ. Then, only growing rules are possible. Thus, if the inference system enjoys the G/S restriction then $\mathcal{D}^R(\phi)$ is decidable when ϕ is finite. We may note that the inference system in page 1 enjoys the G/S restriction and so its deduction relation is indeed decidable.

In the case the inference system has no growing rules, we have decidability even in the presence of a weaker form of *shrinking rules*. We say that a rule is *eq-shrink* whenever the conclusion has an equal or smaller size than one of the premises; moreover all the variables occurring in the conclusion must occur in at least one of the premises. In such a case the decision procedure simply consists of building the transitive closure of the inference rules.

3   Modeling Several Trust Management Languages

Through process algebras, one can formally specify communicating protocols and complex distributed systems. For instance, one could use CryptoCCS to describe the components and the communication interface of an access control mechanism as the Policy Enforcement Point (PEP), the Policy Decision Point (PDP) and the resource to be protected (see [26]).

In Figure 3 we may see the components of a common access control framework. A request is performed by the user to the PEP. The PEP often applies a communication with the user, often performing an authentication protocol. Then, using the information acquired by PEP is sent to the PDP. Eventually the access is granted to the resource.

In particular, in trust management systems, where policies are given through credentials, this allow one to use the inference system of CryptoCCS to model also the trust engine used in these frameworks. Let us see how it works with two well known models.

---

[1] It is worthy noticing that in [13] a similar terminology has been used, and a restriction, called S/G, has been defined. However, this is rather different from ours and it is not well suited to model cryptographic systems.

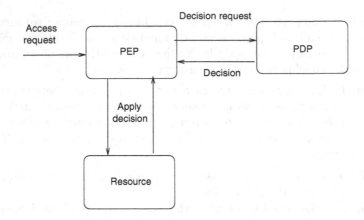

Fig. 3. An access control system.

3.1 RT_0: Role-Based Trust Management

We show how inference rules can be conveniently used to model RT languages for trust management [14–16, 28]. In these languages, credentials carry information on policies to define attributes of principals by starting from assertions of other principals. The notion of attribute is general enough to permit to use RT languages to model Role-based Access Control Mechanisms (RBAC), e.g. see [25]. As a matter of fact, an attribute could be considered as a role. Then one could use RT credential to express how principals are related to roles[2]. More precisely, we denote principals with $A, B, C...$; we denote role names with $r, u, z....$ A role takes the form of a principal followed by a role name, separated by a dot, e.g. $A.r$.

RT assumes four kind of credentials that express possible policy statements.

- $A.r \leftarrow D$ (**simple member**)
  This statement defines that D has role $A.r$.
- $A.r \leftarrow A_1.r_1$ (**simple containment**)
  This statement asserts that if D has role $A_1.r_1$ then it has role $A.r$. This kind of credential can be used to delegate the authentication of attributes from A to A_1.
- $A.r \leftarrow A_1.r_1.r_2$ (**linking containment**)
  This statement asserts that E has role $A_1.r_1$ and D has role $E.r_2$ then D has role $A.r$. This kind of credential may be used to delegate the assignment of $A.r$ role not to specific entities but to entities of a given role.
- $A.r \leftarrow A_1.r_1 \cap A_2.r_2$ (**Intersection containment**)
  This statement asserts that D has role $A_1.r_1$ and $A_2.r_2$ then D has role $A.r$.

Example 4. Consider the following set of credentials.

$$Univ.stud \leftarrow FM$$
$$Shop.discount \leftarrow Univ.stud$$

---

[2] Similarly, credentials and attributes could be used to assign permissions to roles

It follows that FM has role $Shop.discount$. So, the shop offers discounts to the students of the University.

The language for credentials has been equipped with several semantics. In particular, one semantics based on datalog is very similar to our inference rules (that in this case can be seen as datalog rules). So, we define one inference rule for each credential as follows.

$$A.r \leftarrow D \qquad \{D, r\}_A$$

$$A.r \leftarrow A_1.r_1 \qquad \frac{\{y, r_1\}_A}{\{y, r\}_A}$$

$$A.r \leftarrow A_1.r_1.r_2 \qquad \frac{\{z, r_1\}_{A_1} \quad \{y, r_2\}_z}{\{y, r\}_A}$$

$$A.r \leftarrow A_1.r_1 \cap A_2.r_2 \qquad \frac{\{y, r_1\}_{A_1} \quad \{y, r_2\}_{A_2}}{\{y, r\}_A}$$

However, this requires a rule for each credential. We wish to fix from the very beginning the set of inference rules. Thus, we provide a slightly modified version of the inference system where we consider only 3 rules, one for each kind of credential defined in RT_0 (with the exception of the first kind of credentials that are simply messages).

$$A.r \leftarrow D \qquad \{D, r\}_A$$

$$A.r \leftarrow A_1.r_1 \qquad \frac{\{y, r_1\}_A \quad \{r, A_1, r_1\}_A}{\{y, r\}_A}$$

$$A.r \leftarrow A_1.r_1.r_2 \qquad \frac{\{z, r_1\}_{A_1} \quad \{y, r_2\}_z \quad \{r, A_1, r_1, r_2\}_A}{\{y, r\}_A}$$

$$A.r \leftarrow A_1.r_1 \cap A_2.r_2 \qquad \frac{\{y, r_1\}_{A_1} \quad \{y, r_2\}_{A_2} \quad \{r, A_1, A_2, r_1, r_2\}_A}{\{y, r\}_A}$$

Note that, under the common measure of the size of terms, all the previous rules are *eq-shrink* rules and there are no *growing* rules. Thus, establishing whether a given principal, say D, has a certain role in a policy ϕ, i.e. $\{D, r\}_A \in \mathcal{D}(\phi)$ is decidable. This kind of analysis[3] is called *Simple Safety* in [14] and can be performed by our analysis tool PaMoChSA [22].

3.2   Josang *et al.* Topologies

We also show how the trust model of Josang *et al.* [12] can be managed in our framework. The authors suggest trust is always linked to a purpose. The most natural situation is when one trusts another for performing a certain function/task. This may be expressed as $A \xrightarrow{f} D$, i.e. A trusts D for performing f. Moreover, it is often common that one, say A, asks another, say D, for suggesting/reccomendating a third one for doing a given task, i.e. f. This could be expressed by the following credential $A \xrightarrow{r, f} D$.

---

[3] Actually, that work considers a dynamic set of policies. However, the analysis technique adopted is actually based on a subset of the set of prolog rules that represent the initial problem. Thus, we are also able to manage it.

The main idea is that when one calculates whether a given chain trust exists, it must always consider that the last step in the chain is a functional trust one, while all the others are recommendation steps. Thus, we have another kind of credential like $A \xrightarrow{r} B \xrightarrow{f} D$, , expressing the fact that A trusts D for performing f via the recommendation of B.

$$A \xrightarrow{f} D \qquad\qquad \{f,D\}_A$$

$$A \xrightarrow{r,f} D \qquad\qquad \{r,D,f\}_A$$

$$\frac{A \xrightarrow{r,f} B \quad B \xrightarrow{r,f} D}{A \xrightarrow{r,f} D} \quad \frac{\{r,B,f\}_A \quad \{r,D,f\}_B}{\{r,D,f\}_A}$$

$$\frac{A \xrightarrow{r,f} B \quad B \xrightarrow{f} D}{A \xrightarrow{r} B \xrightarrow{f} D} \quad \frac{\{r,B,f\}_A \quad \{f,D\}_B}{\{r,B,f,D\}_A}$$

As in the previous case, the deduction relation of this set of rules is decidable. This gives us an alternative strategy w.r.t. the one presented in [12].

As in [12], one could insert further information into the credentials, as measure of trust. For instance, credentials could be enhanced with such information and rules could derived the trust measure of resulting credentials in the appropriate way. For instance, consider the following credential enhanced with a trust measure, i.e.: $A \xrightarrow{r,f,m} B$. Then the transitive composition rule could be the following:

$$\frac{A \xrightarrow{r,f,m_1} B \quad B \xrightarrow{r,f,m_2} D}{A \xrightarrow{r,f,m_3} D}$$

where m_3 is a function of m_1, m_2, for instance $m_3 = min\{m_1, m_2\}$.

If the set of possible trust values is finite, then the deduction relation is still decidable. More complex trust measures can be found in [11]. Clearly, one may try to define specific strategies for each set of inference rules in order to obtain decidability. However, we argue that the mechanisms we proposed are general enough to deal with common trust management systems.

4   An Application to Automated Trust Negotiation Problems

The usage of credentials for policy decision is useful, but as mentioned before is not the unique part of access control. When one user (i.e., a *requester*) tries to access to a resource controlled by another entity (i.e., *access mediator*) there could be a trust establishment phase where the two entities exchange some credentials in several steps. As a matter of fact, the requester could not know exactly which kind of credential to present. Then, the access mediator could try to help him by prompting the access control policy for its resource. Some user's attributes stated in the credentials used for the negotiation phase could be sensible. Thus, specific procedures for controlling the disclosure of such credentials have been designed. Credentials are managed like resources to be protected, and have their own access (disclosure) control policies. This applies to both the requester and the access mediator. This aspect of trust management is an active topic of investigation and is called in the literature Automated trust negotiation (ATN, for short), e.g. see [3, 27–29].

Since ATN actually deals with protocols for exchanging credentials, it seems natural that it should be modeled in our framework. This has a very nice consequence to make it formal the intuition expressed in [28] that some properties of ATN resemble non-interference ones. We exactly identify a notion that is very good for describing properties of ATN.

We briefly present a slightly simplified version of the theory developed in [28].

A participant in a trust negotiation protocol is described through a finite configuration $G = \langle K_G, E, Policy_G, Ack_G \rangle$, where:

- K_G is the public key of the participant (i.e., the participant knows the corresponding private key);
- E is a set of credentials, where we assume that the subject of each credential is K_G;
- $Policy_G$ is a table where to each entry corresponds a positive propositional logic formula expressing a disclosure policy for attributes (such a logic may be easily modeled through a suitable inference system);
- Ack_G is a partial function mapping attributes to an entry in $Policy_G$. Basically, a credential proving an attribute may be disclosed only if the attributes presented by the other participants satisfy the corresponding (ack-)policy.

The goal is to protect attributes rather than credentials where these attributes are stated (see [28] for a deeper discussion).

A negotiation starts when the requester sends a request to the access mediator and continues by exchanging of messages. Each participant has a local state that keeps track of the negotiation steps. We have two special states: *failure, success*. The negotiation process fails when one of the two participants enters into the failure state. The negotiation process succeeds when the access mediator enters into the success state.

A negotiation strategy *strat* describes the behavior of each negotiator (in contrast to [28] we do not assume it is deterministic).

- $strat.rstart(G, K_O)$ is used by the requester just after the sending of the access request to the access mediator; it returns the requester's initial local state;
- $strat.start(G, pid, K_O)$ is used to respond to the first message from the requester; the access mediator checks the policy associated with the resource (identified by pid) and then determines the next local state and message to be sent to the requester. (The negotiation proceeds only if the state is different from *success* and *failure*.)
- $strat.respond(G, st, msg)$ is used to respond to a message from the other negotiator; it returns the new local state and the next message to be sent. (The negotiation proceeds only if the state is different from *success* and *failure*.)

Using CryptoCCS, we may model the negotiation steps performed by a negotiator starting in a configuration G and using a strategy $strat$ through a term of the process algebra. Note that states simply record the execution history of a negotiation (and the initial request). Thus, by recording the messages received and sent, one may avoid the usage of states. Moreover, note that having in the term algebra a constructor for pairs one may express sequences of messages using a single one. We assume to have two special messages used to encode the success and failure states, and an inference system $\vdash_{G,strat}$ that suitably mimics $strat$ strategy. Eventually, the definition of the term corresponding, for instance, to the requester is as follows:

$$A_{G,rstart} = \overline{c}(resource). \qquad\qquad \text{outpus the resource requests}$$
$$A_{G,respond}(resource, nil) \text{ proceeds to the respond phase}$$

$$
\begin{aligned}
A_{G,respond}(s, r) = c(y). &\qquad\qquad \text{receives the message}\\
[r \quad y \vdash_{pair} r_1] &\qquad\qquad \text{added to received ones}\\
[s \quad z \vdash_{G,strat} x] &\qquad\qquad \text{next message}\\
[x = success]A_{G,success}; (&\qquad\qquad \text{success}\\
[x = failure]A_{G,failure}; (&\qquad\qquad \text{failure}\\
\overline{c}(x). &\qquad\qquad \text{outputs next message}\\
[s \quad x \vdash_{pair} s_1] &\qquad\qquad \text{added to sent ones}\\
A_{G,respond}(s_1, r_1) &\qquad\qquad \text{continues the negotiation}\\
))&
\end{aligned}
$$

In [28] there is an interesting discussion about the privacy issues in ATN. This is out of the scope of this paper. We are simply interested in presenting the main notion of privacy preserving negotiation defined in that paper, i.e., credential-combination-hiding[4].

Roughly, no adversary, using observations it can make during the negotiation phase with the other participant, may infer something about credentials proving attributes it is not entitled to know (i.e., it does not satisfy the appropriate disclosure policies).

We give below a variant of the notion of indistinguishability for non-deterministic strategies originally presented in [28].

Definition 2. *(Indistinguishability) Given an adversary M and a negotiation strategy strat, two configurations $G = \langle K, E, Policy, Ack \rangle$, $G' = \langle K, E', Policy, Ack \rangle$ are indistinguishable under strat by M, if and only if for every attack sequence seq, any possible response sequence induced by seq from G is among the ones induced by seq on G'.*

Clearly, this definition depends on the notion of attack sequence and response. A consequence of using our formalism equipped with a precise operational semantics and an abstract model of cryptography is that these notions come for

---

[4] Note also we are not advocating this property; we simply show how it is possible to relate it to a specific notion of non-interference.

free. (For instance, in [28] a notion of computationally feasible is referred while dealing with cryptography forgery, without mentioning the difficulties on managing it in an automated manner.)

Then, one identifies the set of credentials that can be safely disclosed without revealing information about attributes the adversary M is not entitled to know (i.e., it cannot present the necessary credentials during the negotiation phase). Call this set $Rel_{G,M}$. Then, an adversary should not be able to tell apart two configurations that are equal but for the set of credentials not in the Rel set. Note that here we do not consider the strategy that will be used by M but simply the set of credentials it has at the beginning of the computation (called usually initial knowledge in security protocol analysis, e.g. see [7]).

Definition 3. *(Credential-combination hiding safe) A negotiation strategy strat is* credential-combination hiding safe *if for every pair of configurations* $G = \langle K, E, Policy, Ack \rangle$ *and* $G' = \langle K, E', Policy, Ack \rangle$, *and adversary* M *with* $Rel_{G,M} = Rel_{G',M}$ *then* G *and* G' *are indistinguishable.*

4.1   ATN Properties as Non-interference Properties

To solve the problem of preventing unauthorized information flows, be they direct or indirect, in the last two decades many proposals have been presented, starting from the seminal idea of *non interference* proposed in [8] for deterministic functions. In [4–7], many non interference-like notions in the literature have been uniformly defined in a common process algebraic setting based on CryptoCCS, producing one of the first taxonomies of these properties reported in the literature.

We recall here a notion of secrecy about security protocols defined by Abadi and Gordon [1].

Basically, a protocol $S(x)$ keeps secret the variable x iff for any message M, M' there is no attacker able to tell apart $S(M)$ from $S(M')$. This secrecy property has been nicely modeled by exploiting an equivalence notion, called testing equivalence.

May-Testing Equivalence states that two processes cannot be distinguished by any process (tester). In our framework, it is possible to formally impose the fact that the tester is not able to break cryptography and so to forge credentials.

Consider a special action ω available only to testers. We say that two processes P and Q are may testing equivalent iff for any tester T, $P \,|\, T \stackrel{\omega}{\Longrightarrow} P'$ iff $Q \,|\, T \stackrel{\omega}{\Longrightarrow} Q'$. Basically, the tester plays the role of the adversary. Thus the notion of indistinguishability is similar to the notion of testing equivalence, when one considers as testers only the ones with any credentials able to infer a fixed set of attributes. Eventually, one configuration G and one configuration G' that have the same Rel set and differ on the credentials that cannot be released, may be analyzed by using with a single process $A_{G,Rel}(y)$ that has as parameter y the set of credentials that cannot be disclosed. Thus, this amounts to check whether or not $A_{G,Rel}$ keeps secret such credentials (again we assume that a set of messages may be encoded as a single one).

Probabilistic notions of this property may be easily given by using suitable modifications of the process algebra and of the corresponding may testing equivalence.

5   Conclusions and Future Work

We have shown how the same machinery used for the formal specification and verification of security protocols may be used to analyze a variety of access control approaches based on trust management. In addition, in [5, 7, 21] CryptoCCS has been proposed as a uniform specification and verification framework for security protocols properties and non-interference ones, usually managed with different techniques. This made it very natural for us to model automated trust negotiation problems as proposed in [28] as non-interference ones.

The approach presented in this paper may be considered as a step towards the creation of a uniform and automated verification framework for studying security properties of networked systems. As future work we wish to extend our analysis tool called PaMoChSA [22] to fully support our approach. Moreover, we wish to investigate more deeply the relationships of non-interference with ATN properties.

Acknowledgments

We would like to thank the anonymous reviewers for their helpful comments.

References

1. M. Abadi and A. D. Gordon. A calculus for cryptographic protocols: The spi calculus. *Information and Computation*, 148(1):1–70, 1999.
2. P. A. Bonatti and P. Samarati. Logics for authorizations and security. In *Logics for Emerging Applications of Databases*, LNCS. Springer-Verlag, 2003.
3. R. Dingledine and P. F. Syverson, editors. *Privacy Enhancing Technologies, Second International Workshop, PET 2002, San Francisco, CA, USA, April 14-15, 2002, Revised Papers*, volume 2482 of *Lecture Notes in Computer Science*. Springer, 2003.
4. R. Focardi and R. Gorrieri. Classification of security properties (part i: Information flow). In *Foundations of Security Analysis and Design*, volume 2171 of *Lecture Notes in Computer Science*, pages 331–396, 2001.
5. R. Focardi, R. Gorrieri, and F. Martinelli. Non interference for the analysis of cryptographic protocols. In *Proceedings of 27th International Colloquium in Automata, Languages and Programming*, volume 1853 of *Lectures Notes in Computer Science*, pages 354–372, 2000.
6. R. Focardi, R. Gorrieri, and F. Martinelli. Classification of security properties – Part II: Network security. In *FOSAD school Lectures*, volume 2946 of *LNCS*. Springer-Verlag, 2004.
7. R. Focardi and F. Martinelli. A uniform approach for the definition of security properties. In *Proceedings of World Congress on Formal Methods (FM'99)*, volume 1708 of *Lecture Notes in Computer Science*, pages 794–813, 1999.

8. J. A. Goguen and J. Meseguer. Security policy and security models. In *Proceedings of the 1982 Symposium on Security and Privacy*, pages 11–20. IEEE Computer Society Press, 1982.

9. J. D. Guttman, F. J. Thayer, J. A. Carlson, J. C. Herzog, J. D. Ramsdell, and B. T. Sniffen. Trust management in strand spaces: A rely-gurantee method. In *Proceedings of the European Symposium on Programming (ESOP)*, LNCS, 2004.

10. Halpern and van der Meyden. A logic for SDSI's linked local name spaces. In *PCSFW: Proceedings of The 12th Computer Security Foundations Workshop*. IEEE Computer Society Press, 1999.

11. A. Josang. The consensus operator for combining beliefs. *Artif. Intell.*, 141(1):157–170, 2002.

12. A. Josang, E. Gray, and M. Kinateder. Analysing topologies of transitive trust. In *Proc. of the 1st workshop on Formal Aspects in Security and Trust (FAST2003)*, 2003.

13. D. Kindred and J. M. Wing. Fast, automatic checking of security protocols. In *Second USENIX Workshop on Electronic Commerce*, pages 41–52, Oakland, California, 1996.

14. N. Li, J. Mitchell, and W. H. Winsborough. Beyond proof-of-compliance: Safety and availability analysis in trust management. In *IEEE Symposium on Research in Security and Privacy*. 2003.

15. N. Li and M. V. Tripunitara. Security analysis in role-based access control. In *ACM Symposium on Access Control Models and Techniques (SACMAT 2004)*. 2004.

16. N. Li, W. H. Winsborough, and J. C. Mitchell. Distributed credential chain discovery in trust management. *Journal of Computer Security*, 1:35–86, 2003.

17. G. Lowe. Breaking and fixing the Needham Schroeder public-key protocol using FDR. In *Proceedings of Tools and Algorithms for the Construction and the Analisys of Systems*, volume 1055 of *Lecture Notes in Computer Science*, pages 147–166. Springer Verlag, 1996.

18. F. Martinelli. Towards a uniform framework for the formal analysis for security and trust. Technical Report IIT, 2004. A position paper has been presented at 2nd Workshop on Ubiquitious Networking (Cambridge, UK-Ubinet 2004).

19. F. Martinelli. Languages for description and analysis of authentication protocols. In P. Degano and U. Vaccaro, editors, *Proceedings of 6th Italian Conference on Theoretical Computer Science*, pages 304–315. World Scientific, 1998.

20. F. Martinelli. Symbolic semantics and analysis for crypto-ccs with (almost) generic inference systems. In *Proceedings of the 27th international Symposium in Mathematical Foundations of Computer Sciences(MFCS'02)*, volume 2420 of *LNCS*, pages 519–531, 2002.

21. F. Martinelli. Analysis of security protocols as *open* systems. *Theoretical Computer Science*, 290(1):1057–1106, 2003.

22. F. Martinelli, M. Petrocchi, and A. Vaccarelli. PaMoChSA: A tool for verification of security protocols based on partial model checking. 2001. Tool Demo at the 1st International School on Formal Methods for the Design of Computer, Communication and Software Systems: Process Algebras.

23. R. Milner. *Communication and Concurrency*. International Series in Computer Science. Prentice Hall, 1989.

24. P. Samarati and S. D. C. di Vimercati. Access control: Policies, models, and mechanisms. In R. Focardi and R. Gorrieri, editors, *Foundations of Security Analysis and Design*, LNCS 2171. Springer-Verlag, 2001.

25. R. Sandhu, V. Bhamidipati, E. Coyne, S. Ganta, and C. Youman. The arbac97 model for role-based administration of roles: preliminary description and outline. In *Proceedings of the second ACM workshop on Role-based access control*, pages 41–50. ACM Press, 1997.
26. J. Vollbrecht, P. Calhoun, S. Farrell, L. Gommans, G. Gross, B. de Bruijn, B. C. de Laat, M. Holdrege, and D. Spence. RFC 2904 AAA authorization framework. 2000.
27. W. H. Winsborough and N. Li. Towards practical automated trust negotiation. In *IEEE 3rd Intl. Workshop on Policies for Distributed Systems and Networks (Policy)*, 2002.
28. W. H. Winsborough and N. Li. Safety in automated trust negotiation. In *IEEE Symposium on Security and Privacy*. 2004.
29. M. Winslett. An introduction to automated trust negotiation. In *Workshop on Credential-Based Access Control Dortmund, October 2002*.

A Formal Security Analysis
of an OSA/Parlay Authentication Interface

Ricardo Corin[1], Gaetano Di Caprio[3], Sandro Etalle[1], Stefania Gnesi[2],
Gabriele Lenzini[1,4], and Corrado Moiso[3]

[1] Department of Computer Science, University of Twente
7500 AE Enschede, The Netherlands
{corin,etalle,lenzinig}@cs.utwente.nl
[2] Istituto di Scienza e Tecnologie dell'Informazione, ISTI-CNR
Area della Ricerca di Pisa, Via G. Moruzzi 1, 56124 Pisa, Italy
gnesi@isti.cnr.it
[3] Telecom Italia Lab
Via G. Reiss Romolo 274, 1048 Torino, Italy
{gaetano.dicaprio,corrado.moiso}@tlab.com
[4] Istituto di Informatica e Telematica, IIT-CNR
Area della Ricerca di Pisa, Via G. Moruzzi 1, 56124 Pisa, Italy
gabriele.lenzini@iit.cnr.it

Abstract. We report on an experience in analyzing the security of the
Trust and Security Management (TSM) protocol, an authentication procedure within the OSA/Parlay Application Program Interfaces (APIs)
of the Open Service Access and Parlay Group. The experience has been
conducted jointly by research institutes experienced in security and industry experts in telecommunication networking. OSA/Parlay APIs are
designed to enable the creation of telecommunication applications outside the traditional network space and business model. Network operators consider the OSA/Parlay a promising architecture to stimulate the
development of web service applications by third party providers, which
may not necessarily be experts in telecommunication and security. The
TSM protocol is executed by the gateways to OSA/Parlay networks; its
role is to authenticate client applications trying to access the interfaces of
some object representing an offered network capability. For this reason,
potential security flaws in the TSM authentication strategy can cause
the unauthorized use of the network, with evident damages to the operator and the quality of services. We report a rigorous formal analysis of
the TSM specification, which is originally given in UML. Furthermore,
we illustrate our design choices to obtain the formal model, describe the
tool-aided verification and finally expose the security flaws discovered.

Keywords: Formal Verification of Security, OSA/Parlay API, Industrial
Test Case.

1 Introduction

OSA/Parlay[1] Application Program Interfaces (APIs) [9] are designed for an easy
interaction between traditional IT applications and telecommunication networks.

---

[1] See http://www.parlay.org

M. Steffen and G. Zavattaro (Eds.): FMOODS 2005, LNCS 3535, pp. 131–146, 2005.
© IFIP International Federation for Information Processing 2005

OSA/Parlay APIs are abstract building blocks of network capabilities that developers, not necessarily expert in telecommunications but perhaps with more expertise in the enterprise market, can quickly comprehend and use to generate new applications. Concisely, OSA/Parlay APIs proposes an attractive framework where programmers can develop innovative resources or design new services.

An example of such a service is the retrieval and purchase of goods via a mobile phone. The service could be provided by a third party, different from the mobile operator. In this case, the provider could develop the service by assembling components that control network capabilities and functions, for example, sending/receiving a SMS. These components (in particular, their APIs) are provided by the telecom's operator. For example, the sending/receiving of a SMS could be realized in the following SOAP body that, in XML notation where namespace and encoding descriptors are omitted, appears as follows:

```
<sendSMS>
  <dest_address>
    tel:1234567
  </dest_address>
  <send_address>
    tel:0123456
  </send_address>
  <message>
    Could you please reserve
    two seats for 9 o'clock?
  </message>
</sendSMS>
```

OSA/Parlay APIs can also be used in the development of new web-based services. To this end, the Parlay community has designed specific APIs, called Parlay X APIs, based on web service principles and oriented to the Internet community.

When network resources are broadly accessible, it becomes crucial to define and enforce appropriate access rules between entities offering network capabilities and service suppliers, so that an operator can maintain full control over the usage of her resources and on the quality of service. For instance, it is important that the use of services is guided by a set of rules defining the supply conditions and the reciprocal obligations between the client and the network operator. Service Level Agreements (SLAs) are commonly used to formalize a detailed description of all the aspect of the deal. To avoid that unauthorized entities can sign an agreement and use the network illegally, on-line authentication checks are of primary importance.

Authentication in a distributed setting is usually achieved by the use of cryptographic protocols. Experience teaches that these protocols need to be carefully checked, before being fielded (e.g., [2, 5, 8, 11, 12, 15, 16]), and nowadays developers have access to libraries of reliable protocols for different security goals. For example the Secure Socket Layer (SSL) by Netscape, is widely used to ensure authenticity and secrecy in Internet transactions. Unfortunately, the use of reliable, plugged-in, protocols is not sufficient to ensure security, just like the use of reliable cryptography is not sufficient to ensure secrecy in a communication. As we shall see formal methods can help to validate the correct use of security procedures.

In this paper we discuss the validation of the authentication mechanism in the Trust and Security Management (TSM) protocol in OSA/Parlay APIs [1]. This protocol is designed to protect telecommunication capabilities from unauthorized access and it implements an authentication procedure. TSM is specified in the UML [14], where its composing messages, its interfaces towards the client and the server, and the methods implementing security-critical procedures, are described at different levels of abstraction. The formal validation experiment, conducted within a joint project between research Institutes and Telecom Italia Lab, has revealed some security flaws of the authentication mechanism. From the analysis of the traces showing the attacks, we were able to suggest possible solutions to fix the security weaknesses discovered, and to state a general principle of prudent engineering (in the style of [4]) for improving the security in web-service applications.

2   The OSA/Parlay Architecture

The OSA/Parlay architecture enables service application developers to make use of network functionality through an open standardized interface. OSA/Parlay APIs [1] provide an abstract and coherent view of heterogeneous network capabilities, and they allow a developer to interface its applications via distributed processing mechanisms. The OSA/Parlay architecture, shown in Figure 1, consists of:

- a set of *Client Applications* accessing the network resources;
- a set of *Service Interfaces*, or Service Capability Features (SCFs), that represent interfaces for controlling the network capabilities provided by network resources (*e.g.,* controlling the routing of voice calls, sending/receiving SMSs, locating a terminal, etc.);
- a *Framework*, that provides a modular and "controlled" access to the SCFs.
- *Network Resources*, in the telecommunication network, implementing the network capabilities.

A *Parlay Gateway* includes the framework functions and the Service Capability Services (SCSs), that is the modules implementing the SCFs: it is a logical entity that can be implemented in a distributed way across several systems. Since the target applications could be deployed in an administrative domain different from the one of the Parlay Gateway, the secure and controlled access to the SCFs is a predominant aspect for the Parlay architecture. To get the references of the required SCFs, an application must interact several times with the framework interfaces. For example, the application must carry out an authentication phase before selecting the SCFs required, as described in Section 2.1. In this phase the framework verifies whether the application is authorized to use the SCFs, according to a subscription profile. Finally, an agreement is digitally

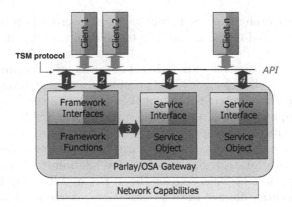

Fig. 1. The OSA/Parlay Architecture. The Trust and Security Management protocol runs between the Framework Interfaces and the Clients.

signed, and the framework gives to the application the references to the required SCFs (*e.g.*, as CORBA interface reference). These references are valid only for a single session of the application. When the framework has to return an SCF reference to an application, it contacts the SCS which implements it, by passing all the configuration parameters, for instance the Service Level Agreement conditions, stored in the subscription profile of the application. The SCS creates a new instance of the SCF, configured with the received parameters, and returns its reference to the framework. Each time the application invokes a method on the SCF instance, the SCS executes it by taking into account the configuration parameters received at instantiation time.

Gateways based on the OSA/Parlay framework here presented have been implemented by, for instance, Ericsson, Alcatel, Lucent, AePONA, and Incomit (though they have not been deployed yet).

2.1   Trust and Security Management Protocol

One of the critical steps for guaranteeing controlled access to the SCFs is the authentication phase between the gateway and the application. It is supported by the protocol implemented by the Trust and Security Management (TSM) API. We focuses on the analysis of the properties of this security protocol, whose behavior is summarized by the message sequence chart in Figure 2. The main steps of the protocol are:

- Initiate Authentication: the client invokes "initiateAuthenticationWith-Version" on the framework's *public* interface (*e.g.*, an URL) to initiate the authentication process. Both the client and the framework provide a reference to their own access interfaces.
- Select Authentication Mechanism: the client invokes "selectAuthentica-tionMechanism" on the framework authentication interface, to negotiate which hash function will be used in the authentication steps.

- The client and the framework authenticate each other. The framework could authenticate the client before (or after) the client authenticates the framework, or the two authentication processes could be interleaved. However, the client shall respond immediately to any challenge issued by the framework, as the framework might not respond to any challenge issued by the client until the framework has successfully authenticated the client. Each authentication step is performed following a one-way Challenge Handshake Authentication Protocol (CHAP) [10], that is by issuing a challenge in the "challenge" method, and checking if the partner returns the correct response. An invocation of the method "authenticationsucceeded" signals the success of the challenge.
- Request an access session: when authenticated by the framework, the client is permitted to invoke "requestAccess" to start an access session. The client provides a reference to its own Access interface, and the framework returns a reference to Access interface, unique for this client.
- The access interface is used to negotiate the signing algorithm to be used in the session and to obtain the references to other framework interfaces (we will call them, *service framework interfaces*), such as service discovery and service agreement management.

Having obtained the reference to a service framework interface the TSM finishes. Note that the references to the interfaces must remain secret: if an intruder got hold of them, it would be able to (abusively) access the services. For this reason our analysis will mainly concentrate on the secrecy of these references.

In fact, after the TSM ends, the client selects the required SCFs by invoking the "selectService" method on the service agreement management interface. The client obtains a service token, which can be signed as part of the service agreement by the client and the framework, through the "signServiceAgreement" and the "signAppServiceAgreement" methods. Generally the service token has a limited lifetime: if the lifetime of the service token expires, a method receiving the service token will return an error code. If the sign service agreement phase succeeds, the framework returns to the client a reference to the selected SCF, personalized with the client configuration parameters.

3   Security Formal Analysis

This section explains in detail the formal analysis of the security of the TSM protocol that we have done. To carry out the verification phase we used CoProVe [6] a constraint-based system for the verification of cryptographic protocols[2]. Co-ProVe has been developed at the University of Twente (NL); it is an improved version of the system designed by Millen and Shmatikov [13]. CoProVe is based on the strand spaces model [17]; it enjoys an efficient implementation, a monotonic behavior which allows to detect flaws associated to partial runs, and an

---

[2] Freely accessible via the web at
http://wwwes.cs.utwente.nl/24cqet/coprove.html

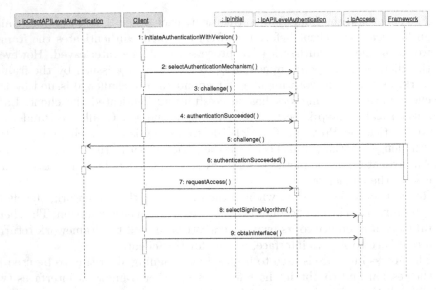

Fig. 2. Message sequence chart describing the steps of the TSM protocol [1].

expressive syntax in which a principal may also perform explicit checks for deciding whether to continue or not with the execution. All these features make CoProVe quite efficient in practice. The intruder model is that of Dolev-Yao [7], where the malicious entity is identified with the communication infrastructure. Protocols are written in Prolog-lake style, and properties are expressed as reachability predicates. In case a security flaw is discovered, CoProVe can show one or all the traces showing the attack.

3.1   Modelling Choices

One of the challenges in applying tools of automatic analysis to industrial architectures lies in translating the (usually less formal) specification into a rigorous formal model. In our experience, translating a complex system design into a formal protocol specification involves many non-trivial steps: software technology concepts such as method invocation and object interfaces have to be "encoded" into an algebraic protocol specification. This encoding phase also forces the engineer to reason about the security implication of using these constructs.

The OSA/Parlay framework APIs specification consists of many pages of UML specification; at this level of abstraction it is difficult to have a good overview of its security mechanisms. In the APIs specification, for instance, there is no explicit transmission of messages: the exchange of one (sometimes even more) messages happens exclusively by the mechanism "invocation of a method over an object interface". Moreover, different levels of abstraction are mixed: for example, the same mechanism of "method invocation" is used both to describe, in one step, the whole set of critical steps of the CHAP handshake and the single message starting of the protocol. More critically, "method invocation" does not specify the confidentiality of the input/output parameters involved. Innocent acknowledgment messages are treated in the same way as references to confidential object interfaces.

The application of clear modeling choices encourages the design of a formal model without the previous ambiguities. In translating the TSM specification in a model we define and apply the following modeling choices.

Modelling Choice 1 *A reference to a (new) private interface, F, is modeled by a (new) shared encryption key, KF.*

Choice 1 reflects the fact that an intruder who does not know the private interface reference cannot infer anything from any method invocation over that interface. This simple, but essential observation will make our security analysis straightforward, as we explain in Section 3.

Modelling Choice 2 *Calling a method, with parameter M, over a private interface F is modeled as sending the message $\{M\}_{KF}$ i.e., M encrypted with KF. Dually, getting the result is translated as receiving a message encrypted with the same KF;*

In Choice 2 we treat a reference to an object interface as a communication port; consequently calling a method equates transmitting a message through that port. Moreover, we model the transmission of a message through F, as the transit of a message encrypted with the key KF. In other words, calling a method over an interface is modeled as a communication encrypted with the interface key. This choice reminds of an observation by Abadi and Gordon [3], who suggest the use of cryptographic keys to model mobility. Our situation is indeed much simpler: the only form of "mobility" we have, is the dynamic creation of a "channel", that is an interface reference.

3.2   Formal Models

We apply Choices 1 and 2 to design the TSM formal *abstract* model written in the usual representation of cryptographic protocols. The obtained model is as follows:

* initiate *
step 1. $C \longrightarrow F : C, KC$
step 2. $F \longrightarrow C : KF$

* select authentication methods *
step 3. $C \longrightarrow F : \{[h, h', h'']\}_{KF}$
step 4. $F \longrightarrow C : \{h\}_{KF}$

* challenge *
step 5. $F \longrightarrow C : \{F, N\}_{KC}$
step 6. $C \longrightarrow F : \{C, h(N, SCF)\}_{KC}$
step 7. $F \longrightarrow C : \{ok/fail\}_{KC}$

* request access *
step 8. $C \longrightarrow F : \{req\}_{KF}$
step 9. $F \longrightarrow C : \{KA/fail\}_{KF}$

* select signing methods *
step 10. $C \longrightarrow F : \{[s, s', s'']\}_{KA}$
step 11. $F \longrightarrow C : \{s\}_{KA}$

* request for service interface *
step 12. $C \longrightarrow F : \{req'\}_{KA}$
step 13. $F \longrightarrow C : \{KS/fail\}_{KA}$

In this abstract model, C represents a client and F the framework, while $C \longrightarrow F : M$ denotes C sending message M to F. With $\{M\}_K$ we indicate the plain-text M encrypted with a key K, while $h(M)$ denotes the result of applying a hash function h to M. In step 1 the client initiates the protocol over the public interface of the framework, by providing its name and a reference to its interface, KC. In step 2 the framework replies by sending a reference, KF, to its own interface.

Remark 1. It may seem odd that despite modelling choice we transmit references to interfaces (represented as keys) in clear. The expectation here is that the challenge response protocol of steps 5-7 would avoid intrusion anyway.

In steps 3 and 4 the client asks the framework to choose an authentication method among h, h' and h''. In steps 5 and 6 the actual CHAP protocol is carried out, using the hash function selected in step 4. Here, SCF represents a shared secret between C and F, required by CHAP [10]. Indeed the UML specification did not provide the details about the CHAP implementation; here we use the version of CHAP where the client and the framework already share the secret SCF. In steps 8 and 9 the client asks for an interface where to invoke the request access for a service. In steps 10 and 11 the framework chooses the interface. Finally in steps 12 and 13 the client sends a request for a service and receives back the reference to the relative framework interface.

The abstract model has been translated into the language required by CoProVe. The result of this translation is a *concrete* formal model; in addition, we encode (in the language of CoProVe) the security properties that we want to check. In Figure 3 we report one of the concrete models we used for checking whether KA remains secret or not.

The specification in Figure 3 involves three principals: one client (c), one framework (f) and eavesdropping agent (sec). Each role is specified by a sequence of send or receive actions that mimic exactly the steps of the abstract model. Symbol "+" is used to denote symmetric encryption using shared keys. Formal parameters (*e.g.,* in the client roleC,F,Kc,Kf,N,Req,Ka,Scf) are used to denote all the objects used in the role specification. In a scenario these parameters are instantiated with actual constants representing real objects (*i.e.,* c,f,_,kf,n,_,ka,scf). Here "_" is used when no instantiation is required, that is when a free variable is involved. The intruder is assumed to know only the client and framework names plus its own name "e". Verification of secrecy consists in asking if there is a trace leading the eavesdropper to know a secret.

3.3   Formal Analysis and Detected Weakness

The analysis performed on the model of TSM protocol, pointed out weaknesses in the security mechanism. In the following we will describe the flaws discovered as a commented list of items. Where significant, we show the output produced by CoProVe and we interpret the output.

Flaw 1. An intruder can impersonate a client and start an authentication challenge with the framework.

```
% Initiator role specification        % scenario specification
client(C,F,Kc,Kf,N,Req,Ka,Scf,[       % pairs [name, Name]
    send([C,Kc]),                     % [label for the role; actual role]
    recv(Kf),                         scenario
    recv([F,N]+Kc),                   ([[c,Client1],
    send([C,sha([N,Scf])]+Kc),         [f,Framew1],
    send(Req+Kf),                      [sec,Secr1]]):-
    recv(Ka+Kf)]).
                                      client(c,f,kc,_,_,req,_,scf,Client1),
% Responder role specification        framewk(c,f,_,kf,n,_,ka,scf,Framew1),
framewk(C,F,Kc,Kf,N,Req,Ka,Scf,[      secrecy(ka, Secr1).
    recv([C,Kc]),
    send(Kf),                         % The initial intruder knowledge
    send([F,N]+Kc),                   initial_intruder_knowledge([c,f,e]).
    recv([C,sha([N,Scf])]+Kc),
    recv(Req+Kf),                     % specify which roles we want
    send(Ka+Kf)]).                    % to force to finish
                                      %(only sec in this example)
% Secrecy check                       has_to_finish([sec]).
%(it is a singleton role)
secrecy(N, [ recv(N) ] ).
```

Fig. 3. The "CoProVe" specification (in two columns) used to check the secrecy of KA. To reduce the search space here we implemented only steps 1-2, 5-6 and 8-9. In other words we assumed: (a) a constant hashing function h; (b) that the framework does not reply (instead of replying "false") if the client answer wrongly to the CHAP challenge.

An intruder can obtain the reference to the interface used by the client to start the authentication challenge (key kf). This happens, unsurprisingly, because the reference kf is transmitted in clear, as the following trace of CoProVe confirms:

```
1.   [c,send([c,kc])]
1'.  [f,recv([c,kc])]
2.   [c,recv(_h325)]
2'.  [f,send(kf)]
```

Each row represents a communication action. For example, c,send[c,kc] represents the action "send" that "c" executes with message "[c,kc]"; c,recv(_h325) represents the results of a "receive" where the client "c" receives the name (in this case generated by the intruder) " _h325". The sequence of actions reveal the attack. It can be visualized in the conventional notation of security protocol (where, we also write _h325 as KE, the intruder key, because this is its understood meaning.):

$$1. \qquad C \longrightarrow I(F) : C, KC \qquad 2. \qquad I(F) \longrightarrow C : KE$$
$$1'. \qquad I(C) \longrightarrow F : C, KC \qquad 2'. \qquad F \longrightarrow I(C) : KF$$

This run comprises two parallel runs of the protocol, in which the intruder plays, respectively, the role of the client against the framework ($I(C)$ in *steps* 1' and 2') and the framework against the client ($I(F)$ in steps 1 and 2).

This flaws is not serious in itself (provided the authentication procedure is able to detect an intruder and close the communication), but it becomes serious when combined with the next weaknesses in the security; by knowing *kf* an intruder is able to grab other confidential information.

Flaw 2. An intruder can impersonate a client, authenticate itself to the framework and obtain the reference to the interface used to request access to a service (key *ka*).

This is a serious flaw that compromises the main goal of the protocol itself. Informally, a malicious application can pass the authentication phase instead of an honest client, and it can obtain a reference to the interface used to request a service (key *ka*). The study of the output of CoProVe (here depicted in two columns) shows the existence of an "oracle" attack, where the intruder uses the client to get the right answer to the challenge:

```
1.   [c,send([c,kc])]          6.   [c,send([c,sha([n,scf])] + kc)]
1'.  [f,recv([c,kc])]          6'.  [f,recv([c,sha([n,scf])] + kc)]
2.   [c,recv(_h325)]           8.   [c,send(req + _h325)]
2'.  [f,send(kf)]              9.   [c,recv(_h391 + _h325)]
5'.  [f,send([f,n] + kc)]      8'.  [f,recv(req + kf)]
5.   [c,recv([f,n] + kc)]      9'.  [f,send(ka + kf)]
                                    [sec,recv(ka)]
```

Using the standard informal notation for describing protocols, the above trace is read as follows:

$$
\begin{array}{llll}
1. & C \longrightarrow I(F) : C, KC & 6. & C \longrightarrow I(F) : \{C, h(N, SCF)\}_{KC} \\
1'. & I(C) \longrightarrow F : C, KC & 6' & I(C) \longrightarrow F : \{C, h(N, SCF)\}_{KC} \\
2. & I(F) \longrightarrow C : KE & 8. & C \longrightarrow I(F) : \{req\}_{KE} \\
2'. & F \longrightarrow I(C) : KF & 9. & I(F) \longrightarrow C : \{fail\}_{KE} \\
5'. & F \longrightarrow I(C) : \{F, N\}_{KC} & 8'. & I(C) \longrightarrow F : \{req\}_{KF} \\
5. & I(F) \longrightarrow C : \{F, N\}_{KC} & 9'. & F \longrightarrow I(C) : \{KA\}_{KF}
\end{array}
$$

This run comprises two parallel runs of the protocol, in which the intruder plays, respectively, the role of the framework against the client and the role of the client against the framework. Searching among the set of attacks returned by CoProVe, we find also the following, straightforward, man-in-the-middle, attack:

```
1.   [c,send([c,kc])]          6.   [c,send([c,sha([n,scf])] + kc)]
1'.  [f,recv([c,kc])]          6'.  [f,recv([c,sha([n,scf])] + kc)]
2'.  [f,send(kf)]              8.   [c,send(req + kf)]
2.   [c,recv(kf)]              8'.  [f,recv(req + kf)]
5'.  [f,send([f,n] + kc)]      9'.  [f,send(ka + kf)]
5.   [c,recv([f,n] + kc)]      9.   [c,recv(_h325)]
                                    [sec,recv(ka)]
```

This trace shows that the intruder can eavesdrop first the key kf, passed in clear, and then steal the message ka+kf. At this point key ka can be obtained by a simple decryption. This attack is obviously straightforward at this point of the analysis, but it became clear as soon as we applied Choice 1.

Flaw 3. An intruder can impersonate a client, authenticate itself to the framework, send a request for a service and obtain the reference to a service framework interface (key *ks*).

This is also a serious flaw that compromises the main goal of the protocol. An intruder can obtain the reference to a service framework interface (key *ks*). It is easy to understand, that this is possible, for example, as a consequence of flaw 1 and 2: once an intruder has authenticated itself instead of the client, it can easily obtain the reference.

Further checks with CoProVe, show that the intruder can even retrieve this reference with a man-in-the-middle attack, for instance, by listening to the communication between the client and the framework and stealing the reference when it is passed in clear. In our model this attack can be explained as follows: the intruder intercepts, by eavesdropping, the message $\{KS\}_{KA}$ and it decrypts it. This is possible because the encryption key KF is passed in clear and, by eavesdropping, the intruder can easily obtain $\{KA\}_{KF}$, and hence KA (flaw 2).

Flaw 4. An intruder can force the framework to use an authentication mechanism of her choice.

This flaw has been discovered using the specification in Figure 4, with two instances of the framework. When a client offers a list of authentication methods, the first instance selects the first method at the head of a list (here consisting of only two items), whereas the second instance chooses the second. In this way we model different choices made by the framework.

The attack is shown by the following CoProVe trace; an intruder can force the framework to select a particular authentication mechanism, by the use of a replay attack.

```
a.1.   [c,send([c,kc])]              a.6'.  [f,recv([c,sha([n,scf])] + kc)
a.1'.  [f,recv([c,kc])]              a.8.   [c,send(req + _h320)]
a.2.   [c,recv(_h320)]               a.9.   [c,recv(req + _h320)]
a.2'.  [f,send(kf)]                  a.8'.  [f,recv(_h404 + kf)]
a.3.   [c,send([a1,a2] + _h320)]     a.9'.  [f,send(ka + kf)]
a.3'.  [f,recv([a1,a2] + kf)]        b.1'.  [f,recv([c,_h487])]
a.4'.  [f,send([a1,a1] + kf)]        b.2'.  [f,send(kf2)]
a.4.   [c,recv([a1,a1] + _h320)]     b.3'.  [f,recv([a1,a1] + kf2)]
a.5'.  [f,send([f,n] + kc)]          b.4'.  [f,send([a1,a1] + kf2)]
a.5.   [c,recv([f,n] + kc)           b.8'.  [f,recv(_h488 + kf2)]
a.6.   [c,send([c,sha([n,scf])] + kc) b.9'. [f,send(ka2 + kf2)]
                                            [sec,recv(ka2)]
```

```
% Initiator role specification
client(C,F,Kc,Kf,N,Req,Scf,
        Ka,A1,A2,A,[
    recv([C,F]),
    send([C,Kc]),
    recv(Kf),
    send([A1,A2]+Kf),
    recv([A,A]+Kf),
    recv([F,N]+Kc),
    send([C,sha([N,Scf])]+Kc)
    send(Req+Kf),
    recv(Ka+Kf)]).

% Responder role specification
framewk(C,F,Kc,Kf,N,Req,Scf,
        Ka,A1,A2,[
    recv([C,Kc]),
    send(Kf),
    recv([A1,A2]+Kf),
    send([A1,A1]+Kf),
    send([F,N]+Kc),
    recv([C,sha([N,Scf])]+Kc),
    recv(Req+Kf),
    send(Ka+Kf)]).

framewk2(C,F,Kc,Kf,N,Req,
        Ka,A1,A2,[
    recv([C,Kc]),
    send(Kf),
    recv([A1,A2]+Kf),
    send([A2,A2]+Kf),
    recv(Req+Kf),
    send(Ka+Kf)]).
```

```
% secrecy check (singleton role)
secrecy(N, [ recv(N) ] ).

% Scenario
scenario([
        [c,Client1],
        [f,Framew1],
        [f,Framew2],
        [sec,Secr1]
        ]) :-
client(c,f,kc,_,_,req,scf,_,a1,
        a2,a1,Client1),

framewk(c,f,_,kf,n,_,scf,ka,_,_,
        Framew1),

framewk2(c,f,_,kf2,n2,_,ka2,_,_,
        Framew2),

secrecy(ka2, Secr1).

% Set up the intruder knowledge
initial_intruder_knowledge([c,f,e]).

% specify which roles we want
% to force to finish
% (only sec in this example)
has_to_finish([sec]).
```

Fig. 4. The "CoProVe" code used to discover flaw 4 (in two columns). The model of the framework includes the "select authentication method" phases of the abstract model and implements steps 1–9 of the abstract model. Step 7 is omitted, *i.e.*, the framework does not reply (instead of sending "fail") in case of failure of the challenge phase. The second instance of the framework models only steps 1–4 and steps 8–9, that is those steps strictly necessary to discover the attack.

The attack can represented in the following abstract steps:

$$
\begin{array}{llll}
\text{a.1} & C \longrightarrow I(F1) : C, KC & \text{a.4'} & F1 \longrightarrow I(C) : \{[a1]\}_{KF} \\
\quad \text{a.1'} & I(C) \longrightarrow F1 : C, KC & [\ldots] \\
\text{a.2} & I(F) \longrightarrow C : KE & \text{b.1'} & I(C) \longrightarrow F2 : C, KE \\
\quad \text{a.2'} & F1 \longrightarrow I(C) : KF & \text{b.2'} & F2 \longrightarrow I(C) : KF2 \\
\text{a.3} & C \longrightarrow I(F1) : \{[a1,a2]\}_{KE} & \text{b.3'} & I(C) \longrightarrow F2 : \{[a1,a1]\}_{KF2} \\
\quad \text{a.3'} & I(C) \longrightarrow F1 : \{[a1,a2]\}_{KF} & \text{b.4'} & F2 \longrightarrow I(C) : \{[a1]\}_{KF2} \\
\end{array}
$$

In the trace the intruder acts as a men-in-the-middle in a communication between the client and the first instance of the framework $F1$ and it learns what method the framework is able to use (sequences $a.i$). In the second run, the intruder acts as a client, and it offers to the second instance of the framework $F2$ the choice that the framework is able to accept (sequences $b.i$). The structure of the attack is such that it can be applied also for forcing the selection of a signing methods, that is steps 10 and 11 of the abstract model.

4 Discussion

The analysis performed so far shows some weaknesses of the protocol, and gives also useful indications on how to improve the robustness of the protocol. This section discusses the weaknesses here presented, and suggests possible solutions to increase the overall security. We start with some preliminary considerations.

The security is weak is because some references to interfaces are passed in the clear. This is because the role of those references has been misunderstood, or under-evaluated, or more probably not recognized in the UML, high-level, object specification. A rigorous, synthetic, formal specification and precise modeling choices helps in giving each object its right role. In our case we were able to identify in the role of some references to object interface the same role that session keys have. This observation can be quoted as a principle:

Independently of their high-level representation, data that directly or indirectly gives access to a secret, must be thought of (hence, modeled) as encryption keys.

This principle plays a role also in fixing the protocol. In fact, the common practice in protocol engineering [4] suggests the use of (other) session keys to protect the confidentiality of sensitive information, which in the case of TSM are the references to interfaces. According to the TSM model, session keys are indeed missing completely from the present implementation[3] while their use could prevent the intruder from gaining a reference to an interface (as shown, by a men-in-the-middle attack).

An additional point of discussion concerns the correct use of a CHAP-based authentication. From the OSA/Parlay documentation ([1] page 19) we read that *security can be ensured if the "challenge" is frequently invoked by the framework to authenticate the client that, in turn, must reply "immediately"*:

Our analysis proves that not only the intruder can act as a client with respect to the framework, but also that it can passively observe, as man-in-the-middle, the framework and a client authenticating each other as many times as they want, and then steal the reference to the service framework interfaces when they are transmitted in clear. At this point the intruder can substitute itself for the client.

---

[3] Do not confuse them with the session keys that appear in the abstract model. Those are part of the model and represent private references to interfaces.

Generally speaking TSM confidentiality improves if the framework encrypts all the messages containing a reference to an interface. Encryption requires that the framework authenticates the client, and later that it agrees upon a session key with the authenticated client. This can be done, for example by "running a Secure Sockets Layer (SSL) protocol at the beginning of the TSM session. The SSL allows two entities, a client and a server, to authenticate each other and to establish session keys. Session keys are then used to ensure confidentiality and integrity in any, next, exchange of messages. As a consequence, the SSL can substitute the CHAP authentication procedure required by the TSM specification. The common use of the SSL sees the client to authenticate the server (*i.e.,* the framework in our case); in the context of the TSM security, is mandatory that the server authenticates the client as well.

Flaw 4 is different in nature, and it teaches that particular care must be paid to the choice of the encryption algorithms or digital signature procedures offered by the framework: for example, the intruder can force the system to use the encryption algorithm that is easier to crack.

5   Conclusions

This paper discusses an industrial experience of formal analysis applied to the security aspects of the OSA/Parlay Trust and Security Management protocol. The protocol is devised to authenticate clients before granting them access to network services. Our experience confirms that formal methods are an invaluable tool for discovering serious security flaws which may be overlooked otherwise. This is true in two respects. First, the use of a formal model, where only the relevant security features are expressed, helps at pointing out what are the critical security component. In an informal description, on the other hand, this information is usually dispersed and difficult to gather. Second, the use of an automatic tool allows one to identify dangerous man-in-the middle attacks, which are notoriously difficult to see on high-level specifications.

From this experience, conducted within a joint project between industry and research institutes, we state a general principle for security in web-services: it is essential to identify clearly the security role of each object involved in service specification. It is vital especially for those objects that abstractly represent encryption keys. This principle helps at simplifying the security analysis. With the application of this principle we discover serious weaknesses more easily, and we are able to discuss how the security of the TSM protocol can be generally improved.

The results of this work has been presented to the join standardization group 3GPP/ETSI/Parlay. They have decided to open a study on how to strengthen the security of OSA/Parlay in the next future.

Acknowledgment

S. Gnesi and G. Di Caprio, and C. Moiso were supported by the MIUR-CNR Project SP4. R. Corin was supported by the IOP GenCom project PAW; S. Etalle was partially supported by the BSIK project BRICKS; G. Lenzini was supported by SP4, PAW and by the IIT-CNR project "Trusted e-services for Dynamic and Mobile Coalitions".

References

1. *Open Service Access (OSA) - Application Programming Interface (API) Mapping for OSA.* http://www.3gpp.org/ftp/Specs/archive/29_series. Release 5.
2. M. Abadi and A. D. Gordon. Reasoning about Cryptographic Protocols in the Spi Calculus. In A. W. Mazurkiewicz and J. Winkowski, editors, *Proc. of 8th Int. Conf. on Concurrency Theory (CONCUR 97), Warsaw, Poland, July 1997, LNCS* 1243, pages 59–73. Springer-Verlag, 1997.
3. M. Abadi and A. D. Gordon. A Calculus for Cryptographic Protocols. The Spi Calculus. TR 149, Digital Equipment Corporation Systems Research Center, Palo Alto, CA, USA 1998.
4. M. Abadi and R. Needham. Prudent engineering practice for cryptographic protocols. *IEEE Transactions on Software Engineering*, 22(1):6–15, 1996. IEEE Computer Society.
5. E. M. Clarke, S. Jha, and W. Marrero. Verifying security protocols with Brutus. *ACM Trans. Software Engineering and Methodology*, 9(4):443–487, 2000. ACM .
6. R. Corin and S. Etalle. An improved constraint-based system for the verification of security protocols. In M. Hermenegildo and G. Puebla, editors, *Proc. of the International Static Analysis Symposium (SAS), Madrid, Spain, Sep. 2002, LNCS* 2477, pages 326–341. Springer-Verlag, 2002.
7. D. Dolev and A. Yao. On the security of public-key protocols. *IEEE Trans. Information Theory*, 29(2):198–208, 1983. IEEE Computer Society.
8. R. Gorrieri, F. Martinelli, M. Petroocchi, and A. Vaccarelli. Formal analysis of some timed security properties in wireless protocols. In *Proc. of the 6th IFIP WG 6.1 Formal Methods for Open Object-Based Distributed Systems (FMOODS 2003) Paris, France, Nov. 2003, LNCS* 2884, pages 139–154. Springer Verlag, 2003.
9. Parlay X Working Group. Parlay apis 4.0: Parlay x web services - white paper. The Parlay Group, 2002. http://www.parlay.org.
10. G. Leduc. Verification of two versions of the challenge handshake authentication protocol (CHAP). *Annals of Telecommunications*, 55(1-2):18–30, 2000. Hermes-Lavoisier.
11. G. Lowe. Breaking and Fixing the Needham-Schroeder Public-Key Protocol using FDR. *Software Concepts and Tools*, 3(17):93–102, 1997. Springer-Verlag.
12. C. A. Meadows. Formal verification of cryptographic protocols: A survey. In J. Pieprzyk and R. Safavi-Naini, editors, *Proc. of the Int. Conf. on the Theory and Application of Cryptology Advances in Cryptology and Information Security, (ASIACRYPT 94), LNCS* 917, pages 135–150. Springer-Verlag, 1994.
13. J. Millen and V. Shmatikov. Constraint Solving for Bounded-Process Cryptographic Protocol Analysis. In P. Samarati, editor, *Proc. of the 8th ACM Conf. on Computer and Communication Security*, pages 166–175. ACM , 2001.
14. UML Resource Page. Unified Modeling Language. http://www.uml.org.

15. A. W. Roscoe. Modelling and Verifying Key-Exchange Protocols using CSP and FDR. In *Proc. of The 8th Computer Security Foundations Workshop (CSFW 95), Kenmare, Ireland, Mar. 1995*, pages 98–107. IEEE Computer Society, 1995

16. S. Schneider. Verifying Authentication Protocols in CSP. *IEEE Trans. Sofware Engineering*, 24(8):743–758, 1998. IEEE Computer Society .

17. J. Thayer, J. Herzog, and J. Guttman. Strand spaces: Why is a security protocol correct? In *Proc. of the 19th IEEE Computer Society Symposium on Research in Security and Privacy (SSP 98), Oakland, CA, USA, May 1998*, pages 160–171. IEEE Computer Society, 1998.

Tracing Integration Analysis
in Component-Based Formal Specifications*

Martín López-Nores, José J. Pazos-Arias, Jorge García-Duque,
Belén Barragáns-Martínez, Rebeca P. Díaz-Redondo, Ana Fernández-Vilas,
Alberto Gil-Solla, and Manuel Ramos-Cabrer

Department of Telematics Engineering, University of Vigo, 36310 Vigo, Spain
{mlnores,jose,jgd,belen,rebeca,avilas,agil,mramos}@det.uvigo.es

Abstract. The correctness of a component-based specification is not guaranteed
by the correctness of its components alone; on the contrary, integration analysis
is needed to observe their conjoint behavior. Existing approaches often leave the
results of the analysis at the level of the integrated system, without tracing them
onto the corresponding components. This effectively results in loss of architecture, as it is no longer possible to reason over those components and evolve their
specification while keeping the results of integration analysis.

This paper presents a formal approach to automatically translate changes on the
integrated system into revisions of the components and the architecture initially
defined by the developers. Several architectural alternatives are provided that,
besides allowing developers to reason about the system from different points of
view, promote its correct modularization in two overlapping perspectives: the encapsulation of crosscutting concerns and the elaboration of the architecture desired for the final implementation.

1 Introduction

Component-based approaches have been around for a long time as a means to split
complexity in software development, promising better understanding of a system by its
developers, improved quality and easier maintenance. A more recent idea to improve
software engineering practice has been to apply incremental development techniques,
which are based on obtaining successive revisions of a system until achieving the desired functionality. These techniques are especially suitable to deal with changeable
specifications, and also with maintenance and evolution tasks.

Due to the well-known problem of *feature interaction*, the correctness of a system
is not guaranteed by the correctness of its parts, considering these in isolation. On the
contrary, certain properties can only be verified by observing the conjoint operation of
several components. This points out the need for *integration analysis*.

Current approaches to component-based development often limit themselves to finding whether integration analysis succeeds. In case of failure, no information is given on
how to modify the components, forcing the developers to attempt manual changes until
getting a positive response, which is clearly unsatisfactory. The ideal would be to determine the changes needed to satisfy the integration properties over the integrated system

* Work partially funded by the Xunta de Galicia Research Project PGIDIT04PXIB32201PR.

M. Steffen and G. Zavattaro (Eds.): FMOODS 2005, LNCS 3535, pp. 147–162, 2005.

(i.e., where the properties can be observed), and then trace those changes automatically to the components. Unfortunately, support for this feature is missing nowadays, resulting in an effective *loss of architecture*, as it is no longer possible to reason over the individual components while keeping the results of integration analysis. So, the ability to trace integration results would represent a major aid to incremental development.

In this paper, we present a formal methodology to tackle this concern. Our proposal is to automatically translate the changes resulting from integration analysis into revisions of the components and the architecture defined by the developers. These are provided with several architectural views, that promote the correct modularization of a system and help to elaborate the architecture wanted for its final implementation.

The paper is organized as follows. Section 2 outlines the development model in which our proposal takes place, with Section 3 describing our methodology to trace integration analysis. Section 4 presents a simple example on applying this methodology, which is later discussed in Section 5. Section 6 comments our ongoing work in the line of this paper, and Section 7 discusses related work. Appendixes A, B and C gather the technical details not included elsewhere.

2   The $(SCTL/MUS)^A$ Context

The context for our work lies in the SCTL-MUS methodology [14], a formal approach to the specification of reactive systems that models the usual way in which a system is specified: starting with an initially rough idea of the desired functionality, this is successively refined until the specification is complete.

SCTL-MUS combines property-oriented and model-oriented formal description techniques: on the one hand, the many-valued logic SCTL (*Simple and Causal Temporal Logic*) is used to express the system's functional requirements; on the other, the graph formalism MUS (*Model of Unspecified States*) is employed to model systems for validation and formal verification purposes.

SCTL statements have the generic form $Premise \oplus Consequence$, with $\oplus$ ranging over the set of temporal operators $\{\Rightarrow, \Rightarrow \bigcirc, \Rightarrow \odot\}$ and the following semantics:

If $Premise$ is satisfied, then [simultaneously ($\Rightarrow$) | next ($\Rightarrow \bigcirc$) | previously ($\Rightarrow \odot$)] $Consequence$ must be satisfied.

This causal semantics allows expressing under what circumstances during the operation of a system shall a given condition be satisfied, so that the premise and the temporal operator of a statement delimit the applicability of its consequence.

Given a set of requirements expressed in SCTL, the synthesis algorithm of SCTL-MUS attempts to generate a MUS graph that adheres to all of them. As a distinctive feature with respect to traditional *Labeled Transition Systems* (LTS), the events of a MUS graph can be not only *possible* (*true*, 1) or *non-possible* (*false*, 0) in the different states; on the contrary, if there are no requirements affecting the specification of an event in a given state, that event is given the value $\frac{1}{2}$ (*not-yet-specified* or *unspecified*) in that state. Figure 1 shows two SCTL requirements and the MUS graph that implements them – note that we do not explicitly represent *unspecified* actions (like a in state s_2), because $\frac{1}{2}$ is the default value; instead, we do represent *false* actions (like b in s_2), placing a symbol like $\neg$ next to every state where a given event is *non-possible*.

$$r_1 \equiv a \Rightarrow (\neg b \wedge \bigcirc c)$$
$$r_2 \equiv c \Rightarrow \bigcirc a$$

Fig. 1. Two SCTL requirements and the MUS graph that implements them

The commented notion of *unspecification* was introduced to deal with the incompleteness inherent to the intermediate stages of an incremental process, so as to enable reasoning about evolutions and satisfaction tendencies in the formal verification process. A partial specification represents all the systems into which it can evolve by adding new requirements, and the MUS formalism was devised to explicitly capture that potentiality. This is achieved through the inclusion of an *unspecified* state – not relevant for the contents of this paper and, therefore, not drawn in the figures – that represents all the states that have not been specified so far (see [14] for the details). With this definition, the addition of new requirements to a specification always results in *losses of unspecification* in the MUS model that implements it (i.e., some *unspecified* events are turned into *possible* or *non-possible* ones), which allows making the synthesis an incremental process. These features are not fully catered for by other formalisms intended to support partial specifications, like KPSs [3] or MTSs [6].

2.1 An Incremental Approach to Component-Based Specification

SCTL-MUS lacks the notion of *architecture*, which hinders the simultaneous work of several developers and makes specifications unmanageable for large systems. Moreover, it only defines mechanisms to handle evolutions of a specification to satisfy new requirements, consistent with the current ones, but provides no support to modify the current requirements so as to solve inconsistencies or revise previous design decisions.

To solve these flaws, we are now working on $(SCTL/MUS)^A$, a fully incremental methodology aimed at facilitating task division and collaborative work. The new methodology, whose motivation was given in [11], inherits most of the philosophy of SCTL-MUS, keeping its dual approach in the use of formal description techniques, its iterative life cycle and its notion of *unspecification*. It also uses the same formalisms (SCTL and MUS), to reason over individual components and their compositions, but extends this basis to handle component-based specifications.

$(SCTL/MUS)^A$ accommodates the multiple parts of a specification in *composition layers* that relate components to the compositions in which they take part, with the overall system at the top. The composition operators allowed have been borrowed from the LOTOS process algebra, though adapting them to the three-valued domain of MUS. This is the key to make compositions reflect the *unspecification* – and, therefore, the potentiality – of their forming components, which is essential to support the incremental approach. Appendix A explains this vision on the *selective parallel composition* operator (denoted by $||[\Lambda]||_{\mathcal{M}}$), which is a powerful way to express the concurrent operation of several components. In brief, a composition $C_1||[\Lambda]||_{\mathcal{M}} C_2$ can advance through an event $a \notin \Lambda$ if a is *possible* in either C_1 or C_2, but it can advance through an event $b \in \Lambda$ only if b is *possible* in both of them; thus, if Λ is the empty set, the effect is that of pure interleaving (in this case, the operator is denoted by $|||_{\mathcal{M}}$).

2.2   Orientation to Aspects

(SCTL/MUS)^A fits within the *Early-Aspects* initiative [16], which aims at extending the principles of aspect-oriented programming [9] to the phases of requirements engineering and architectural design. Aspect-orientation is a way to achieve modularizations that facilitate the management of *crosscutting functionality*, i.e., functionality that appears scattered through the parts of any decomposition in objects. This is done by introducing *aspects* that encapsulate the crosscutting functionality, and by defining mechanisms to *weave* (combine) the aspects with the components they crosscut.

Due to the slight notion of structure available during requirements elicitation tasks, our vision is not to make an explicit distinction between components and aspects; instead, any component that is combined with the composition of several others may be seen as an aspect, because it crosscuts their functionality. Nonetheless, treating a piece of functionality as an aspect is only justified when it can be traced into modifications of the crosscut components as a meaningful addition to their functionality.

In line with the ideas discussed in [13] and the works on *multi-dimensional separation of concerns* [18], the management of aspects in (SCTL/MUS)^A is linked to allowing developers to handle multiple *architectural views*, each one defining a different decomposition of the system or any of its components. Different decompositions enable different reasonings, and it is possible to work over any one of them, since we can propagate what is done on a given view to the others. This way, multiple developers can contribute to construct the desired system by reasoning from different perspectives.

3   A Methodology for Integration Analysis

This section introduces the methodology we have defined to perform integration analysis in (SCTL/MUS)^A, which is targeted at facilitating incremental development. The fundamental idea is that the analysis of a system should not be delayed until its parts have been completely developed, in order to prevent doing much work over incorrect foundations. Consequently, (SCTL/MUS)^A allows integration analysis to be done at intermediate stages of the specification process. Furthermore, it supports analysis at any level of composition, not necessarily on the whole system. Despite, for simplicity, we will refer to the composition being analyzed as *"the system"*.

Figure 2 illustrates the steps of the methodology, which we proceed to describe.

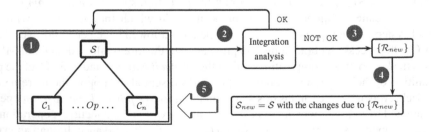

Fig. 2. The complete cycle of integration analysis

3.1 Specification

The starting point (step 1 in Fig. 2) is the specification of the system (S) as the combination of several components (C_i) by means of composition operators (Op). The analysis is done on the MUS graph of the composition, that is computed from the MUS graphs of the components by following the rules of the composition operators. The MUS graphs of the components may have been derived from other components or, for those at the lowest composition levels, synthesized from a set of SCTL requirements.

3.2 Integration Analysis

Once available, the MUS graph of the system is subject to verifying the integration properties (step 2 in Fig. 2), to find whether the system satisfies them (OK) or it does not satisfy them *yet* (NOT OK).

If the system satisfies the properties, the analysis is finished, and the developers can continue working over the unchanged current specification. On the contrary, if the system does not fulfill the properties, an evolution of its specification is needed to satisfy the developers' expectancies. In this case, as commented in Sect. 1, the goal of the methodology is twofold: to find the modifications needed for the system to satisfy the properties stated for it, and to trace those changes onto the components whose conjoint behavior is being analyzed. Our proposal, as explained below, is to aid the developers in the first task, and to fully automate the second.

3.3 The Creative Part

Determining the changes needed for a system to satisfy certain objectives (step 3 in Fig. 2) requires participation from the developers, because many viable alternatives may exist in the general case. To help in this process, we have adapted the *analysis-revision cycle* presented in [5], that automatically provides some of those alternatives.

An important thing to note here relates to the concept of *unspecification* (Section 2), that allows us to conjugate the two main methods proposed in literature to revise the specification of a system: *refinements* [10, 17] and *retrenchments* [15]. Because of *unspecification*, the developers can evolve a system in two different ways:

(i) **By retrenchments, for properties that are explicitly violated.** In this case, the system includes unwanted behavior, that must be eliminated. The analysis-revision cycle points out the circumstances under which the properties are violated, and suggests possibilities to solve the problem.

(ii) **By refinements, for properties that are not explicitly violated *yet*.** These properties, which are neither fulfilled nor violated yet (they are *unspecified*), indicate that behavior must be added to make the specification satisfy them. Here, the analysis-revision cycle identifies evolutions that would make the specification violate the properties, and suggests modifications to conduct it the other way.

Assisted by the suggestions of the analysis-revision cycle on how to evolve the system, the developers are expected to come up with a set of requirements ($\{\mathcal{R}_{new}\}$) that specify the changes to be done on the system.

3.4   The Automated Part (I): Incorporating the New Requirements

Once the changes have been decided, it is easy to apply them over the MUS graph of the integrated system (step 4 in Fig. 2), but the result is no longer obtainable from the MUS graphs of the original components. At most, it can be expressed as a new system where the architecture has been lost: $\mathcal{S}_{new} = \mathcal{S}$ with the changes due to $\{\mathcal{R}_{new}\}$.

3.5   The Automated Part (II): Tracing Changes onto the Original Specification

In order to avoid loss of architecture, and to permit future iterations in the specification of the individual components, our approach traces the changes done on the system into revisions of the original architecture and components (step 5 in Fig. 2). We do this by automatically refactoring $\mathcal{S}_{new}$ into two different architectural views, as shown in Fig. 3:

(i) In the first view, a new component is created that materializes the new requirements and that, combined with the original components, makes the system behave as intended. As shown in Fig. 3, the new architecture only adds the new component ($\mathcal{C}_{n+1}$), preserving the original ones and the ways they were combined (Op).
   The new component, that manifests the crosscutting nature of the integration properties, may have significance in the domain of application of the system, in which case it can be further developed (in functionality and architecture), and may even be reused for other systems.

(ii) Just because the new component may be meaningless in the implemented system, our methodology provides a second architectural view, where its functionality is discharged over the original components. In other words, since the new component may be seen as an aspect ($\mathcal{A}$) that modifies the original components, we offer a view that re-expresses the original architecture in terms of modified components ($\mathcal{C}_i^*$), possibly changing the original composition operators (note the Op'' instead of Op in Fig. 3). We represent the weaving operation by means of a newly-defined operator, that we call "*projection*" and denote by $\leftarrow^*$.

To complete the process of tracing changes, $(\text{SCTL/MUS})^A$ supports the automatic reformulation of the requirements of the original components. Using mechanisms like the ones presented in [5], we modify the SCTL requirements provided by the developers from the transformations done over the MUS models that implement them, which allows the developers to see the changes made to the system expressed in the same language used to specify it. This is an essential aid to go on with the incremental specification process: the requirements are the mechanism by which developers express their conception of the system, and so their formulation holds the key to understand what is being constructed.

Reformulating requirements is necessary in the second architectural view, to enable reasoning about some behavior of a given component that can only be observed in its combination with the aspect. In this case, the requirements for $\mathcal{C}_i^*$ are derived from the requirements of the corresponding $\mathcal{C}_i$. As for the new components $\mathcal{C}_{n+1}$ and $\mathcal{A}$ in Fig. 3, at most we can annotate the situation and the set of requirements that led to their appearance – inventing a set of requirements from which their MUS graphs could be generated is purposeless, because those requirements would not capture any expressive effort from the developers.

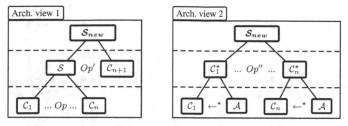

Fig. 3. Two architectural views for the new system

4   An Example on Synchronization Concerns

This section illustrates the methodology presented in Sect. 3, with an example of tracing synchronization requirements over the parallel composition of several components. We describe an evolution of the system based on suppressing unwanted behavior, and show how the two architectural views are automatically computed. These include the restrictions imposed at the composition level while keeping the original architecture. Details about the algorithms applied are left for Appendixes B and C.

4.1   Specification

Let *Sender* be a component whose functionality, at the current stage of development, is "*a Sender starts a transmission when it has data to send; it waits for new data after each transmission*". A system is wanted that defines a communications network with n senders operating on a shared channel. To model this, the developers initially specify the system $\mathcal{S}^n$ as the interleaved combination of n instances of component *Sender*:

$$\mathcal{S}^n \equiv Sender_1 \ldots \|\|_{\mathcal{M}} \ldots Sender_n = \|\|_{\substack{\mathcal{M} \\ i=1\ldots n}} Sender_i \tag{1}$$

Figure 4(a) shows the MUS graph of the i-th sender in the system, in its current status of specification. The sender waits for data in state s_1 (the initial state), and transitions into s_2 when action rdy_i occurs, meaning that new data are available. Once in s_2, the sender can begin transmitting the data by executing ini_i. It stays at s_3 until the transmission finishes (action end_i), and then goes back to s_1 to wait for new data. All the other actions are *not-yet-specified*.

4.2   Integration Analysis

The specification of the senders is not yet complete, because some *unspecification* remains in their MUS graphs. However, it may be wise to analyze their conjoint behavior before completing them, to make sure that what has been specified so far is correct, avoiding futile efforts in evolving incorrect specifications.

As the senders will operate on a shared channel, it is necessary to ensure that it is not possible for several of them to be transmitting simultaneously. According to the MUS graph of Fig. 4(a), a sender is transmitting only when it is in state s_3, and this can

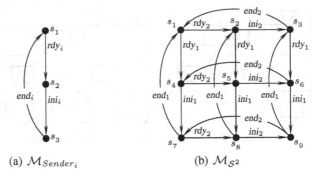

Fig. 4. The MUS graphs of $Sender_i$ and $\mathcal{S}^2 \equiv Sender_1 \,|||_{\mathcal{M}} Sender_2$

be referred to as the only state where action end_i is *possible*. Therefore, for the $n = 2$ case, the developers can specify the desired property as $\mathcal{P} \equiv true \Rightarrow \neg(end_1 \wedge end_2)$ – since the premise ($true$) is satisfied in every state, the property is violated in those states where both end_1 and end_2 are *possible*.

The first step to analyze the satisfaction of $\mathcal{P}$ is to obtain the MUS graph of the system $\mathcal{S}^n$, by combining the graphs of n senders according to the rules of the $|||_{\mathcal{M}}$ operator. Figure 4(b) shows the MUS graph of the network with two senders, $\mathcal{M}_{\mathcal{S}^2}$.

4.3   The Creative Part

Analyzing the property $\mathcal{P}$ reveals that it is explicitly violated in the state s_9 of $\mathcal{M}_{\mathcal{S}^2}$, since both end_1 and end_2 are *possible* there. Therefore, as explained in Sect. 3.3, a retrenchment is needed to ensure proper behavior. From among the possible evolutions suggested by the analysis-revision cycle, the developers decide to incorporate the requirements of Eq. (2), which prevent one sender from starting a transmission while the other is transmitting:

$$\{\mathcal{R}^2_{new}\} = \{\mathcal{R}_1, \mathcal{R}_2\}, \quad \text{where} \quad \begin{cases} \mathcal{R}_1 \equiv end_1 \Rightarrow \neg ini_2 \\ \mathcal{R}_2 \equiv end_2 \Rightarrow \neg ini_1 \end{cases} \tag{2}$$

For the general case of n senders, the new requirements would be those of Eq. (3):

$$\{\mathcal{R}^n_{new}\} = \{\mathcal{R}_i\}_{1 \leq i \leq n}, \quad \text{where} \quad \mathcal{R}_i \equiv end_i \Rightarrow \bigwedge_{j \neq i} \neg ini_j \tag{3}$$

4.4   The Automated Part

To describe how the new requirements are applied onto the MUS graph of the original system ($\mathcal{S}^n$), we consider again the case $n = 2$, without loss of generality. Due to $\mathcal{R}_1$, the specification of action ini_2 changes to *false* in the states s_7, s_8 and s_9 of $\mathcal{M}_{\mathcal{S}^2}$; similarly, $\mathcal{R}_2$ changes the specification of ini_1 to *false* in s_3, s_6 and s_9. The resulting graph ($\mathcal{M}_{\mathcal{S}^2_{new}}$) is shown in Fig. 5, where it can be seen that the problematic state s_9 is now unreachable – this is the desired effect of the new requirements.

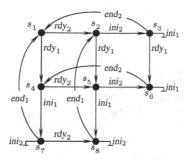

Fig. 5. The MUS graph of the revised overall system, $\mathcal{M}_{\mathcal{S}_{new}^2}$

Returning to the general case, the important thing to note is that, despite $\mathcal{M}_{\mathcal{S}_{new}^n}$ represents the desired functionality, it is not expressed in terms of the original components. In fact, it represents a system without architecture (remember point number 4 in Fig. 2), which prevents from continuing its modular development. $(\text{SCTL/MUS})^A$ addresses this problem by automatically refactoring $\mathcal{S}_{new}^n$ into two architectural views, which are revisions of the original system.

The first architectural view includes a new component, $Synchronizer^n$, that materializes the new requirements and ensures the correct operation of the senders. This view is expressed in Eqs. (4) and (5), where $\Lambda_{sync}^n = \{ini_i, end_i\}_{1 \leq i \leq n}$.

$$\mathcal{S}_{new}^n = \mathcal{S}^n \,||[\Lambda_{sync}^n]||_{\mathcal{M}} \, Synchronizer^n \qquad (4)$$

$$\mathcal{S}_{new}^n = (\,|||_{\mathcal{M}} \, Sender_i) \,||[\Lambda_{sync}^n]||_{\mathcal{M}} \, Synchronizer^n \qquad (5)$$
$$\phantom{\mathcal{S}_{new}^n = (\,}{}_{i=1...n}$$

The $Synchronizer^n$ component, whose MUS graph is shown in Fig. 6(a), and the Λ_{sync}^n set of actions are automatically derived from from $\mathcal{S}^n$ and $\{\mathcal{R}_{new}^n\}$ using the algorithm described in Appendix B. This algorithm guarantees by construction that the MUS graph of the composition $\mathcal{S}^n \,||[\Lambda_{sync}^n]||_{\mathcal{M}} \, Synchronizer^n$ is equal to $\mathcal{M}_{\mathcal{S}_{new}^n}$.

In the second architectural view, $Synchronizer^n$ is seen as an aspect that crosscuts the original senders. This allows re-expressing the system $\mathcal{S}_{new}^n$ as the composition of n modified senders, in a way that resembles the original architecture of Eq. (1). The new expression is shown in Eq. (6), where the Λ_{sync}^n set of actions is the same as above.

$$\mathcal{S}_{new}^n = ||[\Lambda_{sync}^n]||_{\mathcal{M}} \, Sender_{csma_i}^n \qquad (6)$$
$$\phantom{\mathcal{S}_{new}^n = }{}_{i=1...n}$$

We refer to the modified components as $Sender_{csma}^n$, because they have the basic functionality of the original $Sender$, though enhanced with the capability to prevent collisions on a communications channel shared with other $Sender_{csma}^n$ components. Figure 6(b) shows the MUS graph of the i-th instance of $Sender_{csma}^n$ in the system, where it can be seen that the start of a transmission is forbidden while another sender is using the channel (ini_i is *false* in s_4 and s_5). Therefore, a retrenchment of the overall system has led to a loss of *unspecification* of the MUS graphs of its forming components; as noted in Sect. 3.5, this can be translated into a refinement of the requirements provided for those components by the developers.

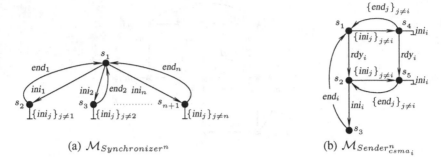

(a) $\mathcal{M}_{Synchronizer^n}$ (b) $\mathcal{M}_{Sender^n_{csma_i}}$

Fig. 6. The MUS graphs of $Synchronizer^n$ and $Sender^n_{csma_i}$

$Sender^n_{csma_i}$ results from weaving $Synchronizer^n$ with the $Sender_i$ components, by applying the *projection* operator as described in Appendix C (again, the composition of the $Sender^n_{csma_i}$ components is guaranteed to yield a MUS graph equal to $\mathcal{M}_{S^n_{new}}$). So, Equation (6) can be rewritten with an additional lower composition layer:

$$S^n_{new} = |[\Lambda^n_{sync}]|_\mathcal{M} \underset{i=1...n}{} (Sender_i \leftarrow^* \ Synchronizer^n) \qquad (7)$$

To sum up, Equations (4) and (5) describe two composition layers in the first architectural view proposed for S^n_{new}, and Eqs. (6) and (7) do the analogous with the second one. These two views are illustrated in Fig. 7.

5 Analyzing the Example

About the Architectural Views. Handling different architectural views of a system is useful to advance towards the architecture desired for its implementation, while keeping the ability to reason about different features of its functionality. In our example, if the developers expect $Synchronizer^n$ to have significance of its own in the implemented system (as an arbitrage mechanism controlling the concurrent execution of the senders), they should continue evolving the first architectural view. Conversely, they should work on the second if synchronization will be up to the senders themselves.

Multiple views also help to gain understanding about the desired functionality, because some evolutions of the system may be easier to identify from certain perspectives. For example, moving from CSMA to CSMA/CD synchronization is easier (and less error-prone) to attain by evolving the $Synchronizer^n$ component and projecting it again over the senders, than by directly modifying these. This witnesses the advantages of encapsulating crosscutting concerns.

Furthermore, from the second architectural view, we can recover the notion of a sender in which the start of a transmission can be delayed due to environmental conditions, a feature that is not present in the other view. Thus, $Sender^n_{csma_i}$ can be taken as a reusable component, with the basic functionality of a generic sender and the added value that, in the presence of other components of the same kind, it incorporates additional functionality to model synchronization. Even the $Synchronizer^n$ component may be reused, since it works as a *mutual exclusion semaphore*.

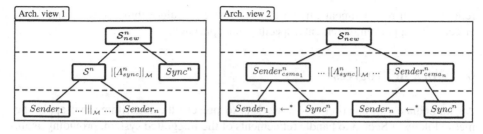

Fig. 7. The two architectural views for the system $\mathcal{S}_{new}^n$

About Tracing Integration Results. Tracing the results of integration analysis back to the composed components is essential to continue their incremental development. It is particularly frequent that a component needs to incorporate considerations from higher layers before doing new iterations of its specification. This would be the case if we wanted to enhance $Sender_{csma_i}^n$ with behavior to execute when the state s_5 is reached (after receiving data to send, the attempt to use the channel is blocked by other sender). Thus, the methodology presented here, together with the management of *unspecification*, endows (SCTL/MUS)^A with great levels of incrementality.

About the Algorithms and Formalisms. Even though the methodology of Sect. 3 is general, we have focused on handling retrenchments over compositions with the $\|[\Lambda]\|_\mathcal{M}$ operator, for which the algorithms described in Appendixes B and C are always valid. This specificity does not imply loss of generality or interest, because parallel composition is, by far, the most important construct in the field of reactive systems (see [1]), being not only valid to model distribution or the concurrent operation of several components, but also for the general management of interacting features.

The algorithm to derive the synchronizer component succeeds at encapsulating the crosscutting concerns. As a proof for this, note that, during integration analysis, the developers referred to the fact that $Sender_i$ was transmitting by the possibility of executing end_i, which would be incorrect if the senders had more actions between *ini* and *end*. Nonetheless, $Synchronizer^n$ remains valid even if new actions are inserted between *ini* and *end* in a posterior evolution. This is because $Synchronizer^n$ captures the intention of the new requirements in the context of their formulation, having nothing to do with the component that would be synthesized from those requirements alone.

On its part, the projection algorithm modifies the original components by adequately introducing *true* and *false* events. It forbids just what the synchronization requirements forbid, and maintains the *unspecification* not affected by those requirements so as not to limit future evolutions unnecessarily. Besides, it does not incorporate irrelevant facts about the environment into the specification of the individual components (note that there is no trace of rdy_j in $Sender_{csma_i}^n$, for any $j \neq i$).

As a final remark, it must be noted that our methodology is not dependent on using SCTL, since other logics could be employed – our use of SCTL is motivated by its causal semantics, which we consider adequate for the first stages of the development process, in line with the comments given in [12]. In contrast, the management of MUS models is indispensable for several reasons: i) to allow deciding when to apply refinements or retrenchments, ii) for the transformation algorithms to work, and iii) to effectively support an incremental specification approach.

6   Work in Progress

An immediate continuation of our work is to present the algorithms that apply the methodology of Sect. 3 to handle refinements of the integrated system, providing again two architectural views: one in which a new component gathers the added behavior, and other in which the new behavior is allotted over the original components. Analogous comments hold for the algorithms that perform the transformations over compositions involving other operators than $|[\Lambda]|_{\mathcal{M}}$.

We are also considering the possibility of offering other meaningful architectural alternatives, besides the two commented here. For instance, while the second view brings into the components what their environment forbids about them, a third one could incorporate what each component prohibits in its environment. Another option would be to discharge the functionality of the aspect onto a subset of the original components, though we conjecture that this may not be possible in all cases.

Our proposal in this paper represents an aid to go from the customers' requirements to a system that satisfies them, allowing to progressively conduct the specification towards the desired architecture while not preventing reasoning over the different concerns in isolation. In this regard, we intend to provide additional assistance by supporting the automatic identification of crosscutting functionality and its posterior extraction into aspects, which may be weaved with the crosscut components through parallel or sequential composition. To handle the first case, we are experiencing with algorithms similar to those of *bipartition* employed in [2], though considering *unspecification* and taking the requirements into account; to handle the second, we are currently involved with the definition of a suitable language for the definition of *pointcuts*.

The identification of aspects will be helpful to assist the developers when they fail to identify a modular decomposition of a system's functionality. As argued in Sect. 5, encapsulating crosscutting concerns is desirable even when they will not represent components in the final implementation. Besides, we remark the importance of an early identification, before the aspects get so tangled in the hierarchy of components that their identification becomes unfeasible – we believe that the incrementality of $(SCTL/MUS)^{\mathcal{A}}$ can be a good basis to advance research in this topic.

7   Related Work

The work presented here is involved with the conjoint treatment of requirements and architecture in the specification of software systems, an area that has received little attention to date. In [20], it is noted that "*little work has been devoted to techniques for systematically deriving architectural descriptions from requirements specifications*", noticing that this is somewhat paradoxical, as long as architecture has a profound impact on the achievement of a system's goals. The same author discusses in [19] the desirability of doing analysis on specification drafts and carrying out development in an incremental fashion, whereas *"many specification techniques require that the specification be complete in some sense before the analysis can start"*.

To the best of our knowledge, ours is the first formal approach that completes the cycle for integration analysis shown in Fig. 2. Elementary approaches finish at step 2, only informing about whether the analysis succeeds or not. In other cases, counterexamples are provided to help finding the source of the errors [7], but this is limited assistance (insufficient to claim step 3), because no guidance is given on how to modify the system. Even when such an aid is provided – as in [4] –, changes are made only at the level being analyzed, not being traced throughout the architecture of the system.

We only found works on traceability within the paradigm of *assume-guarantee reasoning* [8], which attempts to characterize the influence of the environment over the components to guarantee the satisfaction of the integration properties, resembling what we do with our second architectural view. However, the techniques based on this paradigm usually demand manual intervention and great expertise in formal verification, deviating intellectual efforts from the specification tasks. Our proposal addresses these shortcomings by allowing developers to reason continuously over the problem at hands; the key to achieve it is that we lean intermediately against an operational model (MUS) instead of reasoning directly over mathematical formulae (requirements).

Some transformations similar to the ones presented in this paper have been applied in the Lotosphere environment [2], though with remarkable differences. In Lotosphere, transformations were applied to refine abstract specifications into component processes, with those specifications typically describing the service offered by a communications protocol that was completely known in advance. In contrast, the vision in $(SCTL/MUS)^A$ is that no complete idea of the desired functionality is known beforehand, and that developers gain knowledge about the desired system as the development progresses. Thereby, we do not take a top-down approach to development, but an incremental one in which requirements and architecture can be elaborated in parallel. This way, we relate refinements to a progressive removal of incompleteness, which is supported by the management of *unspecification* and the reformulation of the requirements.

References

1. K. Altisen, F. Maraninchi, and D. Stauch. Exploring aspects in the context of reactive systems. In *Proceedings of Workshop on Foundations of Aspect-Oriented Languages (FOAL), in conjunction with AOSD*, pages 45–51, Lancaster, UK, 2004.
2. T. Bolognesi, J. van de Lagemaat, and C. Vissers, editors. *Lotosphere: Software development with LOTOS*. Kluwer Academic Publishers, 1995.
3. G. Bruns and P. Godefroid. Model checking partial state spaces with 3-valued temporal logics. In *Proceedings of the 11th International Conference on Computer-Aided Verification (CAV)*, pages 274–287, Trento, Italy, 1999.
4. A. S. d'Avila Garcez, A. Russo, B. Nuseibeh, and J. Kramer. An analysis-revision cycle to evolve requirements specifications. In *Proceedings of the 16th IEEE International Conference on Automated Software Engineering (ASE)*, pages 354–358, San Diego, USA, 2001.
5. J. García-Duque, J. J. Pazos-Arias, and B. Barragáns-Martínez. An analysis-revision cycle to evolve requirements specifications by using the SCTL-MUS methodology. In *Proceedings of the 10th IEEE International Conference on Requirements Engineering (RE)*, pages 282–288, Essen, Germany, 2002.

6. P. Godefroid, M. Huth, and R. Jagadeesan. Abstraction-based model checking using modal transition systems. In *Proceedings of the 12th International Conference on Concurrency Theory (CONCUR)*, pages 426–440, Aalborg, Denmark, 2001.

7. A. Gurfinkel and M. Chechik. Generating counterexamples for multi-valued model-checking. In *Proceedings of the 12th International Symposium on Formal Methods (FME)*, pages 503–521, Pisa, Italy, 2003.

8. T. A. Henzinger, S. Qadeer, and S. K. Rajamani. You assume, we guarantee: Methodology and case studies. In *Proceedings of the 10th International Conference on Computer-Aided Verification (CAV)*, pages 440–451, Vancouver, Canada, 1998.

9. G. Kiczales, J. Lamping, A. Mendhekar, C. Maeda, C. Videira Lopes, J. M. Loingtier, and J. Irwin. Aspect-oriented programming. In *Proceedings of the 11th European Conference on Object-Oriented Programming (ECOOP)*, pages 220–242, Jyväskylä, Finland, 1997.

10. S. Liu. Capturing complete and accurate requirements by refinement. In *Proceedings of the 8th IEEE International Conference on Engineering of Complex Computer Systems (ICECCS)*, pages 57–67, Maryland, USA, 2002.

11. M. López-Nores and J. J. Pazos-Arias. A Formal Approach to Component-based Specification with Improved Requirements Traceability. In *Proceedings of RE'04 Doctoral Symposium*, Kyoto, Japan, 2004.

12. J. Moffett. A model for a causal logic for requirements engineering. *Journal of Requirements Engineering*, 1:27–46, 1996.

13. B. Nuseibeh. Crosscutting requirements. In *Proceedings of the 3rd International Conference on Aspect-Oriented Software Development (AOSD)*, pages 3–4, Lancaster, UK, 2004.

14. J. J. Pazos-Arias and J. García-Duque. SCTL-MUS: A formal methodology for software development of distributed systems. A case study. *Formal Aspects of Computing*, 13:50–91, 2001.

15. M. Poppleton and R. Banach. Retrenchment: Extending the reach of refinement. In *Proceedings of the 14th IEEE International Conference on Automated Software Engineering (ASE)*, pages 158–165, Florida, USA, 1999.

16. A. Rashid, P. Sawyer, A. Moreira, and J. Araújo. Early aspects: A model for aspect-oriented requirements engineering. In *Proceedings of the 10th IEEE International Conference on Requirements Engineering (RE)*, pages 199–202, Essen, Germany, 2002.

17. S. Schneider. *The B method: An introduction*. Palgrave, 2001.

18. P. Tarr, H. Ossher, W. Harrison, and S. Sutton. N degrees of separation: Multi-dimensional separation of concerns. In *Proceedings of the 21st International Conference on Software Engineering (ICSE)*, pages 107–119, Los Angeles, USA, 1999.

19. A. van Lamsweerde. *The future of software engineering*, chapter Formal specification: A roadmap. ACM Press, 2000.

20. A. van Lamsweerde. Requirements engineering in the year 00: A research perspective. In *Proceedings of the 22nd International Conference on Software Engineering (ICSE)*, pages 5–19, Limerick, Ireland, 2000.

A   Selective Parallel Composition of MUS Graphs

The *selective parallel composition* operator ($|[\Lambda]|$) has been typically defined over *Labeled Transition Systems*. For example, in Fig. 8(a), the overall system $\mathcal{L}_3 = \mathcal{L}_1 |[c]| \mathcal{L}_2$ can evolve through actions a and b in any order, because they are not in the Λ set. In contrast, c must be executed by the two individual processes simultaneously, which

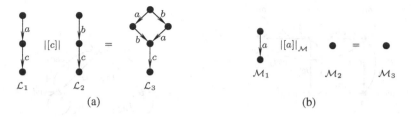

Fig. 8. Parallel composition of LTS and MUS graphs

guarantees that they terminate at the same time. Note that, as LTSs only handle *true* and *false* actions, the actions not explicitly represented are *false*.

Based on the $||[\Lambda]||$ operator, we define $||[\Lambda]||_\mathcal{M}$ by adapting its semantics to deal with *unspecification*. In a composition $\mathcal{M}_1||[\Lambda]||_\mathcal{M}\mathcal{M}_2$, the specification value for an action a is computed as the *minimum* between its values in $\mathcal{M}_1$ and $\mathcal{M}_2$ if $a \in \Lambda$, and as the *maximum* otherwise (note that $0 \le \frac{1}{2} \le 1$). Intuitively, if $a \notin \Lambda$, the two components need no agreement to go on, so it is possible to evolve through a if any of the two components can. On the contrary, if $a \in \Lambda$, the two components have to agree on a. If a is *false* in $\mathcal{M}_2$ and *true* in $\mathcal{M}_1$, the agreement is not possible, but if a were *unspecified* in $\mathcal{M}_2$ (as in Fig. 8(b)), the agreement would be possible if a evolved into *true* in a later iteration of the specification process. This way, the definition of $||[\Lambda]||_\mathcal{M}$ preserves the incompleteness of the components in the composition.

B   Synthesis of the Synchronizer Component

This appendix outlines the algorithm used in Sect. 4 to derive the $Synchronizer^n$ component. This algorithm is applicable whenever the new requirements suppress behavior in the MUS graph of the composition, by turning *true* or *unspecified* actions into *false* ones. For simplicity, we illustrate the steps for the $n = 2$ case.

1. The first step is to turn *false* actions in the starting MUS graph into *unspecified* ones, to distinguish the actions forbidden by the specification of the components from the actions that will be prohibited by the new requirements. In the example, this returns the original MUS graph $\mathcal{M}_{S^2}$ (Figure 4(b)) because it had no *false* actions.
2. Next, the new requirements are materialized over the composition, by turning into *false* all the actions they forbid. As explained in Sect. 4, the new requirements of Eq. 2 lead to the MUS graph of Fig. 5.
3. The MUS graph resulting from the previous step is reduced, to remove the actions whose occurrence is irrelevant for the integration properties. This is done by successively merging contiguous *compatible states*, that is, states in which the specification values of the actions are not contradictory (what is *true* in the one is not *false* in the other) – remark that no reduction would be possible without the management of *unspecification*.

   In the MUS graph of Fig. 5, it is possible, for instance, to merge state s_1 with s_4, s_2 with s_5 and s_3 with s_6, which yields the reduced graph of Fig. 9(a). The process eventually produces the graph of Fig. 9(b).

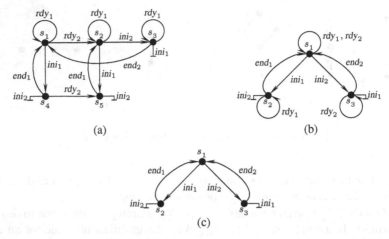

Fig. 9. Synthesis of the synchronizer component

4. To finish, it only remains to turn into *unspecified* the actions that are either *un-specified* or forming unitary loops in all the states – those actions are not rele-vant at the composition level. Then, the Λ_{sync} set of actions is formed by those actions which are *true* or *false* in any state. In the graph of Fig. 9(b), both rdy_1 and rdy_2 can be turned into *unspecified* actions in all the states, leading to the fi-nal component $Synchronizer^2$, shown in Fig. 9(c). The Λ_{sync}^2 set is found to be $\{ini_1, ini_2, end_1, end_2\}$.

C   Projection of the Synchronizer Aspect ($\leftarrow$*)

We briefly describe here how to derive the modified components in the second archi-tectural viewpoint of Sect. 4 by projecting the synchronizer aspect onto the original ones. As shown in Fig. 10, this is achieved by operating the original $Sender_i$ with the $Synchronizer^n$ component using the $|[\Lambda]|_{\mathcal{M}}$ operator, with Λ computed as the intersection of Λ_{sync}^n with the alphabet of actions of each $Sender_i$. This process is applicable whenever the original components are combined with $|[\Lambda]|_{\mathcal{M}}$, for any Λ.

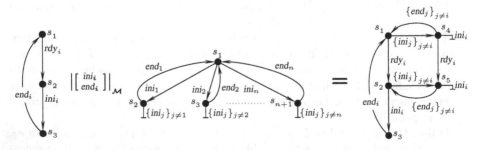

Fig. 10. Projection of the synchronizer aspect

CompAr:
Ensuring Safe Around Advice Composition

Renaud Pawlak[1], Laurence Duchien[1], and Lionel Seinturier[2]

[1] Université de Lille, INRIA Futurs-Jacquard
Bâtiment M3, Villeneuve d'Ascq, 59655, France
[2] Université de Paris 6, LIP6, INRIA Futurs-Jacquard
4, place Jussieu, 75252 Paris, France

Abstract. Advanced techniques in separation of concerns such as
Aspect-Oriented Programming, help to develop more maintainable and
more efficient applications by providing means for modularizing crosscutting concerns. However, conflicts may appear when several concerns
need to be composed for the same application, especially when dealing
with around advice. We call this problem the Aspect Composition Issue (ACI). Based on our experience in programming aspects, this paper
presents a language called CompAr, which allows the programmer to
abstractly define an execution domain, the advice codes, and their execution constraints. The CompAr compiler then evaluates the definitions
in order to check if the execution constraints are fulfilled. Using a concrete AOP case study, we show how to use the CompAr language in order
to detect and avoid ACIs.

1 Introduction

When dealing with complex software, programmers and designers naturally try
to apply the *divide and conquer* principle by splitting the application into small
pieces, which are easier to understand than the whole system. This technique is
referred to as Separation of Concerns (SoC) and has been originally described
in [5, 13]. The goal of SoC is to analyze one of the parts without having to take
the other parts into account. However, in the difficult process of making the
application parts independent, many issues can arise.

Within the last few years, Aspect-Oriented Programming (AOP) [9] has
stressed the point that some concerns are significantly difficult to modularize.
AOP identifies these concerns as crosscutting concerns, i.e. the implementation
of these concerns spans over some modules of the other concerns. AOP and related approached propose some solutions to these issues which would pull out
the crosscutting concerns from the application code, allowing for easier modularization.

Thanks to AOP, some techniques that are used in middleware and other
fields have been highlighted and are becoming more popular. One of the most
important and widely used techniques can be referred to as the *around advising of
the code*; this is an important mechanism used to compose concerns together. It

M. Steffen and G. Zavattaro (Eds.): FMOODS 2005, LNCS 3535, pp. 163–178, 2005.

has been employed under several contexts and can be implemented by wrappers, filters, interceptors, proxies, around code injections, and so on. However, all these implementation techniques face the same issues when composing several concerns. We call this kind of issue the Aspect Composition Issue (ACI) [14]. Unfortunately, little support is provided to solve this problem and, most of the time, it has to be handled manually, without any tools or guidelines.

In this paper, we present a language called CompAr that is able to automatically detect conflicting around advice codes out of an abstract specification of the aspect-oriented program.

In section 2, we define the around advice and give some examples of its use. Then, in section 3, we present our case study, which deals with real-life aspects that we use for reasoning on specific ACIs. In section 4, we define CompAr, our language to specify composition-relevant information. We show how CompAr checks a specification to detect composition issues. Section 5 goes further in studying ACI by focussing on composing all the aspects of our case study by using CompAr. Finally, before concluding, we list some related works in section 6.

2   The Around Advice

Breaking down software into independent modules, objects or components that can be designed or programmed separately, implies a composition phase. In this section, we focus on a useful composition mechanism called around advice; we introduce its mechanisms and common utilizations.

2.1   Introducing Around Advice

When composing several modules together, structural or behavioral composition mechanisms are needed; our focus is on the behavioral compositions. When composing behaviors, the behavior of the target module is modified by another behavior coming from source modules. In order to achieve this, around advice is a convenient mechanism; we describe the device here in an informal manner.

One can apply an around device code to a given target executable element such as a method, a constructor, or a field access; as a result, the target element will be modified transparently for the base program; the target element is said to be advised. Once this element is executed in the program, the flow of execution is the following:

1. the advice code is executed (and can access some contextual information from the base program),
2. when a special instruction called *proceed* is reached, the advice code executes the advised executable element (called *this*),
3. when the advised method ends, the rest of the advice code is executed and can finally return.

Note that an advice code has a *before* part (before the call to *proceed*) and an *after* part (after the call to *proceed*). It is not required to call *proceed* (it then completely replaces the implementation of the advised method).

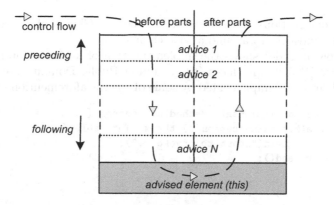

Fig. 1. An around advice chain.

As shown in figure 1, a method can be advised several times; this method then holds an advice chain. Each advice before part is executed in the order defined by the chain (the top advice code is executed first). When the execution of an advice code reaches *proceed*, the control is passed to the next advice of the chain.

The advised element is executed at the end of the chain and returns so that all the advice after parts are executed in the reverse order of the before parts execution order. An advice code can break the regular advice chain control flow by not calling proceed or by throwing an exception.

Note that an advice code is said to *precede* the advice codes that come after it in the chain and to *follow* the advice codes that come before it in the chain.

2.2   Around Advice Utilizations

Even though around advice-related techniques are used in many contexts and languages, the main utilization of around advice is in Aspect-Oriented Programming (AOP) [9]. AOP focuses on solving *crosscutting* of concerns when programming or designing complex applications. In short, AOP solves crosscutting and tangling code issues by allowing the programmer to define *pointcuts*. A pointcut is a set of points (joinpoints) in the base program that are affected by aspect-level advice, including around advice.

Aside from the popular AspectJ [8] language, numerous projects have included AOP features such as JAC [15], CFOM [2], CaesarJ [11], and PROSE [16]. Besides, several other approaches use techniques that can be closely related to around advising, for instance: Composition Filters [2] and Multi-Dimensional Separation of Concerns [12].

When a new language is not available, around advice is usually implemented by using Interception [10] [15], which is a very popular mechanism to implement separation of concerns in middleware environments. In these frameworks, interceptors are regular objects which may intercept the method invocations, the object constructions, and/or the field accesses. Chains of interceptors are functionally equivalent to around advice chains.

The following code[1] shows the implementation of an interceptor using the AOP-Alliance [1] Java interfaces (the common Public Domain interfaces that have been defined and implemented by some of the the aforementioned projects).

```
class MyInterceptor implements MethodInterceptor {
  Object invoke(MethodInvocation i) throws Throwable {
    System.out.println("About to invoke...");
    return i.proceed();
} }
```

3   An AOP Case Study for Composition

This section presents a set of useful generic server-side aspects which are typically used in distributed middleware layers.

For the sake of this paper, we have focused solely on the around devices of the aspects, and have simplified them to keep only the relevant details. Note that we use the AOP Alliance API in order to remain as independent as possible from any specific language or commercial framework. The aspects depicted here are used to illustrate typical composition issues, and they will be formalized in the next sections.

3.1   Logging Aspect

The most well-known and straightforward application of AOP consists of seamlessly introducing logging when needed. By using around advice, the logging aspect can write into files what happens on a server; this can be useful for maintenance (security, performance, debugging). As shown below, the implementation of the logging aspect's around advice is quite simple.

```
class LoggingAspect implements MethodInterceptor {
  Object invoke(MethodInvocation i) throws Throwable {
    Object result=null;
    logEntry(i.getMethod(),i.getParameters());
    result=i.proceed();
    logExit(i.getMethod(),result);
    return result;
  } [...] }
```

3.2   Authentication Aspect

Within a client/server interaction, a server-side authentication aspect checks that the user associated to the current session has the right to access the involved

---

[1] Note that the `throws Throwable` clause is used since `proceed` throws a `Throwable` and that the interceptors most of the time forward the exceptions rather than handling them.

resources. If the current session has no associated user, the authentication aspect may ask the client to authenticate by, for example, asking for a login and a password. If the client does not have the right to perform the current action, the authentication aspect performs an alternative action, such as throwing an exception to notify the client that the rights were not granted.

The implementation of the authentication aspect's logic is mainly done within the following around advice:

```
class AuthenticationAspect implements MethodInterceptor {
  Object invoke(MethodInvocation i) throws Throwable {
    // gets the session from a thread local (set by a client)
    Session s=getThreadLocalAttribute("session");
    if(s.getUser()==null) doAuthentication(s);
    if(canAccess(s.getUser(),i.getMethod())) {
      return i.proceed();
    } else {
      throw new AuthenticationException(
      "user '"+s.getUser()+"' cannot access '"+i.getMethod()+"'");
    }
  } [...] }
```

3.3   Persistence Aspect

On the server, objects can be persistent. Typically, this is achieved by advising all the setters and getters of the objects and by writing or reading the data in a storage (XML files, JDBC data source). In many systems, the object's fields may still be directly accessed on optimization purpose so that the object acts as a cache for the storage. Additionally, any transient object that is referenced by a persistent object (through a reference or a collection) should itself become persistent.

The implementation of the persistence aspect's logic is mainly done within the following around advice:

```
class PersistenceAspect implements MethodInterceptor {
  // advice all the setters, getters, adders, and removers
  Object invoke(MethodInvocation i) throws Throwable {
    Object result=null;
    if (isPersistent(i.getThis()) {
      [...] // Before: read needed data from storage
      result = i.proceed() // read or write the value in memory
      // After: write changed data into storage and
      if(isSetter(i.getMethod())) {
        // make the new referenced object persistent if needed
        if(isStorable(i.getParameters()[0]))
          makePersistent(i.getParameters()[0]);
      [...] } [...]
    } else result = i.proceed(); // Transient object case.
    return result;
  } [...] }
```

3.4   Association Aspect

In object or component models, entities may be related to each other through references or collections. At a higher level, these references or collections can be part of an association; they are then called *roles*.

For instance, an association exists between an employee and a company: an employee *belongs to* a company and a company *employs* several employees; each class (Employee and Company) defines a role field of this association. When a role that is part of an association is set, as through a role setter, it generally means that the other role should be updated in order to preserve the association integrity.

With AOP, it is possible to handle the association integrity concern within an aspect. This concern, which is usually a crosscutting one, can then be cleanly modularized and the maintenance of the application is more straightforward. The main logic of the association integrity concern is programmed in the following around advice:

```
class AssociationAspect implements MethodInterceptor {
  // advice the setters, adders, remover of roles
  Object invoke(MethodInvocation i) throws Throwable {
    Field current = getCurrentRole(i.getMethod());
    if(current!=null) {
      // do not update if we are already within updating
      if (getThreadLocalAttribute("update") ==
          getCurrentRole(i.getMethod()))
        return i.proceed();
      Field opposite = getOppositeRole(i.getMethod());
      try {
        setThreadLocalAttribute("update", opposite);
        doUpdate(opposite, // the opposite role
          i.getThis(), // the object that holds the current role
          current.get(i.getThis()), // the old role value
          i.getParameters()[0]); // the new role value
      } finally { setThreadLocalAttribute("update", null); }
    }
    return = i.proceed();
  } [...] }
```

3.5   Composing Logging, Authentication, and Persistence

As a first introduction to ACIs (Aspect Composition Issues), this section informally shows how to compose the Logging, Authentication, and Persistence aspects. This simple composition problem illustrates the importance of correctly ordering the around advice.

When composing these three aspects, a simple reasoning can help the programmer to find the aspect interactions and thus find out how to solve them. Let us first look at the code of these aspects (see sections 3.1, 3.2, and 3.3). A quick glance shows that the only aspect that does not call proceed all the time is the authentication aspect. This property is important because when an aspect is programmed independently from any context, the programmer assumes that the invocation is actually proceeded to the advised element.

Therefore, if the logging around advice is placed after the authentication advice, then the logging will only be performed if the invocation is authenticated. However, it is not always the behavior that a programmer would expect for the system. Indeed, to detect attack attempts on the server, we may want to log all the requests, even if the associated action is not successfully executed. In contrast, a quick study of the persistence aspect shows that we want to apply the persistence only if the action is successfully executed.

Finally, we are in the presence of three significantly different kinds of around advice.

- The logging has an execution constraint which states that its before part must always be executed. By using first order action logic, this constraint can be expressed as: `beforeLogging`, where `beforeLogging` is true if the before-logging part has been executed at the end of the advice chain execution. We refer to this kind of advice as **obligatory** advice.
- The persistence has an execution constraint which can be expressed as: `[persistent]?this<=>writeStorage:true`, to be read as "if our execution context is `persistent` (boolean), then the execution of `this` advised implies the execution of the `writeStorage` action and vice versa, else the execution constraint is always fulfilled (`true`)". Note that we refer to this kind of advice as **exclusive** advice.
- The authentication does not have an execution constraint, but it does not always call proceed. We refer to this kind of advice as **conditional** advice.

Taking into account all that has been said, in order to fulfill the obligatory and exclusive constraints, the best order for the chain should be: (`Logging > Authentication > Persistence`). Note that we have already informally presented this classification in [14]. This is, on the other hand, a very intuitive result that would need to be validated. Besides, when the number of aspects grows, it can become tedious to manually fulfill all the execution constraints. In the next section, we present CompAr, a language which helps the programmer to find and validate the right composition order in a rigorous way.

4   Supporting Aspects Composition: The CompAr Language

In the previous section, we presented a set of useful aspects for server-side middleware layers: `Logging`, `Authentication`, `Persistence`, and `Association`. Thanks to AOP and around advising, we have been able to separately define these different concerns so that the understanding of the sever-side system is easier. However, as seen in section 3.5 some ACIs are likely to appear when composing the aspects. This is due to the fact that each aspect is programmed independently, and holds some *implicit constraints*.

In this paper, we go far beyond our first paper on the subject [14], which informally introduced the advice types and stated the ACI in a general way. Here, in order to deal with the ACIs, we have defined a language called CompAr (for Composing Around advice). CompAr allows the programmer to specify the advice codes and their implicit constraints. In addition, CompAr checks that a given composition order is valid for a set of execution contexts.

In the rest of this section, we present CompAr (4.1), we define its semantics (4.2), and we apply it to our composition example (4.3).

4.1   The CompAr Language

In order to introduce CompAr, we first show how to specify the composition problem which was informally presented in 3.5. In order to do this, we write the following abstract program:

```
choices: persistent, authenticated;
advice logging:loggingEnter {loggingEnter+loggingExit}
advice authentication { [authenticated]?-+-:throw NotAuthenticated }
advice persistenceSetter:[persistent]?this<=>writeStorage:true {
   [persistent]?-+(caller(persistent=true),writeStorage):-+-}
advised a { logging, authentication, persistenceSetter; }
```

Where the choices command defines the different boolean variables of the execution domain, advice defines a new abstract advice code, and advised defines a composition order to be tested by the compiler. When run, the compiler executes the defined advised in the domain (all the possible combinations of choices values) and checks that the advice definitions are valid. Note that choices can be initialized to true or false in order to restrain the execution domain, but they are usually left undefined, as in this case, to test all the possible executions.

An advice definition contains two parts: an optional post-execution constraint, defined after the advice name and separated from it by a colon; and a body, within curly brackets, which represents the abstract definition of the advice code.

As a result, with CompAr, the logging advice programmed in section 3.1 can be abstractly defined by:

    advice logging:loggingEnter{loggingEnter+loggingExit}.

It means that the body is composed of a loggingEnter before-proceed action and a loggingExit after-proceed action. Besides, when the advice is included in an advised, the post-condition execution constraint ensures that the loggingEnter action has been executed.

The persistence advice is more complicated but follows the same principle:

    advice persistenceSetter:[persistent]?this<=>writeStorage:true
{[persistent]?-+(caller(persistent=true),writeStorage):-+-}

As an execution constraint, we recognize the constraint defined in section 3.5. The body must be understood as follows: "If the execution context is persistent we define a body that does nothing as a before part and that executes two actions as an after part: (1) it sets the calling context to persistent (as an effect, the newly referred object is made persistent), (2) it executes the `writeStorage` action. If the execution context is not `persistent`, we just proceed the execution."

Note that we use - to indicate that the advised body code performs some action that is not relevant for composition.

4.2   The CompAr Semantics

We now give a brief overview of the CompAr semantics by using a denotational semantics. CompAr can be split into two sub-languages: the body language and the constraint language.

To help the semantics understanding, note that the body language syntax is given by the B rule (terminals are lower-cased identifiers and symbols other than '|', ';', and '::='):

```
B ::= E | E+E;
E ::= (E) | - | id | [T]?B:B | id(PARAMS)
          | throw id | (E,E) | caller(PARAMS);
PARAMS ::= PARAMS, ASSIGN | ASSIGN;
ASSIGN ::= id=T;
T ::= (T) | id | T&&T | T||T | !T | true | false;
```

The constraint language syntax is defined by C:

```
C ::= A | A=>A | A<=>A | [T]?C:C | true | false | C&&C | C||C | !C;
A ::= id | ?id | this | ?this;
```

The Body Language Semantics: The body language is inductively defined by three denotation functions: $[\![B]\!]$:*Environment*→*Environment* (body denotation function), $[\![E]\!]$:*Environment*→ *Environment* (expression denotation function), and $[\![T]\!]$:*Environment*→*Boolean* (boolean expression denotation function). For the sake of simplification, we use primitive functions that we informally describe.

The $[\![B]\!]$ denotation function is defined through the $[\![E]\!]$ denotation function:

1. $[\![E1+E2]\!](e) = [\![E2]\!](\mathrm{proceed}([\![E1]\!](e)))$
2. $[\![B]\!](e) = [\![E]\!](e)$

where proceed:*Environment*→*Environment* is the function that corresponds to the denotation function of the next advice body in the chain. For a given advised execution, an environment contains a linked code list, which corresponds to the advice order that has been defined for the advised. Moreover, when the end of the chain is reached and the advised element is executed, a *this* action is set to '*executed*' in the environment.

The $[\![E]\!]$ denotation function (for expressions) is defined as follows and using $[\![B]\!]$ and $[\![T]\!]$:

1. $[\![-]\!](e) = e$ // skip function
2. $[\![(E)]\!](e) = [\![E]\!](e)$
3. $[\![(E1,E2)]\!](e) = [\![E2]\!]([\![E1]\!](e))$
4. $[\![i]\!](e) = e[\text{executed}/i]$
5. $[\![[T]?B1:B2]\!](e) = [\![B1]\!](e)$ if $[\![T]\!](e)$=true, $[\![B2]\!](e)$ otherwise
6. $[\![i(i1=T1,\ldots,in=Tn)]\!](e)$
   $=\text{advised}(i,\text{new}/[\![T1]\!](e)/i1,\ldots,[\![Tn]\!](e)/in],e[\text{invoked}/i])$
7. $[\![\texttt{caller}(i1=T1,\ldots,in=Tn)]\!](e) = \text{parent}(e)/[\![T1]\!](e)/i1,\ldots,[\![Tn]\!](e)/in]$

where advised:$Identifier \times Environment \times Environment \rightarrow Environment$ is the function that initializes a new child environment (new:$\rightarrow Environment$) with the linked code that corresponds to the advised identified by i. It then proceeds the first linked code of the chain in the new environment. Note that '*advised*' sets the i action state to '*invoked*' in the parent environment. This i action state will be set to '*executed*' in the parent environment by the '*proceed*' function whenever the advised element is executed in the child environment.

Note that two types of environment changes can be performed: an action state change, where an action can be set to '*executed*' or '*invoked*', and a choice boolean value assignment. This assignment can be done in a new context, during an '*advised*' invocation, or in a calling context, during a `caller` instruction.

We do not formally define the throwing of exceptions since it is easy to understand intuitively. When a exception is thrown, the program terminates its execution and the environment is returned as is.

Finally, we do not define the denotation function $[\![T]\!]$ because it is a classical boolean expression denotation function.

The Constraint Language Semantics: When a CompAr program is executed, it is important to note that some choices may be left undefined. As a consequence, the compiler creates all the possible environments in order to cover the domain and check out all the possible executions. For instance, when an invocation towards an advised is done, a new set of environmental contexts is created and the invocation is performed for all these contexts. Hence, the compiler creates an execution tree rather than a simple execution.

When the execution tree is created, the compiler inspects all the final environmental contexts (one per tree node) and checks, for each one, that the advice post-execution constraints are fulfilled. For a given environment, we define the $[\![C]\!]$ denotation function, which is used for constraint verification.

1. $[\![[T]?C1:C2]\!](e) = [\![C1]\!](e)$ if $[\![T]\!](e)$=true, $[\![C2]\!](e)$ otherwise
2. $[\![i]\!](e) = true$ if get$(i)(e)$=executed, *false* otherwise
3. $[\![?i]\!](e) = true$ if get$(i)(e)$=invoked, *false* otherwise
4. $[\![C1 \texttt{=>} C2]\!](e) = [\![C1]\!](e) \Rightarrow [\![C2]\!](e)$
5. $[\![C1 \texttt{<=>} C2]\!](e) = ([\![C1]\!](e) \Rightarrow [\![C2]\!](e)) \wedge ([\![C2]\!](e) \Rightarrow [\![C1]\!](e))$
... the rest is regular boolean expressions

4.3   Testing Our Case Study with CompAr

Note that the CompAr language and all the examples used in this paper are available for download at [4].

If we compile the program defined in section 4.1, we can check that our informal reasoning led in section 3.5 is correct. The compiler then writes out:

```
[START] checking 'a' advised execution constraints...
   [OK] [0] {persistent=true, authenticated=true}
   [OK] [0] {persistent=true, authenticated=false}
   [OK] [0] {persistent=false, authenticated=true}
   [OK] [0] {persistent=false, authenticated=false}
[END] no composition errors found while checking 'a'
```

As we can see, the compiler checked the post-execution constraints for the domain, which is formed out of the combination of the persistent and authenticated choices possible values. Here, since the values are undefined, there are four possible executions and they all fulfill the constraints for the advised: ordered as logging, authentication, persistenceSetter.

Next, if we try an invalid order such as persistenceSetter, authentication, logging, the compiler reports an error for each execution that does not fulfill all the constraints:

```
[START] checking 'a' advised execution constraints...
   [OK] [0] {persistent=true, authenticated=true}

   [ERROR] [0] constraint unfulfilled in 'logging' (loggingEnter)
    - final context:
       choices: {persistent=true, authenticated=false}
       actions: {}
    - execution trace:
       test([persistent]?(-+caller([persistent=true]),writeStorage)
                         :(-+-)=>true)
       enter(a.persistenceSetter=>before)
       test([authenticated]?(-+-):(throw NotAuthenticated)=>false)
     * throw(throw NotAuthenticated)

   [OK] [0] {persistent=false, authenticated=true}

   [ERROR] [0] constraint unfulfilled in 'logging' (loggingEnter)
   [...]

[END] 2 composition error(s) found while checking 'a'
```

Here, we see that the loggingEnter constraint defined by the logging advice is not fulfilled when authenticated=true.

5   Using CompAr to Solve Complex ACIs

In this section, we finalize our case study which had started in sections 3.5 and 4.3 by adding the association aspect of section 3.4. As we will see next, adding this final aspect induces a difficult ACI that we manage to detect and solve with CompAr.

5.1   Composing the Association

For the association, the advice code, applied on a role setter, is active only if the advised method is a `role` (part of an association), and if we are not already in an `update` process. Further, in the case that the `role&&!update` condition is fulfilled, the association is exclusive – the opposite role of an association has to be updated only if the current role itself is updated. As a consequence, a possibly valid order for the `roleSetter` advice can be defined in the `total` advised: `advised total { logging, authentication, persistenceSetter, roleSetter; }`.

More precisely, by using CompAr, the association around advice can be abstractly specified as:

```
advice roleSetter : [role && !update]?this <=> total:true {
    ([role && !update]?total(update=true):-) + -
}
```

where `total` is the name of the advised that defines the full order of our four aspects. The association specification should be read as follows: "the before part does nothing except proceeding; the after part invokes recursively the advised `total` if we are in a role and not in an updating process (`role && !update` condition)".

Note that this definition makes the total `advised` definition recursive. The infinite recursion is avoided by the `update=true` assignment which restricts the domain of the `total` invocation and prevents having to re-apply the `roleSetter` advice.

However, the `total` ordering leads to a conflict that we explain in the next section.

5.2   The Persistence and Association Conflict

Let us imagine that we want to apply our aspects to two objects o1 and o2, where o1 and o2 can be linked through an association. This association has two roles r1 and r2. A method `setR2` can be called on o1 in order to set the association's role and a method `setR1` can be called on o2 in order to set the association's opposite role. Let us also assume our initial conditions imply that o2 is persistent, that o1 is not persistent, and that o1.r2 and o2.r1 are `null`.

Figure 2 shows the execution flow when `setR2(o2)` is invoked on o1 and when the advice chain is the one suggested by the `total` advised of the previous section. Note that x refers to a memory variable, whereas x̲ refers to the corresponding variable in the persistent storage.

As seen in the figure, the composition of the aspects as they are produces a side-effect that breaks the implicit persistence constraint; the final storage state

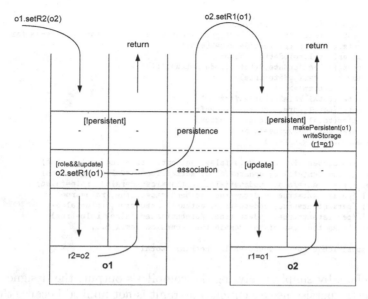

Fig. 2. Example of conflict between persistence and association.

(o1.r2=null) differs from the final memory state (o1.r2=o2). This composition error is mainly a result of the condition [persistent] being global to the before and after parts of the persistent advice code. As a consequence, the persistence after code, which is supposed to write the value of the r2 role in the storage, is never executed.

5.3   Solving the Conflict by Using CompAr

In the previous section, we have seen that the persistence and the association conflict. Detecting this conflict requires a great deal of analysis and understanding from the aspect designer. However, by using CompAr, this conflict can be automatically detected. In fact, if we run CompAr on the total advised as defined in section 5.1, it gives the following output:

```
[START] checking 'total' advised execution constraints...
   [OK] [O] {persistent=true, update=true, authenticated=true, role=true}
   [OK] [O] {persistent=true, update=true, authenticated=true, role=false}
   [OK] [O] {persistent=true, update=true, authenticated=false, role=true}
   [...] // checks the rest of the domain...

   [ERROR] [O] constraint unfulfilled in 'persistenceSetter'
              ([persistent]?(this<=>writeStorage):(true))
   - initial context:
        choices: {persistent=false, update=false, authenticated=true, role=true}
        actions: {}
   - final context:
        choices: {persistent=true, update=false, authenticated=true, role=true}
        actions: {loggingEnter=EXECUTED, total=EXECUTED, loggingExit=EXECUTED, this=EXECUTED}
   - execution trace:
          enter(total.logging=>before)
        * execute(loggingEnter)
          test([authenticated]?(-+-):(throw NotAuthenticated)=>true)
```

```
    enter(total.authentication=>before)
    test([persistent]?(-+caller([persistent=true]),writeStorage):(-+-)=>false)
    enter(total.persistenceSetter=>before)
    enter(total.roleSetter=>before)
    test([role&&!update]?(total(update=true)):(-)=>true)
  * invoke(total(update=true))
  * execute(total=>this)
    enter(total.roleSetter=>after)
    enter(total.persistenceSetter=>after)
    enter(total.authentication=>after)
    enter(total.logging=>after)
  * execute(loggingExit)

[OK] [0] {persistent=false, update=false, authenticated=true, role=false}
[OK] [0] {persistent=false, update=false, authenticated=false, role=true}
[OK] [0] {persistent=false, update=false, authenticated=false, role=false}
[OK] [1] {persistent=true, update=true, authenticated=true, role=true}
[OK] [1] {persistent=true, update=true, authenticated=true, role=false}
[OK] [1] {persistent=true, update=true, authenticated=false, role=true}
[...] // checks the rest of the domain for recursion level 1...

[END] 1 composition error(s) found while checking 'total'
```

Therefore, by simply analyzing the compiler's output, the designer can deduce that the persistence execution constraint is not fulfilled because the action writeStorage is not executed at level 0 of the recursive evaluation (the final context contains a list of the executed actions). A simple solution to solve this conflict is to decouple the [persistent] condition. In fact, by specifying the persistence body as, ([persistent]?-:-)+([persistent]?(caller(persistent= true),writeStorage):-), the compiler does not report any more errors. It is then easy for the designer to report this design change in the persistence implementation of section 3.3.

6   Related Works

Some important studies on aspect interaction are conducted in [6]. This work, which is based on a more precise definition of the AOP's pointcuts semantics, allows their authors to automatically detect the points where a potential conflict may occur (the points where several advice codes are applied). However, it does not give solutions for ordering the advice codes. We believe that this work and our work are complementary.

As shown in [7], *superimpositions* define program modules that can augment distributed programs (defined as processes and modules) with added functionalities. Some calculi are available to combine superimpositions and to perform semantic checks so that the expected properties of the final program and the superimposed modules are verified. Our approach focuses on the around advice and is more usable by the end programmer since superimpositions require the programmer to define a great deal of semantics, which can make the approach difficult to understand and to use in practice.

Also, some core composition mechanisms are defined in the Composition Filter model [3]. These mechanisms rely on the definitions of workflows which define how filters interact. However, it is tricky to define a given workflow and make sure that it will be valid and usable in any case. Besides, the chosen approach makes the implementation quite difficult to read an maintain.

Finally, besides validation of aspect compositions, the strength of our approach comes from its simplicity: it can be straightforwardly mapped to a plain implementation, without having to use complex paradigms and API within the program.

7   Conclusion

In this paper, we study the Aspect Composition Issues (ACIs) when using the around advice construct, which is a significant construct for separating concerns, especially for AOP and related approaches. Our work defines a language called CompAr that allows the specification of composition-relevant information that includes boolean choices (forming the execution domain), action executions or invocations, and post-execution constraints. Our compiler then evaluates the specification within the defined domain and checks that all the execution paths fulfill the constraints.

Our study of the four real-life aspects (logging, authentication, persistence, and association) shows that our approach helps to detect and solve ACIs (see the persistence/association ACI of section 5). Besides, the fact that we define a new language makes the approach independent from existing concrete environments or languages. CompAr can then be used as a complementary tool or a DSL for helping the designers.

Finally, even though CompAr is a research prototype, our study is a proof of concept that validation of AO programs is possible. For instance, it would be possible, for a tool or language editor, to generate the abstract CompAr specification out of a real program. One could argue that we could face a state explosion problem when executing the specification (especially if we wanted to test all the possible orders). However, since the abstract specification focuses only on composition-relevant information, and that the number of around advice codes it somehow restrained in real systems, we think that this method is applicable in most cases.

We are currently working on several improvements of the language. For instance, we would like to introduce missing constructs such as exception catches, that have not been implemented yet. Modeling other kind of advice such as before, after, cflow, and call-located advice would be quite straightforward. Indeed, before and after advice are subcases of around once; cflow can be modeled by defining specific choices; call-located advice (in this paper we focus on execution-located advice) can be modeled using a proxy-like design. More importantly, we also would like to enhance the post execution constraint sub-language to allow TLA-like expressions. This would allow the designer to specify advice where the performed actions must be executed in a certain order. For instance, a security aspect should always execute the `crypt` action before the `decrypt` action.

References

1. AOP-Alliance. http://aopalliance.sf.net.
2. L. Bergmans, M. Aksit, and B. Tekinerdogan. *Software Architectures and Component Technology*, chapter Aspect Composition Using Composition Filters, pages 357–382. Kluwer Academic Publishers, 2001.
3. L. Bergmans and M. Aksits. Composing crosscutting concerns using composition filters. *CACM*, 44(10):51–57, 2001.
4. CompAr. http://www.lifl.fr/~pawlak/compar.
5. E. Dijkstra. *A Discipline of Programming*. Prentice Hall, 1976.
6. R. Douence, P. Fradet, and M. Südholt. Composition, reuse and interaction analysis of stateful aspects. In *Proceedings of the 3rd Int. Conf. on Aspect-Oriented Software Development (AOSD'04)*, Mar. 2004.
7. M. Katara and S. Katz. Architectural views of aspects. In *Proceedings of the 2nd international conference on Aspect-oriented software development*, pages 1–10. ACM Press, 2003.
8. G. Kiczales, E. Hilsdale, J. Hugunin, M. Kersten, J. Palm, and W. Griswold. Getting started with AspectJ. *Communications of the ACM*, 44(10):59–65, 2001.
9. G. Kiczales, J. Lamping, A. Mendhekar, C. Maeda, C. Lopes, J. Loingtier, and J. Irwin. Aspect-oriented programming. In *Proceedings of the European Conference on Object-Oriented Programming (ECOOP'97)*, 1997.
10. R. Lämmel. A semantical approach to method-call interception. In *Proceedings of the 1st international conference on Aspect-oriented software development*, pages 41–55. ACM Press, 2002.
11. M. Mezini and K. Ostermann. Conquering aspects with Caesar. In *Proceedings of the 2nd International Conference on Aspect-Oriented Software Development (AOSD'03)*, 2003.
12. H. Ossher and P. Tarr. Using multidimensional separation of concerns to (re)shape evolving software. *Communications of the ACM*, 44(10):43–50, 2001.
13. D. L. Parnas. On the criteria to be used in decomposing systems into modules. *Communications of the ACM*, 15(12):1053–1058, 1972.
14. R. Pawlak, L. Duchien, and G. Florin. An automatic aspect weaver with a reflective programming language. In *Proceedings of Reflection'99*, July 1999.
15. R. Pawlak, L. Seinturier, L. Duchien, and G. Florin. Jac: A flexible solution for aspect-oriented programming in java. In *Proceedings of Reflection 2001*, LNCS 2192, pages 1–21, May 2001.
16. A. Popovici, G. Alonso, and T. Gross. Just-in-time aspects: Efficient dynamic weaving for java. In *Proceedings of the 2nd international conference on Aspect-Oriented Software Development*, pages 100–109. ACM Press, 2003.

Guaranteeing Resource Bounds
for Component Software

Hoang Truong

Department of Informatics, University of Bergen,
PB.7800, N-5020 Bergen, Norway
hoang@ii.uib.no

Abstract. Component software is software that has been assembled from various pieces of standardized, reusable computer programs, so-called components. Executing component software creates instances of these components. For several reasons, for example, limited resources and/or application requirements, it can be important to have control over the number of such instances.

In the previous work [3], we have given an abstract component language and a type system which ensures that the number of simultaneously active instances of any component never exceeds a sharp bound expressed in the type. The language featured instantiation and reuse of components, as well as sequential composition, choice and scope.

This work extends the previous one to include a parallel composition. Moreover, we improve on the operational semantics by using a small-step reduction relation. As a result, we can prove the soundness property of our static type system using the technique of Wright and Felleisen.

1 Introduction

Component software is built from various components, possibly developed by third-parties [15], [20], [17], [8]. These components may in turn use other components. Upon execution instances of these components are created. For example, when we launch a web browser application it may create an instance of a dial-up network connection, an instance of a menubar and several instances of a toolbar, among others. Each toolbar may in turn create its own control instances such as buttons, addressbars, bookmarks, and so on.

The process of creating an instance of a component x does not only mean the allocation of memory space for x's code and data structures, the creation of instances of x's subcomponents (and so on), but possibly also the binding of other system and hardware resources. Usually, these resources are limited and components are required to have only a certain number of simultaneously active instances. In the above example, there should be only one instance of a menubar and one instance of a modem for network connection. Other examples come from the singleton pattern and its extensions (multitons), which have been widely discussed in literature [10], [9]. These patterns limit the number of objects of a certain class dynamically, at runtime.

M. Steffen and G. Zavattaro (Eds.): FMOODS 2005, LNCS 3535, pp. 179–194, 2005.

When building large component software it can easily happen that different instances of the same component are created. Creating more active instances than allowed can lead to errors or even a system crash, when there are not enough resources for them. An example is resource-exhaustion DoS (Denial of Service) attacks which cause a temporary loss of services. There are several ways to meet this challenge, ranging from testing, runtime checking [9], to static analysis.

Type systems are a branch of static analysis. Type systems have traditionally been used for compile-time error-checking, cf. [4]. Recently, there are several works on using type systems for certifying important security properties, such as performance safety, memory safety, control-flow safety [14], [6], [5]. In component software, typing has been studied in relation to integrating components such as type-safe composition [19] or type-safe evolution [13]. In this paper we explore the possibility of a type system which allows one to detect *statically* whether or not the number of simultaneously active instances of specific components exceeds the allowed number. Note that here we only control resources by the number of instances. However, we can extend to more specific resources, such as memory, by adding annotations to components using such resources.

For this purpose we have designed a component language where we have abstracted away many aspects of components and have kept only those that are relevant to instantiation and composition. In the previous work [3], the main features are instantiation and reuse, sequential composition, choice and scope. In this work we add a parallel composition, which allows two expressions running independently at the same time. At the first look, the parallel composition seems adding only a small difficulty to the type system. However, we have found that we have to make substantial changes to the type system to obtain sharp upper bounds as in [3]. As before, reusing a component means to use an existing instance of the component if there is already one, and to create a new instance only if there exists none. Though abstract, the strength of the primitives for composition is considerable. Choice allows us to model both conditionals and non-determinism (due to, e.g., user input). It can also be used when a component have several compatible versions and the system can choose one of them at runtime. Scope is a mechanism to deallocate instances but it can also be used to model method calls. Sequential composition is associative.

The operational semantics in this work has also been improved as compared to the previous one. Instead of using a big-step operational semantics, here we use a small-step reduction relation and as a result, we can prove the soundness of our type system using the technique of Wright and Felleisen [18].

The type inference algorithm for this system is almost the same as in [3]. We still have a polynomial time type inference algorithm but we leave it out here for the sake of brevity.

The paper is organized as follows. Section 2 introduces the component language and a small-step operational semantics. In Section 3 we define types and the typing relation. Properties of the type system and the operational semantics are presented in Section 4. Last, we outline some future directions.

2   A Component Language

2.1   Terms

Component programs, declarations and expressions are defined in Table 1. In the definition we use extended Backus-Naur Form with the following meta-symbols: infix | for choice and overlining for Kleene closure (zero or more iterations).

Table 1. Syntax

Prog	::=	$Decls; E$	Program
Decls	::=	$\overline{x \prec E}$	Declarations
$A, .., E$	::=		Expressions
		ϵ	Empty expression
		new x	New instantiation
		reu x	Reuse instantiation
		$E\,E$	Sequential composition
		$(E + E)$	Choice composition
		$(E \parallel E)$	Parallel composition
		$\{E\}$	Scope

We use $a, b, .., z$ for component names and $A, .., E$ for expressions. We collect all component names in a set $\mathbb{C}$.

We have two primitives (**new** and **reu**) for creating and (if possible) reusing an instance of a component, and four primitives for composition (sequential composition denoted by juxtaposition, + for choice, $\parallel$ for parallel, and $\{\ldots\}$ for scope). Together with the empty expression ϵ these generate so-called *component expressions*. A *declaration* $x \prec E$ states how the component x depends on subcomponents as expressed in the component expression E. If x has no subcomponents then E is ϵ and we call x a *primitive component*. Upon instantiation or reuse of x the expression E is executed. A *component program* consist of declarations and ends with a *main expression* which sparks off the execution, see Section 2.2.

The following example is a well-formed component program:

$$d \prec \epsilon \quad e \prec \epsilon \quad a \prec (\,\mathbf{new}\,d \parallel \{\,\mathbf{reu}\,d\}\,\mathbf{reu}\,e)$$
$$b \prec (\,\mathbf{reu}\,d\{\,\mathbf{new}\,a\} + \mathbf{new}\,e\,\mathbf{new}\,a)\,\mathbf{reu}\,d; \quad \mathbf{reu}\,b$$

In this example, d and e are primitive components. Component a is the parallel composition of **new** d and $\{\,\mathbf{reu}\,d\}\,\mathbf{reu}\,e$. Component b has a choice expression before reuse of an instance of d. The first subexpression of the choice expression is **reu** $d\{\,\mathbf{new}\,a\}$.

We can view $\{\,\mathbf{new}\,a\}$ in this expression as a function call $f()$ (in traditional programming languages). Function f then has body **new** a, which means $f()$ needs a new instance of a to carry out its task. We abstract from the details of this job, the only relevant aspect here is that it involves a new instance of a which will be deallocated upon exiting f.

The example is simple, but as we will see in the next section, there are many possible runs of the program, resulting in difference numbers of instances for each component during and after each run.

2.2   Operational Semantics

The operational semantics is based on a reduction relation and a structural congruence. The reduction relation is a set of small-step reduction rules between *configurations*. The structural congruence, essentially commutativity of $+$ and $\|$, allows us to rearrange the structure of a configuration so that reduction rules may be applied. In the sequel we assume that we are working with a program $Prog = Decls; E$ and $x \prec A \in Decls$ denotes that $x \prec A$ is a declaration in $Decls$.

Before going into the details of congruence and reduction rules, we define our notion of configuration and its relevant components. A configuration is a binary tree $\mathbb{T}$ of threads. A thread is a stack ST of pairs of a local store and a expression (M, E), where M is a multiset over component names $\mathbb{C}$, and E is an expression as defined in Table 1. A thread is *active* if it is a leaf thread. Reduction always occurs at one of the leaf/active threads. A configuration is *terminal* if it has only one thread of the form (M, ϵ). Stacks and configurations are defined as follows:

$$
\begin{array}{llll}
ST & ::= (M_1, E_1) \circ \dots \circ (M_n, E_n) & \text{Stack} \\
\mathbb{T}, \mathbb{S} ::= & & \text{Configurations} \\
& \mathsf{Lf}(ST) & \text{Leaf} \\
\mid & \mathsf{Nd}(ST, \mathbb{T}) & \text{Node with one branch} \\
\mid & \mathsf{Nd}(ST, \mathbb{T}, \mathbb{T}) & \text{Node with two branches}
\end{array}
$$

Multisets are denoted by $[\dots]$, where sets are denoted, as usual, by $\{\dots\}$. $M(x)$ is the multiplicity of element x in multiset M and $M(x) = 0$ if $x \notin M$. The operation $\cup$ is union of multisets: $(M \cup N)(x) = max(M(x), N(x))$. The operation $\uplus$ is additive union of multisets: $(M \uplus N)(x) = M(x) + N(x)$. We write $M + x$ for $M \uplus [x]$ and when $x \in M$ we write $M - x$ for $M - [x]$.

We assign to each node in our tree a *location*. Let α, β range over locations. A location is a sequence over $\{l, r\}$. The root is assigned the empty sequence. The locations of two direct nodes from the root are l and r. The locations of the two direct child nodes of l are ll and lr, and so on. In general, αl and αr are the locations of the direct children of α. We write $\alpha \in \mathbb{T}$ when α is a valid location in tree $\mathbb{T}$. Whenever a new node is created, a location is assigned to it and this location will not be changed by rule conBranch.

Since the location of a parent node is a subsequence of the location of its children (direct and indirect), we define the following binary prefix ordering relation $\leq$ over locations. For location $\alpha = s_0 s_1 .. s_n$ where $s_i \in \{l, r\}$, $\alpha' \leq \alpha$ if $\alpha' = s_0 s_1 .. s_m$, $0 \leq m \leq n$. The set of all locations in a tree and this binary relation form a partially ordered set [7]. A maximal element of this partially ordered set is the location of a leaf. We denote by leaves($\mathbb{T}$) the set of locations of all the leaves of $\mathbb{T}$.

We denote by $\mathbb{T}(\alpha)$ the stack at location α in $\mathbb{T}$. We write $ST = (M_1, E_1) \circ .. \circ (M_n, E_n)$ for a stack of n elements where (M_1, E_1) is the bottom and (M_n, E_n) is the top of the stack. '$\circ$' is the stack separator. We call $\alpha.k$ the *position* of the kth element (from the bottom) of the stack $\mathbb{T}(\alpha)$. Again the set of all positions $\alpha.k$ in tree $\mathbb{T}$ is a partially ordered set with the following binary relation. $\alpha_1.k_1 \leq \alpha_2.k_2$ if either $\alpha_1 = \alpha_2$ and $k_1 \leq k_2$, or $\alpha_1 < \alpha_2$. We denote by hi(ST) the height of the stack and $ST|_k$ is the stack of from bottom to the kth element: $ST|_k = (M_1, E_1) \circ .. \circ (M_k, E_k)$. By $[ST|_k]$ we denote the multiset of active instances in $ST|_k$, so $[ST|_k] = M_1 \uplus .. \uplus M_k$. We simply write $[ST]$ when $k = $ hi(ST). We denote by $[\mathbb{T}]$ the multiset of all active instances in $\mathbb{T}$: $[\mathbb{T}] = \biguplus_{\alpha \in \mathbb{T}} [\mathbb{T}(\alpha)]$

Table 2. Reduction rules

(osNew)　　$x \prec A \in Decls$
$\mathbb{T}[\mathsf{Lf}(ST \circ (M, \mathtt{new}\, xE))]_\alpha \longrightarrow \mathbb{T}[\mathsf{Lf}(ST \circ (M + x, AE))]_\alpha$

(osReu1)　　$x \prec A \in Decls$　$x \notin \mathsf{reuLf}_\mathbb{T}(\alpha.\mathsf{hi}(\mathbb{T}(\alpha)))$
$\mathbb{T}[\mathsf{Lf}(ST \circ (M, \mathtt{reu}\, xE))]_\alpha \longrightarrow \mathbb{T}[\mathsf{Lf}(ST \circ (M + x, AE))]_\alpha$

(osReu2)　　$x \prec A \in Decls$　$x \in \mathsf{reuLf}_\mathbb{T}(\alpha.\mathsf{hi}(\mathbb{T}(\alpha)))$
$\mathbb{T}[\mathsf{Lf}(ST \circ (M, \mathtt{reu}\, xE))]_\alpha \longrightarrow \mathbb{T}[\mathsf{Lf}(ST \circ (M, AE))]_\alpha$

(osChoice)
$\mathbb{T}[\mathsf{Lf}(ST \circ (M, (A + B)E))]_\alpha \longrightarrow \mathbb{T}[\mathsf{Lf}(ST \circ (M, AE))]_\alpha$

(osPush)
$\mathbb{T}[\mathsf{Lf}(ST \circ (M, \{A\}E))]_\alpha \longrightarrow \mathbb{T}[\mathsf{Lf}(ST \circ (M, E) \circ ([], A))]_\alpha$

(osPop)
$\mathbb{T}[\mathsf{Lf}(ST \circ (M, E) \circ (M', \epsilon))]_\alpha \longrightarrow \mathbb{T}[\mathsf{Lf}(ST \circ (M, E))]_\alpha$

(osParIntr)
$\mathbb{T}[\mathsf{Lf}(ST \circ (M, (A \parallel B)E))]_\alpha \longrightarrow \mathbb{T}[\mathsf{Nd}(ST \circ (M, E), \mathsf{Lf}(([], A)), \mathsf{Lf}(([], B)))]_\alpha$

(osParElim1)
$\mathbb{T}[\mathsf{Nd}(ST \circ (M, E), \mathbb{S}, \mathsf{Lf}((M', \epsilon)))]_\alpha \longrightarrow \mathbb{T}[\mathsf{Nd}(ST \circ (M \uplus M', E), \mathbb{S})]_\alpha$

(osParElim2)
$\mathbb{T}[\mathsf{Nd}(ST \circ (M, E), \mathsf{Lf}((M', \epsilon)))]_\alpha \longrightarrow \mathbb{T}[\mathsf{Lf}(ST \circ (M \uplus M', E))]_\alpha$

(osCong)　　$\mathbb{S} \equiv \mathbb{S}'$
$\mathbb{T}[\mathbb{S}]_\alpha \longrightarrow \mathbb{T}[\mathbb{S}']_\alpha$

The next notion is that of *reusable instances* because the primitive $\mathtt{reu}$ depends on the state of the configuration. In our model, the instantiation always occurs at the top of a leaf stack, for the moment we only need the concept of reusable instances for an expression at a leaf node. Later, we will extend the notion of reusable instances to non-leaf nodes. The multiset of reuseable instances at level k of the leaf stack α is the collection of all existing instances in

Table 3. Structural congruence: basic axioms

(conChoice)
$\mathsf{Lf}(ST \circ (M,(A+B)E)) \equiv \mathsf{Lf}(ST \circ (M,(B+A))E)$
(conBranch)
$\mathsf{Nd}(ST, \mathsf{Lf}(ST), \mathbb{T}) \equiv \mathsf{Nd}(ST, \mathbb{T}, \mathsf{Lf}(ST))$

all the predecessor nodes $\beta < \alpha$ and all the existing instances from the bottom of stack $\mathbb{T}(\alpha)$ up to k (inclusion).

$$\mathsf{reuLf}_{\mathbb{T}}(\alpha.k) = \biguplus_{\beta < \alpha} [\mathbb{T}(\beta)] \ \uplus \ [\mathbb{T}(\alpha)|_k]$$

The reduction relation is defined in terms of a rewriting system [16]. By $\mathbb{T}[]_\alpha$ we denote a tree with a hole at the leaf location α. Filling this hole with a (sub)tree $\mathbb{T}'$ will be denoted by $\mathbb{T}[\mathbb{T}']_\alpha$.

Table 2 defines the reduction rules. Each reduction rule has two lines. The first line contains a rule name followed by a list of conditions. The second line has the form $\mathbb{T} \longrightarrow \mathbb{T}'$, which states that if the configuration has the form $\mathbb{T}$ and the condition in the first line holds, then we can move to configuration $\mathbb{T}'$. As usual, $\longrightarrow^*$ is the reflexive and transitive closure of $\longrightarrow$. One step reduction is defined first by choosing an arbitrary active thread. Then depending on the pattern of the expression at the top of the chosen thread and the state of the configuration, the appropriate rewrite rule is selected. If necessary the configuration is rearranged using the congruence rules. By the rules osNew, osReu1, osReu2, and osChoice we only rewrite the element at the top of the stack. The rule osPush adds an element to the top of the leaf stack. The rule osPop only removes the element at the top of the stack when the stack has at least two elements. That means no stack in any configuration is empty. By the rule osParIntr, a leaf is replaced by a branch of a node and two leaves. In contrast, by the rules osParElim1, osParElim2, a leaf is removed from the tree and its parent node may be promoted to be a leaf if it is the case (osParElim2). The rule osCong allows the configuration to be rearranged so that reduction rule can be applied.

The structural congruence relation $\equiv$ is defined in Table 3. By the congruence rules, we can replace the left hand side of $\equiv$ by the right hand side in the reduction rule osCong.

The example at the end of Section 2.1 is used to illustrate the operational semantics. There are many possible runs of the program due to the choice composition and when a configuration has more than one leaf thread, the number of possible runs can be exponential as active threads have the same priority. Here we only show one of the possible runs. To make it easier to follow, we represent the trees graphically instead of using the formal syntax; '⌣' and '⟨' denote branches with one and two child nodes, respectively. At the starting point, the configuration has one leaf $\mathsf{Lf}([], \mathbf{reu}\,b)$. After the first step, there are two possibilities because we can apply the congruence rule conChoice before the rule osChoice.

$\quad$ (Start) $\quad$ $([], \text{reu}\, b)$

$\quad$ (osNew) $\longrightarrow$ $([b], (\text{reu}\, d\{\text{new}\, a\} + \text{new}\, e\, \text{new}\, a)\, \text{reu}\, d)$

$\quad$ (osChoice) $\longrightarrow$ $([b], \text{reu}\, d\{\text{new}\, a\}\, \text{reu}\, d)$

$$(\text{or } ([b], \text{new}\, e\, \text{new}\, a\, \text{reu}\, d))$$

Now we continue with the first possibility. When there are two or more leaves, we draw a box around the leaf which is to be executed in the next step.

$$([b], \boxed{\text{reu}\, d\{\text{new}\, a\}}\, \text{reu}\, d)$$

$\quad$ (osReu1) $\longrightarrow$ $([b, d], \{\text{new}\, a\}\, \text{reu}\, d)$

$\quad$ (osPush) $\longrightarrow$ $([b, d], \text{reu}\, d) \circ ([], \text{new}\, a)$

$\quad$ (osNew) $\longrightarrow$ $([b, d], \text{reu}\, d) \circ ([a], (\text{new}\, d \parallel \{\text{reu}\, d\}\, \text{reu}\, e))$

$\quad$ (osParIntr) $\longrightarrow$ $([b, d], \text{reu}\, d) \circ ([a], \epsilon) \langle \begin{array}{l} ([], \text{new}\, d) \\ \boxed{([], \{\text{reu}\, d\}\, \text{reu}\, e)} \end{array}$

$\quad$ (osPush) $\longrightarrow$ $([b, d], \text{reu}\, d) \circ ([a], \epsilon) \langle \begin{array}{l} \boxed{([], \text{new}\, d)} \\ ([], \text{reu}\, e) \circ ([], \text{reu}\, d) \end{array}$

$\quad$ (osNew) $\longrightarrow$ $([b, d], \text{reu}\, d) \circ ([a], \epsilon) \langle \begin{array}{l} ([d], \epsilon) \\ \boxed{([], \text{reu}\, e) \circ ([], \text{reu}\, d)} \end{array}$

$\quad$ (osReu1) $\longrightarrow$ $([b, d], \text{reu}\, d) \circ ([a], \epsilon) \langle \begin{array}{l} \boxed{([d], \epsilon)} \\ ([], \text{reu}\, e) \circ ([], \epsilon) \end{array}$

$\quad$ (osElim1) $\longrightarrow$ $([b, d], \text{reu}\, d) \circ ([a, d], \epsilon) \leftharpoonup ([], \text{reu}\, e) \circ ([], \epsilon)$

$\quad$ (osPop) $\longrightarrow$ $([b, d], \text{reu}\, d) \circ ([a, d], \epsilon) \leftharpoonup ([], \text{reu}\, e)$

$\quad$ (osReu) $\longrightarrow$ $([b, d], \text{reu}\, d) \circ ([a, d], \epsilon) \leftharpoonup ([e], \epsilon)$

$\quad$ (osParElim2) $\longrightarrow$ $([b, d], \text{reu}\, d) \circ ([a, d, e], \epsilon)$

$\quad$ (osPop) $\longrightarrow$ $([b, d], \text{reu}\, d)$

$\quad$ (osReu2) $\longrightarrow$ $([b, d], \epsilon)$ $\quad$ (terminal)

Last, we should note that we could model our operational semantics slightly simpler by using only *complete binary trees*. A complete binary tree is a binary tree with the additional property that every node must have exactly two children if an internal node, and zero children if a leaf node. Then we have only one rule for truncating the tree:

(osParElim)
$$\mathbb{T}[\text{Nd}(ST \circ (M, E), \text{Lf}((M', \epsilon)), \text{Lf}((M'', \epsilon)))]_\alpha \longrightarrow \mathbb{T}[\text{Lf}(ST \circ (M \uplus M' \uplus M'', E))]_\alpha$$

However, doing in this way reduces the reuse capability because two sibling threads cannot reuse instances of each other, after one has terminated before the other. In our model this is possible as a leaf can return its instances to its parent and the other sibling branch can reuse the instances from its parent.

3   Type System

We start this section by describing informally types and gives some intuitive examples. Then we will define and explain the typing rules in more details.

Definition 1 (Types). *Types of component expressions are tuples*

$$X = \langle X^i, X^o, X^j, X^p, X^l \rangle$$

where X^i, X^o, X^j, X^p and X^l are finite multisets over $\mathbb{C}$. We let $U, V, \ldots, Z$ range over types.

Let us first explain informally why multisets, which multisets and why five. The aim is to have an upper bound of the number of simultaneously active instances of any component during the execution of the expression (X^i). Multisets are the right data structure to collect and count such instances.

In addition, we want compositionality of typing, that is, we want the types to be computable from types of subexpressions. Since subexpressions may be scoped, it is necessary to have an upper bound of the number of instances that are still active *after* the execution of an expression (X^o). Pairs $\langle X^i, X^o \rangle$ sufficed for the purpose of the paper [2]. Here we consider also reusing instances of components and this depends on whether there is already such an instance or not. More concretely, in a sequential composition of A and B, the behaviour of **reu**'s in B depends on the instances that are active *after* the execution of A, which would violate the compositionality. In order to save the compositionality, we have to add three more multisets to the types, denoted by X^j, X^p and X^l. The first two multisets X^j, X^p express the same bounds as X^i, X^o, but with respect to executing the expression in a state where every component has already one active instance.

Without the parallel composition, these four multisets $\langle X^i, X^o, X^j, X^p \rangle$ sufficed for the purpose of [3] since the difference between $X^i(x)$ and $X^j(x)$ as well as between $X^o(x)$ and $X^p(x)$ is at most one for every x. With the new parallel composition, these differences may be greater than one, and note that due to the non-determinism of the choice composition, the surviving instances after executing A is also non-deterministic. In order to obtain a sharp bound for x, we need to know whether B can always reuse x after executing A or not. Because if it is the case, the maximum number of additional instances of x generated by B is only $Y^j(x)$, where Y is the type of B. Therefore, we need the last component X^l in the type expression. X^l is the set of instances which always active after executing A. Although X^l can be a set, we let X^l be a multiset so that the multiset operations in the later sessions can be applied without any conversion.

Based on the above intuitions, the following typings are easy:
new $d : \langle [d], [d], [d], [d], [d] \rangle$, $\{$**new** $d\} : \langle [d], [], [d], [], [] \rangle$, **reu** $d : \langle [d], [d], [], [], [d] \rangle$,
reu $d\{$**new** $d\} : \langle [d, d], [d], [d], [], [d] \rangle$, **reu** $d\{$**new** $a\} : \langle [a, d, d], [d], [a, d], [], [d] \rangle$,
$($**reu** $d \parallel$ **new** $e) : \langle [d, e], [d, e], [e], [e], [d, e] \rangle$, $($**reu** $d +$ **new** $e) : \langle [d, e], [d, e], [e], [e], [] \rangle$,
where $d \prec \epsilon$ and $a \prec$ **new** d like in the example program in Section 2.1.

The intuitions from the above paragraphs will be indispensable for understanding the typing rules later in this section, in particular the sequencing rule.

We will explain more when describing each typing rule, but before that we have to prepare with some preliminary definitions.

Let $\mathcal{R}$ be the requirement that some components in $\mathbb{C}$ can have at most a certain number of simultaneous instances. $\mathcal{R}$ can be viewed as a total function from $\mathbb{C}$ to $\mathbb{N} \cup \{\infty\}$. Then $\mathcal{R}(x) \in \mathbb{N}$ is the maximum allowed number of simultaneously active instances of x; $\mathcal{R}(x) = \infty$ expresses that x can have any number of instances. By convention $n < \infty$ for all $n \in \mathbb{N}$. For any multiset M, we denote $M \subseteq \mathcal{R}$ when $M(x) \leq \mathcal{R}(x)$ for all $x \in M$.

A *basis* or an *environment* is an list of declarations: $x_1 \prec A_1, \ldots, x_n \prec A_n$ with distinct variables $x_i \neq x_j$ for all $i \neq j$, as in [1]. Let Γ, Δ range over bases. The domain of basis $\Gamma = x_1 \prec A_1, \ldots, x_n \prec A_n$, denoted by $Dom(\Gamma)$, is the set $\{x_1, \ldots, x_n\}$. A typing judgment is a tuple of the form

$$\Gamma \vdash_{\mathcal{R}} A : X$$

and it asserts that expression A has type X in the environment Γ, with respect to requirement $\mathcal{R}$. We leave out subscript $\mathcal{R}$ when $\mathcal{R}$ is clear from context.

Definition 2 (Typing rules). *Type judgments $\Gamma \vdash A : X$ are derived by applying the typing rules in Table 4 in the usual inductive way.*

In rule Seq in Table 4, expression $M!_N$, where M, N are multisets, is defined as follows:

$$(M!_N)(x) = \begin{cases} 0, & \text{if } x \in N \\ M(x), & \text{otherwise} \end{cases}$$

Besides the intuition given in the beginning of this section, some further explanation of these typing rules is in order. The rule Axiom requires no premise and is used to take-off. The rules New and Reu allow us to type expressions $\mathbf{new}\,x$ and $\mathbf{reu}\,x$, respectively. The rule Weaken is used to expand bases so that we can combine typings in the other rules. The side condition $x \notin Dom(\Gamma)$ in the rules Weaken, New and Reu keeps the expanded basis well-formed. The rules Choice and Scope are easy to understand recalling the semantics of the corresponding reduction rules osChoice, osPush and osPop. In the rule Parallel, since we have no specific schedule for two parallel threads, both can generate their maximum numbers of instances for any component. To be on the safe side, we have to prepare for the worst case and therefore the type of two parallel expressions is additive union of their types. The side condition follows naturally.

The most critical rule is Seq because sequencing two expressions can lead to increase in instances of the composed expression. Let us start with the first component of type expression for AB. After expression A is executed, there are at most $X^o(x)$ instances of component x. If x is not in the system state after the execution of A, then at most $Y^i(x)$ instances of x can be created when executing B. Otherwise, at most $Y^j(x)$ additional instances of x can be created. If we take the maximum of $(X^o \uplus Y^j)(x)$ and $Y^i(x)$ to be the maximum number of x which can be created after the execution of A and during the execution of B, then we do not obtain the *sharp* upper bound. For example, let $A = \mathbf{reu}\,x$

Table 4. Typing rules

(Axiom)   (Weaken)
$$\frac{\Gamma \vdash A : X \quad \Gamma \vdash B : Y \quad x \notin Dom(\Gamma)}{\Gamma, x \prec B \vdash A : X}$$

$$\vdash \epsilon : \langle [], [], [], [], [] \rangle$$

(New)
$$\frac{\Gamma \vdash A : X \quad x \notin Dom(\Gamma)}{\Gamma, x \prec A \vdash \mathbf{new}\, x : \langle X^i + x, X^o + x, X^j + x, X^p + x, X^l + x \rangle}$$

(Reu)
$$\frac{\Gamma \vdash A : X \quad x \notin Dom(\Gamma)}{\Gamma, x \prec A \vdash \mathbf{reu}\, x : \langle X^i + x, X^o + x, X^j, X^p, X^l + x \rangle}$$

(Seq)
$$\frac{\Gamma \vdash A : X \quad \Gamma \vdash B : Y \quad X^o \uplus Y^j \subseteq \mathcal{R} \quad A, B \neq \epsilon}{\Gamma \vdash AB : \langle X^i \cup (X^o \uplus Y^j) \cup Y^i !_{X^l}, (X^o \uplus Y^p) \cup Y^o !_{X^l}, X^j \cup (X^p \uplus Y^j), X^p \uplus Y^p, X^l \cup Y^l \rangle}$$

(Choice)
$$\frac{\Gamma \vdash A : X \quad \Gamma \vdash B : Y}{\Gamma \vdash (A + B) : \langle X^i \cup Y^i, X^o \cup Y^o, X^j \cup Y^j, X^p \cup Y^p, X^l \cap Y^l \rangle}$$

(Parallel)
$$\frac{\Gamma \vdash A : X \quad \Gamma \vdash B : Y \quad X^i \uplus Y^i \subseteq \mathcal{R}}{\Gamma \vdash (A \parallel B) : \langle X^i \uplus Y^i, X^o \uplus Y^o, X^j \uplus Y^j, X^p \uplus Y^p, X^l \cup Y^l \rangle}$$

(Scope)
$$\frac{\Gamma \vdash A : X}{\Gamma \vdash \{A\} : \langle X^i, [], X^j, [], [] \rangle}$$

and $B = (\mathbf{reu}\, x \parallel \mathbf{reu}\, x)$. Executing B alone can create two instances of x. However, executing AB creates only one instance of x.

To remedy the situation we need to know whether an instance of x is always in the system state after the execution of A or not. If it is, then we know that at most $Y^j(x)$ additional instances can be created; otherwise, $Y^i(x)$ additional instances can be created when executing B. Therefore the maximum number of x after execution of A and during execution of B are $(X^o \uplus Y^j)(x)$, or $(X^l \uplus Y^j)(x)$ if $X^l(x) \geq 1$, or $Y^i(x)$ if $X^l(x) = 0$. Since $X^o \supseteq X^l$, the number becomes $((X^o \uplus Y^j) \cup Y^i !_{X^l})(x)$.

In addition, because executing A can create at most $X^i(x)$ instances, the first component of type of AB is the maximum of $X^i(x)$ and $((X^o \uplus Y^j) \cup Y^i !_{X^l})(x)$. Last, since X^i and Y^i satisfy the requirement $\mathcal{R}$, we only require an additional side condition $X^o \uplus Y^j \subseteq \mathcal{R}$ which means $X^o(x) + Y^j(x) \leq \mathcal{R}(x)$ for each $x \in \mathbb{C}$.

Analogously, after executing AB, the maximal number of surviving instances of x are $X^o(x) + Y^p(x)$, or $Y^o(x)$ if there is a run of A which ends with no surviving instance of x. Hence the surviving instances of AB are $(X^o \uplus Y^p) \cup Y^o !_{X^l}$.

By a similar reasoning, when we start with a stack containing at least one instance of every component, we can calculate the second and the last components in the type expression for AB and the whole type expression of AB is $\langle X^i \cup (X^o \uplus Y^j) \cup Y^i !_{X^l}, (X^o \uplus Y^p) \cup Y^o !_{X^l}, X^j \cup (X^p \uplus Y^j), X^p \uplus Y^p, X^l \cup Y^l \rangle$.

Using the example in Section 2.1 with assumption that $\mathcal{R} = \{b \mapsto 1, e \mapsto 2, a, d \mapsto 4\}$, we derive type for $\mathbf{reu}\, b$. Note that we omitted some side conditions as they can be checked easily and we shortened the rule names to the first two characters. The rule Axiom is also simplified.

$$\text{We} \dfrac{\text{Sc} \dfrac{\text{Re} \dfrac{\vdash \epsilon : \langle [], [], [], [], [] \rangle}{d \prec \epsilon \vdash \mathbf{reu}\, d : \langle [d], [d], [], [], [d] \rangle}}{d \prec \epsilon \vdash \{\mathbf{reu}\, d\} : \langle [d], [], [], [], [] \rangle} \quad \text{We} \dfrac{\vdash \epsilon : \langle [], [], [], [], [] \rangle}{d \prec \epsilon \vdash \epsilon : \langle [], [], [], [], [] \rangle}}{d \prec \epsilon, e \prec \epsilon \vdash \{\mathbf{reu}\, d\} : \langle [d], [], [], [], [] \rangle} \tag{1}$$

$$\text{Se} \dfrac{(1) \quad \text{Re} \dfrac{\text{We} \dfrac{\vdash \epsilon : \langle [], [], [], [], [] \rangle \quad \vdash \epsilon : \langle [], [], [], [], [] \rangle}{d \prec \epsilon \vdash \epsilon : \langle [], [], [], [], [] \rangle}}{d \prec \epsilon, e \prec \epsilon \vdash \mathbf{reu}\, e : \langle [e], [e], [], [], [e] \rangle}}{d \prec \epsilon, e \prec \epsilon \vdash \{\mathbf{reu}\, d\}\, \mathbf{reu}\, e : \langle [d, e], [e], [], [], [e] \rangle} \tag{2}$$

$$\text{Ne} \dfrac{\text{Pa} \dfrac{\text{We} \dfrac{\text{Ne} \dfrac{\vdash \epsilon : \langle [], [], [], [], [] \rangle}{d \prec \epsilon \vdash \mathbf{new}\, d : \langle [d], [d], [d, [d], [d]] \rangle}}{d \prec \epsilon, e \prec \epsilon \vdash \mathbf{new}\, d : \langle [d], [d], [d, [d], [d]] \rangle} \quad (2)}{d \prec \epsilon, e \prec \epsilon \vdash (\mathbf{new}\, d \parallel \{\mathbf{reu}\, d\}\, \mathbf{reu}\, e) : \langle [d, d, e], [d, e], [d], [d], [d, e] \rangle}}{d \prec \epsilon, e \prec \epsilon, a \prec (\mathbf{new}\, d \parallel \{\mathbf{reu}\, d\}\, \mathbf{reu}\, e) \vdash \mathbf{new}\, a : \langle [a, d, d, e], [a, d, e], [a, d], [a, d], [a, d, e] \rangle}$$

Similarly, we can derive $\Gamma \vdash \mathbf{reu}\, b : \langle [b, a, d, d, e], [b, a, d, e], [a, d, e], [a, d, e], [a, b, d, e] \rangle$ where $\Gamma = d \prec \epsilon, e \prec \epsilon, a \prec (\mathbf{new}\, d \parallel \{\mathbf{reu}\, d\}\, \mathbf{reu}\, d), b \prec (\mathbf{reu}\, d\{\mathbf{new}\, a\} + \mathbf{new}\, e\, \mathbf{new}\, a)\, \mathbf{reu}\, d$.

In this example expression $\mathbf{reu}\, b$ is typable. If $\mathcal{R}(d) = 1$, the expression would not be typable as the side condition when paralleling $\mathbf{new}\, d$ and $\{\mathbf{reu}\, d\}\, \mathbf{reu}\, e$ would not be satisfied. Also, note that the above type derivation is not the only one but, as we will see later, the type for any expression is unique.

As mentioned at the Section 1, we can infer specific resource consumption from our types by adding annotations to the source programs. For example, if component a and d each create a database connection, then from the type of b, we know that the program, in particular the main expression $\mathbf{reu}\, b$, may need three database connections (since the first component in the type of b has one a and two d's). From another point of view, we view d as a database connection component, then we know that the program needs two database connections.

We end this section with the definition of *well-typed program*.

Definition 3 (Well-typed programs). *Let $\mathcal{R}$ be a requirement. Program $Prog = Decls; E$ is well-typed w.r.t. $\mathcal{R}$ if there exists a reordering Γ of declarations in Decls such that $\Gamma \vdash_R E : X$.*

4   Formal Properties

4.1   Type Soundness

A fundamental property of static type systems is *type soundness* or *safety* [4]. It states that well-typed programs cannot cause type errors. In our case, type errors occur when a configuration violates requirement $\mathcal{R}$, that is, there exists a component x whose the number of its active instances is greater than the allowed number, $\mathcal{R}(x)$.

Our proof of the type soundness is based on the approach of Wright and Felleisen [18]. We will prove two main lemmas: Preservation and Progress. The first lemma states that well-typedness is preserved under reduction. The latter guarantees that well-typed programs cannot get stuck, that is, move to a non-terminal state, from which it cannot move to another state. In order to use this technique, we need to define the notion of *well-typed configuration*. Before giving the formal definition of well-typed configuration we need some auxiliary definitions.

The first notion is *subtree*. Given a tree $\mathbb{T}$ and a set of positions $\mathcal{L} = \{\alpha_i.k_i \in \mathbb{T} \mid 1 \leq i \leq m\}$ such that $\alpha_i.k_i \not\leq \alpha_j.k_j$ for all $i \neq j$ and for all leaf $\alpha \in \mathsf{leaves}(\mathbb{T})$ there exists a h such that $\alpha \geq \alpha_h \in \mathcal{L}$. That means for every path from the root of $\mathbb{T}$ to one of its leaves we select one and only one position for set $\mathcal{L}$. In the sequel, we assume that $\mathcal{L}$ always satisfies these conditions. The tree $\mathbb{S}$ obtained from $\mathbb{T}$ by keeping only elements at positions $\alpha.k \leq \alpha_i.k_i$ for $1 \leq i \leq m$ is a subtree of $\mathbb{T}$, notation $\mathbb{S} \sqsubseteq_{\mathcal{L}} \mathbb{T}$. Consequently, $\mathsf{leaves}(\mathbb{S}) = \{\alpha_1, .., \alpha_m\}$ and $\mathsf{hi}(\mathbb{S}(\alpha_i)) = k_i$ for all $1 \leq i \leq m$.

The next one is the notion of the reusable instances for the expression E at an arbitrary position $\alpha.k$. Recall that we have defined the reusable instances for an expression in a leaf node in Section 2.2. Now we extend this notion for an arbitrary position $\alpha.k$. Due to the nondeterminism of our operational semantics, the collection of reusable instances for an expression in a non-leaf node is also non-deterministic, but we can calculate its sharp upper bound and a lower bound. Note that due to the semantics of $\mathtt{reu}$, it is enough for the latter being a collection of instances which E can always reuse; it needs not to be a sharp lower bound. We define the latter first and denote this collection by $\mathsf{reu}|_{\mathbb{T}}(\alpha.k)$.

The element of $\mathsf{reu}|_{\mathbb{T}}(\alpha.k)$ is not only those in $\mathsf{reuLf}_{\mathbb{T}}(\alpha.k)$ but also ones returned from its child nodes, $\mathsf{retl}_{\mathbb{T}}(\alpha.k)$ (see the rules $\mathsf{osParElim1}, \mathsf{osParElim2}$ in Table 2.)

$$\mathsf{reu}|_{\mathbb{T}}(\alpha.k) = \mathsf{reuLf}_{\mathbb{T}}(\alpha.k) \cup \mathsf{retl}_{\mathbb{T}}(\alpha.k)$$

The set of instances returned to $\alpha.k$ is empty if $\alpha.k$ is not at the top of α. Otherwise, it contains instances which will be generated at the bottom of its child nodes. Since the child nodes may have more children, we need to make recursive calls to them.

$$\mathsf{retl}_{\mathbb{T}}(\alpha.k) = \begin{cases} [], & \text{if } k < \mathsf{hi}(\mathbb{T}(\alpha)) \text{ or } \alpha.k \notin \mathbb{T} \\ \bigcup_{\beta \in \{\alpha l, \alpha r\}} ([\mathbb{T}(\beta.1)] \cup X^l \cup \mathsf{retl}_{\mathbb{T}}(\beta.1)), & \text{otherwise} \end{cases}$$

where X is the type of the expression at position $\beta.1$ and $\mathbb{T}(\beta.1)$ is the multiset at position $\beta.1$.

Analogously, for the sharp upper bound, the maximal number of instances returned to a position $\alpha.k$ ($\mathsf{retop}_{\mathbb{T}}(\alpha.k)$) is zero if k is not at the top of the stack at α. Otherwise, it contains the one in the multisets at the bottom of its child nodes and the maximal number of instances which survive the expressions here. This number, $\mathsf{op}_{\mathbb{T}}(\alpha.k)$, is calculated as in the sequencing typing rule Seq. Last, the child nodes of $\alpha.k$ may received instances from its child nodes and so on, so we need to call the function recursively. To simplify the definition of the function retl and retop with recursion, we let the function return an empty multiset for invalid positions $\alpha.k \notin \mathbb{T}$.

$$\mathsf{retop}_{\mathbb{T}}(\alpha.k) = \begin{cases} [], & \text{if } k < \mathsf{hi}(\mathbb{T}(\alpha)) \text{ or } \alpha.k \notin \mathbb{T} \\ \biguplus_{\beta \in \{\alpha l, \alpha r\}} ([\mathbb{T}(\beta.1)] \uplus \mathsf{op}_{\mathbb{T}}(\beta.1) \uplus \mathsf{retop}_{\mathbb{T}}(\beta.1)), & \text{otherwise} \end{cases}$$

where
$$\mathsf{op}_{\mathbb{T}}(\alpha.k) = X^p \cup X^o!_{\mathsf{reul}_{\mathbb{T}}(\alpha.k)}$$

Here X is the type of the expression at position $\alpha.k$.

We are going to define the central notion of well-typed configuration. Its main statement is that the total number of active instances in the configuration respects the requirement $\mathcal{R}$. Since the leaves of the configuration tree may generate more instances, we need to include these instances to the above total number. Furthermore, because the tree can shrink and when it shrinks, some nodes eventually become leaves we need to prove for these future states also. The function $\mathsf{ij}_{\mathbb{T}}(\alpha.k)$ below returns a multiset which is the maximal number of instances which can be generated by the expression at the position $\alpha.k$. As in the sequencing typing rule Seq, this number is bounded by the maximal number returned from its child nodes ($\mathsf{retop}_{\mathbb{T}}(\alpha.k)$) and the additional instances (X^j) for components that indeed are reused, where X is the type of the expression at position $\alpha.k$. For runs after which x may not be in the set of reusable instances, an additional bound $X^i(x)$ should be taken into account. This explains the definition of the function ij.

$$\mathsf{ij}_{\mathbb{T}}(\alpha.k) = (\mathsf{retop}_{\mathbb{T}}(\alpha.k) \uplus X^j) \cup X^i!_{\mathsf{reul}_{\mathbb{T}}(\alpha.k)}$$

Now we are ready to define the notion of a *well-typed configuration*. The first clause requires that all expressions in the configuration are well-typed. The second one contains the safety behaviour of the configuration. It requires that the total number of existing instances in the configuration and the ones which may be generated by expressions in the future still respect the requirement $\mathcal{R}$.

Definition 4 (Well-typed configuration). *Let Γ be a legal basis. Configuration $\mathbb{T}$ is well-typed with respect to requirement $\mathcal{R}$ if*

1. for every E occurring in $\mathbb{T}$ there exists X such that $\Gamma \vdash E : X$, and
2. for all $\mathbb{S} \sqsubseteq_{\mathcal{L}} \mathbb{T}$:

$$[\mathbb{S}] \uplus \biguplus_{\alpha.k \in \mathcal{L}} \mathsf{ij}_{\mathbb{T}}(\alpha.k) \subseteq \mathcal{R}$$

Having the definition of well-typed configuration, the two main lemmas mentioned at the beginning of the section are stated as follows.

Lemma 1 (Preservation). *If $\mathbb{T}$ is a well-typed configuration and $\mathbb{T} \longrightarrow \mathbb{T}'$, then $\mathbb{T}'$ is well-typed.*

Lemma 2 (Progress). *If* $\mathbb{T}$ *is a well-typed configuration, then either*

1. *there exists configuration* $\mathbb{T}'$ *such that* $\mathbb{T} \longrightarrow \mathbb{T}'$ *or*
2. $\mathbb{T}$ *is terminal.*

Finally, the type soundness property allows us to safely execute well-typed component programs. That is, during the execution of the programs the number of active instances of any component never exceeds the allowed number.

Theorem 1 (Soundness). *Let* $\mathcal{R}$ *be a requirement,* Γ *be a basis,* E *be an expression and suppose* $\Gamma \vdash_{\mathcal{R}} E : X$ *for some* X. *Let* $\mathbb{T} = \mathsf{Lf}([], E)$. *Then for every sequence of reductions* $\mathbb{T} \longrightarrow^* \mathbb{T}'$ *we have* $[\mathbb{T}'] \subseteq \mathcal{R}$.

4.2   Other Properties

The section lists some fundamental properties of our type system. These properties are needed to prove the lemmas and theorem in the previous section. Most of these properties are analogous to those in [3]. We start by giving some definitions. In the sequel we use X^* for any of X^i, X^o, X^j, X^p and X^l.

Following [1] we fix some terminology on bases or environments.

Definition 5 (Bases). *Let* $\Gamma = x_1 {\prec} A_1, \ldots, x_n {\prec} A_n$ *be a basis.*

– Γ *is called* legal *if* $\Gamma \vdash A : X$ *for some expression* A *and type* X.
– *A declaration* $x {\prec} A$ *is in* Γ, *notation* $x {\prec} A \in \Gamma$, *if* $x \equiv x_i$ *and* $A \equiv A_i$ *for some* i.
– Δ *is* part *of* Γ, *notation* $\Delta \subseteq \Gamma$, *if* $\Delta = x_{i_1} {\prec} A_{i_1}, \ldots, x_{i_k} {\prec} A_{i_k}$ *with* $1 \leq i_1 < \ldots < i_k \leq n$. *Note that the order is preserved.*
– Δ *is an* initial segment *of* Γ, *if* $\Delta = x_1 {\prec} A_1, \ldots, x_j {\prec} A_j$ *for some* $1 \leq j \leq n$.

For any expression E, let $\mathsf{var}(E)$ denote the set of variables occurring in E:

$$\mathsf{var}(\mathbf{new}\,x) = \mathsf{var}(\mathbf{reu}\,x) = \{x\}, \quad \mathsf{var}(\{A\}) = \mathsf{var}(A),$$
$$\mathsf{var}(AB) = \mathsf{var}((A+B)) = \mathsf{var}((A \parallel B)) = \mathsf{var}(A) \cup \mathsf{var}(B)$$

The following lemma collects a number of simple properties of a typing judgment. It also shows some relations among multisets of A and any legal basis always has distinct declarations.

Lemma 3 (Legal typing). *If* $\Gamma \vdash A : X$, *then*

1. *elements of* $\mathsf{var}(A)$, X^* *are in* $Dom(\Gamma)$,
2. $\Gamma \vdash \epsilon : \langle [], [], [], [], [] \rangle$,
3. *every variable in* $Dom(\Gamma)$ *is declared only once in* Γ,
4. $X^o \subseteq X^i \subseteq \mathcal{R}$ *and* $X^p \subseteq X^j \subseteq \mathcal{R}$,
5. $X^j \subseteq X^i$, $X^p \subseteq X^o$, *and* $X^l \subseteq X^o$.

The following lemma is important in that it allows us to find a syntax-directed derivation of the type of an expression and hence it allows us to calculate the types of sub-expressions and is used in type inference. This lemma is sometimes called the *inversion lemma of the typing relation* [12].

Lemma 4 (Generation).

1. If $\Gamma \vdash \mathbf{new}\, x : X$, then $x \in X^p$ and there exists bases Δ, Δ' and expression A such that $\Gamma = \Delta, x \prec A, \Delta'$, and $\Delta \vdash A : \langle X^i - x, X^o - x, X^j - x, X^p - x, X^l - x \rangle$.

2. If $\Gamma \vdash \mathbf{reu}\, x : X$, then $x \in X^o$ and there exists bases Δ, Δ' and expression A such that $\Gamma = \Delta, x \prec A, \Delta'$, and $\Delta \vdash A : \langle X^i - x, X^o - x, X^j, X^p, X^l - x \rangle$.

3. If $\Gamma \vdash AB : Z$ with $A, B \neq \epsilon$, then there exists X, Y such that $\Gamma \vdash A : X$, $\Gamma \vdash B : Y$ and $Z = \langle X^i \cup (X^o \uplus Y^j) \cup Y^i!_{X^l}, (X^o \uplus Y^p) \cup Y^o!_{X^l}, X^j \cup (X^p \uplus Y^j), X^p \uplus Y^p, X^l \cup Y^l \rangle$.

4. If $\Gamma \vdash (A + B) : Z$, then there exists X, Y such that $\Gamma \vdash A : X$, $\Gamma \vdash B : Y$ and $Z = \langle X^i \cup Y^i, X^o \cup Y^o, X^j \cup Y^j, X^p \cup Y^p, X^l \cap Y^l \rangle$.

5. If $\Gamma \vdash (A \parallel B) : Z$, then there exists X, Y such that $\Gamma \vdash A : X$, $\Gamma \vdash B : Y$, and $Z = \langle X^i \uplus Y^i, X^o \uplus Y^o, X^j \uplus Y^j, X^p \uplus Y^p, X^l \cup Y^l \rangle$.

6. If $\Gamma \vdash \{A\} : \langle X^i, [], X^j, [], [] \rangle$, then there exists multisets X^o, X^p, and X^l such that $\Gamma \vdash A : X$.

The next lemma stresses the significance of the order of declarations in a legal basis in our type system. Besides, because of the weakening rule, there can be many legal bases under which a well-typed expression can be derived. Thus, its 'inversion' is stated in the lemma following.

Lemma 5 (Legal monotonicity).

1. If $\Gamma = \Delta, x \prec E, \Delta'$ is legal, then $\Delta \vdash E : X$ for some X.
2. If $\Gamma \vdash E : X$, $\Gamma \subseteq \Gamma'$ and Γ' is legal, then $\Gamma' \vdash E : X$.

Lemma 6 (Strengthening). If $\Gamma, x \prec A \vdash B : Y$ and $x \notin \mathsf{var}(B)$, then $\Gamma \vdash B : Y$ and $x \notin Y^i$.

Last, in our type system, when an expression has a type this type is unique. This property is stated in the following proposition.

Proposition 1 (Uniqueness of types). If $\Gamma \vdash A : X$ and $\Gamma \vdash A : Y$, then $X^i = Y^i$, $X^o = Y^o$, $X^j = Y^j$, $X^p = Y^p$, and $X^l = Y^l$.

5   Research Directions

In a slightly more liberal approach one leaves out the side condition from the typing rule Seq and takes the types as counting the maximum number of simultaneously active instances of each component. These maxima can then be compared to the available resources.

We are well aware of the level of abstraction of the component language and plan to incorporate more language features. These include recursion in component declarations, explicit deallocation primitive, and communication among threads. For example, suppose d, e are primitive components, then $a \prec (\{\mathbf{new}\, d\}$ $\mathbf{reu}\, a + \mathbf{new}\, e)$ is bounded by $\{a, e, d\}$, despite that it has one infinite execution trace.

References

1. H. Barendregt. Lambda Calculi with Types. In: Abramsky, Gabbay, Maibaum (Eds.), *Handbook of Logic in Computer Science*, Vol. II, Oxford University Press. 1992.
2. M. Bezem and H. Truong. A Type System for the Safe Instantiation of Components. In *Electronic Notes in Theoretical Computer Science* Vol. 97, July 2004.
3. M. Bezem and H. Truong. Counting Instances of Software Components, In *Proceedings of LRPP'04*, July 2004.
4. L. Cardelli. Type systems. In A. B. Tucker, editor, *The Computer Science and Engineering Handbook*, chapter 103, pages 2208-2236. CRC Press, 1997.
5. K. Crary, D. Walker, and G. Morrisett. Typed Memory Management in a Calculus of Capabilities. In *Twenty-Sixth ACM SIGPLAN-SIGACT Symposium on Principles of Programming Languages*, pages 262-275, San Antonio, TX, USA, January 1999.
6. K. Crary and S. Weirich. Resource Bound Certification. In *the Twenty-Seventh ACM SIGPLAN-SIGACT Symposium on Principles of Programming Languages*, pages 184-198, Boston, MA, USA, January 2000.
7. B. Dushnik and E. W. Miller. *Partially Ordered Sets*, American Journal of Mathematics, Vol. 63, 1941.
8. R. Englander. *Developing Java Beans*. 1st Edition, ISBN 1-56592-289-1, June 1997.
9. E. Gamma, R. Helm, R. Johnson, and J. Vlissides. *Design Patterns - Elements of Reusable Object-Oriented Software*, Addison-Wesley, Reading, Mass., ISBN 0201633612, 1994.
10. E. Meijer and C. Szyperski. Overcoming Independent Extensibility Challenges, *Communications of the ACM*, Vol. 45, No. 10, pp. 41–44, October 2002.
11. R. Milner, M. Tofte, R. Harper, and D. MacQueen. *The Definition of Standard ML (Revised)*. MIT Press, 1997.
12. B. Pierce. *Types and Programming Languages*. MIT Press, ISBN 0262162091, February 2002.
13. J. C. Seco. Adding Type Safety to Component Programming. In *Proc. of The PhD Student's Workshop* in FMOODS'02, University of Twente, the Netherlands, March 2002.
14. F. Smith, D. Walker and G. Morrisett. Alias Types. In *European Symposium on Programming*, Berlin, Germany, March 2000.
15. C. Szyperski. *Component Software: Beyond Object-Oriented Programming*, 2nd edition, Addison-Wesley, ISBN 0201745720, 2002.
16. Terese. *Term Rewriting Systems*, Cambridge Tracts in Theoretical Computer Science, Vol. 55, Cambridge University Press, 2003
17. T. L. Thai, Hoang Lam. *.NET Framework Essentials*. 3nd Edition, ISBN 0-596-00302-1, August 2003.
18. A. K. Wright and M. Felleisen, A Syntactic Approach to Type Soundness. In *Information and Computation*, Vol. 115, No. 1, pp. 38–94, 1994.
19. M. Zenger, Type-Safe Prototype-Based Component Evolution. In *Proceedings of the European Conference on Object-Oriented Programming*, Malaga, Spain, June 2002.
20. M. Zenger, Programming Language Abstractions for Extensible Software Components, PhD Thesis, No. 2930, EPFL, Switzerland, March 2004.

Specification and Verification
of Encapsulation in Java Programs

Andreas Roth

Institut für Logik, Komplexität und Deduktionssysteme
Universität Karlsruhe, Germany
aroth@ira.uka.de

Abstract. Encapsulation is a major concept in object-oriented designs as design pattern catalogues, approaches for alias control, and the need for modular correctness of components demonstrate. The way encapsulation can be formally *specified* in existing approaches has several shortcomings. We show how encapsulation in sequential Java programs is specified by means of a new concept, called *encapsulation predicates*, in a clearly defined and comprehensible way, well fitting into the concept of *design by contract*. Encapsulation predicates extend existing functional specification languages. There are two kinds: basic predicates, which provide the actual extension, and convenience predicates, which are abbreviations for often used specification patterns. With encapsulation predicates, encapsulation properties in design patterns can be modelled and approaches to control aliasing can be simulated. Specifications containing encapsulation predicates are deductively checkable, but can also be tackled by static analysis methods which are similar to alias control approaches.

1 Introduction

Encapsulation plays a major role in object-oriented software development for at least one important reason: Without it, the complexity of inter-object relations would become uncontrollable, and one of the most basic concepts of computer science, the division of tasks into subtasks, indispensable to master complex problems, would be impossible.

It is thus quite striking that formal methods for software development have discovered only relative lately this problem for real-world object-oriented languages, and have so far provided solutions that are only partially satisfactory (Sect. 2.2).

A successful concept for formal methods in object-oriented software development is the notion of a (formal) *contract* [14]. It provides formal specifications in a way that perfectly reflects the way programmers informally reason about objects: namely by mutual responsibilities and services between objects. Surprisingly the concept of *design by contract* has so far only been applied to pure functional properties and not yet to properties of encapsulation. Our work contributes to the formalisation of encapsulation properties in the natural way of contracts by enriching specification languages with *encapsulation predicates*.

M. Steffen and G. Zavattaro (Eds.): FMOODS 2005, LNCS 3535, pp. 195–210, 2005.

Programs can be verified with respect to formal contracts in a mathematically rigorous way. We thus provide means for making our formal specification of encapsulation properties checkable: We provide a deductive approach to realise this as well as sketch how existing methods from the static program analysis area can be integrated.

As basis of our reasoning we have chosen to investigate single-threaded programs in the language Java [9] for its widespread use in research and practice. The results should however be transferable to similar object-oriented languages.

2   Encapsulation as Important Object-Oriented Concept

The importance of encapsulation in object-oriented programs is a rather empirical phenomenon. It is manifested in properties of "good" software designs (documented in design pattern catalogues), other approaches to restrict aliasing (*alias control*), and the need for encapsulation in object-oriented components. The properties occurring in these areas are analysed in this section and serve as a basis to validate our solution in Sect. 6.

2.1   Design Patterns

We investigate the design pattern catalogues [6, 8, 10] for encapsulation properties. A selection of patterns that affect encapsulation is listed below; the list is far from complete, though these patterns are very clear manifestations of encapsulation properties in designs:

Whole-Part. This is a structural pattern [6] which provides a very strict encapsulation policy. There is an *aggregate object* (`Whole`) at work which hides access to other objects, called `Part`s: "Clients should see the aggregate object as an atomic object that does not allow any direct access to its constituent parts." [6]

Copy Mutable Parameters and

Return New Objects from Accessor Method. These two patterns [10] ensure that, at a method call, the passed mutable objects are copied before being stored at field locations and the returned objects are copied before being returned. The purpose of both patterns is to achieve encapsulation: No client of an object is allowed to directly access its internals.

Iterator. This behavioural pattern [8] ensures that an aggregate object, such as a linked list, does not expose its internal structure, though it provides an `Iterator` object that traverses the aggregate. Other clients of the list than iterators are not allowed to access its internals. They must however be enabled to put elements into the list, which makes the objects referenced by the internals also referenced by the clients.

These – and many other, e.g. the *Memento* [8] or the *Proxy* [8] – patterns have in common that they require some objects to be hidden from others in one or the other way. If the graphs made up by the references between objects in all states of a system have such a property we speak of *encapsulation*: **An encapsulation property describes under which circumstances it is forbidden to have a reference from one object to another.** Obviously, the above mentioned patterns have properties that satisfy this – purposely rather vague – condition.

We believe that there is no sharp distinction between encapsulation properties and functional properties. To require, e.g., an object stored in the field of an object o to be different in all visible states from an object p can be considered both an encapsulation property (since we restrict the accessibility between objects) *and* a traditional functional invariant property.

Example 1. To be more concrete, we take up the example of an application of the Whole-Part pattern given in [6]. We have an object `Triangle` whose instances contain each three references (`p0`, `p1`, `p2`) to objects of class `Point`. Points themselves consist of a pair of primitive integer fields `x` and `y`. Though immutable `Point` objects would be preferable, we explicitly allow in our design that `Points` are mutable. Applying the Whole-Part pattern, `Triangle` should play the role of a `Whole` object and `Point` should play the role of a `Part`.

Following the pattern, the `Point` objects must not be shared among other graphical objects, since otherwise, e.g., a `rotate` operation on another object could unintendedly change the shape of the `Triangle`. Fig. 1 (without the grey parts) shows a UML class diagram of the design and an object diagram for a snapshot of the system; we disallow the reference labelled with ①.

For a comprehensive specification of the design, we want to specify, in addition to the mere functional behaviour (such as an invariant that the nodes of a triangle are not collinear), that instances of `Point` cannot be accessed by any other object than the specific triangle which it is a node of. Since the desired property describes a behaviour that must be observed in any visible state of a `Triangle` object, we would like to describe it as a class invariant of `Triangle`.

Example 2. To increase the level of complexity a bit, we assume now that, in addition to Example 1, `Point` contains additional references to other objects, such as to instances of `Colour`; the colour of the triangle is determined to be the "gradient" of the colours of its nodes. The representation of a `Colour` object is left open, it may consist of an "RGB" triple of primitive integer fields, or may have references to further objects.

A possible design decision would be to make `Colours` in general sharable among other graphical objects such as `Points`, but not if they belong to `Points` that are constituent parts of *different* `Triangles`. This restriction still allows `Points` of the same triangle to reference the same `Colour`. So modifying a colour not belonging to a triangle t does not affect the state of t: Each node together with its associated colour is in fact a true part of the triangle, as the Whole-Part pattern requires. Like in the previous settings, `Point` objects being part of a `Triangle` must not be shared among other graphical objects.

Fig. 1 (including the grey extension) illustrates the design. The references ① and ② are not allowed in our design.

Again we would like to specify this more challenging encapsulation policy by means of an invariant of `Triangle`.

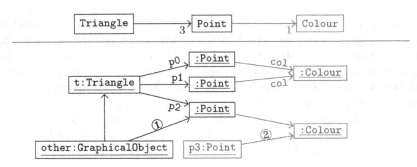

Fig. 1. UML class diagrams (top) and object diagrams (bottom) for Example 1, extensions for Example 2 are grey

The brief investigation of patterns should have shown:

(DP1) Encapsulation is the result of purposely made design decisions.

(DP2) There is not *the* encapsulation property, but there are many varying – and arbitrarily complex – encapsulation properties.

(DP3) There is no sharp line between functional and encapsulation properties.

2.2   Alias Control: Related Work on Encapsulation

Quite a number of techniques have been published in recent years that aim at reducing the complexity introduced by aliasing in programs with pointers, as for example *islands* [12], *balloons* [2], *uniqueness* [5], and different types of *ownership* [7, 15]. We refer to them as *alias control policies*. Overviews are, e.g., in [17]. According to our criteria, these policies ensure properties that can be classified as encapsulation properties.

Most, if not all, of these policies are however technology driven, that is the properties are mostly statically checkable (e.g. by means of a type checker), which is the major justification that the approach exists. We claim that we can formulate each of the properties summarised in [17] with our approach, and we will demonstrate this in some examples below. Moreover we can observe that the investigated design patterns require more generality concerning their encapsulation properties than the existing encapsulation policies provide. Finally, users are facing two ways of writing specifications: the one they are usually used to, *design by contract*, writing invariants and pre-/postcondition contracts, and on the other hand, a completely different way of denoting encapsulation properties, e.g., by labelling fields with a special modifier. We believe that this distinction is unnecessary and unnatural, thus confusing for developers, especially for those who are sceptical towards formal specification anyway.

To sum up, we can state the following weaknesses of the existing *alias control* approaches to master encapsulation:

(AC1) There is an irritating difference between how functional properties and how encapsulation properties are specified in recent approaches.

(AC2) The way encapsulation properties are specified is closely coupled to technologies that check them, which makes it likely that not all desired properties can be formulated.

2.3 Components

Encapsulation is indispensable for the specification and verification of object-oriented software components. Let A be a component that is used by component B and let C be a component that uses both A and B. Assumed that B's methods preserve an invariant φ. Also, φ holds in initial states of B's objects. However, if φ includes statements about the state of objects from A, then these assumptions will *not* ensure that B's invariant holds whenever B is used, since it might be possible that during the use of B in C φ gets violated due to modifications of objects from A which "bypass" B. This undesired behaviour can only be prevented modularly if there is more encapsulation: all uses of A in B that affect B's invariant must only be accessible by means of B.

This observation means however that guarantees on functional properties of components ("trusted components") can only be made if there is a sufficient – and equally well guaranteed – degree of encapsulation to ensure *modular correctness*. More on this issue, in particular on the question of *which* objects are to be encapsulated, can be found in [18].

3 Outline

Taking the results of our reviews of design patterns and alias control policies into account, the central idea of our work is thus: Programmers know how they encapsulate data (DP1), they should be enabled to easily specify their encapsulation concept formally and to check these properties with machine assistance. Especially, (AC1) and (DP3) encourage us to make encapsulation specifiable in a way traditional functional properties are, i.e. by applying *design by contract* and extending a specification language. Moreover, this has the flexibility required by (DP2) and the independence from concrete techniques required by (AC2).

The obvious way to get new features, such as encapsulation properties, into specification languages is to make them accessible as special predicates of the specification language. As any other predicate they can then be connected with other expressions of the language. Language expressions containing the predicates may serve as preconditions, postconditions, or class invariants.

Basically two predicates, *acc* and *reachable* which we will introduce in Sect. 5 are needed to express any encapsulation property we can reasonably expect. They are usually not available in specification languages such as JML[1] [13] or UML/OCL [20]. Since these predicates are most probably hard to handle and do not intuitively reflect the way one wants to specify encapsulation, there is a second layer on top of these basic predicates. Predicates defined in this layer can easily be applied to the reference patterns and alias control properties from above, as demonstrated in Sect. 6.

Finally, in Sect. 7, we investigate how feasible it is to check encapsulation predicates. Since it was left open which technology to use (AC2), we will consider both a deductive approach and approaches from the static analysis area.

First we have a look at the formal basis of our reasoning.

---

[1] In fact, there is an equivalent for the predicate *reachable* available in JML.

4   Formal Background

This work has been done in the context of KeY [1], a project to establish formal specification and deductive verification within commercial software development. The KeY prover, integrated in a CASE tool or an IDE, enables developers to prove properties of Java[2] programs using a program logic called JavaDL [4]. JavaDL expressions may, in KeY, either be the result of a translation from specification languages such as UML/OCL or JML or of direct specification. Functional properties expressible in the aforementioned specification languages are as well expressible in JavaDL, and the other way round, extensions made to (the first order fragment of) JavaDL concerning additional predicates, can also be made to those languages. In this paper we rely on the JavaDL logic and trust in the ability of the reader to translate the definitions to his favourite language.

As follows, some formal properties of a first-order fragment[3] JavaFOL* of JavaDL [4] are defined, which will be extended by encapsulation predicates in the following sections. Note, that these properties are necessary to consolidate encapsulation predicates (Sect. 5) and their axiomatisation (Sect. 7.1).

We assume to have fixed a Java program (i.e. set of classes) P. By *available types* we characterise the Java types declared by P and the built-in Java types. The set *Term* of terms is built inductively from program variables, logical variables, the literal `null`, the `boolean`, `int`, and `String` literals, and in addition: $a_C \in Term$ for static fields $C.a$ of P, $t.a_C \in Term$ for terms t and (instance) fields a declared in class C of P[4], and $t_0[t_1] \in Term$ for terms t_0 and terms t_1.

The formulae *Fma* of JavaFOL* are constructed as usual from terms with user-defined predicate symbols, the predicate $\doteq$, junctors $\neg, \wedge, \vee, \rightarrow, \leftrightarrow$, and quantifiers $\forall$ and $\exists$ which bind logical variables. More precisely, each quantifier is indexed with one of the available types, i.e. for every available type tp there are quantifiers $\forall \colon tp$ and $\exists \colon tp$. $\forall x$ is an abbreviation for $\forall x \colon$ `java.lang.Object` for every logical variable x. Additionally there is the unary predicate $instanceof_{tp}(\cdot)$ for every available type tp.

The semantics is defined by mapping terms to the domain $\mathcal{D}$ of Java objects or values and by the validity relation $\models$ for formulae. Both depend on a state s and a variable assignment β. For undefinedness a choice function ch is employed which delivers, for a term t, an arbitrary unknown but fixed domain element $ch(t)$ as advocated in [11]. The valuation $val_{s,\beta} : Term \rightarrow \mathcal{D}$ is defined as follows:

- for local variables and static fields $\underline{v}$: $val_{s,\beta}(\underline{v})$ is the object or value assigned to the variable (or static field) v in state s.
- for a logical variable x: $val_{s,\beta}(x) = \beta(x)$
- for a term $t.\underline{a}$: $val_{s,\beta}(t.\underline{a}) = \begin{cases} val_{s,\beta}(t).a & \text{if } a \text{ is defined for } val_{s,\beta}(t) \\ ch(t.\underline{a}) & \text{otherwise} \end{cases}$

---

[2] More precisely, only the sequential subset JavaCard is considered.

[3] Though JavaDL is a typed logic, our presentation provides a version that has no types on the syntax level.

[4] The subscript C is skipped if it is clear from the context where a field is declared.

– for a term $t_0[t_1]$:

$$val_{s,\beta}(t_0[t_1]) = \begin{cases} val_{s,\beta}(t_0)[val_{s,\beta}(t_1)] & \text{if } val_{s,\beta}(t_0) \text{ is of an array type} \\ & \text{and } val_{s,\beta}(t_1) \text{ is an int value } i \\ & \text{with } 0 \leq i < val_{s,\beta}(t_0).\texttt{length} \\ ch(t_0[t_1]) & \text{otherwise} \end{cases}$$

The validity $\models$ of formulae is (for formulae φ, terms t_1, t_2, logical variables x):

– $s, \beta \models t_1 \doteq t_2$ iff $val_{s,\beta}(t_1) = val_{s,\beta}(t_2)$
– $s, \beta \models \neg\varphi$ iff not $s, \beta \models \varphi$, etc.
– $s, \beta \models \exists x \colon tp\ \varphi$ iff there is an initialised object $d \in \mathcal{D}$ which is assignment compatible [9] to type tp such that $s, \beta_x^d \models \varphi$, analogously for $\forall x \colon tp\ \varphi$
– $s, \beta \models instanceof_{tp}(t)$ iff $s, \beta \models \exists x \colon tp\ x \doteq t \wedge \neg(t \doteq \texttt{null})$

If $s, \beta \models \varphi$ holds for all β, we just write $s \models \varphi$. In the sequel sets of fields A are considered. A is partitioned in sets A^{inst} and A^{stat} such that A^{stat} contains all the static fields of A and $A^{inst} = A \backslash A^{stat}$. We further denote the set of all fields of a program P as $Fields(P)$.

5 Basic Encapsulation Predicates

In this section, the two basic encapsulation predicates, the *acc* and the *reachable* predicate, are defined for JavaFOL*. As already mentioned, they can likewise be defined for any specification language that is capable of making statements about program states, such as JML or UML/OCL. In Sect. 6 they are complemented with a mere convenience layer, i.e. we provide handy abbreviations. This however means that this section presents all the needed extensions to express encapsulation properties. All applications to design patterns and alias control properties shown in Sect. 6 could be done with the basic predicates of this section only. The formulae would just be more intricate.

5.1 The *acc* Predicate

In object-oriented specification languages as well as in JavaDL there are only means to reason about concrete field accesses but there is no way to talk about an *arbitrary* field access, such as "there is a field such that. . .". Without getting too much into the spheres of higher order logic, this restriction needs to be relaxed by defining an *acc* predicate. It defines the relation of objects which can be accessed with exactly one field or array access from a list of allowed fields.

Definition 1 (Syntax of acc). *Let A be a set of fields defined in a Java program P, and t_1 and t_2 JavaFOL* terms for P. Then $acc[A](t_1, t_2)$ is a formula of JavaFOL*. For a program P, $acc(t_1, t_2)$ is regarded as abbreviation for $acc[Fields(P)](t_1, t_2)$.*

What does *accessibility* between two objects exactly mean? Since our goal is to cope with the design patterns mentioned above, we clarify the question by looking at one of them more carefully. In the Whole-Part pattern, the restricted accessibility is supposed to ensure that the state of Parts cannot be modified by clients others than from the corresponding Whole. State changes on a Part object p are performed by invoking methods of p or directly assigning to a field or to an array slot of p. Both possibilities require that the object that performs the modification holds a reference to p. References may be held either in a local variable, a field, or an array slot. Like when invariants are considered, we are however only interested in states directly before and after method invocations (*visible states*). Since such a method invocation cannot change the assignments to local variables of the caller with the exception of the returned value, all local variables but the one assigned to by the call, can be ignored. The return value can be taken into consideration if we, without loosing generality, look at method calls that assign to a field of an anonymous class (see Sect. 7). This justifies the following two possibilities of how to access an object e_1 directly from a given one e_0: e_1 may be stored in a field of a class instance e_0 or e_0 is an array object of which one slot stores e_1.

In addition we say that e_1 is accessed from e_0 if there is some static field that references e_1. For encapsulation this is crucial: With static fields, encapsulation is practically completely compromised since they provide global access to the object of question. In fact, it would be sufficient only to consider *visible* static fields. For simplicity, the slightly more conservative approach to take *all* static fields into account is taken here.

The three possibilities for an access are reflected in the semantics of *acc*:

Definition 2 (Semantics of acc). $s, \beta \models acc[A](t_1, t_2)$ *is defined to hold for a state s iff $(val_{s,\beta}(t_1), val_{s,\beta}(t_2)) \in Acc[A]$. $Acc[A]$ is defined to be a relation on D (that is a subset of $\mathcal{D} \times \mathcal{D}$) with $(e_0, e_1) \in Acc[A]$ iff*

- e_0 *is a class instance (i.e. not an array object) and there exists $a \in A^{inst}$ with $e_1 = e_0.a$, or*
- *there exists $a \in A^{stat}$ with $e_1 = val_{s,\beta}(\underline{a})$, or*
- e_0 *is an array and there exists $j \in \{0, \dots, e_0.\texttt{length}\}$ with $e_1 = e_0[j]$.*

5.2   The *reachable* Predicate

Reasoning about encapsulation often means reasoning about restricted reachability. In this section a *reachable* predicate is defined that can be used to reason about these restrictions. Essentially, reachability is the reflexive and transitive closure of the *acc* relation defined in the last section. So we define *reachable*, a binary predicate for each set of fields, as follows:

Definition 3 (Syntax and Semantics of reachable). *Let A be a set of fields defined in a Java program P, and t_1 and t_2 JavaFOL* terms for P. Then reachable $[A](t_1, t_2)$ is a formula of JavaFOL*. Again reachable (t_1, t_2) is considered to be an abbreviation for reachable $[Fields(P)](t_1, t_2)$.*

For a state s and a variable assignment β, $s, \beta \models$ reachable $[A](t_1, t_2)$ iff there is a finite sequence of objects $(e_0, e_1, \dots e_k)$ $(k \in \mathbb{N})$ such that $e_0 = val_{s,\beta}(t_1)$ and $e_k = val_{s,\beta}(t_2)$ and for all $i = 1, \dots, k$: $(e_{i-1}, e_i) \in Acc[A]$.

6   Applications and Convenience Encapsulation Predicates

Though the predicates *acc* and *reachable* provide a basic vocabulary for specifying encapsulation behaviour, their use is still tedious. We thus provide handy abbreviations, or *convenience encapsulation predicates*, for useful application patterns. Below, their practicability is measured by formulating properties of the design patterns and the alias control approaches. In the end, all predicates introduced throughout this section are summarised in Table 1.

6.1   The *guardAcc* and *uniqueAcc* Predicates

We define an abbreviation for specifying the following property: If there is a direct reference between an arbitrary *guard* object x and an object u then x must satisfy $\varphi(x)$. In JavaFOL* we formalise this property as

$$guardAcc_x[A; \varphi(x)](u) \leftrightarrow \forall y\big(acc[A](y, u) \rightarrow \varphi(y)\big) \ .$$

As before the parameter A is optional and skipping it can be seen as abbreviation for using $Fields(P)$. The formula $\varphi(x)$ is the characteristic function of those objects, the *guard* objects, which are allowed to hold a reference to u. In the easiest and most common case, $\varphi(x)$ will consist just of an equality $x \doteq g$, thus having just one guard object g. This specification pattern is in fact so common that we introduce another convenience predicate called *uniqueAcc* which is defined by the equivalence

$$uniqueAcc(g, u) \leftrightarrow guardAcc_x[g \doteq x](u) \ .$$

Alias Control: Unique Pointer. A *unique object* is an object that is referenced by at most one object [5]. The *guardAcc* predicate can easily be used to model this property, e.g. to say that u is a unique object, we require that for every object z that has a direct reference to u, all other objects referencing u must be equal to z. Or simpler: z is the only guard object. Moreover there is an equivalent formulation with *uniqueAcc*:

$$\forall z(acc(z, u) \rightarrow guardAcc_x[x \doteq z](u)), \qquad \forall z(acc(z, u) \rightarrow uniqueAcc(z, u)) \ .$$

By inserting the definition of *guardAcc* and simplifying we get the following formula, which obviously fits our expectations of a unique object:

$$\forall z \forall y\big(acc(z, u) \wedge acc(y, u) \rightarrow y \doteq z\big) \ .$$

Pattern: Whole-Part. The *guardAcc* or the *uniqueAcc* predicate can be employed for simple versions of the Whole-Part pattern, namely if the part's state does not depend on additional objects. In this case, the Whole-Part pattern forbids direct access to the parts (instances of `Part`), only indirect accesses through the `Whole` object are allowed. We can now formally note this property as

$$\forall p{:}\,\texttt{Part}\ \exists w{:}\,\texttt{Whole}\ guardAcc_x[x \doteq w](p) \ .$$

or if we already know that the value in field `p` is a part of a `Whole` and using *uniqueAcc*, we write simpler: $\forall w{:}\,\texttt{Whole}\ uniqueAcc(w, w.\underline{\texttt{p}})$.

Example 3. For the settings in Example 1, we would require the following invariant:

$$\forall t\colon \mathtt{Triangle}\ \big(uniqueAcc(t, t.\underline{\mathtt{p0}}) \wedge uniqueAcc(t, t.\underline{\mathtt{p1}}) \wedge uniqueAcc(t, t.\underline{\mathtt{p2}})\big)\ .$$

This exactly describes the desired property that nodes may only be accessed by means of `Triangle`. It is however *not* sufficient for the settings of Example 2 since then references to `Colour` objects would be allowed, even if they "bypass" the corresponding `Triangle` object.

Patterns: Copy Mutable Parameters, Return New Objects from Accessor Method. These two patterns ensure that an object stored in a field a of object o is only accessed through o itself, denoted in JavaFOL* as $guardAcc_x[x \doteq o](o.\underline{a})$. In contrast to many other patterns, these two patterns exactly define *how* encapsulation must be achieved, namely by copying parameters and return values. Only the effect of the pattern can be specified with encapsulation predicates.

Alias Control: Confinement. The formula that specifies the confinement [19] aliasing policy demonstrates that it is useful to have the possibility to use a formula $\varphi(x)$ to qualify guard objects.

We assume that we have a unary predicate $confined_p$ which holds for every object whose type is confined to package p. Let $tp_1, \ldots, tp_n$ be the classes in package p. Only these classes may access types confined to p. The following formula describes this property:

$$\forall y\big(confined_p(y) \rightarrow guardAcc_x[instanceof_{tp_1}(x) \vee \ldots \vee instanceof_{tp_n}(x)](y)\big)\ .$$

6.2   The *guardReg* and *uniqueReg* Predicates

The *guardAcc* predicate restricts the accessibility of one single object. Often however, it is necessary to restrict the access to *all* objects (indirectly) referenced by a particular one. To ensure, e.g., that in the object graph of Fig. 1 references ① and ② are not allowed, it must be required that all objects reachable from `t.p0` are only reachable through `t`. No restriction should however be imposed on references within the group of objects reachable from `t.p0`. Using the *guardAcc* predicate we can formalise such properties as follows and define the *guardReg* predicate, an informal description follows afterwards:

$$guardReg_x[A; \varphi(x)](u) \leftrightarrow$$
$$\forall z\big(reachable[A](u, z) \rightarrow z \doteq u \vee guardAcc_x[\varphi(x) \vee reachable[A](u, x)](z)\big)$$

or equivalently:

$$guardReg_x[A; \varphi(x)](u) \leftrightarrow$$
$$\forall y\forall z\big((reachable[A](u, z) \wedge acc(y, z)) \rightarrow (z \doteq u \vee reachable[A](u, y) \vee \varphi(y))\big)\ .$$

In this formalisation one can associate the objects of the protected "region" as those objects z which are reachable with fields A starting from an object u. For

u itself no restriction regarding incoming references is imposed (this explains $z \doteq u$ on the right side of the implication). Any reference from an object y to such a z must either satisfy $\varphi(y)$ or is itself part of this region (i.e. reachable from u via fields A).

Like there was a *uniqueAcc* predicate introduced for the *guardAcc* predicate we define a *uniqueReg* predicate as follows to capture the most common application of *guardReg*:

$$uniqueReg(g, u) \leftrightarrow guardReg_x[x \doteq g](u) .$$

Again, a survey of design patterns and alias control policies follows, to demonstrate the usefulness of the two additional convenience predicates. In addition, we mention how the predicate enables us to formally specify *compositions* of the modelling language UML.

Alias Control: Islands. An object *bridge* plays the role of a bridge if in all states the formula *uniqueReg(bridge, bridge)* holds [12]. By applying the definition and simplifying we get:

$$\forall y \forall z \big((reachable(bridge, z) \wedge acc(y, z)) \rightarrow (z \doteq bridge \vee reachable(bridge, y)) \big) .$$

Alias Control: Balloons. For balloons, it is required [2] that for an object b of a balloon type and the objects B indirectly referenced by b the property holds: b is referenced at most once, the referencing object is not in B, and all objects in B are only referenced by objects in $B \cup \{b\}$. Formalised in JavaFOL*, this property is:

$$uniqueReg(b, b) \wedge \forall v \big(acc(v, b) \rightarrow (uniqueAcc(v, b) \wedge \neg reachable(b, v)) \big) .$$

Pattern: Whole-Part. The Whole-Part pattern requires that there is no direct access to the parts (instances of `Part`), only indirect accesses through the `Whole` object are allowed. For simple structures, we have already observed above that it is sufficient to use a formulation using the *guardAcc* predicate.

If, however, the `Part` objects' representations consist of a more complex object structure, this formulation is insufficient as Example 3 has illustrated. Instead, we can express the desired property with the help of *guardReg*. The basic formalisation is:

$$\forall p\text{:}\mathtt{Part}\ \exists w\text{:}\mathtt{Whole}\ uniqueReg(w, p) . \tag{1}$$

The validity of this formula implies that all objects that are (indirectly) referenced by a `Part` are only accessed among each other or by a particular `Whole` object. For patterns like the *Proxy* or the *Memento* pattern similar conditions can be formalised with *guardReg*, and even variations (like that some objects may bypass a *Proxy*) are possible to formalise.

Example 4. We take up the settings of Example 2. The special variant of the Whole-Part pattern imposed there is that parts of the same aggregate may access internals of each other. The guard object is thus not only the `Whole` but also all objects reachable from the parts, i.e. those x satisfying

$$\varphi_g := x \doteq t \vee reachable(t.\underline{\mathtt{p0}}, x) \vee reachable(t.\underline{\mathtt{p1}}, x) \vee reachable(t.\underline{\mathtt{p2}}, x)$$

The desired property is now formalised in JavaFOL* as follows:

$$\forall t\!:\!\texttt{Triangle}\ (\ guardReg_x[\varphi_g](t.\underline{\texttt{p0}})\wedge$$
$$guardReg_x[\varphi_g](t.\underline{\texttt{p1}})\wedge guardReg_x[\varphi_g](t.\underline{\texttt{p2}}))\ .$$

Pattern: Iterator. With this pattern, we show that the parameterisation of the predicate with a set of fields A is in fact useful. The objects protected by guard objects are the internals of the aggregate. For simplicity, we assume that the aggregate object is a linked list implemented in a class `LinkedList` (like the Java implementation `java.util.LinkedList`). We assume that the internals of the list are made up by objects of a class `Entry` connected by a `next` field. The first object of the internals is stored in the `header` field of a `LinkedList`. The guard objects are both the `LinkedList` instance and the `ListItr` iterator object (this could be made more precise by describing only `ListItr` instances of the particular list). The encapsulation property for the Iterator pattern is thus:

$$\forall l\!:\!\texttt{LinkedList}\ guardReg_x[\{\texttt{next}\}; x \doteq l \vee instanceof_{\texttt{ListItr}}(x)](l.\texttt{header})\ .$$

UML Compositions. In the modelling language UML, classes and their interrelation can be modelled in class diagrams. The relation between instances of classes are represented as *associations* between classes. *Compositions* are special kinds of associations, which are depicted with a filled diamond adornment (see Fig. 2).

Fig. 2. UML composition

They emphasise that one partner in the relation has sole responsibility for managing the parts of the other partner. As a consequence, accessing these objects directly is forbidden. This property can be formally captured as in (1):

$$\forall p\!:\!\texttt{Part}\ \exists w\!:\!\texttt{AClass}\ uniqueReg(w,p)\ .$$

6.3   Direct Applications of the Basic Predicates

Ownership. We assume to have given an acyclic partial function *own* [15], which we formalise as predicate: $own(t_1,t_2)$ holds iff an object t_1 owns t_2 or t_1 is *null* and t_2 is not owned. We assume that the acyclicity of *own* is checked externally before, since this is out of reach of a first order formulation, and can in fact be enforced [15]. With the *acc* predicate, the ownership relation of [15] can simply be written down in JavaFOL*:

$$\forall e \forall e'\ acc(e,e') \rightarrow \Big(own(e,e') \vee \exists e_0 \big(own(e_0,e) \wedge own(e_0,e')\big)\Big)\ .$$

7   Checking Encapsulation Predicates

This section deals with the question how specifications containing encapsulation predicates can be checked against an implementation. Using deduction for this is

Table 1. Overview of encapsulation predicates

Predicate	Definition
$acc[A](t_1, t_2)$	(Axiom, "there are direct references from t_1 to t_2")
$reachable[A](t_1, t_2)$	(Axiom, "there are access paths from t_1 to t_2")
$guardAcc_x[A; \varphi(x)](u)$	$\forall y (acc[A](y, u) \rightarrow \varphi(y))$
$uniqueAcc(g, u)$	$guardAcc_x[g \doteq x](u)$
$guardReg_x[A; \varphi(x)](u)$	$\forall y \forall z ((reachable[A](u, z) \wedge acc(y, z))$
	$\rightarrow (z \doteq u \vee reachable[A](u, y) \vee \varphi(y)))$
$uniqueReg(g, u)$	$guardReg_x[g \doteq x](u)$

most natural, since this is the preferred way to verify programs w.r.t functional specifications; encapsulation properties can, as shown above, be formulated in the very same way. Static analysis has the appeal of a fully automated technique which should thus be made use of whenever possible. Our approach aims at a framework which integrates both techniques. Due to space restrictions, we can only give a brief impression of our approach and do not show correctness proofs.

7.1 Deductive Approach

The two predicates defined in Sect. 5 must be axiomatised to deductively treat encapsulation predicates. Both *acc* and *reachable* predicates are challenging, since both are beyond the original JavaDL expressibility (for the need to identify *all* fields in the program) and the latter has no complete axiomatisation.

The acc Predicate. The following axiom for the *acc* predicate is correct:

$$\forall x \forall y \Big(acc[A](x, y) \;\leftrightarrow\; \big(\quad \exists i{:}\,int\, (x[i] \doteq y) \tag{2}$$
$$\vee \bigvee_{a \in A^{stat}} \underline{a} \doteq y \quad \vee \bigvee_{a \in A} x.\underline{a} \doteq y\big)\Big) .$$

In contrast to the logic presented in Sect. 4, the logic implemented in the KeY prover is a *typed logic*, so even on the syntactic level there are types. Then, for every s, β and every term t of type tp, $val_{s,\beta}(t)$ is always assignment compatible to tp, so basically they are subtypes. This gives rise to an optimisation. It is obvious that we do not need to generate sub-formulae $x.\underline{a} \doteq y$ if we already know by the (static) type of x that x can not have a field a. By similar considerations we can skip one disjunct of (2) since we know, just by considering the type of x, that a term is either of an array type or not, and so one disjunct is irrelevant.

The *reachable* Predicate. The *reachable* predicate is axiomatised in a similar way as other attempts in literature [16]. Basically it is the reflexive and transitive closure of *acc*. The following axiomatisation is correct:

$$\forall x \forall y \left(reachable[A](x, y) \leftrightarrow (x \doteq y \vee \exists z(acc[A](x, z) \wedge reachable[A](z, y)))\right)$$
$$\forall x \forall y \left(reachable[A](x, y) \leftrightarrow \exists z(reachable[A](x, z) \wedge reachable[A](z, y))\right) .$$

It is well known that there is no complete axiomatisation of the transitive closure, and thus of *reachable*, in first order logic since the access graph may contain cycles and our domain is infinite [3]. However, it seems that the above (incomplete) axiomatisation is sufficient for practical purposes.

Proving Encapsulation Properties of Programs. For treating programs we need more than the first order fragment JavaFOL* used so far, that is full JavaDL plus the extensions made in the last two sections. On the syntactic level, JavaDL introduces a modality $\langle \cdot \rangle$: For every JavaDL formula φ and every sequence α of (correctly typed) Java statements, $\langle \alpha \rangle \varphi$ is a JavaDL formula. JavaDL semantics [4] is defined formally in terms of Kripke structures. Here, we just say informally that $\langle \alpha \rangle \varphi$ denotes the property of α to terminate in a state in which φ holds (total correctness). So $\psi \to \langle \alpha \rangle \varphi$ means (similar to a Hoare triple) that, if ψ holds initially then α terminates and afterwards φ holds.

With the axiomatisation of encapsulation properties and modalities, we can prove with a theorem prover that methods preserve encapsulation properties. If all public methods and constructors preserve an encapsulation property the property holds in all visible states of the program.

In order to prove the preservation of an (encapsulation) property φ for a method call `e.m(e`$_0$`, ..., e`$_n$`);` we have the following proof obligation:

$$\varphi \to \langle \texttt{Ano.o = e.m(e}_0\texttt{, ..., e}_n\texttt{);} \rangle \varphi . \tag{3}$$

Since our notion of accessibility refers only to field or array accesses, and deliberately *not* to local variables, the method call we investigate assigns its return value to a suitable static field of an "anonymous" class `Ano` which is unused in the rest of the code. This reflects the fact that callers of the method may reference the returned object and, thus, have direct access to it.

We have extended the KeY prover [1] with some of the predicates from above. The example below reports on a sample application.

Example 5. Let us take up the settings from Example 1. To class `Triangle`, we add a method `getPoint0()`. Our first attempt is to attach to `getPoint0()` the implementation `return p0;`. This is however not acceptable since callers reference `p0` after `getPoint0()` has terminated, though the encapsulation specification requires unique access through the `Triangle` object.
Proof obligation (3), instantiated as follows, can thus not be proven:

$$\forall t\colon \texttt{Triangle } guardAcc_x[x \doteq t](t.\underline{\texttt{p0}})$$
$$\to \langle \texttt{Ano.o = tria.getPoint0();} \rangle \forall t\colon \texttt{Triangle } guardAcc_x[x \doteq t](t.\underline{\texttt{p0}}) .$$

Implementing `getPoint0()` with `return new Point(p0.getX(),p0.getY());` makes the proof obligation however – as desired – provable. The KeY prover requires some manual, though trivial, quantifier instantiations to close the proof.

7.2   Static Analysis Techniques

Sect. 2.2 already referenced static analysis techniques called *alias control policies* and the encapsulation properties they check. Though encapsulation predicates provide a much more general framework than these rather specialised properties, the use of deductive verification to prove properties expressed by means of encapsulation predicates has a major disadvantage compared to the static analysis techniques employed for *alias control*: In general, deduction requires user inter-action, which is especially in the case of treating *reachable* non-trivial, while the techniques to prove *alias control* properties are usually fully automated static analyses. Automated techniques can nevertheless be used even in the general set-ting of encapsulation predicates. By a simple type checker like algorithm (similar to those of ownership type systems) we can, e.g., check that a piece of code α preserves the property $uniqueReg(w, w.p)$. So, instead of deductively verifying this, this algorithm can be invoked by the following "sequent calculus rule":

$$\frac{\Gamma, uniqueReg(w, w.p) \vdash \#analyse(\langle\alpha\rangle uniqueReg(w, w.p)), \Delta}{\Gamma, uniqueReg(w, w.p) \vdash \langle\alpha\rangle uniqueReg(w, w.p), \Delta}.$$

If the static check is successful $\#analyse(\dots)$ is rewritten to *true*, otherwise the argument $\langle\alpha\rangle uniqueReg(w, w.p)$ is returned.

8 Future Work and Conclusions

This work contributes to the application of formal methods to object-oriented software development by

- emphasising the importance of encapsulation properties for the formally cor-rect realisation of design decisions,
- giving specifiers means to easily formulate a wide range of encapsulation properties *within* the traditional methodology *design by contract* by using basic and convenience *encapsulation predicates*,
- providing means to verify encapsulation properties from within an interactive theorem prover and integrating static analysis methods.

We have demonstrated that the approach is suited to formulate encapsulation properties occurring in relevant software designs by formalising design patterns.

As future work, we want to further work on integrating advanced static pro-cedures into our framework to resolve encapsulation properties. Moreover, we envisage the automated generation of a formal encapsulation specification from software components with an attached formal specification. As pointed out in Sect. 2.3 such an encapsulation specification of a component is a major step towards components with guaranteed functionality.

Acknowledgements

Thanks are due to Richard Bubel for great help with the *reachable* predicate, and to him, Steffen Schlager, and the anonymous reviewers for helpful comments and corrections.

References

1. W. Ahrendt, T. Baar, B. Beckert, R. Bubel, M. Giese, R. Hähnle, W. Menzel, W. Mostowski, A. Roth, S. Schlager, and P. H. Schmitt. The KeY tool. *Software and System Modeling*, 4:32–54, 2005.

2. P. S. Almeida. Controlling sharing of state in data types. In M. Aksit and S. Matsuoka, editors, *ECOOP '97–Object-Oriented Programming*, volume 1241 of *Lecture Notes in Computer Science*, pages 32–59. Springer, 1997.
3. T. Baar. The definition of transitive closure with OCL – limitations and applications. In *Proceedings, Fifth Andrei Ershov International Conference, Perspectives of System Informatics, Novosibirsk, Russia*, volume 2890 of *Lecture Notes in Computer Science*, pages 358–365. Springer, July 2003.
4. B. Beckert. A dynamic logic for the formal verification of Java Card programs. In I. Attali and T. Jensen, editors, *Java on Smart Cards: Programming and Security. Revised Papers, Java Card 2000, International Workshop, Cannes, France*, volume 2041 of *Lecture Notes in Computer Science*, pages 6–24. Springer, 2001.
5. J. Boyland. Alias burying: Unique variables without destructive reads. *Software – Practice and Experience*, 31(6):533–553, May 2001.
6. F. Buschmann, R. Meunier, H. Rohnert, P. Sommerlad, and M. Stal. *Pattern-Oriented Software Architecture - A System of Patterns*. John-Wiley and Sons, 1996.
7. D. Clarke, J. Potter, and J. Noble. Ownership types for flexible alias protection. In *ACM Conference on Object-Oriented Programming Systems, Languages and Applications (OOPSLA'98)*, Vancouver, Canada, October 1998.
8. E. Gamma, R. Helm, R. Johnson, and J. Vlissides. *Design Patterns: Elements of Reusable Object-Oriented Software*. Addison-Wesley, Reading/MA, 1995.
9. J. Gosling, B. Joy, G. Steele, and G. Bracha. *The Java Language Specification*. Addison Wesley, 2nd edition, 2000.
10. M. Grand. *Patterns in Java*, volume 1 and 2. John Wiley & Sons, 1998 and 1999.
11. D. Gries and F. B. Schneider. Avoiding the undefined by underspecification. In J. van Leeuwen, editor, *Computer Science Today*, volume 1000 of *Lecture Notes in Computer Science*, pages 366–373. Springer, 1995.
12. J. Hogg. Islands: Aliasing protection in object-oriented languages. In *Conference proceedings on Object-oriented programming systems, languages, and applications*, pages 271–285. ACM Press, 1991.
13. G. T. Leavens, A. L. Baker, and C. Ruby. Preliminary design of JML: A behavioral interface specification language for Java. Technical Report 98-06z, Iowa State University, Department of Computer Science, Dec. 2004. See www.jmlspecs.org.
14. B. Meyer. Applying "design by contract". *IEEE Computer*, 25(10):40–51, Oct. 1992.
15. P. Müller. *Modular specification and verification of object-oriented programs*. Springer-Verlag New York, Inc., 2002.
16. G. Nelson. Verifying reachability invariants of linked structures. In *Proceedings of the 10th ACM SIGACT-SIGPLAN symposium on Principles of programming languages*, pages 38–47. ACM Press, 1983.
17. J. Noble, R. Biddle, E. Tempero, A. Potanin, and D. Clarke. Towards a model of encapsulation. In *International Workshop on Aliasing, Confinement, and Ownership (IWACO)*, Darmstadt, Germany, July 2003.
18. A. Roth and P. H. Schmitt. Ensuring invariant contracts for modules in java. In *Proceedings of the ECOOP Workshop FTfJP 2004 Formal Techniques for Java-like Programs*, number NIII-R0426 in Technical Report, University of Nijmegen, pages 93–102, June 2004.
19. J. Vitek and B. Bokowski. Confined types in Java. *Software – Practice and Experience*, 31(6):507–532, 2001.
20. J. Warmer and A. Kleppe. *The Object Constraint Language: Precise Modelling with UML*. Object Technology Series. Addison-Wesley, Reading/MA, 1999.

Detecting Errors in Multithreaded Programs by Generalized Predictive Analysis of Executions

Koushik Sen, Grigore Roşu, and Gul Agha

Department of Computer Science,
University of Illinois at Urbana-Champaign
{ksen,grosu,agha}@cs.uiuc.edu

Abstract. A predictive runtime analysis technique is proposed for detecting violations of safety properties from apparently successful executions of concurrent systems. In this paper we focus on concurrent systems developed using common object-oriented multithreaded programming languages, in particular, Java. Specifically, we provide an algorithm to *observe* execution traces of multithreaded programs and, based on appropriate code instrumentation that allows one to atomically extract a partial-order causality from a linear sequence of events, we predict other schedules that are compatible with the run. The technique uses a weak *happens-before* relation which orders a write of a shared variable with all its subsequent reads that occur before the next write to the variable. A permutation of the observed events is a *possible execution* of a program if and only if it does not contradict the weak happens-before relation. Even though an observed execution trace may not violate the given specification, our algorithm infers other possible executions (consistent with the observed execution) that violate the given specification, if such an execution exists. Therefore, it can *predict* concurrency errors from non-violating runs.

1 Introduction

In multithreaded systems, threads can execute concurrently communicating with each other through a set of shared variables, creating the potential for subtle errors. The large number of potential interleavings makes it infeasible to check all possible executions before deployment. Ordinary testing of such systems, on the other hand, can be quite ineffective in practice, because of its low coverage with respect to the number of interleavings and because of the difficulty to reproduce many concurrency errors. The work presented in this paper builds upon our experience with *predictive runtime analysis* (or *predictive testing*) techniques, whose aim is to increase the effectiveness of testing by analyzing a class of possible executions that are causally equivalent to the particular observed one. What makes predictive analysis techniques appealing is the fact that some of the causally equivalent executions may violate the requirements of the system even though the observed execution does not.

Unlike model checking, predictive monitoring is not comprehensive. However, it is far more efficient than model checking because it does not execute the program but relies only on the information that is already available in a run-time

M. Steffen and G. Zavattaro (Eds.): FMOODS 2005, LNCS 3535, pp. 211–226, 2005.

execution. Specifically, we use a relatively non-restrictive semantic precedence relation, extracted entirely automatically at runtime via appropriate program instrumentation, to cluster events into equivalence classes. We then allow permutations of these equivalence classes and show how these permutations can be used to determine the effect of a large number of alternate schedules of threads.

Example. Consider an execution of the multithreaded program in Figure 1 for airplane landing. Suppose in an execution, one thread (t2) in the program sets the variable `permit` to `false` (event e'). Another thread (t1) in the program checks with the control tower to see if the plane has permission to land. It then sets a variable `permit` to `true` (event e_1). At a subsequent point, the thread t1 reads the variable `permit` (event e_2), checks if `permit` is `true`, and sets the variable `landing` to `true` (event e_3).

Suppose we want to check that the property that "if `landing` then immediately before `permit` is `true`". For the observed execution e', e_1, e_2, e_3, the property holds. However, since there is no causal connection between e' and e_1, and they are executed by different threads, we may permute these writes. Permuting only the writes would require us to actually execute the program along a different path (as in model checking). This would be inefficient and generally not feasible at runtime. We avoid doing so by requiring all associated reads (i.e., all reads of a variable that follow the latest preceding write of the variable) to also be permuted. This allows us to construct an alternate execution path, e_1, e_2, e', e_3 and the monitor infers that the property could be violated at e_3 and produces the trace as a witness.

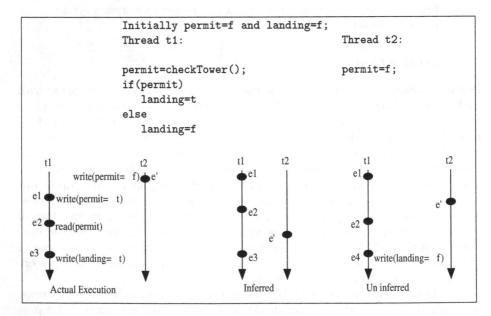

Fig. 1. Time increases downward and is assumed to be the same across the threads.

Observe that, given the semantics of the program, the order of events could also have been: $e_1, e', e_2, ..$ in which case `landing` would never be set to `true`. We do not infer this path because doing so would require actually running the program with a different schedule (or semantically analyzing it) to determine which event happens instead of e_3. In particular, this means that violations of some properties may never be detected. For example, consider the property that "if `landing` is modified then `landing` is true or always in the past `permit` was false". This property is not violated by either the execution we observed, nor the alternate execution we constructed. However, it would be violated by the execution trace $e_1, e', e_2, ..$ and a model checker could detect this and our method could not, unless a related trace was one of the test cases. However, we show that our generalized analysis can very efficiently uncover many errors that standard testing would not with the same set of test cases.

2 Related Work

A number of runtime monitoring tools have been developed. These tools include NASA's JPAX [10], University of Pennsylvania's JAVA-MAC [13], Bell Labs' PET [9], and the commercial analysis systems Temporal Rover and DBRover [6, 7]. Our work builds on experience with related techniques and tools–namely, JAVA PATHEXPLORER (JPAX) [10] and its sub-system EAGLE [2]. These tools treat the execution of a program essentially as a flat, sequential trace of events or states. We proposed *predictive runtime analysis* in [17, 18]. The technique was based on checking a specification against executions that are *causally consistent* with a given execution – i.e., executions that do not permute writes to the same shared variable.

In this paper, we have significantly extended the strength of our prediction by abstracting a multithreaded computation in terms of two novel relations: *weak-happens-before* relation and *atomicity* relation on post-write set of read events. As a consequence of abstracting multithreaded computations this way, we are able increase the coverage of runtime analysis of multithreaded programs by being able to predict more valid multithreaded runs from a given single execution. In particular, in the example described above, the existing predictive technique would not have detected a violation of our specification.

3 Monitors for Safety Properties

Safety properties form an important class of properties in monitoring. This is because once a system violates a safety property, there is no way to continue its execution to satisfy the safety property later. Therefore, a monitor for a safety property can precisely say at runtime when the property has been violated, so that an external recovery action can be taken. From a monitoring perspective, what is needed from a safety formula is a succinct representation of its *bad prefixes*, which are finite sequences of states leading to a violation of the property. Therefore, one can abstract away safety properties by languages over finite words. Nondeterministic automata are a standard means to succinctly represent languages over finite words. We next define a suitable version of automata, called *monitor*, with the property that it has a "bad" state from which it never exits:

Definition 1. *Let E be a finite or infinite set, that can be thought of as the set of events generated by the program to monitor. Then an E-monitor or simply a monitor, is a tuple $\mathcal{M}on = \langle \mathcal{M}, m_0, b, \rho \rangle$, where*

- *$\mathcal{M}$ is the set of states of the monitor;*
- *$m_0 \in \mathcal{M}$ is the initial state of the monitor;*
- *$b \in \mathcal{M}$ is the final state of the monitor, also called bad state; and*
- *$\rho: \mathcal{M} \times E \to 2^{\mathcal{M}}$ is a non-deterministic transition relation with the property that $\rho(b, e) = \{b\}$ for any $e \in E$.*

Sequences in $E^\star$, where ϵ is the empty one, are called (execution) traces. A trace π is said to be a bad prefix in $\mathcal{M}on$ iff $b \in \rho(\{m_0\}, \pi)$, where $\rho: 2^{\mathcal{M}} \times E^\star \to 2^{\mathcal{M}}$ is recursively defined as $\rho(M, \epsilon) = M$ and $\rho(M, \pi e) = \rho(\rho(M, \pi), e)$, where $\rho: 2^{\mathcal{M}} \times E \to 2^{\mathcal{M}}$ is defined as $\rho(\{m\} \cup M, e) = \rho(m, e) \cup \rho(M, e)$ and $\rho(\emptyset, e) = \emptyset$, for all finite $M \subseteq \mathcal{M}$ and $e \in E$.

$\mathcal{M}$ is not required to be finite in the above definition, but $2^{\mathcal{M}}$ represents the set of *finite* subsets of $\mathcal{M}$. In practical situations it is often the case that the monitor is *not* explicitly provided in a mathematical form as above. For example, a monitor can be just any program whose execution is triggered by receiving events from the monitored program; its state can be given by the values of its local variables, and the bad state has some easy to detect property, such as a specific variable having a negative value. There are fortunate situations in which monitors can be *automatically generated* from formal specifications [2, 11, 16], thus requiring the user to focus on system's formal safety requirements rather than on low level implementation details.

Example 1. Let us consider the program given in Figure 2. It consists of two threads t1 and t2 accessing the variables x, y, and z. Let the safety property that we want to monitor be "if x becomes positive then eventually in the past x became negative" which can be written in past-time temporal logic as the formula $F = p \to \Diamond q$, where p represents the event that x becomes positive and q represents the event that x becomes negative. The monitor automaton for this formula is given in Figure 2. State 4 in this automaton represents the bad state. Suppose that one runs the program and observes the execution t1: x=-1; t1: z=x+3; t2: x=1; t2: y=x+z; in that order; then, the safety property is not violated for this execution. Moreover, with the "happens-before" relation given in [17, 18] which disallows any permutation of two accesses of the same variable except when both of them are reads, one cannot predict any other possible valid run (obtained through a different scheduling) that violates the property. However, as shown later in this paper, our approach allows an observer of the execution above to predict another possible valid run that violates the safety property, namely the one in which t2 executes first. The interesting aspect here is that the observer *does not see the code*, but only the flat sequence of read and write events of shared variables, time-stamped appropriately.

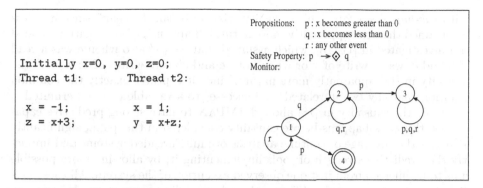

Fig. 2. Two threads t1 and t2 and a monitor.

4   Abstracting Multithreaded Computations

A multithreaded program consists of n threads t_1, t_2, ..., t_n that execute concurrently and communicate with each other through a set of shared variables. The computation of each thread is abstracted out in terms of *events*, while the multithreaded computation is abstracted out in terms of a partial order $\prec$ on events. There can be three types of events: an *internal* event, a *read* or a *write* of a shared variable. Internal events can be reads or writes of local variables, calling a function, the value of a variable crossing some threshold, etc. We use e_i^j to represent the jth event generated by thread t_i since the start of its execution. When the thread or position of an event is not important we can refer to it generically, such as e, e', etc.; we may write $e \in t_i$ when event e is generated by thread t_i. Let us fix an arbitrary but fixed multithreaded execution and let S be the set of all variables that are shared by more than one thread in the execution.

We can define a special "happens-before" relation over the accesses to each shared variable: we say e x-happens-before e', written $e <_x e'$, iff e is a write of x and e' is a read of x such that the latest write to x that happens-before e' is e. In other words, we say that $e <_x e'$ if and only if the value of x read by event e' is the value written by the event e on variable x. This can be realized by maintaining a counter for each shared variable, which is incremented at each variable write. If the value of the counter at the read event e' of x is same as the counter value after the write event e of x, we say that $e <_x e'$. Let E_i denote the set of events of thread t_i and let E denote $\bigcup_i E_i$. Also, let $< \subseteq E \times E$ be defined as follows:

1. $e < e'$ when e and e' are events of *the same thread* and e happens immediately before e';
2. $e < e'$ whenever there is an $x \in S$ with $e <_x e'$.

The partial order $\prec$ is the transitive closure of the relation $<$. Let $\preceq$ be the transitive, reflexive closure of $<$. We say $e||e'$ if $e \npreceq e'$ and $e' \npreceq e$, i.e., the events e and e' are causally unrelated. The partial order $\prec$ captures a special causal "happens-before" relation among the events in different threads, which we call *weak-happens-before*. This causality relation is called "weak" since it is less constrained than the apparently more natural "happens-before" relation defined and investigated in [17, 18], which assumed that $e \prec_x e'$ also when e was a read of x and e' was a write of x or when both e and e' were writes of x; we call the causality in [18] apparently more natural since it captures exactly the common intuition that any two unrelated read accesses to a variable can be permuted.

While the causality in [18] allowed JMPAX to have strong predictive capabilities, the weak-happens-before causality considered in this paper significantly increases the coverage of runtime analysis of multithreaded systems and implicitly the predictive strength of tools implementing it, by allowing more possible runs to be inferred from just one observed execution of the system. All these predicted runs can occur under different thread scheduling or interleavings, meaning that *the increase in coverage comes at no expense*, that is, our technique is still free of false alarms. The fact that there are more possible execution traces to analyze must be clearly regarded as an advantage in the context of predictive runtime analysis; if, in the context of a highly unsynchronized multithreaded program, one finds the number of possible runs too large to analyze effectively, then one has the option to discard online as many of those "uninteresting" runs as needed. JMPAX already provides this functionality by allowing its users to tune an analysis breadth "knob", ranging from only one possible execution (the observed one), like in testing, to all possible executions, like in model-checking.

Unlike in [18], the weak-happens-before relation above is *not sufficient* to completely describe the multithreaded computation; if e and e' are two events such that $e \prec_x e'$ and e'' is another event writing x such that $e''||e$ and $e''||e'$, one *cannot* interleave e'' between e and e'. This is because if e'' happens in between e and e', then by the definition of $\prec_x$, it is the case that $e'' \prec_x e'$, which contradicts $e''||e'$. This observation suggests that given a write event, say e, of x, the set $\{e\} \cup \{e' \mid e' \in E \wedge e \prec_x e'\}$ should be regarded as *atomic* with respect to any other event outside the set that reads or writes x. Such a set is called an *atomic set* for the variable x. Therefore, each atomic set of $x \in S$ contains exactly one write and the corresponding reads. Any set which is a proper subset of an atomic set is called an *incomplete* atomic set. The atomic sets define another relation, called *atomicity relation* over the set of events E. We say that two events e and e' are *x-atomically related*, denoted by $e \updownarrow_x e'$, if and only if e and e' belong to the same "atomic set" for the variable x. Formally, $e \updownarrow_x e'$ if an only if there exists an event e'' such that both e and e' belong to the set $\{e''\} \cup \{e''' \mid e''' \prec_x e''\}$. Therefore, $\updownarrow_x$ is an equivalence relation on E. Let $[e]_x$ denote the corresponding *atomic equivalence class* of an event $e \in E$.

The structure described by $\mathcal{C} = (E, \prec, \updownarrow)$ is called a *multithreaded computation*. A possible linearization of the events in E is *consistent* with $\prec$ if for any two events e and e' in E, $e \prec e'$ implies that e appears before e' in the linearization. Similarly, a linearization of the events in E is consistent with $\updownarrow$ if for any two events e and e' and an arbitrary shared variable x, $e \updownarrow_x e'$ implies that any other access (read or write) event e'' of x, such that $e'' \not\updownarrow_x e$, appears either before or after both e and e' in the linearization. Combining the two conditions, we say that a linearization of the events E is consistent with a multithreaded computation $\mathcal{C} = (E, \prec, \updownarrow)$ if and only if it is consistent with both $\prec$ and $\updownarrow$. Any such linearization of events consistent with the multithreaded computation is called a *consistent multithreaded run*, or simply, a *multithreaded run*.

A multithreaded computation can be thought of as the *most general assumption* that an observer of the multithreaded execution can make about the system without knowing what it is supposed to do. Indeed, an external observer simply *cannot disregard* the order in which the same variable is modified and used within the observed execution, because this order can be part of the semantics of the multithreaded program. However, multiple consecutive writes of the same variable can be permuted provided that the set of a write and all reads following the write occur atomically. As seen in Section 6, by allowing an observer to analyze *multithreaded computations* rather than just *multithreaded executions*, one gets the benefit of *predicting errors* from analyzing successful executions, errors which can occur under a different thread scheduling.

5   Capturing Multithreaded Computations

To capture and transmit to an external observer the weak-happens-before and atomicity relations in a multithreaded computation, we use data-structures such as *vector clocks* and *atomicity identifiers*, respectively, as explained below. The algorithm based on vector clocks, which correctly and efficiently implements the weak-happens-before relation, is motivated by related work [1, 3, 8, 14]. However, the vector clock algorithm described in this paper differs from the algorithms described in previous works, because our focus here is to implement a different, less usual but more powerful w.r.t. monitoring "happens-before" relation. Let a vector clock $V : ThreadId \rightarrow Nat$ be a *partial* map from thread identifiers to natural numbers. We call such a map a *dynamic vector clock (DVC)* because its partiality reflects the intuition that threads are dynamically created and destroyed. To simplify the presentation, we assume that each DVC V is a total map, where $V[t] = 0$ when V is not defined on thread t.

We associate a DVC with every thread t_i and denote it by V_i. Moreover, we associate a DVC V_x with every shared variable x. All the DVCs V_i are kept empty at the beginning of the computation, so they do not consume any space. For DVCs V and V', we say that $V \leq V'$ if and only if $V[j] \leq V'[j]$ for all j, and we say that $V < V'$ iff $V \leq V'$ and there is some j such that $V[j] < V'[j]$; also, $\max\{V, V'\}$ is the DVC with $\max\{V, V'\}[j] = \max\{V[j], V'[j]\}$ for each j.

Further, we associate a counter, called *atomicity identifier*, with every shared variable. Let c_x denote the counter associated with a shared variable x. These counters are initialized to 0. An atomicity counter associated with a variable keeps track of its atomic sets. A set of events corresponding to a read or write of x belong to an atomic set if and only if the atomicity identifiers associated with the variable x at those events are the same.

At every event in the multithreaded computation the DVCs and the atomicity identifiers are updated according to the following algorithm, which acts as a program instrumentation technique to emit events to an external observer of the system. If a thread t_i with current DVC V_i processes event e_i^k then

1. $V_i[i] \leftarrow V_i[i] + 1$;
2. if e_i^k is a write of a shared variable x then
   $V_x \leftarrow V_i$
   $c_x \leftarrow c_x + 1$;
3. if e_i^k is a read of a shared variable x then
   $V_i \leftarrow \max\{V_i, V_x\}$;
4. if e_i^k is a read or write of a shared variable x
   then send message $\langle e_i^k, i, V_i, x, c_x \rangle$ to observer
   else send message $\langle e_i^k, i, V_i, \perp, -1 \rangle$ to observer.

Intuitively, at every write event of a shared variable x, the DVC of x is updated with the DVC of the thread writing x. Thus, the thread passes its current time-stamp to the variable. This ensures that every event of the thread t_i till e_i^k happens before any event that reads the value written to x. The atomicity identifier is incremented by 1 to indicate that a new atomic set is starting; all the following read events, before another write of the same variable, will share the same atomicity identifier. At a read event of a variable x, the DVC of the reading thread is updated with the maximum of the DVC of the thread and the DVC of the variable x. This ensures that the read event happens after any previous event of the thread and the last write event of the variable x.

Theorem 1. *After event e_i^k is processed by thread t_i,*

a) *$V_i[j]$ equals the number of events of t_j that "weak-happens-before" e_i^k; if $j = i$ then this number is k;*

b) *$V_x[j]$ is the number of events of t_j that "weak-happens-before" the most recent write of x; if $i = j$ and e_i^k is a write of x then this number also includes e_i^k.*

Therefore, if $\langle e, i, V, x, c \rangle$ and $\langle e', j, V', x', c' \rangle$ are different messages sent by the algorithm, then $e \prec e'$ if and only if $V[i] \leq V'[i]$; if i and j are not given, then $e \prec e'$ if and only if $V < V'$. Moreover, $e \Updownarrow_x e'$ if and only if $x = x' \neq \perp$ and $c_x = c'_{x'}$.

Therefore, the code instrumentation algorithm above correctly implements the weak-happens-before and the atomicity relations.

6   Runtime Model Generation and Predictive Analysis

We now consider what happens at the observer's site, which receives messages $\langle e, i, V, x, c \rangle$ from the running multithreaded program, and which, because of Theorem 1, can infer the weak-happens-before and atomicity relations on these events. The observer can effectively, *online* and *in parallel*, analyze all possible interleavings of events that are consistent with the weak-happens-before and atomicity relations. Only one of these corresponds to the real execution. Since the other interleavings correspond to other possible executions, the presented technique has the capability to *predict* violations from successful executions.

6.1   Multithreaded Computation Lattice

Inspired by [1], we show how to incrementally generate an abstract model from a multithreaded computation, the *computation lattice*, with the properties: (1) every path in the computation lattice corresponds to a consistent multithreaded run; (2) every node in the computation lattice represents a set of events that can be observed as a prefix of a consistent multithreaded run. Our purpose in this paper is to check safety requirements against *all consistent* multithreaded runs of a system by systematically and efficiently exploring the computation lattice.

Let us fix an arbitrary multithreaded computation $C = (E, \prec, \updownarrow)$. Let e_i^k be the kth event generated by the thread t_i since the start of its execution. A *cut* Σ is a subset of E such that for all $i \in [1, n]$, if $e_i^k \in \Sigma$ then $e_i^l \in \Sigma$ for all $l < k$. Let $\Sigma^{k_1 k_2 \cdots k_n}$ denote the cut containing the latest events $e_1^{k_1}, e_2^{k_2}, \ldots, e_n^{k_n}$ from each of the threads. If a thread i has not seen any event then k_i is considered 0.

Definition 2 (Consistent Cut). *A cut Σ is **consistent** if for all $e, e' \in E$,*

(a) if $e \in \Sigma$ and $e' \prec e$ then $e' \in \Sigma$, and
(b) if $e, e' \in \Sigma$ and $e \, \updownarrow_x \, e'$ for some $x \in S$, then $[e]_x \subseteq \Sigma$ or $[e']_x \subseteq \Sigma$.

(a) says that a consistent cut is closed under the weak-happens-before relation, and *(b)* says that a consistent cut can contain at most one incomplete atomic set for any shared variable. Indeed, if *(b)* fails, then there is no way to reorder the remaining events in $E - \Sigma$ without violating the atomicity relation.

Definition 3. *An event e_i^l is **enabled** for a consistent cut $\Sigma = \Sigma^{k_1 k_2 \cdots k_n}$ iff*

(a) $l = k_i + 1$,
(b) for all events $e \in E$, if $e \prec e_i^l$ then $e \in \Sigma$, and
(c) if e_i^l is an access (read or write) event of an $x \in S$ and e is any access event of x in Σ then either $e_i^l \in [e]_x$ or $[e]_x \subseteq \Sigma$.

Since e_i^l can be in at most one atomic set for a given shared variable, the above actually says that e_i^l can be safely considered a next event in the execution. Indeed, the following can be regarded as an equivalent definition of enabledness:

Proposition 1. *e_i^l is enabled for a consistent Σ iff $\Sigma \cup \{e_i^l\}$ is also consistent.*

Proof. Since Σ is a cut, all the events $e_i^1, e_i^2, \ldots, e_i^{k_i}$ are in Σ. Therefore, $\Sigma \cup \{e_i^l\}$ contains all events e_i^m, for $m < l$, if $l = k_i + 1$. This implies that $\Sigma \cup \{e_i^l\}$ is a cut. Since Σ is a consistent cut, for all events $e \in \Sigma$, if $e' \prec e$ then $e' \in \Sigma$. It is given that for all events $e' \prec e_i^l$, $e' \in \Sigma$. Therefore, for all events $e \in \Sigma \cup \{e_i^l\}$, if $e' \prec e$ then $e' \in \Sigma$. This is the first condition for $\Sigma \cup \{e_i^l\}$ being a consistent cut. Let e be any access event of x in Σ. Given that Σ is a consistent cut, if $e_i^l \in [e]_x$ then the second condition for the definition of consistent cut continues to hold for $\Sigma \cup \{e_i^l\}$ because the addition of e_i^l to Σ cannot create a new atomic set for x. Otherwise, if $e_i^l \notin [e]_x$ then we know that $[e]_x \subseteq \Sigma$. This implies that $[e]_x \subseteq \Sigma \cup \{e_i^l\}$ or $[e_i^l]_x \subseteq \Sigma \cup \{e_i^l\}$. Hence, the second condition for the definition of consistent cut holds for $\Sigma \cup \{e_i^l\}$. Since both the first and second conditions for the definition of consistent cut holds for the cut $\Sigma \cup \{e_i^l\}$, $\Sigma \cup \{e_i^l\}$ is a consistent cut. $\qquad\square$

Definition 4. *If* $\Sigma = \Sigma^{k_1 k_2 \cdots k_n}$ *is consistent and* e_i^l *is enabled for* Σ, *then let* $\delta(\Sigma, e_i^l)$ *denote the consistent cut* $\Sigma \cup \{e_i^l\}$, *that is,* $\Sigma^{k_1 k_2 \cdots k_{i-1}(k_i+1)k_{i+1}\cdots k_n}$.

Therefore, δ maps a consistent cut Σ and a corresponding enabled event e into another consistent cut, which can be regarded as the result of executing e after executing all the events in Σ in some consistent way. Let $\Sigma^{K_0} = \Sigma^{00\cdots0}$ be the consistent cut at the beginning of the computation. Then

Proposition 2. *A consistent multithreaded run* $R = e_1 e_2 \ldots e_{|E|}$ *generates a sequence of consistent cuts* $\Sigma^{K_0} \Sigma^{K_1} \ldots \Sigma^{K_{|E|}}$ *such that for all* $r \in \overline{1,|E|}$, $\Sigma^{K_{r-1}}$ *is a consistent cut,* e_r *is enabled for* $\Sigma^{K_{r-1}}$, *and* $\delta(\Sigma^{K_{r-1}}, e_r) = \Sigma^{K_r}$.

Proof. The proof is by induction on r. By definition Σ^{K_0} is a consistent cut. Moreover, it is easy to see that e_1 is enabled in Σ^{K_0}. Since Σ^{K_0} is a consistent cut and e_1 is enabled in Σ^{K_0}, $\delta(\Sigma^{K_0}, e_1)$ is defined. Let $\Sigma^{K_1} = \delta(\Sigma^{K_0}, e_1)$.

Let us assume that $\Sigma^{K_{r-1}}$ is a consistent cut, e_r is enabled in $\Sigma^{K_{r-1}}$, and $\delta(\Sigma^{K_{r-1}}, e_r) = \Sigma^{K_r}$. Therefore, by Proposition 1, $\delta(\Sigma^{K_{r-1}}, e_r) = \Sigma^{K_r}$ is also a consistent cut. Let $\Sigma^{K_r} = \Sigma^{k_1 k_2 \cdots k_n}$ and $C = \Sigma^{K_r}$. We want to prove that e_{r+1} is enabled in Σ^{K_r}. Let $e_{r+1} = e_i^l$ for some i and l i.e. e_{r+1} is the lth event of thread t_i. For every event e_i^k, such that $k < l$, $e_i^k \prec e_i^l$. Therefore, by the definition of consistent run, in R, e_i^k appears before e_i^l for all $0 < k < l$. This implies that all e_i^k for $0 < k < l$ are included in C. Therefore, $k_i = l - 1$. Thus the first condition for e_{r+1} being enabled for Σ^{K_r} is met. Since C is a consistent cut, for all events e and e', if $e \neq e_i^l$ then $(e \in C \cup \{e_i^l\}) \wedge (e' \prec e) \rightarrow e' \in C \cup \{e_i^l\}$. Otherwise, if $e = e_i^l$ then by the definition of consistent run, if $e' \prec e_i^l$ then e' appears before e_i^l in R. This implies that e' is included in $C \cup \{e_i^l\}$. Therefore, for all events e and e', if $e \in C \cup \{e_i^l\}$ and $e' \prec e$ then $e' \in C \cup \{e_i^l\}$. Thus the second condition for e_{r+1} being enabled for Σ^{K_r} is met. Let e_{r+1} be access event of a shared variable x. Let e be an event in the incomplete atomic set (if exists) for x in C. If $e \Updownarrow_x e_{r+1}$, the third condition for the enabledness of an event is not violated. If $e \not\Updownarrow_x e_{r+1}$ and $\exists e' \in E - (C \cup \{e_i^l\})$ such that $e \Updownarrow_x e'$ then any run that extends $e_1 e_2 \ldots e_{r+1}$ will be inconsistent with respect to the "atomicity" relation. Therefore, if $e \not\Updownarrow_x e_{r+1}$ then $[e]_x \subseteq C \cup \{e_{r+1}\}$. Thus the third condition for e_{r+1} being enabled for Σ^{K_r} is met. Therefore, we proved that e_{r+1} is enabled for the consistent cut Σ^{K_r}. Since, Σ^{K_r} is a consistent cut and e_{r+1} is enabled in Σ^{K_r}, $\delta(\Sigma^{K_r}, e_{r+1})$ is defined. We let $\delta(\Sigma^{K_r}, e_{r+1}) = \Sigma^{K_{r+1}}$.
□

From now on, we identify sequences $\Sigma^{K_0} \Sigma^{K_1} \ldots \Sigma^{K_{|E|}}$ as above with multithreaded runs, and simply call them *runs*. We say that Σ *leads-to* Σ', written $\Sigma \rightsquigarrow \Sigma'$, when there is some run in which Σ and Σ' are consecutive consistent cuts. Let $\rightsquigarrow^*$ be the reflexive transitive closure of the relation $\rightsquigarrow$. The set of all consistent cuts together with the relation $\rightsquigarrow^*$ forms a *lattice* with n mutually orthogonal axes representing each thread. For a consistent cut $\Sigma^{k_1 k_2 \cdots k_n}$, we call $k_1 + k_1 + \cdots k_n$ its *level*. A *path* in the lattice is a sequence of consistent cuts where the level increases by 1 between any two consecutive consistent cuts in the path. Therefore, a run is just a path starting with $\Sigma^{00\cdots0}$ and ending with $\Sigma^{r_1 r_2 \cdots r_n}$, where r_i is the total number of events of thread t_i in the multithreaded computation. This lattice, called *computation lattice*, can be regarded as an *abstract model* of the running multithreaded program.

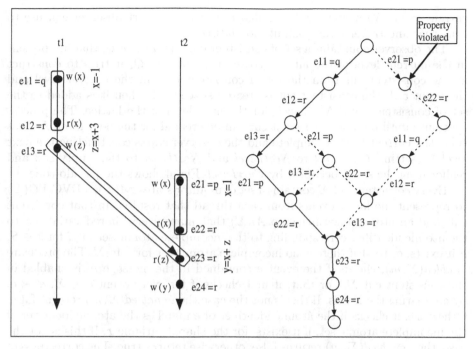

Fig. 3. Successful Execution and Computation Lattice.

Figure 3 shows the weak-happens-before and atomicity relations on the events generated by the multithreaded execution in Example 1, together with the corresponding computation lattice. The rectangular boxes enclose the atomic sets $\{e_1^1, e_1^2\}$, $\{e_1^3, e_2^3\}$, and $\{e_2^1, e_2^2\}$. The actual execution is marked with solid edges in the lattice. It can be readily seen that the temporal property defined in Example 1 holds on the actual execution of the program, but that it is violated on some other consistent run represented by the sequence of events $e_2^1, e_2^2, e_1^1, e_1^2, e_1^3, e_2^3, e_2^4$.

6.2   Level by Level Analysis of the Computation Lattice

A naive observer of a multithreaded program would just check the observed execution trace against the monitor for the safety property, say $\mathcal{M}on$, and would maintain at each moment a set of states, say *MonStates*, in $\mathcal{M}on$. When a new event e arrives, it would replace *MonStates* by $\rho(MonStates, e)$. If the bad state b occurs in *MonStates* then a property violation error would be reported, meaning that the current execution trace led to a bad prefix of the safety property. Here we assume that the events are received in the order in which they are emitted.

A smart observer, as seen next, analyzes not only the observed execution trace, but also all the other consistent runs of the multithreaded system, thus being able to *predict* violations from successful executions. The observer receives the events from the running program and enqueues them in an event queue Q. At the same time, it traverses the computation lattice level-by-level and checks whether the bad state of the monitor can be hit by any of the runs up to the current level. We next provide an algorithm that a smart observer can use to construct and traverse the computation lattice.

The observer maintains a set of consistent cuts, ($CurrLevel$), that are present in the current level of the lattice. For each event e in Q, it tries to construct a new consistent cut from the set of consistent cuts in the current level and the event e. If the consistent cut is created successfully then it is added to the set of consistent cuts ($NextLevel$) for the next level of the lattice. The process continues until no more consistent cut can be created for the next level. At that time, the current level is complete and the observer starts constructing the next level by setting $CurrLevel$ to $NextLevel$ and $NextLevel$ to the empty set, and reallocating the space occupied by $CurrLevel$. Fig. 4 shows the pseudo-code.

Every consistent cut Σ contains a set of monitor states $\mathcal{M}(\Sigma)$, a DVC $VC(\Sigma)$ to represent the latest events from each thread that resulted in that consistent cut, and an atomic identifier map $AI(\Sigma)$ that maps every shared variable x to the atomic identifier corresponding to the incomplete atomic set in Σ for $x \in S$, if it exists, or to -1 if there is no incomplete atomic set for x in Σ. The predicate $enabled(\Sigma, m)$, checks if the event e contained in the message m is enabled in the consistent cut Σ. For that, it first checks if for every event $e' \in \Sigma$, $e' \prec e$, by comparing the DVCs. If this is not the case then $enabled(\Sigma, m)$ returns false. Otherwise, it checks if the atomic identifier of e matches the atomic identifier of the incomplete atomic set, if it exists, for the shared variable x. If this is not the case, then $enabled(\Sigma, m)$ returns false; otherwise returns true. The correctness of the function follows from Theorem 1 and the definition of enabledness of an event

```
while(not empty(Q)){
  monitorLevel()
}


State cut(Σ,m,Q){
  create Σ' such that
    VC(Σ') = VC(Σ)
    and AI(Σ') = AI(Σ)
  let m is of the form ⟨e,i,V,x,c⟩
  VC(Σ')[i] ← VC(Σ)[i] + 1
  if c ≥ 0 and
    ∃⟨e',i',V',x,c'⟩ ∈ Q such that
    V' ≰ max(VC(Σ),V) and c = c'{
      AI(Σ')[x] ← c
  }
  for each s ∈ M(Σ){
    M(Σ') ← M(Σ') ∪ ρ(s,e)
    if b ∈ M(Σ')
      output 'property violated'}
  return Σ'
}


boolean monitorLevel(){
  for each m ∈ Q and Σ ∈ CurrLevel{
    if enabled(Σ,m) {
      NextLevel ← NextLevel ⊎ cut(Σ,m,Q)}}}
  Q ← removeUselessMessages(CurrLevel,Q)
  CurrLevel ← NextLevel
  NextLevel ← ∅
}


boolean enabled(Σ,m){
  let m is of the form ⟨e,i,V,x,c⟩
  if not(∀j ≠ i : VC(Σ)[j] ≥ V[j] and
    VC(Σ)[i] + 1 = V[i]) return false
  if c ≥ 0 and AI(Σ)[x] ≥ 0 and AI(Σ)[x] ≠ c{
    return false
  }
  return true
}
```

Fig. 4. Level-by-level traversal.

for a consistent cut. It essentially says that event e can generate a consecutive consistent cut from the consistent cut Σ iff Σ "knows" everything e knows about the current evolution of the multithreaded system except for the event e itself. Note that e may know less than Σ knows with respect to the evolution of other threads in the system, because Σ has global information.

The function $cut(\Sigma, m, Q)$, which implements the function δ in Definition 4, creates a new consistent cut Σ', as the consistent cut resulting from Σ after adding the event e of message m. It first copies the DVC and the atomic identifier map associated with Σ to Σ'. Then it increments the ith element of the DVC of Σ' and updates the atomic identifier map of Σ' for variable x with the atomic identifier of e if Σ' still contains an incomplete atomic set for x. For every monitor state s in $\mathcal{M}(\Sigma)$, it applies the monitoring function ρ to s and e and adds the resulting states in the set $\mathcal{M}(\Sigma')$. After the update, if $\mathcal{M}(\Sigma')$ contains the bad state b then a 'property violated' error is raised.

The merging operation $nextLevel \uplus \Sigma$ adds the consistent cut Σ to the set $nextLevel$. If Σ is already present in $nextLevel$, it updates the existing cut's $MonStates$ with the union of the existing state's $MonStates$ and the $Monstates$ of Σ. Two consistent cuts are the same if their DVCs are equal. The function $removeUselessMessages(CurrLevel, Q)$ removes from Q all the messages that cannot contribute to the construction of any cut at the next level. To do so, it creates a DVC V_{min} for which each component is the minimum of the corresponding component of the DVCs of all the consistent cuts in the set $CurrLevel$. It then removes all the messages in Q whose DVCs are less than or equal to V_{min}. This function makes sure that we do not store any unnecessary messages.

6.3   Handling Synchronization Constructs

In Java, one can synchronize blocks of statements by using the keyword synchronize with an object over which the block is synchronized. When the execution enters the synchronized block, it acquires the lock associated with the object and releases the lock when it exits the block. The main goal of synchronization is to attain atomicity: if two synchronized blocks over the same lock are executed by two different threads, then their execution cannot be interleaved. This atomicity can be naturally achieved in our approach by generating dummy write and read events of the lock variable when the lock is acquired or released, respectively. In particular, since in Java synchronized blocks holding the same lock cannot be interleaved, so corresponding events cannot be permuted, locks are considered shared variables and a write event of a lock is generated whenever a lock is acquired, and a read event of the lock is generated whenever a lock is released. This way, we make a block holding a lock atomic with respect to any other block holding the same lock, thus avoiding reporting any false alarms.

7   Application to Data-Race Detection

Since the predictive runtime analysis approach discussed in the previous sections is parameterized by a very generic concept of monitor as a nondeterministic finite state machine of bad prefixes, it can be applied to predict violations of requirements specifications given in a variety of formalisms. Temporal logics and regular expressions are just special cases. In particular, our technique can be used as a complementary approach to model-checking, when the total number of states to be model-checked is prohibitively large.

We next discuss another interesting application of our runtime analysis technique, namely in predicting data-races from data-race-free executions. The idea is to specify some simple temporal logic formulae, which, if violated, imply the existence of data-races in a multithreaded computation. A data-race occurs when two threads access a shared variable simultaneously without any synchronization and at least one of the accesses is a write. Data-races can lead to very unexpected behaviors of concurrent systems, and are notorious for their difficulty to detect. Plain testing can easily escape data-races, due to their dependency on thread-scheduling. For example, suppose that two threads increment a shared variable x simultaneously by executing statements $x++$ without any synchronization. If the initial value of x is 0 then at the end of the execution the value of x can be 1 or 2. The former is obviously wrong, but hard to catch during testing.

It has been broadly recognized that tools capable of detecting data-races automatically in programs at runtime can be very valuable. There has been a substantial effort dedicated to developing tools and techniques that detect data-races online, such as those based on "happens-before" relations over locks [5], or those based on *locksets*, such as Eraser [15]. We next show how one can use our predictive runtime analysis technique to *precisely* detect data-races in a way somewhat similar to [5]. An advantage of our technique over the former approaches based on "happens-before" causality, such as the one in [5], is that we can *permute two synchronized blocks* holding the same lock due to our less constrained weak-happens-before relation. For example, if one sees the execution trace t1: z=1; t1: lock(l); t1: x=0; t1: unlock(l); t2: lock(l); t2: y=10; t2: unlock(l); t2: z=0;, then the "happens-before" data-race detection algorithm in [5] cannot detect the potential data-race over the variable z. However, it is easy to see that our approach can construct the consistent run t2: lock(l); t2: y=10; t2: unlock(l); t2: z=0; t1: z=1; t1: lock(l); t1: x=0; t1: unlock(l); that exhibits the data-race over z. Moreover, since we do the analysis at runtime, we can take a necessary recovery action whenever we find a data-race.

We conservatively say that two accesses of a shared variable x, of which at least one is a write, by two threads are *in data-race conflict*, if one can permute events consistently with the multithreaded computation such that the two accesses become consecutive events. Using our predictive monitoring approach, one can detect such data-race conflicts by monitoring the following simple property for every shared variable x and for every pair of threads t_i and t_j:

$$(\text{write}(x, t_i) \rightarrow \neg \odot \text{write}(x, t_j)) \wedge (\text{write}(x, t_i) \rightarrow \neg \odot \text{read}(x, t_j))$$
$$\wedge (\text{read}(x, t_i) \rightarrow \neg \odot \text{write}(x, t_j))$$

where the temporal operator $\odot F$ means "F holds at the previous event", the events $\text{read}(x, t)$ (or $\text{write}(x, t)$) are generated whenever the thread t reads (or writes) x. The first conjunct in the formula states the absence of write-write data-races. A write-write data-race happens if there is a consistent run in which two different threads write a variable x consecutively. Similarly, the second and the third conjunct state the absence of write-read and read-write data-races. Using our approach, by monitoring the above formulae, one can detect data-races in multithreaded programs precisely, that is, without false positives.

8   Implementation

We have implemented this novel predictive runtime analysis technique as part of version 3.0 of the tool Java MultiPathExplorer (JMPaX) [12], designed to monitor multithreaded Java programs. The current implementation is written in Java and it removes the previous limitation of version 2.0 that all the shared variables are static and of type int. The tool has three main modules, the *instrumentation* module, the *observer* module and the *monitor* module.

The instrumentation module takes a specification file and a list of class files as command line arguments, and it instruments each class file provided as argument to send messages to the observer module whenever a relevant read, write, or internal event occurs at runtime. The instrumentation module uses the BCEL Java library [4] to modify Java class files.

The *observer* module generates the lattice level-by-level as the events are received from the instrumented program. The *monitor* module reads the requirements specification file, currently using either linear temporal logic or regular expression formalism, and generates the non-deterministic monitor corresponding to the bad prefixes of the specification. An implementation of the monitor transition function ρ is provided as an interface method to the *observer* module. This method raises an exception if at any point the set of states returned by ρ contains the "bad" state of the monitor. The system being modular, the user can plug in his/her own *monitor* module for his/her logic of choice.

9   Conclusion

We have developed a simple and efficient technique to predict violations of safety properties of concurrent object-oriented programs. Our algorithm requires maintaining an atomic identifier map for every consistent cut. The size of this map is linearly proportional to the number of shared variables. This can lead to consumption of a large amount of memory space if the number of shared variables is large and slow down the monitoring process. As an aside, this reinforces the view that avoiding unnecessary sharing of variables is good software practice; in this case, fewer variables will improve the efficiency of monitoring (as well as reduce the chances of errors). While our technique will not find all errors, it can be applied to detect important software errors such as unintended data-race conditions which may otherwise be missed. The technique is, however, sound: it does not produce any false positives (any errors predicted could actually occur in a different execution).

References

1. O. Babaoğlu and K. Marzullo. Consistent global states of distributed systems: Fundamental concepts and mechanisms. In S. Mullender, editor, *Distributed Systems*, pages 55–96. 1993.
2. H. Barringer, A. Goldberg, K. Havelund, and K. Sen. Rule-based runtime verification. In *Proc. of 5th International Conference on Verification, Model Checking and Abstract Interpretation (VMCAI'04)*, volume 2937 of *LNCS*, pages 44–57, 2004.
3. H. W. Cain and M. H. Lipasti. Verifying sequential consistency using vector clocks. In *Proceedings of the 14th annual ACM Symposium on Parallel Algorithms and Architectures*, pages 153–154. ACM, 2002.
4. M. Dahm. Byte code engineering with the BCEL API. Technical Report B-17-98, Freie Universitat at Berlin, Institut für Informatik, April 2001.
5. A. Dinning and E. Schonberg. Detecting access anomalies in programs with critical sections. In *Proc. of the ACM/ONR Workshop on Parallel and Distributed Debugging*, 1991.
6. D. Drusinsky. Temporal Rover. http://www.time-rover.com.
7. D. Drusinsky. The Temporal Rover and the ATG Rover. In *SPIN Model Checking and Software Verification*, volume 1885 of *LNCS*, pages 323–330, 2000.
8. C. J. Fidge. Partial orders for parallel debugging. In *Proceedings of the 1988 ACM SIGPLAN and SIGOPS workshop on Parallel and Distributed debugging*, pages 183–194. ACM, 1988.
9. E. L. Gunter, R. P. Kurshan, and D. Peled. PET: An interactive software testing tool. In *Proc. of Computer Aided Verification (CAV'00)*, volume 1885 of *LNCS*, pages 552–556, 2000.
10. K. Havelund and G. Roşu. Monitoring Java Programs with Java PathExplorer. In *Proc. of Workshop on Runtime Verification (RV'01)*, volume 55 of *ENTCS*, 2001.
11. K. Havelund and G. Roşu. Synthesizing monitors for safety properties. In *Tools and Algorithms for Construction and Analysis of Systems (TACAS'02)*, volume 2280 of *LNCS*, pages 342–356, 2002.
12. Java MultiPathExplorer (JMPaX). Download: http://fsl.cs.uiuc.edu/jmpax/.
13. M. Kim, S. Kannan, I. Lee, and O. Sokolsky. Java-MaC: a Run-time Assurance Tool for Java. In *Proceedings of the 1st Workshop on Runtime Verification (RV'01)*, volume 55 of *ENTCS*, 2001.
14. F. Mattern. Virtual time and global states of distributed systems. In *Parallel and Distributed Algorithms: proceedings of the International Workshop on Parallel and Distributed Algorithms*, pages 215–226. Elsevier, 1989.
15. S. Savage, M. Burrows, G. Nelson, P. Sobalvarro, and T. Anderson. Eraser: A dynamic data race detector for multithreaded programs. *ACM Transactions on Computer Systems*, 15(4):391–411, 1997.
16. K. Sen and G. Roşu. Generating optimal monitors for extended regular expressions. In *Proc. of the 3rd Workshop on Runtime Verification (RV'03)*, volume 89 of *ENTCS*, pages 162–181, 2003.
17. K. Sen, G. Roşu, and G. Agha. Runtime safety analysis of multithreaded programs. In *Proceedings of 4th joint European Software Engineering Conference and ACM SIGSOFT Symposium on the Foundations of Software Engineering (ESEC/FSE'03)*. ACM, 2003.
18. K. Sen, G. Roşu, and G. Agha. Online efficient predictive safety analysis of multithreaded programs. In *Proc. of 10th International Conference on Tools and Algorithms for the Construction and Analysis of Systems (TACAS'04)*, volume 2988 of *LNCS*, pages 123–138, 2004.

Transforming Information in RDF
to Rewriting Logic*

Alberto Verdejo[1], Narciso Martí-Oliet[1], Tomás Robles[2], Joaquín Salvachúa[2],
Luis Llana[1], and Margarita Bradley[1]

[1] Universidad Complutense de Madrid
{alberto,narciso,llana,bradley}@sip.ucm.es
[2] Technical University of Madrid
{robles,jsr}@dit.upm.es

Abstract. RDF looks like the first step to build the Semantic Web vision. Our long-term goal is to have a sound way to verify and validate the semantic web interactions that applications and agents may develop in a distributed environment. The first step for reaching this goal is to provide a useful semantic support to RDF itself. Based on this formal support, properties may be analyzed, as well as transformations and verifications can be performed. In this paper we propose an *intuitive* and *formal* semantics for RDF by means of a translation of RDF documents into *executable* object-oriented modules in the formal language Maude. This translation provides a semantics for RDF documents and allows programs managing them to be expressed in the same formalism, since Maude specifications are executable. Moreover, due to the reflective features of Maude, this translation can be implemented in Maude itself. Finally, translated RDF documents are integrated in an agent application written in Mobile Maude, that is, the same framework is used for both translating RDF documents and expressing the programs that manipulate them.

Keywords: RDF, Semantic Web, formal methods, rewriting logic, Maude.

1 Introduction

The current human-centered web is still largely encoded in HTML. Over the past few years, XML has been proposed as an alternative encoding which is intended also for efficient machine processing. It has become the standard for the exchange of information on the Internet. However, it is not a final solution because it only gives support for syntactic representation of information, but not for its meaning. RDF (Resource Description Framework) [12] and RDFS (RDF Schema) [5] represent an attempt to resolve these deficiencies by building on top of XML, although they are still a bit limited for knowledge representation.

* Research supported by MCyT projects *AMEVA: Desarrollo Formal de Sistemas Basados en Agentes Móviles* (TIC2000–0701–C02–01) and *MIDAS: Metalenguajes para el diseño y análisis integrado de sistemas móviles y distribuidos* (TIC2003–01000).

M. Steffen and G. Zavattaro (Eds.): FMOODS 2005, LNCS 3535, pp. 227–242, 2005.

Tim Berners-Lee conceives the Semantic Web as a layered architecture [3]. At the lowest level RDF provides a simple data model and a standardized syntax for *metadata* (data about data) about web resources by providing the language for writing down factual statements. The next layer is the *schema* layer where the definition of concrete vocabularies is given by means of the RDF Schema language. The final layer is the *logical* layer given by a formal knowledge representation language. It is important that each layer is an extension of RDF.

Our long-term goal is to have a sound way to verify and validate the Semantic Web *interactions* that service agents may develop in a distributed environment, for example as part of web services management. This will enable the possibility of reasoning about the information that is being exchanged allowing all the involved partners to have a common understanding. One first step for reaching this goal is to provide a *formal*, *intuitive*, and *executable* semantics to RDF and RDFS. The "official" model-theoretic semantics for RDF and RDFS is presented in [11] (more on this at the end of next section).

We propose in this paper an alternative semantic support to RDF by means of Maude, which is a formal language based on a first-order rewriting logic [7, 16] with well-defined syntax, formal models, and corresponding soundness and completeness theorems. Maude provides an executable language integrated in a global framework including functional elements and concurrency facilities. Using these facilities mobile agents and other advanced elements may be managed as natural elements into the logic of Maude. Maude includes in the same declarative framework both *logic* and *control*, which is a key difference with respect to other logic-based languages. We use the language Maude for:

- giving semantics to RDF documents by translating them into executable object-oriented Maude modules;
- implementing this translation; and
- implementing the applications that make use of the translated documents.

Under this formalized approach, RDF documents can be easily translated into Maude modules and therefore they may be data for Maude applications, as we show in Sections 4 and 5. Translating RDF documents into Maude allows their integration with web agents also defined in Maude. Hence, the development of web agents and their behavior is fully integrated and formally defined in a simple framework, as we will see in Section 5. One of the key features of our approach is that it is object-oriented, so the full power of object-orientation is supported, including inheritance.

In Section 2 RDF and RDFS are briefly introduced. In Section 3 the language Maude is presented by showing its syntax and key features. We pay special attention to object-oriented Maude modules. In Section 4 we describe the proposed translation that provides a semantics for RDF and RDFS documents, and how this translation is implemented by using Maude itself. A case study is presented in Section 5, where the translation is used by agents in a mobile system. We conclude with some comments on future work in Section 6.

2   RDF and RDFS: Syntax and Semantics

The Resource Description Framework (RDF) [19] is a general-purpose language for representing information in the World Wide Web. It provides a common framework for expressing this information in such a way that it can be exchanged between applications without loss of meaning, by providing a simple way to state properties of *web resources*, that is, objects that are uniquely identifiable by a Uniform Resource Identifier (URI) [18].

RDF is based on the idea that the things we want to describe have properties which have values (which can be literals or other resources), and that resources can be described by making statements that specify those properties and values. A statement has three components: a specific resource (subject), a property (predicate), and the value of this property for that resource (object). A collection of these statements that refers to the same resource is called a *description*. A concrete machine-readable syntax using XML is defined in [12]. For example, the following RDF document describes a laser printer:

```
<rdf:RDF xmlns:rdf="http://www.w3.org/1999/02/22-rdf-syntax-ns#"
         xmlns:ps="http://printers.org/schema/">
  <ps:LaserPrinter about="http://HPprinters/HPLaserJet1100" >
    <ps:PrinterTechnology>Laser Jet</ps:PrinterTechnology>
    <ps:PrinterResolution>600 dpi</ps:PrinterResolution>
    <ps:Price>399</ps:Price>
  </ps:LaserPrinter>
</rdf:RDF>
```

In order to uniquely identify properties and their meaning, RDF uses the XML namespaces mechanism [4]. Meaning in RDF is expressed through reference to a *schema* (see below). For example, in the previous example the resource `LaserPrinter` and the property `Price` are imported from `http://printers.org/schema`. The statements in a `Description` refer to the resource determined from the `about` attribute (interpreted as a URI).

Two important RDF concepts are *containers*, used to hold collections of resources, and *reification*, used for making statements about other statements (for a more detailed explanation of these two concepts we refer to [12]).

RDF user communities require the ability to say certain things about certain kinds of resources. The declaration of these properties (attributes) and kinds of resources (classes) is done by means of an *RDF schema* (RDFS) [5]. This mechanism provides a basic *type system* for use in RDF models. Instead of defining a class in terms of the properties its instances may have, an RDF schema will define properties in terms of the classes of resources to which they apply.

The following RDFS document[1] describes a class of printers with a subclass of laser printers, and a printer property, namely, its price (the rest of properties could be defined in the same way):

---

[1] We use `&rdfsns;` as an abbreviation of `http://www.w3.org/2000/01/rdf-schema`.

```
<rdf:RDF xmlns:rdf="http://www.w3.org/1999/02/22-rdf-syntax-ns#"
         xmlns:rdfs="http://www.w3.org/2000/01/rdf-schema#">
  <rdfs:Class rdf:ID="Printer">
    <rdfs:subClassOf rdf:resource="&rdfsns;#Resource"/>
  </rdfs:Class>
  <rdfs:Class rdf:ID="LaserPrinter">
    <rdfs:subClassOf rdf:resource="#Printer"/>
  </rdfs:Class>
  <rdfs:Property rdf:ID="Price">
    <rdfs:domain rdf:resource="#Printer"/>
    <rdfs:range rdf:resource="&rdfsns;#Literal"/>
  </rdfs:Property>
  ...
</rdf:RDF>
```

The **domain** property is used to indicate the class on whose members a property can be used. The **range** property is used to indicate the class that the values of a property must be members of.

In [11] a model-theoretic semantics for RDF and RDFS is presented. The semantic definition translates an RDF graph into a logical expression "with the same meaning." Basically, a graph arc is mapped to an atomic assertion and the complete graph is mapped to the existential closure of the conjunction of the translations of all the arcs in the graph. Also a notion of entailment in RDF is studied. A similar approach is followed in [10] where an axiomatization for RDF is provided by specifiying a mapping of a set of descriptions into a logical theory expressed in first-order predicate calculus. This translation not only specifies the intended meaning of the descriptions, but also produces a representation of the descriptions from which inferences can automatically be made using traditional automatic theorem provers and problem solvers. Although these approaches have different important strengths of their own, they are not well suited for directly executing a system.

In our approach we translate into a *formal language*, but where the translations can be *executed*. So we gain both the advantages of moving into a formal world where properties can be formally verified, and the advantages of being able to implement *prototypes* with which we get confidence of our systems specifications and implementations. The fact of having executable specifications is important not from the point of view of RDF documents that specify data, but from using the same framework both for translating RDF documents and for expressing the programs that manipulate them.

3   Rewriting Logic and Maude

Maude [7] is a high level, general purpose language and high performance system based on rewriting logic [16], a logic *of change* in which deduction directly corresponds to the change [13]. Among the advantages of rewriting logic, we may emphasize the following:

- *It has a simple formalism,* with only a few rules of deduction that are easy to understand and justify;
- *It is very flexible and expressive,* capable of representing change in systems with very different structure;
- *It allows user-definable syntax,* with complete freedom to choose the operators and structural properties appropriate for each problem;
- *It is intrinsically concurrent,* representing concurrent change and supporting reasoning about such change;
- *It supports modelling of concurrent object-oriented systems* in a simple and direct way;
- *It has a semantics based on initial models* that support a "no junk, no confusion" version of the closed world assumption;
- *It is realizable in a wide spectrum logical language (Maude)* supporting executable specification and programming.

In rewriting logic the state of a system is formally specified as an algebraic data type by means of an equational specification. In this kind of specifications we can define new types (by means of keyword `sort(s)`); subtype relations between types (`subsort`); operators (`op`) for building values of these types, giving the types of their arguments and result, and which may have attributes such as being associative (`assoc`) or commutative (`comm`), for example; and equations (`eq`) that identify terms built with these operators. The following *functional* module (with syntax `fmod...endfm`) defines the natural numbers with an addition operation:

```
fmod NAT is
  sort Nat .
  op 0 : -> Nat .
  op s : Nat -> Nat .
  op _+_ : Nat Nat -> Nat [assoc comm] .
  vars N M : Nat .
  eq 0 + N = N .
  eq s(N) + M = s(N + M) .
endfm
```

Equations are assumed to be confluent and terminating, that is, we can use the equations to reduce a term t to a unique, canonical form t' that is equivalent to t (they represent the same value). The Maude system does not check these properties of equational specifications, but there are related tools that can be used for that purpose.

The *dynamic* behavior of such a distributed system is then specified by rewrite rules of the form $t \longrightarrow t'$, that describe the local, concurrent transitions of the system. That is, when a part of a system matches the pattern t, it can be transformed into the corresponding instance of the pattern t'. Rewrite rules are included in *system* modules (with syntax `mod...endm`). For example, the next module defines nondeterministic natural numbers and nondeterministic choice. A module can import, or include, the definitions of another module by means of keyword `inc`.

```
mod ND-NAT is
  inc NAT .
  sort NdNat .
  subsort Nat < NdNat .
  op _?_ : NdNat NdNat -> NdNat [assoc comm].
  var N : Nat .   var ND : NdNat .
  eq N ? N = N .
  rl [choice] : N ? ND => N .
endm
```

A set of natural numbers is regarded as a nondeterministic natural number of sort NdNat, that is, a number that could be anyone of those in the set. The operation _?_ denotes the union of nondeterministic natural numbers, which is associative and commutative, and obeys also an idempotence equation. The choice rule provides nondeterministic choice.

Rewriting logic has revealed itself to be a general and flexible logical and semantic framework [14], in which many different logics, models of computation, and a wide range of languages can be represented, can be given a precise semantics, and can be executed. In this paper we claim that it can also be used to give semantics to metadata description frameworks such as RDF.

One of the main properties of Maude (and rewriting logic) is that it is reflective, that is, Maude can be represented into itself in such a way that a program (or module) M in Maude may be data for another Maude program, which can modify M, obtain information about it, or ask to *execute* it.

In Maude, key functionality of this reflective power has been efficiently implemented in the functional module META-LEVEL, where Maude terms are reified as elements of a data type Term, Maude modules are reified as terms in a data type Module, the process of reducing a term to normal form is reified by a function metaReduce, and the process of rewriting (executing) a term by applying the rewrite rules of a module is reified by a function metaRewrite [7]. We use these features in the implementation of the translation from RDF into object-oriented Maude modules, and when the translation is used in an example about a mobile agent system in Section 5.2.

3.1   Object-Oriented Specification in Maude

In an object-oriented Maude module (a special kind of system module, with syntax omod...endom) classes are declared with the syntax class $C \mid a_1 : S_1, \ldots,$ $a_n : S_n$, where C is the class name, a_i is an attribute identifier, and S_i is the sort of the values this attribute can have. An *object* in a given state is represented as a term $< O : C \mid a_1 : v_1, \ldots, a_n : v_n >$, where O is the object's name (belonging to a set Oid of object identifiers), and the v_i's are the current values of its attributes. *Messages* are defined by the user for each application (introduced with syntax msg). Subclass relations can also be defined, with syntax subclass.

In a concurrent object-oriented system the concurrent state, which is called a *configuration*, has the structure of a multiset made up of objects and messages that evolves by concurrent rewriting (modulo the multiset structural axioms of

Table 1. RDF concepts translated into Maude.

RDF/RDFS	Maude
RDF document	Object-oriented module
Class	Class
Resource	Object
Property	Attribute
Container	Abstract data type
URI	Object identifier

associativity, commutativity, and identity) using rules that describe the effects of *communication events* between some objects and messages. The rewrite rules in the module specify in a declarative way the behavior associated with the messages. The general form of such rules is

$$M_1 \ldots M_n \langle O_1 : F_1 \mid atts_1 \rangle \ldots \langle O_m : F_m \mid atts_m \rangle$$
$$\longrightarrow \langle O_{i_1} : F'_{i_1} \mid atts'_{i_1} \rangle \ldots \langle O_{i_k} : F'_{i_k} \mid atts'_{i_k} \rangle$$
$$\langle Q_1 : D_1 \mid atts''_1 \rangle \ldots \langle Q_p : D_p \mid atts''_p \rangle$$
$$M'_1 \ldots M'_q \quad if \ C$$

where $k, p, q \geq 0$, the M_s are message expressions, $i_1, \ldots, i_k$ are different numbers among the original $1, \ldots, m$, and C is a rule condition. The result of applying a rewrite rule is that the messages $M_1, \ldots, M_n$ disappear; the state and possibly the class of the objects $O_{i_1}, \ldots, O_{i_k}$ may change; all the other objects O_j vanish; new objects $Q_1, \ldots, Q_p$ are created; and new messages $M'_1, \ldots, M'_q$ are sent.

We will use this kind of system modules to provide the semantics for RDF documents and to implement the examples.

Later, in Section 5.2 we will integrate the translated RDF documents in an agent application written using Mobile Maude. This extension of Maude provides some new concepts related with mobility (mobile objects and processes) that are expressed in Maude itself, as explained in Section 5.1.

4   RDF/RDFS Translation into Maude

The main pieces in an RDF document are resources, properties, containers, URIs, and classes. We identified which elements of a Maude module could correspond naturally to these RDF pieces. The principal result is that Maude object-oriented modules are a good choice to represent RDF documents in Maude by giving them the natural, intuitive meaning. Table 1 shows the correspondence between RDF pieces and Maude elements.

In this section we describe the translation of RDF (including reification and containers) and RDFS documents into object-oriented modules in Maude. The driving idea is that an RDF description of a resource will be translated into an object in Maude.

Maude modules are used for describing RDF schemas. Those modules will be included in the translation of any particular RDF document using the predefined vocabulary. The following module defines the basic vocabulary for RDFS. It defines a data type for URI references and declares that they can be used as object identifiers (Oid). A class for resources is defined with several attributes. Every described resource will be an instance of this class, although we have used the same relaxed idea used by RDF of what an instance is. An object O is an instance of class C if it is declared as belonging to this class and it only has attributes defined for this class (or any of its superclasses), but not all the attributes have to be initialized. Apart from this consideration, all the power of object-orientation is supported, including inheritance (as explained in Section 5.2). URI references and instances of the class of resources are put together in a general type Resource. A class for properties is defined, and it is declared as a subclass of resources. There is also a data type for representing literals, which uses the predefined type of quoted identifiers (Qid).

```
omod http://www.w3.org/2000/01/rdf-schema is
  inc QID .
  sorts URI Resource .   subsort URI < Oid .
  op uri : Qid -> URI .
  class ResourceClass | comment : Literal,  label : Literal,
                        seeAlso : Resource, isDefinedBy : Resource .
  subsorts URI ResourceClass < Resource .
  class Property .
  subclass Property < ResourceClass .
  sort Literal .
  op literal : Qid -> Literal .
endom
```

There is another module defining the predefined vocabulary for RDF. A class Statement is declared for representing RDF statements, that is, a *reified statement* will be represented as an instance of this class. The class has three attributes: subject, predicate, and object. The module also declares classes for the different RDF containers by giving precise definitions of what they mean. For example, there is a class for bag containers which are described in [12] as "unordered lists of resources or literals." In Maude, we can define what this exactly *means* by defining a data type for *multisets* of resources and literals, with a constant operator mt for the empty multiset and a union operator _&_ which is declared to be associative, commutative, and with the empty multiset as identity element. There are similar classes for sequences and alternatives, although in each case the union operator is defined in a different way. For example, the union operator for sequences is declared as associative and with identity the empty sequence, but it is not declared as commutative, because a sequence is "an ordered list of resources or literals" [12].

```
omod http://www.w3.org/1999/02/22-rdf-syntax-ns is
  inc http://www.w3.org/2000/01/rdf-schema .
  class Statement | subject : Resource, predicate : Property,
                    object : Resource .
  *** containers
```

```
  class Container .  subclass Container < Resource .
  class Bag | val : BVal .  subclass Bag < Container .
  sort BVal .  subsorts Literal Resource < BVal .
  op mt : -> BVal .
  op _&_ : BVal BVal -> BVal [assoc comm id: mt] .
  ...
endom
```

The translation of a user-defined RDF document into an object-oriented module of Maude is summarized in Table 1. Let us see some examples for illustrating the translation of user-defined RDF documents. The RDF document describing a laser printer in Section 2 is translated into the following object-oriented module in Maude:

```
omod example is
  inc http://www.w3.org/1999/02/22-rdf-syntax-ns .
  inc http://printers.org/schema .
  op http://HPprinters/HPLaserJet1100 : -> Object .
  eq http://HPprinters/HPLaserJet1100 =
  < uri('http://HPprinters/HPLaserJet1100) : LaserPrinter |
    PrinterTechnology : literal('Laser'Jet),
    PrinterResolution : literal('600'dpi),
    Price : literal('399) > .
endom
```

The two namespaces used in the RDF document have been translated to module inclusions. The resource has been translated to an object constant and one equation defining it. This object has three attributes whose values are literals.

Anonymous resources are also supported and translated to object constants as above, although instead of a URI we use a local identifier to name them. Container descriptions are translated to objects of a class like the class Bag commented above, and the enumerated items are included in its attribute as a value built by using the corresponding union operator.

The RDFS description of printers in Section 2 is translated as follows:

```
omod Printers is
  inc http://www.w3.org/1999/02/22-rdf-syntax-ns .
  inc http://www.w3.org/2000/01/rdf-schema .
  class Printer | Price : Literal,
                  PrinterTechnology : Literal,
                  PrinterResolution : Literal .
  subclass Printer < ResourceClass .
  class LaserPrinter .
  subclass LaserPrinter < Printer .
endom
```

The namespaces have been translated into module inclusions, as above. The RDFS class declarations have been translated into Maude class declarations, and the subclass properties have been translated into subclass declarations in the Maude module. When a subclass relation is declared as `subclass` C `<` C', the class C is the subclass and the class C' is the superclass. The effect of a subclass declaration is that the attributes, messages, and rules of the superclass are inherited by the subclass. The property `Price`, with domain `Printer` and range `Literal`, has been translated into an attribute declaration of class `Printer` whose values can be of sort `Literal`. The other two properties are translated similarly.

By using the reflective features of rewriting logic and Maude, and moving up to the metalevel, where Maude modules become data that can be manipulated, we can equationally define operations that perform the translation described above in an *automatic* way. These operations traverse the elements of an RDF value and build the module step by step by including the translation of each element, as explained by means of examples above. The complete Maude code implementing this translation together with the predefined modules described above can all be found in `http://www.ucm.es/sip/alberto/semantic-web`.

5   Case Study

In this section we present a simple application of the translation process. The proposed translation has been used in an example where a buyer agent visits several sellers which give him their printers information in RDF. The buyer keeps the price of the cheapest printer. The example has been implemented using Mobile Maude, a Maude extension that supports mobile computation.

5.1   Mobile Maude

The flexibility of rewriting logic for representing very different styles of communication, either synchronous or asynchronous, its facility for supporting distributed, concurrent object-oriented systems, and its reflective capabilities for supporting metaprogramming and dynamic reconfiguration, make it a very suitable formalism for the specification of distributed systems based on mobile agents, on which the proof of properties about security, correctness, and performance, can be based.

Mobile Maude [8] is an extension of the Maude language supporting mobile computation. It is appropriate for the specification and prototyping of distributed systems based on mobile agents, where data, states, and programs can be moved. Moreover, it has a *formal basis* for the development of security models and the verification of properties for such models. The key entities in Mobile Maude are *processes* and *mobile objects*. Both are defined as classes in Maude. Processes are computational environments where mobile objects evolve and communicate with each other. Mobile objects are created inside a process, they can move to another process, they can operate inside a process, and they can send (receive) messages to (from) other mobile objects in the same process or in other

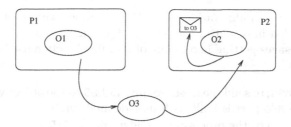

Fig. 1. A view of processes and mobile objects.

processes[2]. This is illustrated in Figure 1, where there are two processes (P1 and P2) and three mobile objects (O1, O2, and O3). Mobile object O3 is moving from process P1 to process P2, while the object O2 has just sent a message addressed to the moving object O3.

Processes and mobile objects are defined in Maude as classes P and MO, respectively. The class P of processes is declared as follows:

```
class P | cnt : Nat, cf : Configuration, guests : Set[Mid],
          forward : PFun[Nat, Tuple[Pid, Nat]] .
```

The main attribute is cf, the configuration of guest mobile objects. The attribute guests is the set of identifiers of mobile objects that currently reside in the process; cnt is the counter of mobile objects created in the process; and forward is a function used to locate the mobile objects created in the process. The names of processes range over the sort Pid, whereas the names of mobile objects range over the sort Mid and have the form o(PI,N), where PI is the name of the object's parent process, that is, the process where it was created, and N is a number that distinguishes the children of PI.

The class MO of mobile objects is defined as follows:

```
class MO | mod : Module, s : Term, p : Pid,
           hops : Nat, gas : Nat, mode : Mode .
```

The mobile object's module that defines a mobile object behavior must be object-oriented, and mod is the metarepresentation of that module. The term s is the metarepresentation of the actual configuration of the mobile object; this configuration has the following form: C & C', where C' is the outgoing messages tray (a multiset of outgoing messages) and C contains the state of the mobile object (as defined in the module mod) and a multiset of unprocessed incoming messages. The rest of the attributes in the class are: p, the identifier of the process where the mobile object currently is; hops, a natural number indicating the number of hops between processes that the object has performed so far; gas, a natural number that limits the rewrite steps that the object can do; and mode, that indicates if the process is active or not.

---

[2] Some mobile agents languages, as Cardelli's Ambient Calculus [6], forbid this last kind of communication, allowing only communications inside the same process.

Messages in the configuration and in the module may be of any form, but those being pulled in or out of the mobile object must have a specific form. In particular, messages getting in and out of mobile objects must be of one of the following forms:

- `to MID : MSG`, to send the message content `MSG` to the object whose identifier is `MID`. The `MSG` part is built with user-defined syntax.
- `go(PID)`, to go to the process whose identifier is `PID`.
- `go-find(MID, PID)`, to go to the process where the object `MID` is, trying as first alternative the process `PID`.
- `newo(MOD, OBJ, OID)`, to create a mobile object where `MOD` is the metarepresentation of the module where the object is defined, `OBJ` is the initial state of the object to be created, and `OID` is its identifier.

When a mobile object wants to deliver messages of this kind it puts them in its outgoing messages tray.

The complete Mobile Maude *system code*, plus some related information, can be found in `http://maude.cs.uiuc.edu/maude1/mobile-maude`.

The code describing the behavior of mobile objects is called *application code*. In the next section we will present several examples of this kind of code.

In [9] a case study using Mobile Maude is presented, and it is shown how an object-oriented specification in Maude can be made mobile. An ambitious wide area application, namely the reviewing system for a conference, going from its announcement to the edition of the proceedings, is specified and implemented. Such example was proposed by Cardelli in [6] as a challenge for any wide area language to demonstrate its usability, although it was previously used by different authors. Mobile Maude was used successfully to implement this system. Moreover, the Maude formal specification of Mobile Maude was used to execute the example. This case study and the possibility of executing it allowed us to test different alternatives both in the language and in the specification of the system. Although in the actual specification RDF documents are not used (different agents communicate with each other with a pre-established small vocabulary), it can be easily modified in such a way that agents communicate by means of RDF documents. Then the translation presented in this paper could be used by the agents to translate and understand the received information.

5.2   Buying Printers

In this example we have two different classes of mobile objects: sellers and buyers. Although in the simple example described here sellers do not move, they have to be mobile objects because they communicate with other mobile objects, so they have to be recognized as mobile objects by the Mobile Maude system. There is another class of objects, the comparers, that are used by buyers to compare printers. These are not mobile objects, as described below. A buyer visits several sellers. The buyer asks each seller he visits for the description of the seller's printer. The seller sends this description in RDF format, which the buyer translates and gives to his comparer, that keeps the price of the cheapest printer.

First we define the sellers. They are static agents whose behavior is defined in the following module. The class `Seller` has an attribute `description` with the RDF description of the printer it sells, using the schema in Section 2. When a seller receives a description request, it sends the description in RDF form.

```
omod SELLER is
  inc RDF-SYNTAX .
  class Seller | description : RDF .
  op get-printer-description : Oid -> Contents .
  op printer-description : RDF -> Contents .
  vars S B : Oid .   var D : RDF .
  rl [get-des] : (to S : get-printer-description(B))
       < S : Seller | description : D > & none
    => < S : Seller | > & (to B : printer-description(D)) .
endom
```

Note how the seller's state is described in rule `get-des` by means of the `_&_` operator in order to separate the inner state and incoming messages from the outgoing messages. Due to that we can use this module to build mobile objects in Mobile Maude.

Before defining the buyers, we define the class `Comparer` whose instances are able to compare different printers, keeping the price of the cheapest printer. When a comparer is near a printer, it looks the price of the printer, and compares it with the best printer it knows, updating its knowledge if necessary. Note that the printer object disappears, because it does not represent a real printer, but a printer information, that is useless after the comparer has looked up its information.

```
omod COMPARER is
  inc Printers .
  inc DEFAULT[Nat] .
  class Comparer | best : Default[Nat] .
  var P C : Oid .   var Q : Qid .   var N : Nat .
  var Atts Atts' : AttributeSet .
  rl [compare] : < P : Printer | Price : literal(Q), Atts >
       < C : Comparer | best : N, Atts' >
    => < C : Comparer | best : if (convert(Q) < N) then
                          convert(Q) else N fi, Atts' > .
endom
```

A comparer is not a mobile object of Mobile Maude. It does not move independently, and cannot send or receive messages from other mobile objects. It is a Maude object that will travel inside a buyer's attribute, as we will see below.

Note how the variable `Atts` of sort `AttributeSet` is used in the printer object. By using this variable, the rule can be applied to any printer with *at least* an attribute `Price`; if the printer has more attributes, they will be caught by the variable `Atts`.

This style of programming is quite useful for the Semantic Web. If a seller has defined its own RDF schema, extending the one presented in Section 2 by defining a subclass of printers with new properties which are important for him, it will send printer descriptions with some properties unknown for our comparer. But the above implementation will also be useful in this case, because the extra properties (attributes) will be caught by the variable `Atts`.

Finally, we define the buyers. The module `BUYER` describes the behavior of a buyer agent. It has a list `IPs` with the addresses of the sellers. It has to visit all the sellers, asking each one for the description of the printers. The buyer has an attribute `app-state` with the current state of its comparer, metarepresented. It has to be metarepresented because the buyer wants to be able to execute the comparer. Each time it receives a new description, it translates the RDF description into a Maude module M with a `Printer` object. It puts this object together with the current state of its comparer, and asks to rewrite them (by using `metaRewrite`, see Section 3) in the Maude module obtained by joining M with the module containing the comparer code.

```
omod BUYER is
  inc RDF-Translation .
  sort Status .
  ops onArrival asking done : -> Status .
  class Buyer | IPs : List[Oid], status : Status, app-state : Term .
  op get-printer-description : Oid -> Contents .
  op printer-description : RDF -> Contents .
  var PD : RDF .   var Ss : List[Oid] .   vars B S : Oid .
  var PI : Pid .   var N : Nat .   var T : Term .
  rl [move] : < B : Buyer | IPs : o(PI,N) + Ss, status : done > & none
    => < B : Buyer | status : onArrival > & go-find(o(PI,N),PI) .
  rl [onArrival] : < B : Buyer | IPs : S + Ss, status : onArrival > & none
    => < B : Buyer | status : asking > &
       (to S : get-printer-description(B)) .
  rl [new-des] : (to B : printer-description(PD))
       < B : Buyer | IPs : S + Ss, app-state : T, status : asking >
    => < B : Buyer | IPs : Ss, app-state : metaRewrite(
          addDecls(up(COMPARER), translate('Printer,PD)),
          '__[T,extractResources(translate('MOD,PD))],0), status : done > .
endom
```

The first rewrite rule, `move`, handles the travels of the buyer: if it has finished in the current process (its status is `done`) and there is at least one seller name in the `IPs` attribute, it asks the system to take it to the host where the seller is. On arrival, the buyer asks the seller for the printer description, giving the seller's name. When the RDF description arrives, the buyer translates it to Maude, extracts the resource corresponding to the printer description, puts it together with the comparer, and asks to rewrite the result in the module with the comparer's behavior, which will change the comparer's state.

The full code of this example can be found in http://www.ucm.es/sip/alberto/semantic-web.

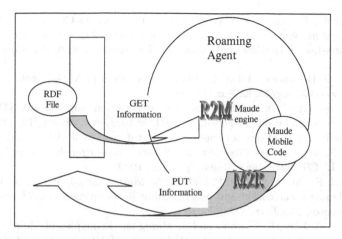

Fig. 2. DF $\leftrightarrow$ Maude translations.

6   Conclusions and Future Work

In this paper we presented the first results of a translation from RDF/RDFS to the language Maude. This translation produces a formal version of the original RDF/RDFS data, without requiring any extra information in the original RDF/RDFS documents, thus preserving compatibility with other approaches. We think this approach offers a sound way for formalizing the Semantic Web.

A key point for success of our translation model is to integrate the approach using Maude with the real Web, as described in Figure 2, where an agent with Mobile Maude code interacts with usual Internet services by getting the RDF file that contains all the required information. Then an RDF2Maude translation will be carried out. After operating, one or more result files will be produced. These files will be translated into RDF by a Maude2RDF translation. This approach will allow the formalized service to interact with the usual Web applications and services. Maude has already been integrated with real Web applications in [1, 2].

The work presented here is the first step to allow a formal model for Web services. This promising area will be enriched with the Semantic Web services approach by enriching not only the services with a semantic definition over RDF or OWL-S [15], but also allowing to access a specification of the dynamic semantics of the operations carried out by this service.

We plan to carry out further research in order to integrate our work with the OWL specification [17] and specially with OWL-S, to extend it on a formal way in order to enable a possible wide future of new formal Semantic Web services.

References

1. A. Albarrán, F. Durán, and A. Vallecillo. From Maude specifications to SOAP distributed implementations: a smooth transition. In *Proceedings VI Jornadas de Ingeniería del Software y Bases de Datos, JISBD 2001, Almagro, Spain*, 2001.

2. A. Albarrán, F. Durán, and A. Vallecillo. Maude meets CORBA. In *Proceedings 2nd Argentine Symposium on Software Engineering*, Argentina, 2001.
3. T. Berners-Lee, J. Hendler, and O. Lassila. The semantic web. *Scientific American*, 2001.
4. T. Bray, D. Hollander, and A. Layman. Namespaces in XML, 1999. http://www.w3.org/TR/REC-xml-names.
5. D. Brickley and R. Guha. RDF vocabulary description language 1.0: RDF Schema. W3C Recommendation, 10 February, 2004. http://www.w3.org/TR/rdf-schema.
6. L. Cardelli. Abstractions for mobile computations. In J. Vitek and C. Jensen, editors, *Secure Internet Programming: Security Issues for Mobile and Distributed Objects*, LNCS 1603, pages 51–94. Springer, 1999.
7. M. Clavel, F. Durán, S. Eker, P. Lincoln, N. Martí-Oliet, J. Meseguer, and J. Quesada. Maude: specification and programming in rewriting logic. *Theoretical Computer Science*, 285(2):187–243, 2002.
8. F. Durán, S. Eker, P. Lincoln, and J. Meseguer. Principles of Mobile Maude. In D. Kotz and F. Mattern, eds., *Agent Systems, Mobile Agents, and Applications, ASA/MA 2000*, LNCS 1882. Springer, 2000.
9. F. Durán and A. Verdejo. A conference reviewing system in Mobile Maude. In F. Gadducci and U. Montanari, eds., *Proceedings Fourth International Workshop on Rewriting Logic and its Applications, WRLA 2002*, ENTCS 71, pages 79–95. Elsevier, 2002.
10. R. Fikes and D. MacGuinness. An axiomatic semantics for RDF, RDF-S, and DAML+OIL. W3C Note, 2001. http://www.w3.org/TR/daml+oil-axioms.
11. P. Hayes. RDF semantics. W3C Recommendation, 10 February, 2004. http://www.w3.org/TR/rdf-mt.
12. F. Manola and E. Miller. RDF primer. W3C Recommendation, 10 February, 2004. http://www.w3.org/TR/rdf-primer.
13. N. Martí-Oliet and J. Meseguer. Action and change in rewriting logic. In *Dynamic Worlds: From the Frame Problem to Knowledge Management*, pages 1–53. Kluwer Academic Publishers, 1999.
14. N. Martí-Oliet and J. Meseguer. Rewriting logic as a logical and semantic framework. In D. M. Gabbay and F. Guenthner, editors, *Handbook of Philosophical Logic, Second Edition, Volume 9*, pages 1–87. Kluwer Academic Publishers, 2002.
15. D. Martin, editor. OWL-S: Semantic Markup for Web Services. http://www.daml.org/services/owl-s/1.1/overview.
16. J. Meseguer. Conditional rewriting logic as a unified model of concurrency. *Theoretical Computer Science*, 96(1):73–155, 1992.
17. D. McGuinness and F. van Harmelen. OWL Web Ontology Language. W3C Recommendation, 10 February, 2004. http://www.w3.org/TR/owl-features.
18. IETF Uniform Resource Identifiers (URI) Working Group, 2000. http://ftp.ics.uci.edu/pub/ietf/uri/.
19. Resource Description Framework (RDF) / W3C Semantic Web Activity. http://www.w3.org/RDF.

Modeling- and Analysis Techniques for Web Services and Business Processes

Wolfgang Reisig

Humboldt-Universität zu Berlin

Abstract. Open distributed systems include in particular Web services and business processes. There is a need of techniques to model such systems formally, and to derive decisive properties from such models. Three such techniques are presented in this paper, exemplified by help of realistic examples, and mutually related w.r.t. their respective expressive power and the availability of analysis techniques.

1 Web Services and Business Processes

The term *Web service* describes a wide range of software architectures, and has no entirely clear-cut definition. But most experts in the field would agree that the following two aspects are essential for Web services:

Firstly, a Web service has a *technological basis*, which is a systematic combination of conventional middleware components for transport (e.g. TCP/ IP), messaging (e.g. SOAP, XML), description (WSDL), quality of service (e.g. WS-coordination, WS-transaction) and integration (UDDI). This combination of technologies has occasionally been denoted as the "technology stack" of Web services. Business processes as well as other distributed services can then be implemented on top of this. Hence, the technological basis of Web services is a combination of existing middleware. The essential idea of Web services is however not merely the middleware components and their combination in the technology stack, but the second aspect of Web services, its *abstraction* from its technological basis.

Web services are a prominent example for the paradigm of service oriented architectures. They in turn are intended to overcome well known problems of updating or replacing single components of conventional, monolithic IT systems. Abstracting from their technological basis, Web services themselves provide the ground for further abstractions, in particular abstractions from the technological foundation of business processes. Such abstractions turn high-level objects and operations into elementary notions. Typical examples include objects like "client" and "message to client", and operations such as "to answer a client's recent request". This kind of objects and operations are elementary in the world of business process. Their implementation in the technological basis of Web services remains irrelevant for the user of business processes.

M. Steffen and G. Zavattaro (Eds.): FMOODS 2005, LNCS 3535, pp. 243–258, 2005.

2   Modeling- and Analysis Techniques

The definition of a Web service must be communicated among its designers, implementers, users, etc. This requires a language, i.e. a meta-model, capable to represent Web services intuitively and uniquely. A commonly accepted meta-model does not exist, however. Instead, notions and notations in the area of Web services emerged quickly and, occasionally, with little mutual recognition. Quoting the W3C consortium, and specifically the group involved in the Web service activity [17], a web service is "a software application identified by a URI, whose interfaces and bindings are capable of being defined, described and discovered by XML artefacts. A Web service supports direct interactions with other software agents, using XML-based messages exchanged via Internet-based protocols." Hence, a meta-model for Web services must in particular be capable of describing interfaces and bridging of services, in addition to abstract objects as described in Section 1.

Specification languages for Web services and business processes differ fundamentally from conventional programming languages: The semantical basis of a conventional programming language essentially consists of objects such as symbols, sequences of symbols, binary integer representations, and operations such as composing and comparing symbol sequences. The corresponding theoretical framework is the world of computable functions. This framework can however not be employed as the semantical basis of specification languages for Web services and business processes, because elementary objects can be *any* items, and elementary operations can be *any* operations. We consider two approaches to tackle this problem: The first one starts out with the observation that many questions can be stated and answered without detailed semantical aspects, focusing only onto the *control structure* of services. Typical examples of such questions include necessary conditions for proper termination, usability and equivalence. Low-level Petri nets turned out to be particularly useful for this purpose. This line of research has mainly been started by [15], [16], and continued by e.g. [6], [7], [9], [8], [13], and [14]. The second solution to the above stated problem applies a kind of mathematics that has been designed to cope with any kind of items and operations on then: General Algebra and first order logic. This kind of mathematics, however, describes *static* structures, whereas we have to tackle dynamic behavior. This goal is achieved by two formalisms, *high-level Petri nets* and Gurevich's *Abstract State Machines*. Each of the three modeling techniques trades expressivity for analysis techniques: The more expressive the modeling technique, the less it offers specific analysis techniques.

Various versions of automata and process algebras have been suggested to model web services and business processes. They do not decisively contribute to the aspects considered in this paper.

3   Low-Level Petri Nets for Business Processes

We start out with the quite elementary technique of *business process nets (BP nets)*, a special class of elementary Petri nets. BP nets model the structure of control within a single business process, as well as control of communication among processes.

Elementary Petri nets have frequently been advocated to model control aspects of communicating business processes. (e.g. [15], [16], [9]) We suggest a variant that is technically simpler, and slightly more general.

A reasonable well structured business process exhibits a number of regularities and important properties: It can properly terminate in combination with any "serving" environment, it may exhibit a "most liberal" serving environment and a most abstract "public view". One business process may simulate or be equivalent to an other business process. Business processes may be composed to larger business processes, thereby systematically transferring important properties of the component processes to the composed process. It should be possible to decide those properties and to derive those processes from a representation of given processes. A number of reasons favors *low-level Petri nets* as an adequate technique for many of those questions:

- Many of those questions depend essentially on the *control structure* only, i.e. are independent of concrete data and operations.
- The paradigm of message passing of business processes ignores concrete delays among processes. In particular, the order of sent messages may swap upon their arrival. This corresponds naturally to the behavior of tokens in the places of Petri nets.
- Composition of business processes correlates exactly with gluing interface places of the corresponding Petri nets.
- In business processes, in particular in cooperating, distributed processes, actions occur locally and causally independently. Petri nets support and describe this kind of behavior by help of *distributed runs*.
- Criteria for selecting an activity out of a set of alternative in a business process, are frequently not fully characterized. Nondeterministic choice of conflicting transitions of a Petri net adequately simulate this kind of behavior.
- There exits a number of specific analysis tools for Petri nets, well applicable to Petri net models of business processes.

3.1 Business Process Nets

As mentioned above, a business process is intended to begin its activities in a definite *start* state and to terminate in a definite *stop* state. Activities include message exchange with an appropriately cooperating *environment*. This fixes the structure of Petri net models of the control structure of business processes. A simple example is

$$(1)$$

The places a and c are *input places*, and b is an *output place* of the net. Furthermore, the net has a *start marking*, with one token at place α_1 and no tokens elsewhere. Furthermore, the *stop marking* of this net has a token on place ω_1, and no tokens elsewhere. We assume the reader be familiar with the basics of elementary Petri nets, and define the general pattern of a *business process net* (a BP net, for short) N as a Petri net structure, consisting as usual of places (circles), transitions (squares) and arcs (arrows) together with

- a distinguished subset of its places where no arcs end, called the *input places of N*
- a distinguished subset of its places where no arcs start, called the *output places on N*
- a *start* marking, $start_N$, and a *stop* marking, $stop_N$, both with empty input- and output places.

The input- and output-places form together the *environment places* (also called the *channels*) of N; all other places are *inner* places. $start_N$ often has tokens only on a set of inner places without ingoing arcs, usually denoted by the (indexed) symbol "α". $stop_N$ often has tokens only on a set of inner places without outgoing arcs, usually denoted by the (indexed) symbol "ω". We follow the convention to draw α and ω at the left and right margin of graphical representations, respectively. This implies control flowing from left to right. (1) follows this convention. This definition of BP nets, as well as the forthcoming definition of their composition, is more liberal than corresponding definitions of [15], [7] and [13]. It is technically simpler and intuitively more natural, while preserving all relevant properties.

3.2 Closed Business Processes

Business process nets without input- and output places are useful for a number of purposes. Such a net is *closed*; here an example:

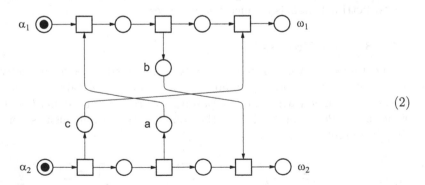

$$(2)$$

Its start marking has tokens on α_1 and α_2, its stop marking has tokens on ω_1 and ω_2.

We will see later on that a closed net may result from composing two business process nets. By construction, a closed net remains if we skip the environment places of a BP net N, retaining the *inner subnet of N*, written $inner(N)$.

3.3 Composition

Cooperation of business processes is properly reflected by the composition of business process nets. Without loss of generality we assume for any two BP nets M and N that a place or a transition of M does not belong to inner(N) and vice versa: Otherwise one may construct *two* instances. Formulated differently, M and N share only places in their environments.

Composition $M \cdot N$ of M and N is then a BP net again, defined by identifying shared places. This way, an input place of M that coincidently is an output place of N, evolves into an inner place of $M \cdot N$.

As an example, one may compose (1) with the BP net

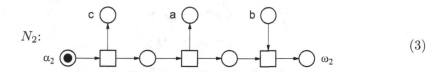

$$N_2: \tag{3}$$

The resulting net $N_1 \cdot N_2$ is the closed BP net (2). Fig. 1 shows a further example.

Composition of BP nets is commutative, i.e. for any BP nets M and N holds

$$M \cdot N = N \cdot M \tag{4}$$

Furthermore, for any three BP nets L, M and N with no interface place shared by all three processes, the product is also *associative*, i.e.

$$(L \cdot M) \cdot N = L \cdot (M \cdot N) \tag{5}$$

3.4 Well-Formed Business Process Nets

We focused the *static structure* of BP nets so far, in particular their input- and output-places, their start- and stop marking, and their composition. Now we consider aspects of *dynamic behavior*, i.e. reachable states, runs, termination etc.

The most important property of a BP net, concerning its dynamic behavior, is *termination*: A BP net N *can terminate* if for each marking m reachable from $start_N$, the marking $stop_N$ is reachable from m. This definition reflects potential loops of N.

Occasionally we require each component of a BP net to be "useful": A BP net N is *covered* in case each transition t of N occurs at least in one occurrence sequence

$$start_N \longrightarrow \ldots \overset{t}{\longrightarrow} \ldots \longrightarrow stop_N. \tag{6}$$

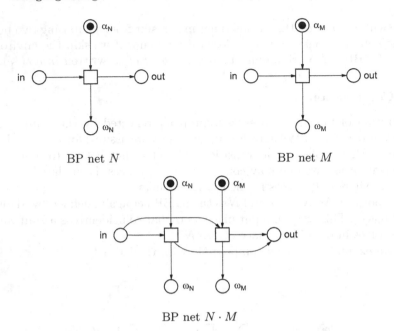

Fig. 1. Composition of BP nets.

It is furthermore reasonable to assume unambiguous start- and stop mark-ings: A BP net N is *unambiguous* if there exist sets α and ω of inner places of N such that

- $start_N$ is the only reachable marking with tokens on all places of α
- $stop_N$ is the only reachable marking with tokens on all places of ω.

The above three conditions define the important class of well formed BP nets: A BP net N is *well formed* if N can terminate, is covered, and is unambiguous.

Any reasonable, closed business process has a well formed model. It remains to decide whether or not a given BP net is well formed. [15] reduces this problem to classical problems of Petri nets: Given a BP net N, he suggests to construct a Petri net N^* from N, by an additional transition t that leads the stop marking ω back to the start marking α. N is then shown to be well formed iff N^* is live and safe. (As a technicality, [15] and others restrict α and ω to one place. Our definition appears technically simpler, in particular the definition of composition, while all analysis techniques are retained).

3.5   Usable Business Process Nets

A well-formed bp exhibits a reasonable inner structure. In this section we ask for "reasonable" behavior w.r.t. the partners in the environment of a BP net.

Two BP nets are *partners* if they together can reach their joint *stop* state. As an example, (1) and (3) are partners.

More precisely formulated, two BP nets M and N are *partners* if $M \cdot N$ is unambiguous and can terminate (as defined in 3.4). We do not expect M and N together can employ all alternatives of M and of N. Hence we do not require $M \cdot N$ be covered.

Based on the above notion of partners, we can now define the central notion of *usability*: A BP net is *usable* if there exists at least one partner of N. As an example, (1) is usable due to its partner (3).

Here an example of a BP net that is *not* usable:

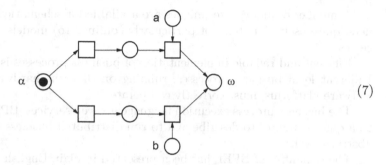

$$(7)$$

Intuitively formulated, this business process decides whether to expect a or b from its environment. The process fails to propagate this decision to its environment. But the environment needs this information to act accordingly. In contrast, the following BP net is very well usable, e.g. by (3):

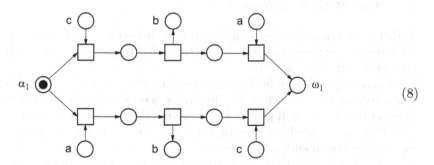

$$(8)$$

This rises the quest for an algorithm to decide whether or not a BP net is usable. In fact, such algorithms have been constructed (e.g. in [7]).

3.6   Further Properties

Usability is a fundamental property; but a number of other non-trivial properties and derived artefacts are likewise important, including *equivalence, abstract views, operating guidelines, fault handling,* and *transactions.* Various algorithms to decided those properties and to generate those artefacts have been published, including [4], [9], [10], and [14].

4 High-Level Petri Nets for BPEL

Here we suggest *schematic high-level Petri nets* as a modeling technique that is expressive enough to model quite complex behavior, such as essentials of the semantics of the *business process execution language*, BPEL. The core concept of schematic high-level Petri nets are symbols to be interpreted by *any* item or operation, not confined to conventional data structures. In analogy to low-level Petri nets as considered above, this technique fits perfectly to model business processes.

A number of analysis techniques are available for schematic high-level Petri nets, quite useful for (but not particularly confined to) models of business processes.

Efficient and reliable implementation of business processes is a tedious task. Different local business processes, running on different hardware on different software platforms, must correctly co-operate.

The business process execution language for web services, BPEL [3] has risen to a quasi-standard to describe and to run distributed business processes on an abstract level.

The semantics of BPEL has been presented in plain English, with some ambiguities, in particular when it comes to the *compensation* of activities.

By help of a small example we will show in the sequel, why high-level Petri nets provide adequate means to formulate the semantics of BPEL.

4.1 The BPEL Language

A BPEL program describes the structure of a business process as a particular Web service, and specifies the interaction of a business process with partner processes in its environment.

A central problem of business processes is *compensation* of already executed sub-activities (e.g. canceling an already booked flight) whenever it turns out later on that the overall goal fails (e.g. no hotel room was available).

BPEL consequently distinguishes *positive* control flow of a business process, formulating the intended activities to achieve its goal, and *negative* control flow, managing the case of faults, in particular the problems of compensation.

4.2 Activities

A core construct of BPEL are *activities*: An activity may be *elementary* (e.g. it may receive a message from its environment), or it may be *composed* from elementary activities. There are different ways to compose activities. They essentially correspond to control structures of conventional programming languages, i.e. sequences, loops and conditional alternative. In the next section we will consider one of them, called *scope*. An activity may be *executed*. Execution of an elementary activity strongly resembles conventional programming languages, and will not be considered in detail here. Executing a composed activity means to iteratively select the next component activity to be executed, in accordance with the activity's control structure, and governed by actual values and predicates.

An execution of an activity can come to an end in three different manners:

- it terminates successfully
- it causes a fault
- it is canceled by a stop signal from its environment

The activity would signal to its environment the manner of ending. Actually, it is not activities but *instances of activities* that are executed. Various instances of an activity may co-exist and be executed concurrently. The phrase "to execute an activity" stands for "to execute one of the activity's instances". As it is intuitive and convenient, we will apply the shorthand whenever confusion can be ruled out.

4.3   Scopes

As mentioned above already, a set of activities may be combined in a *scope*. In addition to its "ordinary" activities, a scope includes a *fault handler* managing fault signals sent from the scope's ordinary activities. In particular, the fault handler may cancel all activities of the scope. Consequently, each activity must be prepared to accept a stop signal, and to process it accordingly.

A message m, as controlled by a scope, has two components: Its *contents* which is irrelevant in the sequel, and its *correlation set, cor(m)*. Details of the correlation set will not be relevant in the sequel. We only must be able to decide whether or not two correlation sets are equal. So, it suffices to represent each correlation set as a symbol.

4.4   The Activity receive

A typical activity is receive. Its instances access three components of the receive activity, provided by the overall process : an *input channel*, carrying messages to be processed by receive, a *correlation set* to direct incoming messages to the corresponding instance, and a *variable* to store the last accepted message.

Each instance i of receive processes an incoming message, m. If the correlation set $cor(m)$ of m and the correlation set of i coincide, the variable of receive is updated and given the message m as its new value. Otherwise the message is extinguished and a "failed" message is generated. As described above, there is always a chance for the fault handler to stop running instances of receive.

We are now prepared to state the problem to be solved: How can activities such as receive be described? This includes in particular

- to properly administer the various instances of receive
- to provide a *composition* technique for descriptions, that reflect the cooperation of activities.

In the next chapter we show that *high-level Petri nets* provide a more than adequate technique to model such systems.

4.5   A Model for Receive

Fig. 2 shows a high-level Petri net model for the *receive* activity. The reader familiar with high-level Petri nets will easily grasp this model. Other readers are helped by the following explanations. One may conceive those explanations as coincidentally providing an introduction to high-level Petri nets.

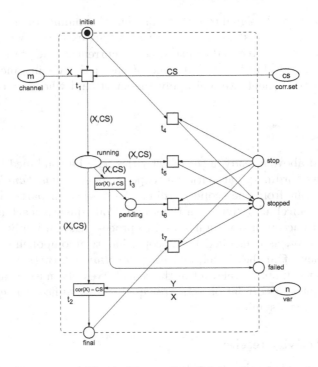

Fig. 2. The receive activity.

In Fig. 2, the dotted frame separates the inner components of the model from its surface and its environment. The five circles on the frame's surface (initial, stop, stopped, failed, final) are places, intended to exchange black dot tokens with other activities. Tokens on these places represent control signals to trigger activities, as discussed above. The three ellipses outside the frame (channel, corr.set, var) are places that model the activities' communication with the overall process: The activity may receive a message along the place channel. The process furthermore provides an initial correlation set at the place corr.set, and an initial value at var. This place represents a variable that always carries the last acceptable message.

Fig. 2 shows a typical state where the activity is ready to act: Some other activity has triggered receive (black dot token on initial) and the scope has sent a message, (token m on channel) A correlation set *cs* is anyway assumed at place corr.set, as well as some value, n, at the place var.

Describing the behavior of the net, we start with the intended, positive control flow. The state shown in Fig. 2 enables the transition t_1, provided the variables X and CS are properly valuated: X by m, and CS by cs, respectively. Occurrence of t_1 then

- removes the black dot token from initial, and the m token from channel
- produces the pair (m, cs) as a token at place running
- retains the cs token at corr.set, as $\longleftrightarrow$ is a *read arc*.

In this situation, to continue one has to evaluate the predicates inscribed in t_2 and t_3, again with $X = m$ and $CS = cs$. If the correlation set $cor(m)$ of the message m coincides with the correlation set cs provided by the environment, the transition t_2 is enabled. Occurrence of t_2 then updates the value at the place var. With the fresh value $X = n$, given the old value $Y = m$, the execution terminates (black dot token at final). If the predicate inscribed in t_2 fails with $X = m$ and $CS = cs$, t_3 is enabled and "throws a fault", i.e. triggers some other activity (black dot token on failed). This token will eventually, via the fault handler activity, cause a token on stop, thus enabling t_6. The activity then terminates with a black dot token at stopped. This completes description of the positive control flow.

A stop token may arrive any time. Hence at any state, the activity may leave its positive control flow by one of the transitions t_4, t_5 or t_7, resulting in a stopped token.

During execution of receive, a fresh message, l, may arrive and another activity may provide a fresh start signal to the *receive* activity. This is the situation where a new instance of *receive* must be created, executing concurrently to the existing one.

In the Petri net of Fig. 2, this may be modeled by a token "l" on the channel place, and another black dot token at the place initial. Concurrent execution of the two instances is then properly modeled by the Petri net, due to the definition of *distributed runs*, not considered here.

Schematic Petri nets come with a number of useful analysis techniques. For example, for the model of the *receive* activity as given in Fig. 2, one may prove that the token m, initially at the channel, eventually reaches the place var, or the system fails. Technically, this is represented by the temporal logic formula

$$(\text{channel}.X \wedge \text{initial} \wedge |\text{corr.set}| \geq 1) \longmapsto (\text{var}.X \vee \text{stopped})$$

with "$\longmapsto$" denoting the "leads-to" operator. This formula can be proven to be valid in Fig. 2, by the help of techniques described e.g. in [11].

4.6   Lessons Learned

The above example provides a first glimpse at schematic high-level Petri nets, and the motivation to model business processes with this kind of Petri nets. Here the most important aspects:

- Elementary objects and operations of business processes are fairly abstract. Examples are "message", "correlation set of an activity", or "correlation set of a message", but also "reply to a quest" or "cancel an order". All these objects and operations, though elementary in the given context, come without any fixed or agreed representation in conventional data structures. High-level Petri nets, in their *schematic* setting as applied in Fig. 2, support this approach.
- The paradigm of business processes ignores delays of messages passing between processes. In particular, messages may "overtake". The semantics of Petri nets, with tokens residing at a place without any order, correspond naturally to this paradigm.
- Single business processes cooperate along message channels: An output channel of one process serves as an input channel of another process. This is mimicked in Petri nets by glueing (identifying) the corresponding places.
- Activities of different business processes operate locally and independently. This is reflected in Petri nets by the occurrence rule for transitions: The behavior of a transition depends only on and only affects the adjacent places. No notion of global state or global time is required.
- Generation of instances of a business process, to occur concurrently, are perfectly modeled in Petri nets by more than one initiating tuple of transitions, and the notion of distributed runs. We refrain from details here.
- Analysis techniques as available for schematic high-level nets, are useful to verify business processes.

5   ASMs for Web Services

As a most universal modeling technique we suggest Gurevich's Abstract State Machines (ASM). The demand of ASM to be "most universal" has been justified in [5]. We refrain from details here. But we show that ASM in fact are expressive enough to model a wide range of Web Service oriented Systems in a natural way.

5.1   The Abstract Basis of Web Services

The monograph [1] provides a comprehensive view on Web services. Concepts are presented in plain English, supported by various kinds of graphical representations, in about 140 Figures. About half of the figures show static, mainly hierarchical structures. The rest of the figures show dynamic behavior, both of middleware components (i.e. the technological basis of Web services) and of abstract components (in particular, components for business processes).

Web services are usually implemented on top of some middleware. Any formal description of the semantics of Web services hence must rely on a formal semantics of those middleware components. Fortunately, the semantics of Web services requires only quite abstract aspects of middleware semantics. What is needed, however, is a formalism to adequately represent those aspects of middleware. This comes in addition, of course, to an adequate representation of the Web service components themselves.

5.2   The Core Idea of ASM

The above problem can be solved by help of an idea that we applied in the context of high-level Petri nets already: Items and operations are symbolically represented, leaving their semantical aspect to be defined elsewhere. For example, in Fig. 2, m is a constant symbol and $cor(m)$ is a term. We only informally specified what a "message" is assumed to be; we only assume that a message has a correlation set, and that the term $cor(m)$ represents the correlation set of m. This idea of "pseudo code" used to represent dynamic behavior, given meaning only up to the interpretation of the involved symbols. It is central to the specification technique of *Abstract State Machines (ASM)*. An ASM is essentially a set of conditional assignment statements, to be executed in parallel. Condition, left side, and right side of each assignment statement are terms over a signature (i.e. a set of symbols, each with an arity). An ASM can be executed for *any* arity respecting interpretation of its symbols. Details on the ASM method can be found e.g. in [2].

ASM provide in fact an adequate framework to formally represent Web services.

5.3   A Small Case Study

Here we consider a small example, taken from [1]. This case study assumes a scenario where a *customer* and a *supplier* communicate along the web. The customer starts an interaction, sending a request for an offer (a *quote request*) to a supplier. After receiving a quote from the supplier, the customer returns and order, and after receipt of the ordered goods, submits his payment. Fig. 3 outlines this behavior, as given in [1], page 198.

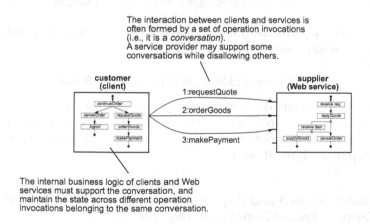

Fig. 3. A sample conversation between a customer (client) and a supplier (Web service).

The supplier Web service offers three operations, symbolically represented as *requestQuote*, *orderGoods* and *makePayment* to the customer. The customer is allowed to envoke the operations only in the order as fixed by the supplier. This order is denoted as *conversation*. To demonstrate the ASM method, we just model the – admittedly quite simple – customer behavior.

We first consider the items we speak about. Each time the customer starts a conversation, he newly chooses the goods he wants to order, as well as the supplier for those goods. In the ASM formalism, this is modeled by the two constant symbols Goods and SupplierMsg. One may have expected variables at this point. But the idea is that the value of a constant symbol is fixed upon the start of an ASM program. Each time the forthcoming ASM *conversation* is started, it starts in a different *initial state*. Each initial state interprets the above mentioned two constant symbols by a newly chosen set of goods, and a newly chosen supplier. We assume corresponding messages to be sent from the client to the supplier Web service. Technically, Messages represents the set of potential messages symbolically. The *undefined* element, symbolically undef, is also assumed as a message. Furthermore, we assume the two constant symbols, true and false, to be always interpreted as expected. Finally, we assume two further constant symbols, GoodsOrdered and GoodsPayed, each to be initially valuated by a truth value.

The next issue to be tackled are the necessary functions. The first function is, symbolically,

$$\text{RequestQuote} : \text{Messages} \times \text{Messages} \rightarrow \text{Messages}$$

Semantically, the parameters should be the supplier to offer a quote, and the goods. The function should return the quote as given by the supplier.

The second function is

$$\text{OrderGoods} : \text{Messages} \times \text{Messages} \rightarrow \text{Boolean}$$

This is merely a predicate, expecting a supplier and an order, and declares whether goods have been ordered already.

Finally,

$$\text{MakePayment} : \text{Messages} \times \text{Messages} \rightarrow \text{Boolean}$$

is again a predicate and declares whether goods have been payed.

We are now ready to formulate the ASM. This is a program, i.e. a text, using the above introduced constant- and function symbols, together with the keywords **par**, **endpar**, **if**, **and**, $\neq$:

```
par
    if (Goods ≠ undef) and (SupplierMsg ≠ undef) and (Quote = undef)
        Quote := RequestQuote(SupplierMsg, Goods)
    if (Quote ≠ undef) and (GoodsOrdered ≠ true)
        GoodsOrdered := OrderGoods(SupplierMsg, Quote)
    if (GoodsOrdered = true) and (GoodsPayed ≠ true)
        GoodsPayed := MakePayment(SupplierMsg, Quote)
endpar
```

Constant symbols play the role of variables of programming languages here.

In general, an ASM may employ *any* kind of terms also on the left side of an assignment statement. Variables are used in ASM as bounded by a quantifier, as usual in logic.

Further examples of ASM models for Web services business processes, and the language BPEL can be found in [12], [4].

6   Conclusion

Service orientation is a principle to organize software architectures, independent of platforms, programming languages, and any other implementation oriented aspect. Service oriented architectures nevertheless deserve a unique representation, i.e. a formal model. This raises the quest for adequate techniques to formulate such models.

In this paper we advocate three such techniques, spanning from a very specific class of low-level Petri nets up to the most universal technique of Abstract State Machines. High-level Petri nets are located somewhere in the middle of the spectrum.

Each modeling technique trades expressivity for analysis techniques. This implies the following rule of thumb: To cover a specific problem, choose a modeling technique expressive enough to represent all relevant aspects intuitively and comprehensively. Coincidently, the chosen modeling technique should be as restrictive as possible, thus exploiting particular structures and regularities for verification issues.

Business process nets have been defined as a special class of elementary Petri nets. Consequently, their distinguished structure is exploited in the definition of derived notions such as well formedness, usability, etc. This structure has furthermore been exploited in analysis algorithms.

One my define corresponding classes of schematic high-level Petri nets and Abstract State Machines, together with corresponding analysis algorithms.

The above outlined spectrum of modeling techniques may cover *operational* models. One my wonder what other models may be useful. An example may be *logic based models*, with Lamport's *Temporal Logic of Actions* as a typical representative. It was particularly useful in this context, would composition of specifications just turn out as conjunction, and implementation as implication. These principles have been advocated by Abadi and Lamport in the early 1990ies already.

References

1. G. Alonso, C. Casati, H. Kuno, and V. Machirajv. *Web Services*. Springer Verlag, 2004.
2. E. Börger and R. Stärk. *Abstract State Machines – A Method for High-Level System Design and Analysis*. Springer-Verlag, 2003.

3. F. Curbera, Y. Goland, J. Klein, F. Leymann, D. Roller, and S. Weerawarana. Business Process Execution Language for Web Services Version 1.1. Specification, BEA Systems, IBM, Microsoft, SAP, Siebel, 05 May 2003. http://msdn.microsoft.com/library/default.asp?url=/library/en-us/dnbiz2k2/html/bpel1-1.asp.
4. D. Fahland and W. Reisig. ASM based semantics of Web services: the negative control flow. International conference, ASM05, Paris, March 2005.
5. Y. Gurevich. Sequential Abstract-State Machines Capture Sequential Algorithms. *ACM Tranactions on Computational Logic*, Vol.1 No.1:77–111, July 2000.
6. Ekkart Kindler, Axel Martens, and Wolfgang Reisig. Inter-operability of Workflow Applications: Local Criteria for Global Soundness. In *Business Process Management*, LNCS 1806, pages 235–253, 2000.
7. Axel Martens. On Usability of Web Services. In *Proceedings of WQW 2003*, Rome, Italy, 2003. IEEE Computer Society Press.
8. Axel Martens. Analyzing Web Service based Business Processes. In *Proceedings of Intl. Conference on Fundamental Approaches to Software Engineering (FASE'05)*, Edinburgh, Scotland, April 2005. Springer-Verlag.
9. Axel Martens. Consistency between Executable and Abstract Processes. In *Proceedings of IEEE International Conference on e-Technology, e-Commerce and e-Service (EEE'05)*, Hong Kong, China, March 2005. IEEE Computer Society Press.
10. P. Massuthe and K. Schmidt. Operating guidelines – an alternative to public view. Internal report, Humboldt-Universität zu Berlin, 2005.
11. W. Reisig. *Elements of Distributed Systems*. Springer Verlag, 1997.
12. W. Reisig and A. Brade. ASM models of Web Services. Technical report, Humboldt-Universität zu Berlin, Computer Science Institute, December 2004. No. 181.
13. W. Reisig, K. Schmidt, and Chr. Stahl. Geschäftsprozesse modellieren und analysieren auf der Basis von Petri-Netzen. Technical report, Humboldt-Universität zu Berlin, Computer Science Institute, December 2004. No. 182.
14. Karsten Schmidt and Christian Stahl. A Petri net Semantic for BPEL4WS - Validation and Application. In Ekkart Kindler, editor, *Proceedings of the 11th Workshop on Algorithms and Tools for Petri Nets (AWPN'04)*, pages 1–6. Universität Paderborn, October 2004.
15. W.M.P. van der Aalst. Structural Characterization of Sound Workflow Nets. Technical report, Eindhoven University of Technology, Dept. of Mathematics and Computing Science, 1996. Computing Science Report 96/23.
16. W.M.P. van der Aalst. The Application of Petri Nets to Workflow Management. *Journal of Circuits, Systems, and Computers*, 8(1):21–66, 1998.
17. W3C. Web Services Architecture Requirements. Working group note, W3C, October 2002. http://www.w3.org/TR/wsa-reqs/.

A Distributed Implementation
of Mobile Nets as Mobile Agents

Nadia Busi and Luca Padovani

University of Bologna, Department of Computer Science
Mura Anteo Zamboni 7, 40127 Bologna, Italy
{busi,lpadovan}@cs.unibo.it

Abstract. Mobile nets arise as a combination of the name managing techniques of the π-calculus with the representation of concurrency and locality of Petri nets. We propose MAGNETs, a variant of mobile nets that are suitable for an effective, distributed implementation. Such implementation extends an implementation of the Join calculus virtual machine with dynamic reconfiguration features.

1 Introduction

Service Oriented Computing is an emerging paradigm for developing autonomous computational elements in a wide-area, distributed setting. Web Services provide an important instantiation of such paradigm, and are supported by a number of standardized technologies for specifying service interfaces, interaction between services, service discovery, service composition and orchestration.

In this context, a variety of languages and infrastructures for Web Services have been recently proposed by leading consortia of industries and organizations. However, before the Service Oriented Computer paradigm becomes reality, there is a number of challenging issues that need to be addressed, including a formal framework for the rigorous specification of their semantics, as well as prototype implementations.

Petri nets [16] and the π-calculus [15] are the most prominent candidates for the definition of a formal semantics of Web Services infrastructures [1].

Petri nets are a widespread formalism for the representation of the behavior of concurrent systems. Since their introduction, they have been deeply studied, providing a variety of analysis techniques and making them suitable for industry applications. However, they fall short in modelling the dynamic features arising in systems for Service Oriented Computing: these systems are characterized by an evolving structure, where both the number of the involved components and the links between them may change during the computation. The π-calculus [15] has been specifically introduced to deal with dynamically evolving systems: dynamicity is achieved by means of transmission of channel names, in combination with a name scoping mechanism. A modeling weakness of the π-calculus is the lack of support for advanced synchronization patterns, for which Petri nets provide a direct, natural representation [1].

Mobile nets [2, 7] arise as an attempt to combine Petri nets with the name managing techniques of the π-calculus, yielding a formalism that is suitable to modelling systems with an evolving structure, while retaining the natural representation of concurrency and locality typical of Petri nets.

M. Steffen and G. Zavattaro (Eds.): FMOODS 2005, LNCS 3535, pp. 259–274, 2005.

From a practical point of view, both the π-calculus and Petri nets (hence Mobile nets also) exhibit complex conflict and contact situations that hinder an effective distributed implementation. In the context of mobile calculi, the Join calculus [9] solves this problem by providing a local management of conflicting reaction rules.

The aim of this paper is to provide MAGNETs, a variant of Mobile nets that is suitable for a distributed implementation. The peculiar properties of MAGNETs are the following: we prevent the need to resolve distributed conflicts by enforcing locality of transition guards in the model, and we enable a constrained form of mobility that preserves the locality property. We support the effectiveness of MAGNETs by providing a distributed implementation, which is based on an enhancement of the Join calculus virtual machine developed in [17].

The paper is organized as follows: in the next section we present an informal overview of MAGNETs; the syntax and the semantics are presented in Section 3; the features of these nets are further explored by two examples in Section 4, while the distributed implementation is described in Section 5. We conclude with a comparison of related literature.

2   An Overview of MAGNETs

A system is modeled as a dynamic pool of net systems, each net system being essentially a mobile net. The pool is dynamic in the sense that new net systems may be created during the computation. Each net system is a triple with three components: a set of *places*, a set of *transitions*, and a *marking*. As for classical Petri nets, the marking, i.e., the distribution of tokens in the places, represents the current state of the system, and the system evolution is represented by firing, i.e., execution of the transitions.

Tokens coloring. As in Colored Petri Nets [11], tokens carry information; the "color" of a token is a (possibly empty) tuple of (place) names, either referring to local places of the nets or to remote places, belonging to another net of the configuration. The main differences between Mobile Nets and classical and Colored Petri Nets regard transitions, whose key features are listed below.

Local versus remote tokens. A transition can produce tokens for local places (places belonging to the net system where the transition resides) as well as for remote places (places belonging to a different net system). Consider the configuration $C_1 = N_a, N_b$, consisting of two mobile nets N_a and N_b, which are defined as follows:

$$N_a = [\{a_1, a_2\}, \{a_1 \mapsto a_2 b_1\}, a_1]$$
$$N_b = [\{b_1, b_2, b_3\}, \{b_1 \mapsto b_2, b_2 \mapsto b_3 a_1\}, b_3 b_3]$$

The net N_a consists of two places, a_1 and a_2, a transition $a_1 \mapsto a_2 b_1$ and an initial marking containing one uncolored token (or, equivalently, colored with the empty tuple) in place a_1. The net N_b consists of three places, two transitions, and an initial marking with two tokens in place b_3. The transition $t_a = a_1 \mapsto a_2 b_1$ in N_a is enabled in the current marking of N_a: when t fires, the token in a_1 is consumed, and two new tokens are produced: one is produced locally in place a_2 whereas the other is a token for the remote place b_1, belonging to N_b. When the token b_1 reaches the net N_b, the transition $t_b = b_1 \mapsto b_2$ becomes enabled (whereas the other transition of N_b, $t_b' = b_2 \mapsto b_3 a_1$, is still disabled); transition t_b has only a local effect on the marking of N_b, whereas transition t_b' also produces a token for a remote place of net N_1.

Mobility. Besides being used to determine the color of the tokens produced by a transition – as in colored nets – the color of the tokens consumed by a transition can be used to determine the place where the transition puts the produced tokens. Consider the configuration $C_2 = N_a, N_b$, consisting of the following nets:

$$N_a = [\{a_1, a_2\}, \{a_1(x) \mapsto x\langle b_2\rangle\}, a_1\langle a_2\rangle a_1\langle b_1\rangle]$$
$$N_b = [\{b_1, b_2\}, \{b_1(x) \mapsto b_2\langle x\rangle\}, \emptyset]$$

The marking of N_a contains the tokens $a_1\langle a_2\rangle$ and $a_1\langle b_1\rangle$, hence the transition $t_a = a_1(x) \mapsto x\langle b_2\rangle$ can consume either the token $a_1\langle a_2\rangle$, thus producing a local token $a_2\langle b_2\rangle$ (i.e., a token colored with b_2 in the local place a_1), or it can consume the token $a_1\langle b_1\rangle$, thus producing a remote token $b_1\langle b_2\rangle$ for the net N_b.

Dynamicity. The last key feature of MAGNETs regards their dynamicity: not only the marking, but also the structure of the mobile nets may vary during the computation. A change in the structure of the nets is carried out by transitions: a transition can add a new transition (either to the net which it belongs to or to a remote net), or spawn a new (part of a) net. More precisely, the firing of a transition may produce either a new mobile net, or a set of places and transitions to be added to an existing net. Consider the configuration $C_3 = N_a$, where

$$N_a = [\{a_1, a_2\}, \{a_1 \mapsto \{\{b_1, b_2\}, \{b_1 \mapsto b_2 a_1\}, b_1\}, a_1]$$

When transition $t = a_1 \mapsto \{\{b_1, b_2\}, \{b_1 \mapsto b_2 a_1\}, b_1\}$ fires, the token in place a_1 is consumed and the new mobile net

$$N_b = [\{b_1, b_2\}, \{b_1 \mapsto b_2 a_1\}, b_1]$$

is added to the configuration. In other words, configuration C_3 evolves to configuration N_a', N_b, where N_a' is the evolution of net N_a after the firing of transition t, that removes token a_1 from the marking of N_a:

$$N_a' = [\{a_1, a_2\}, \{a_1 \mapsto \{\{b_1, b_2\}, \{b_1 \mapsto b_2 a_1\}, b_1\}, \emptyset]$$

Consider now the configuration $C_4 = N_a, N_c$, where

$$N_a = [\{a_1, a_2\}, \{a_1 \mapsto \{\{b_1, b_2\}, \{b_1 c_1 \mapsto b_2 a_1\}, b_1\}, a_1]$$
$$N_c = [\{c_1\}, \{c_1 \mapsto c_1\}, c_1]$$

The firing of transition $t_a = a_1 \mapsto \{\{b_1, b_2\}, \{b_1 c_1 \mapsto b_2 a_1\}, b_1\}$ produces a so called pre–net $N = \{\{b_1, b_2\}, \{b_1 c_1 \mapsto b_2 a_1\}, b_1\}$; such a pre–net has a transition $t_b = b_1 c_1 \mapsto b_2 a_1$ whose pattern contains both a place of the pre–net and a place of the existing net N_c; hence, the places and the transitions of the pre–net N will be added to the net N_c. The configuration C_4 evolves to the configuration N_a', N_c', where N_a' is obtained from N_a by removing the consumed token a_1, and N_c' is obtained from N_c by adding the places, transitions and tokens in the pre–net N:

$$N_a = [\{a_1, a_2\}, \{a_1 \mapsto \{\{b_1, b_2\}, \{b_1c_1 \mapsto b_2a_1\}, b_1\}, \emptyset]$$
$$N_c = [\{c_1, b_1, b_2\}, \{c_1 \mapsto c_1, b_1c_1 \mapsto b_2a_1\}, c_1b_1]$$

Locality and linearity of patterns. One of the peculiar differences of MAGNETS w.r.t. the previous definitions of Mobile Nets [2, 7] consists in the locality and linearity of patterns. Patterns locality means that – given a transition $t = p \mapsto N'$ belonging to a net system $N = [S, T, m]$ – all the place names in the pattern p are local to N; in other words, each place from which transition t consumes tokens belongs to the set S of local places of the net system. This feature turns out to be crucial in the implementation of MAGNETS, as the conflict between transitions competing for the same resource can be resolved locally, with no need for an agreement between the distributed components of the system.

The behavior of a transition that produces a pre–net is driven by the locality requirement on patterns. If each transition in a pre–net $\{S', T', m'\}$ consumes tokens only from local places belonging to S', then the pre–net will evolve in a stand-alone net system (see configuration C_3 above). On the other hand, if some transition in the pre–net requires token consumption from a remote place (i.e., a place not in S'), and all the remote places occurring in patterns of transitions in T' belong to the same net system $N = [S, T, m]$, then the components of the pre–net are added to the net system N, which roughly evolves to the net system $[S \cup S', T \cup T', m \cup m']$ (see configuration C_4). If the remote places occurring in the patterns of transitions in T' belong to at least two different net systems, there is no way to add the components of the pre–net to an existing net system, while respecting the locality condition and avoiding to merge the two existing, distinct nets into a single one. In such a case, the pre–net $\{S', T', m'\}$ can neither evolve to a stand-alone net system, nor being added to an existing net system; hence, the transitions in T' will never fire and the tokens in m' will never become available. As an example, consider the configuration $C_5 = N_a, N_c$, where

$$N_a = [\{a_1, a_2\}, \{a_1 \mapsto \{\{b_1, b_2\}, \{a_1c_1 \mapsto b_2\}, a_1\}, a_1]$$
$$N_c = [\{c_1\}, \{c_1 \mapsto c_1\}, c_1]$$

When transition $t = a_1 \mapsto \{\{b_1, b_2\}, \{a_1c_1 \mapsto b_2\}, a_1\}$ fires, the following pre–net is produced:

$$\{\{b_1, b_2\}, \{a_1c_1 \mapsto b_2\}, a_1\}$$

Note that, for transition $u = a_1c_1 \mapsto b_2$ to fire, both a token from place a_1 of the net N_a and a token from place c_1 of net N_c are necessary. Hence, such a pre–net will never evolve to a (part of a) net system.

Pattern linearity requires that the bound names in a pattern are pairwise different. Linearity simplifies the implementation of the firability check for a transition; for linear patterns, this check can be carried out independently on each place in the pattern. Consider the transition $a(x)b(y) \mapsto c\langle x, y \rangle$: the firability check consists in looking for a token in place a and a token in place b (both colored with a single place name). On the other hand, if we consider the nonlinear pattern of transition $a(x)b(x) \mapsto c\langle x, y\rangle$, the firability check becomes more involved, as it amounts to finding two tokens, one in place a and the other one in place b, with the *same* color.

3 Syntax and Semantics

We start with some auxiliary definitions. The names for the places in the nets are taken from a denumerable set. Markings and quasi–patterns are essentially multisets: a marking represents the distribution and the color of tokens in the places of a net, whereas quasi–patterns are an auxiliary notion useful for defining patterns: a pattern is a quasi–pattern for which the linearity condition holds.

Definition 1. *Let S be a denumerable set of place names; $s, s', \ldots, a, b, \ldots, x, y, \ldots$ range over S, while S, S' range over sets of place names. Let S^* be the set of sequences over S; $\bar{s}, \bar{s}' \ldots, \bar{a}, \bar{b}, \ldots, \bar{x}, \bar{y}, \ldots$ range over S^*.*
A quasi–pattern is generated by the following grammar:

$$p ::= a(\bar{x}) \mid p \oplus p$$

A marking is generated by the following grammar:

$$m ::= \emptyset \mid a\langle\bar{b}\rangle \mid m \oplus m$$

The definition of linearity requires a definition of the *bound* names occurring in a quasi–pattern:

Definition 2. *The set of bound names in quasi–patterns is defined as follows:*

$$bn(a(x_1 \ldots x_n)) = \{x_1, \ldots, x_n\}$$
$$bn(p \oplus p') = bn(p) \cup bn(p')$$

The set of linear quasi–patterns is the least set satisfying the following conditions:

- $a(x_1 \ldots x_n)$ *is a linear quasi–pattern if $\forall 1 \le i, j \le n$: $x_i = x_j$ implies $i = j$;*
- $p \oplus p'$ *is a linear quasi–pattern if p and p' are linear quasi–patterns and $bn(p) \cap bn(p') = \emptyset$.*

We are now ready to introduce the main notions of MAGNETs: patterns, transitions, net expressions, net systems and configurations. A transition is a pair composed by a pattern – specifying the tokens to be consumed – and a net expression – specifying the tokens and the new components that are produced when the transition fires. A net expression is essentially a multiset, whose elements are tokens, transitions, and pre-nets. A net system represents a single component of the system; a net system is a triple composed by the set of local places, the set of transitions and the current marking of the local places. A (system) configuration represents the distributed system, and consists of a multiset of net systems.

Definition 3. *A pattern is a quasi–pattern that is linear. A transition has the form $t ::= p \mapsto N$ where p is a pattern and N is a net expression. We use $T, T', \ldots$ to range over sets of transitions. A net expression is generated by the following grammar:*

$$
\begin{array}{lll}
N ::= & \emptyset & \text{the empty net} \\
\mid & a\langle \bar{b} \rangle & \text{a token} \\
\mid & t & \text{a transition} \\
\mid & \{S, T, m\} & \text{a pre–net} \\
\mid & N \oplus N & \text{a composition of nets}
\end{array}
$$

A net system *is a triple $[S, T, m]$, where S is the set of places of the net, T is the set of transitions and m is the current marking. A* system configuration *is generated by the following grammar:*

$$
C ::= [S, T, m] \mid N \mid C \oplus C
$$

The notions of bound (bn) and free (fn) names occurring in (components of) configurations are as usual and we omit them here for brevity. The set of *place names* in a pattern is the set of places from which the pattern consumes tokens. The set of place names in a marking is the set of places that are not empty in such a marking. Finally, the set of place names in the preset of a transition is the set of places from which the transition consumes tokens, i.e., is the set of place names in the pattern of the transition.

Definition 4. *The set of place names in patterns and markings is defined as follows:*

$$
\begin{array}{ll}
places(a(\bar{x})) = \{a\} & places(\emptyset) = \emptyset \\
places(p \oplus p') = places(p) & places(a\langle b \rangle) = \{a\} \\
\qquad \cup\, places(p') & places(m \oplus m') = places(m) \\
& \qquad \cup\, places(m')
\end{array}
$$

The set of place names in the preset of a transition (of a set of transitions) is

$$
pre(p \mapsto N) = places(p) \qquad pre(T) = \cup_{t \in T} pre(t)
$$

To lighten the definition of the semantics, we reason up to the structural congruence $\equiv$, defined as the least congruence satisfying the commutative monoidal laws for the (overloaded) composition operator $\oplus$.

Definition 5. *Let $\equiv$ be the least congruence over configurations (net expressions, patterns, markings) satisfying the following axioms:*

$$
C \oplus \emptyset \equiv C \qquad C \oplus C' \equiv C' \oplus C \qquad C \oplus (C' \oplus C'') \equiv (C \oplus C') \oplus C''
$$

To lighten the notation, we usually drop the composition operator. E.g., $a(x)\, b(y)$ denotes $a(x) \oplus b(y)$. We also drop the token color, if this is the empty tuple. E.g., $ab(\bar{y})$ denotes $a()b(\bar{y})$, and abb denotes $a\langle\rangle b\langle\rangle b\langle\rangle$.

We introduce a notion of *well–formedness* for net systems and configurations; this notion is needed for a correct definition of the semantics. The set of places of a net system consists of the places that are managed locally in the net, i.e., the tokens in such places are consumed only by local transitions. Thus, a net system $[S, T, m]$ is well–formed if all the tokens in its marking and the place names in its transitions belong to the set of places S. A configuration is well–formed if its net system components are well–formed, the set of places in its components are pairwise disjoint, and all the free place names occurring in tokens, transitions or pre–nets that are moving towards their destination are names occurring in the set of places of some component. Well–formedness of configurations ensures that each place in the configuration is managed by a unique net system; hence, the destination of a remote token, transition or pre–net is uniquely determined.

Definition 6. *A net system $[S, T, m]$ is* well–formed *if $places(m) \subseteq S$ and $pre(T) \subseteq S$. A system configuration C is* well–formed *if $C \equiv N \oplus \bigoplus_{i=1}^{k} [S_i, T_i, m_i]$, and the following conditions are satisfied:*

- $\forall i : 1 \leq i \leq k \Rightarrow [S_i, T_i, m_i]$ *is well–formed, and*
- $S_i \cap S_j = \emptyset$ *for $1 \leq i, j \leq k$, $i \neq j$, and*
- $fn(N) \subseteq \bigoplus_{i=1}^{k} S_i$

In the following, we assume that the net systems and the configurations we deal with are well–formed.

We recall the standard notion of substitution, that will be used in the semantics:

Definition 7. *A substitution ρ on S is a partial function from S to S with finite domain (i.e., the set $dom(\rho) = \{x \mid \exists y : (x, y) \in \rho\}$ is finite).*

We say that a substitution ρ is applicable *to a net expression if, for all $x \in dom(\rho)$, each free occurrence of x in the expression does not lie within the scope of a binder $\rho(x)$. If ρ is applicable to a net expression N, then the application of ρ to the expression N – notation $N\rho$ – is obtained from N by simultaneous substitution of each free occurrence of x with $\rho(x)$, for all $x \in dom(\rho)$. Before performing a substitution, it may be necessary to perform alpha conversion to satisfy the applicability condition.*

We use the notation $\{x/y\}$ as a shorthand for the substitution $\{(x, y)\}$.

To define the firing rule, we need the following definitions. A pattern instantiation for a pattern is a substitution that renames the bound names of the pattern (i.e., the placeholders for token colors). An instance of a pattern is a multiset satisfying the requirements specified by the patterns, i.e., containing the exact number of tokens, and such tokens are decorated with a tuple of the right length.

Definition 8. *A pattern instantiation for a pattern p is a substitution ρ on S such that $dom(\rho) = bn(p)$. The instance of p via ρ, denoted by $p[\rho]$ is the marking defined as*

$$a(x_1 \ldots x_n)[\rho] = a\langle \rho(x_1) \ldots \rho(x_n) \rangle$$
$$(p \oplus p')[\rho] = p[\rho] \oplus p'[\rho] .$$

For example, the substitution $\rho = \{a/x, b/y, b/z\}$ is a pattern instantiation for pattern $p = c(x, y)d(z)$, and $c\langle a, b \rangle d\langle b \rangle$ is the instance of p via ρ.

Now we are ready to define the semantics of configurations. The reduction relation is the least relation satisfying the axioms and rules reported in Table 1.

Table 1. Operational semantics of MAGNETs.

$$(1) \quad \frac{p \to N \in T}{[S,T,m \oplus p[\rho]] \to [S,T,m] \oplus N\rho} \qquad (2) \quad \frac{s \in S}{[S,T,m] \oplus s\langle \bar{s} \rangle \to [S,T,m \oplus s\langle s \rangle]}$$

$$(3) \quad \frac{places(p) \subseteq S}{[S,T,m] \oplus (p \mapsto N) \to [S,T \cup (p \mapsto N), m]}$$

$$(4) \quad \frac{S \text{ fresh} \wedge \forall t \in T \forall s \in S : s \in pre(t) \Rightarrow pre(t) \subseteq S}{\{S,T,m\} \to [S,\emptyset,\emptyset] \oplus T \oplus m}$$

$$(5) \quad \frac{S \text{ fresh} \wedge pre(T) \cap S' \neq \emptyset \wedge \forall t \in T \forall s \in S : s \in pre(t) \Rightarrow pre(t) \subseteq S \cup S'}{\{S,T,m\} \oplus [S',T',m'] \to [S \cup S',T',m'] \oplus T \oplus m}$$

$$(6) \quad \frac{C \to C'}{C \oplus C'' \to C' \oplus C''} \qquad (7) \quad \frac{C \equiv C' \quad C' \to C'' \quad C'' \equiv C'''}{C \to C'''}$$

Firing rule (1). If the marking of a net system contains the tokens required by the pattern of a transition $t = p \mapsto N$ (i.e., there exists a pattern instantiation such that the instance p is contained in the marking) then the transition is enabled. When t fires, the tokens required by the pattern are removed from the marking, and the (tokens, transitions and pre–nets contained in the) net expression $N\rho$, obtained by application of the pattern instantiation to N, is produced. All the components of the net expression are treated in the same way, regardless whether they are local (i.e., belong to the net system of transition t) or remote. The components will reach the net system to which they belong by axioms (2) and (3)[1].

Token and transition migration (2,3). The tokens, as well as the new transitions, produced by a firing of a transition reach the proper net system by application of this reduction.

Net creation (4). If the environment contains a pre–net whose transitions consume tokens only from places local to the pre–net, then such a prenet evolves in a new net system. The transitions and the marking of the pre–net are produced in the environment, as they may refer to another, already existing net system. Such components will reach the right net system by axioms (2) and (3). The freshness condition on the set of places of the pre–net, that can be enforced by performing alpha conversion, ensures the well–formedness of the reached configuration. The condition $\forall t \in T \forall s \in S : s \in pre(t) \Rightarrow pre(t) \subseteq S$ requires that all the transitions that will be local to the newly created net

---

[1] An alternative, equivalent semantics for the firing rule consists in partitioning the components of the net expression in two sets: the components that must be added to the net system of transition t, and those that must migrate to a remote net system. Then, the local components are directly added to the net system, while the remote components are released in the environment. This alternative semantics is closer to the implementation, while our choice provides a simpler rule.

do not consume tokens from remote places belonging to other existing nets. However, the pre–net may contain a transition u consuming all its token from places of another existing net; this is permitted, as the transition u will migrate to the proper net system after creation of the new net.

Net extension (5). If the transitions of a pre–net consume tokens from places of an already existing net system, then the components of the pre–net are added to the net system. The condition $pre(T) \cap S' \neq \emptyset$ requires that at least one transition in the pre–net consumes a token from a place of an existing net system (otherwise, the pre–net evolves in a new, independent net system by axiom (4)). The condition $\forall t \in T \forall s \in S :$ $s \in pre(t) \Rightarrow pre(t) \subseteq S \cup S'$ requires that all the transitions, that will be local to the net obtained by adding the pre–net to the existing net system, do not consume tokens from remote places.

Composition (6). This rule permits the application of the axioms independently of the presence of other components in the configuration.

Structural congruence (7). Structurally congruent configurations behave equivalently.

The following proposition ensures that the well-formedness is preserved by the structural congruence relation and by the reduction semantics.

Proposition 1. *Let C be a well–formed configuration. If $C \equiv C'$, then C' is a well–formed configuration. If $C \rightarrow C'$, then C' is a well–formed configuration.*

4 Examples

4.1 Applet

In the first example we model the execution of some code *à la Java*, where an *applet* is downloaded from a server, and the computation occurs in the client:

$$Client = [\{runHere\}, \ldots, appletX \langle runHere \rangle runHere]$$
$$Server = [\{appletX\}, \{appletX(run) \mapsto \{\emptyset, \{run \mapsto \ldots\}, \emptyset\}\}, \emptyset]$$

The applet download is triggered by a token in place *appletX*. The token carries the client's location in its color (*runHere*). The applet code, which is contained in the spawned pre–net, is executed after the applet has migrated to the client.

4.2 Web Service Generation

The second example models a scenario in which some Web Services are generated from the corresponding factories. The idea in this case is that some services may be computationally too expensive to be carried over the server side. Instead, the Web Service is forked off its origin site and migrates to the client, where the computation occurs. A *service factory* is a net system with a transition expecting two place names *in* and *out* representing the place where the service expects its input and the place where the result

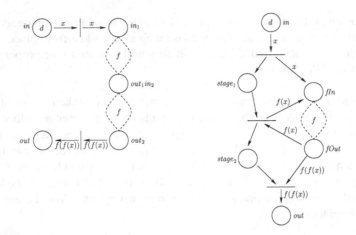

Fig. 1. Two different ways of combining services for computing $f \circ f$.

will be produced, once the computation is finished. These two places will usually be local to the client, thus forcing the generated service to move.

The following are service factories for the x^2 and $\sin x$ functions:

$$[\{squareFactory\}, \{squareFactory(in, out) \mapsto$$
$$\{\{tmp\}, \{in(x) \mapsto tmp\langle \ldots x \ldots \rangle, tmp(y) \mapsto out\langle \ldots y \ldots \rangle\}, \emptyset\}\}, \emptyset]$$

$$[\{sinFactory\}, \{sinFactory(in, out) \mapsto \{\emptyset, \{in(x) \mapsto out\langle \ldots x \ldots \rangle\}, \emptyset\}\}, \emptyset]$$

Next we show how to model a second-order Web Service generator *twiceFactory* which, given a service factory for a generic function f, generates a service for the function $f \circ f$. In fact, there are at least two possible ways for modelling *twiceFactory*. In the first solution, the factory for f is invoked twice, and the two services are sequentially composed by means of a common place $out_1 in_2$ (left hand side of Figure 1):

$$[\{twiceFactory_1\},$$
$$\{twiceFactory_1(in, out, fFactory) \mapsto \{ \{in_1, out_1 in_2, out_2\},$$
$$\{in(x) \mapsto in_1\langle x \rangle, out_2(x) \mapsto out\langle x \rangle\},$$
$$fFactory\langle in_1, out_1 in_2 \rangle$$
$$fFactory\langle out_1 in_2, out_2 \rangle\}, \emptyset]$$

In the second solution the factory for f is invoked only once, and the iterated application is enforced by means of an appropriate control flow in the generated service (right hand side of Figure 1):

$$[\{twiceFactory_2\},$$
$$\{twiceFactory_2(in, out, fFactory) \mapsto \{ \{fIn, fOut, stage_1, stage_2\},$$
$$\{in(x) \mapsto stage_1 \, fIn\langle x \rangle,$$
$$stage_1 \, fOut(r_1) \mapsto stage_2 \, fIn\langle r_1 \rangle,$$
$$stage_2 \, fOut(r_2) \mapsto out\langle r_2 \rangle\},$$
$$fFactory\langle fIn, fOut \rangle\}, \emptyset]$$

Roughly speaking, the two solutions resemble the differences between function in-lining and function call.

The following is a possible invocation of $twiceFactory_1$ with the $squareFactory$ service, which yields a service for the computation of the x^4 function:

$$[\{in, out\}, \emptyset, twiceFactory_1 \langle in, out, squareFactory \rangle]$$

5   Implementation

Entities in the formal model and their representation in the implementation have been purposefully given different names: not every entity in the implementation is paired with an entity in the abstract model, or the correspondence is only approximate.

5.1   Overall Organization of the Virtual Machine

The *virtual machine* that implements MAGNETs consists of the following kinds of objects.

Locations.   Locations represent nets: the name "location" enforces the idea of a well-defined boundary that discriminates what is part of a net from what is not. Each location consists of a set of *ports*, representing places, a set of *rules*, representing transitions, and a set of running *threads*, representing ongoing computations. *Migration* of locations is controlled by the move instruction. Location handles have type *lid*.

Threads.   Threads represent units of sequential computation within a location. As such, threads have no direct counterpart in the formal model. One can think of a thread as a sequence of actions implementing the semantics associated with a transition, once this has fired. A thread is made of

- a *code segment*, containing the list of virtual machine instructions to be executed;
- a *data segment*, containing the associations between names occurring in the thread and values;
- a *stack*, used for storing temporary data.

Thread handles have type *tid*.

Rules.   Rules represent transitions. Each rule depends on a multiset of ports indicating the incoming transition arcs and has an associated blocked thread. Upon firing of the transition, the thread is spawned and its data segment enriched with the newly determined associations between names and values received from the ports.

Ports.   Ports represent places. Each port has an associated queue of messages and has references to all the rules which depend upon it. Port handles have type *pid* and are made of the identifier of the location the port resides in, and a hidden, local port identifier.

Messages. Messages represent tokens. Messages can be sent to any known port, regardless of the location the port resides in.

5.2 Virtual Machine Instructions

The virtual machine is stack-based: every instruction takes its operands and produces results on a stack, just like the Java virtual machine does. Values of the virtual machine include port, thread, and location handles, as well as native data types (not shown for the sake of brevity). Table 2 lists the instructions of the virtual machine, as well as their signature specifying how the instruction manipulates the stack. The notation $x :: S$ represents a stack whose topmost value is x and where the stack underneath x is S.

Table 2. Instructions of the virtual machine.

Instruction	Stack before	Stack after
port	S	$pid :: S$
thread(n) c	$x_1 :: \cdots :: x_n :: S$	$tid :: S$
rule(n)	$tid :: pid_1 :: \cdots :: pid_n :: S$	S
location	S	$lid :: S$
send(n)	$pid :: x_1 :: \cdots :: x_n :: S$	S
spawn	$lid :: tid :: S$	S
load(n)	S	$x :: S$
store(n)	$x :: S$	S
whereis	$pid :: S$	$lid :: S$
move	$lid :: S$	S

What follows is an informal description of the semantics of the instructions. When talking about the values consumed or produced by instructions of the virtual machine, we will usually say "port" instead of "port handle". We will abuse the language similarly when referring to locations and threads. We will say "current thread" for the thread executing the instruction and "current location" for the location where the current thread is running:

port creates a new port in the current location. The port handle is pushed onto the stack;

thread(n) c creates a new thread, without executing it. The thread's code segment is c (a list of instructions), its environment is made of the x_i's vales on the stack ($i = 1, \ldots, n$). The thread handle is pushed onto the stack;

rule(n) creates a new rule in the current location involving the n ports on the stack. As soon as there is at least one message in the queue of each of the n ports, the specified thread is spawned;

location creates a new, empty location as a child of the current location. The new location is pushed onto the stack;

send(n) sends a tuple of n values to the port on the stack;

spawn causes the specified thread to be spawned in the specified location, which must be either an ancestor of the current location, or the current location itself;

load(x) pushes the value associated with the name x in the data segment onto the stack;
store(x) associates the name x with the topmost value on the stack;
whereis pops a port from the stack and pushes the port's location onto the stack;
move causes the current location to migrate inside location found on top of the stack.

5.3 Compiling MAGNETs

We now show the compilation rules for MAGNETs, that is how a net in the formal
model is translated into instructions of the virtual machine. For the sake of brevity,
only the most significant rules are presented here. We denote lists of instructions as
$[i_1; i_2; \ldots; i_n]$ and we use @ for the usual append operation over lists.

A marking is compiled as a message communication. The names to be sent as well
as the destination port are pushed onto the stack, and then the send instruction is executed:

$$[\![x\langle y_1, \ldots, y_n\rangle]\!] = [\mathsf{load}(y_n); \ldots; \mathsf{load}(y_1); \mathsf{load}(x); \mathsf{send}(n)]$$

Message communication is asynchronous, that is the send instruction is nonblocking.

A transition $p \mapsto N$ is compiled as a rule that associates the places in the pattern
$places(p)$ with a thread that "implements" N. In order to create such thread, any free
name occurring in N and that is not bound by p must be loaded onto the stack, so that
an appropriate closure is created. Let $\{z_1, \ldots, z_k\} = fn(N) \setminus bn(p)$, we have

$$[\![x_1(\overline{y_1}), \ldots, x_n(\overline{y_n}) \mapsto N]\!] =$$
$$[\mathsf{load}(x_n); \ldots; \mathsf{load}(x_1); \mathsf{load}(z_k); \ldots; \mathsf{load}(z_1); \mathsf{thread}(k) \, [\![N]\!]; \mathsf{rule}(n)]$$

It is an error to create a rule for a pattern including ports that are not local to the
current location. If this situation occurs, the current location "dies".

Consider now a prenet $\{S, T, m\}$ such that $pre(T) \subseteq S$. This net is unrelated to
any other net since its set of transitions only involve ports that are locally defined. The
net is represented as a fresh location within which an initialization thread is spawn. The
thread creates the ports in S, stores them in its data segment, creates the rules for the
transitions in T and finally sets the places with the initial marking. Let $\{z_1, \ldots, z_l\} =
fn(\{S, T, m\})$, we have

$$[\![\{\{x_1, \ldots, x_n\}, \{t_1, \ldots, t_k\}, m\}]\!] =$$
$$[\mathsf{load}(z_l); \ldots; \mathsf{load}(z_1);$$
$$\mathsf{thread}(l) \, [\mathsf{port}; \mathsf{store}(x_1); \ldots; \mathsf{port}; \mathsf{store}(x_n)]@[\![t_1]\!]@ \cdots @[\![t_k]\!]@[\![m]\!];$$
$$\mathsf{location}; \mathsf{spawn}]$$

The last interesting case we examine is that of a net extension, that is a prenet
$\{S, T, m\}$ connected with an existing net. This condition is formally specified as $S \subsetneq
pre(T)$, or equivalently there exists a place $z \in pre(T) \setminus S$ that belongs to a different
net. As in the case of a standalone net, a fresh location is created. However, this location must first migrate into the location owning z. Once it has reached z's location, a
new locally spawned thread takes care of creating the new rules. Let $\{y_1, \ldots, y_l\} =
fn(\{S, T, m\})$, we have

$$\llbracket \{\{x_1, \ldots, x_n\}, \{t_1, \ldots, t_k\}, m\} \rrbracket =$$
$$[\mathsf{load}(y_l); \ldots; \mathsf{load}(y_1); \mathsf{thread}(l)$$
$$[\mathsf{load}(z); \mathsf{whereis}; \mathsf{move}; \mathsf{load}(y_l); \ldots; \mathsf{load}(y_1); \mathsf{thread}(l)$$
$$[\mathsf{port}; \mathsf{store}(x_1); \ldots; \mathsf{port}; \mathsf{store}(x_n)]@\llbracket t_1 \rrbracket @ \cdots @ \llbracket t_k \rrbracket @ \llbracket m \rrbracket;$$
$$\mathsf{load}(z); \mathsf{whereis}; \mathsf{spawn}];$$
$$\mathsf{location}; \mathsf{spawn}]$$

Finally, the composition of two nets N_1 and N_2 simply amounts at appending the code resulting from compiling N_1 and N_2 in isolation:

$$\llbracket N_1 \oplus N_2 \rrbracket = \llbracket N_1 \rrbracket @ \llbracket N_2 \rrbracket$$

5.4   Remarks

Synchronous communication. As it is stated, the formal model imposes a continuation-passing style arrangement of any sequential computation. As this imposes a considerable overhead in terms of both time and resource consumption (the creation of several temporary, short-living ports), we have enriched the actual implementation with primitive instructions for synchronous communication. Each thread is equipped with a *continuation port* that is used any time synchronization is required. The model syntax can be consequently enriched so as to provide a more comfortable (and familiar) programming framework for MAGNETs.

Rule matching. No mention has been made to the technicalities of pattern matching compilation but a number of optimizations can improve the naive algorithm that checks every rule upon reception of a message (see [14]). We briefly introduce two of them:
Simple port optimization. A *simple port* is a port occurring alone in one pattern only. Roughly speaking, such a place denotes a function as it is normally understood in conventional, sequential programming languages and the action of "firing" corresponds to function application. In this case, no pattern matching is actually necessary, and "firing" can be optimized to a real function call.
Static analysis of net configuration. Places whose names are not communicated outside the net where they reside can undergo a number of optimizations, since their interaction with other places is statically determined by the net configuration. In these cases, some places might be better represented as "net data", possibly protected by a locking mechanism that preserves atomic access.

Migration. The move instruction is by far the most unusual instruction in the virtual machine. One might argue that the compilation rules we have presented do not highlight sufficiently the complexity that underlies migration. Although the implementation of the move instruction indeed raises lots of technical issues, in particular the marshalling and unmarshalling of information, according to the experience gained from our development we can state that the main difficulty of mobile computation is not mobility *per se*. As soon as we have a neat definition of the boundaries of what we want to move, it does not make a great difference whether we move data, or code, or working environments.

Message routing. As locations migrate, the physical location of ports therein contained changes over time. In our implementation, each instance of the virtual machine keeps track of outgoing migrations. When a message is received for a port hosted in a location that has moved, the virtual machine does two things: first, it forwards the message to the site where the location has migrated to, thus ensuring that the message is eventually delivered; second, it notifies the sender with the new physical location of the destination port, so that subsequent communications can be direct and no routing is necessary.

6 Conclusion

MAGNETs are a formal model for the representation of systems with an evolving structure, suitable for a distributed implementation.

In the last years several extensions of Petri nets, dealing with mobility and/or dynamicity, have been proposed. Most of these extensions are devoted to adding object-oriented features on top of (colored) Petri nets (see e.g. [4, 6, 8, 12, 13, 18]): the object structure is represented through a net, and dynamic reconfiguration features are obtained by some mechanism external to the net. There are two main differences w.r.t. our approach: first, our model lies at a lower level of abstraction, because the object-oriented features are not embedded in MAGNETs, but they need to be encoded; second, our aim is to embody dynamicity in our model, not to add it by an external structure.

Some recent extensions are devoted to the modeling of mobile agents in the so called *nets-within-nets* approach [5, 10, 20–22]: mobile agents are modeled as nets that move inside an environment, represented by a net. The two main differences w.r.t. MAGNETs are concerned with the technique adopted to obtain mobility and dynamicity. While MAGNETs borrows the name managing techniques of mobile process calculi, in the nets-within-nets approach mobility and dynamicity are achieved through an higher-order technique: namely, the tokens of the "environment" net are themselves nets. The extension of MAGNETs with higher-order features is a challenging endeavor, for which we plan further investigation.

Another extension, which is closer to the spirit of our model, is given by Self Modifying Nets [19]; in this case, the main difference regards the "locality" of transitions: while in Self Modifying nets the pre and post sets of a transition depend on the whole marking of the net, in MAGNETs they depend only on the color of the consumed tokens.

Finally, we should remark the close relationship between MAGNETs and the Join calculus [9]. MAGNETs extend the Join calculus by allowing join definitions (reaction sites in the CHAM) to evolve at runtime, still preserving the locality constraints, and by having a weaker notion of pattern linearity. Another difference is given by the definition of the boundaries that mark a mobile agent. In the Join calculus with mobile agents there is an explicit notion of *named location*, and locations move by means of a primitive go operation of the formal model. In MAGNETs, there is no need to define such primitive operation, nor there is any need to give nets a name. Migration occurs transparently depending on the use of remote place names. To cope with these differences the implementation of the Join calculus with mobile agents presented in [17] has been suitably adapted.

References

1. W. M. P. van der Aalst, "Pi calculus versus Petri nets: Let us eat "humble pie" rather than further inflate the "Pi hype".
   http://tmitwww.tm.tue.nl/staff/wvdaalst/pi-hype.pdf
2. A. Asperti, N. Busi, "Mobile Petri Nets", Technical Report UBLCS-96-10, dept. of Computer Science, University of Bologna, Italy, 1996.
3. C. Fournet, G. Gonthier, J.-J. Levy, L. Maranget, D. Remy, "A Calculus of Mobile Agents", Proceedings of the 7th International Conference on Concurrency Theory (CONCUR'96)
4. E. Battiston, A. Chizzoni, F. De Cindio, "Inheritance and Concurrency in CLOWN", First Workshop on Object-Oriented Programming and Models of Concurrency, June 1995.
5. M. A. Bednarczyk, L. Bernardinello, W. Pawłowski, L. Pomello, "Modelling mobility with Petri hypernets", in Proc. WADT 2004, LNCS, Springer, to appear.
6. D. Buchs, N. Guelfi, "CO-OPN: a concurrent object-oriented Petri nets approach" , in Proc. 12th Int. Conf. on Appl. and Theory of Petri Nets, Gjern, June 1991.
7. N. Busi. "Mobile Nets", in Proc. FMOODS'99, Kluwer, 1999.
8. J. Engelfriet, G. Leih, G. Rozenberg, "Net based description of parallel object-based systems, or POTs and POPs", LNCS 489, pp.229-273, Springer , 1991.
9. C. Fournet, G. Gonthier, "The reflexive CHAM and the Join calculus", POPL'96, 1996.
10. M. Köhler, D. Moldt, H. Rölke, "Modelling mobility and mobile agents using nets within nets", in Proc. ICATPN 2003, LNCS 2679, Springer, 2003.
11. K. Jensen. "Coloured Petri Nets", EATCS Monographs in Computer Science, Springer, 1992.
12. C. A. Lakos, "Object Petri Nets – Definition and Relationship to Coloured Nets", Technical Report TR94-3, Computer Science Department, University of Tasmania, 1994.
13. C. A. Lakos, "From Coloured Petri Nets to Object Petri Nets", in Proc. 16th Int. Conf. on Appl. and Theory of Petri Nets, LNCS 935, pp. 278-297, Springer Verlag, Turin, Italy, 1995.
14. L. Maranget, F. le Fessant, "Compiling Join Patterns", HLCL '98, volume 16(3) of Electronic Notes in Theoretical Computer Science, Nice, France, Sept. 1998.
15. R. Milner, J. Parrow, D. Walker, "A Calculus of Mobile Processes", in Information and Computation 100, pp.1-77, 1992.
16. C. A. Petri, "Kommunikation mit Automaten", PhD Thesis, Institut für Instrumentelle Mathematik, Bonn, Germany, 1962.
17. L. Padovani, "A Distributed Language with Mobile Agents: Design and Implementation", Master Thesis Dissertation, March 1998.
    http://www.cs.unibo.it/~lpadovan/master_thesis/main.pdf
18. C. Sibertin-Blanc, "Cooperative Nets", in Proc. 15th Int. Conf. on Appl. and Theory of Petri Nets, LNCS 815, pp.471-490, Springer Verlag, Zaragoza, Spain, 1994.
19. R. Valk, "Generalizations of Petri Nets", in Proc. MFCS'81, LNCS 118, 1981.
20. R. Valk, "On Processes of Object Petri Nets", Bericht Nr. 185, Fachbereich Informatik, Universitat Hamburg, 1996.
21. R. Valk, "Petri nets as token objects: An introduction to elementary object nets", in Proc. ICATPN 1998, LNCS 1420, Springer, 1998.
22. R. Valk, "Concurrency in communicating object Petri nets", in *Concurrent Object-Oriented Programming and Petri Nets: Advances in Petri Nets*, LNCS 2001, Springer, 2001.

On Correctness of Dynamic Protocol Update*

Paweł T. Wojciechowski and Olivier Rütti

Ecole Polytechnique Fédérale de Lausanne (EPFL)
1015 Lausanne, Switzerland
{Pawel.Wojciechowski,Olivier.Rutti}@epfl.ch

Abstract. Replacing or adding *network protocols* at runtime is problematic – it must involve synchronization of the protocol switch with ongoing local and network communication. We define a formal mathematical model of *dynamic protocol update (DPU)* and use it to define two DPU algorithms. The algorithms are based on fully-synchronized and lazy strategies. The two strategies implement updates with respectively, *strong* and *weak* safety properties. Our model allowed us to express the properties and the DPU algorithms clearly and abstractly, aiding algorithm design and correctness proofs.

1 Introduction

There is an important class of distributed applications that must run "non-stop". This is especially true of time-critical services, such as financial transactions, telephone switch systems, flight reservations and air traffic control systems. The service providers must be able to update their software, e.g. to fix program bugs, improve performance, and expand functionality. Unfortunately, stopping the system results in loss of service and revenue; it may also compromise safety. Moreover, systems that modify their behavior based on changes in the environment, require the ability to update their functionality *dynamically*, with minimal service interruption. There are quite a number of relevant implementations and techniques (e.g. [1, 4, 6, 9]). Software components can be rebound on-the-fly, using a mechanism of dynamic class loading and linking [10, 15].

In this paper, we focus on global update of *network components* that assumes modification of a network protocol implemented by the components. Such type of update introduces a new problem, however. Replacement of network components involves delicate synchronization (or coordination) of local updates which, if not handled appropriately, could easily prove so disruptive as to, at best, shut the system down, and, at worst, introduce malicious behaviour. Synchronizing local updates so that all software components in the distributed system end up updated in a consistent manner, and doing this while the system continuously provides service, represent serious challenges. It is therefore important to understand what are the minimal properties which must be satisfied by dynamic protocol update (DPU), and what is the range of possible DPU strategies?

* Research supported by the Swiss National Science Foundation under grant number 21-67715.02 and Hasler Stiftung under grant number DICS-1825.

M. Steffen and G. Zavattaro (Eds.): FMOODS 2005, LNCS 3535, pp. 275–289, 2005.

Most of software update implementations concentrate on bug-fixes or software upgrades that do not alter the communication protocol. Thus, coordinating the protocol switch with ongoing communication can be done locally. Few implementations provide solutions to the problem described in this paper. Examples are implementations of dynamic protocol adaptation using Ensemble [21] and Cactus [6] protocol frameworks. They implement complex *DPU algorithms* for global synchronization of local updates. However, they lack both simplicity and generality and it is not clear what properties are actually guaranteed. Therefore, we believe a formal, mathematical model of DPU should be developed, in order to understand by both users and implementors of DPU technology what design choices can be considered, and what impact they have on DPU complexity and scalability. Unfortunately, little formalization work has been carried out to date (e.g. [3, 8, 19]; we discuss this work in Section 8). However, we are not aware of past efforts that have formalized the algorithms for global coordination of local updates or the DPU correctness properties.

A critical safety property of many network services is *message order* preservation. Consider *group communication* middleware [14] that can be used for replicating servers in order to make them tolerant to server crashes. Each replica in the system is guaranteed to receive all messages in the same order. Any update of middleware protocols must not affect this semantics. In this paper, we explain what it really means in case of updating *any* kind of protocols. For this, we construct a model of DPU and use it to define two synchronization-extreme DPU algorithms: a fully-synchronized algorithm that satisfies the message order property but seems impractical for Internet-wide update, and a synchronization-free, lazy algorithm that is scalable but does not guarantee this property.

What are the significant results of our work? Firstly, the lazy DPU strategy does not require any distributed infrastructure, which means that update with weak semantics is no more difficult than a local update. Secondly, the fully-synchronized and lazy strategies define the design space for more practical DPU algorithms that use only as much synchrony as required in a given case. We have actually designed and implemented such algorithms for updating protocols of the group communication middleware. In the end of this paper, we summarize results of this experiment; a complete report is also available [16]. It was somewhat surprising to us that the design space can be indeed usefully explored, leading to specialized DPU algorithms that are more efficient than the fully-synchronized strategy but preserving properties required by correct global update.

Our model abstracts away from any concrete implementation of modular protocols and of the DPU technology. We only make sure that our network communication is directly implementable above standard networks, such as Internet. For this, we assume that protocols use asynchronous, unordered, point-to-point messages; this is a realistic assumption about wide-area networks and common middleware services, where communication delays are not predictable. Our model abstracts away however from any unnecessary details of this communication. For instance, message addressing and message routing are the details of protocols themselves that we do not model here.

Symbols

Service names	$x, y \in Mvar$
Required services	$R \in 2^{Mvar}$
Messages	m
Protocol modules	a, b, c
Module types	$t ::= (x, R) \quad x \notin R$
Module bindings	$w ::= \updownarrow \mid \uparrow$

Terms

Protocol stacks	$P = \{a\,w, ..., b\,w'\}$
Module a in stack P	$P.a$
Peer modules of a	$\delta(a) = \{P.a'\,w \text{ for any } P \mid a' : (x, R)\}$ where $a : (x, R)$
Distributed protocols	$\mathcal{D} = \{P_1, ..., P_n\}$ or $\mathcal{D} = \{\delta(a), ..., \delta(b)\}$
Messages sent $to\ a, .., b$	$S_S = (m^{P.a}, ..., m'^{P'.b})$
Messages delivered $by\ a, .., b$	$S_D = (m^{P.a}, ..., m'^{P'.b})$
Message history	$S = (S_S, S_D)$
Sub-histories $(i = S, D)$	$S_i \mid a = \{m^{P.a'} \text{ for any } P \mid m^{P.a'} \in set(S_i),\ a' : (x, R)\}$
	where $a : (x, R)$
	$S_i \mid P.a = \{m^{P.a} \mid m^{P.a} \in set(S_i)\}$
Protocol states	$\mathcal{D}, S$
Call service x in P	$P.x(m)$
Deliver m using a in P	$[m]P.a$

Fig. 1. The DPU model: Symbols and terms.

The paper is organized as follows. Section 2 and Section 3 define our model. Section 4 specifies DPU, and Section 5 defines its correctness properties. Section 6 defines two DPU algorithms. Section 7 sketches our implementation work, Section 8 contains related work, and Section 9 concludes.

2   Model

In this section, we define basic notions of protocol modules and protocol stacks in our DPU model. All symbols and terms are in Fig. 1.

Protocol stacks. *Protocol services* (or *services* in short), denoted by metavariables x, y, are programming abstractions implemented by network protocols. Example services are "send a message reliably", "broadcast a message with FIFO guarantee", etc. Services can be *called* as functions, as in $x(m)$, where m is a *message*. No protocol data persist after the call returns.

We assume that protocols are *modular*, i.e. they can be composed from communicating *protocol modules* (or *modules* in short), denoted a, b. Modules are *typed* using pairs (x, R), where x is the name of a single service provided by the module, and R is a set of names of services that are required by the module in order to handle a call of x ($x \notin R$). We say that x is a module's *interface*.

Protocol stacks (or *stacks*), denoted P, are sets of modules accompanied by module bindings w, as in $P = \{a\ w, ..., b\ w'\}$; two kinds of bindings ($\updownarrow$ and $\uparrow$) will be explained in Section 3. We write $P.a\ w$ to denote a module a in stack P with binding w. We often omit bindings or stack names if we mean any binding or any stack, or the stack is known from the context. We abstract away in the model from physical machines – intuitively, stacks are located on machines that are interconnected via network.

Distributed protocols.   *Distributed protocols*, denoted $\mathcal{D}$, can be defined vertically or horizontally, i.e. either as sets of stacks $\{P_1, ..., P_n\}$, or as sets of logical protocols $\{\delta(a), ..., \delta(b)\}$, where a *logical protocol* $\delta(a)$ is a set of *peers* of module a, i.e. all modules in the system that have the same type as a. Each logical protocol defines a level of abstraction in a stack. Unless a distributed protocol is being updated, any two stacks are exactly the same.

For clarity, we assume in this paper a system model with no failures, where messages are not lost nor duplicated, and stacks are basically reliable. In our implementation of DPU, however, stacks may *crash* while a protocol is being updated, with a guarantee that all non-crashed stacks get updated.

3   Operational Semantics

Actions.   Interaction between protocol modules (and stacks) is by means of *asynchronous messages*. We use two kinds of actions to express the communication: a service call and a message delivery.

Service call $P.x(m)$ requests a service x of a stack P to deliver a fresh message m in one or many stacks, depending on if the communication is point-to-point or multicast. The call therefore appends to a global list of *sent messages* S_S, a list $(m^{P'.a'}, ..., m^{P''.a''})$ of duplicated messages m decorated with all modules $a', ..., a''$ of type (x, R) for some R, that should be used to deliver m in stacks $P', ..., P''$. Note that our stacks are *symmetric*: modules that are used to output and to deliver a message have the same type.

Message delivery $[m]P.a$ denotes delivery of a message m in a stack P using a module a. The intended semantics is that m is delivered by a to some other module in the local stack that can use m. We assume that the name of this module has been encoded in the message itself. We do not model it explicitly, however, as we only need to know who delivers a message. The delivery adds (using a Lisp-like constructor "::") an element $m^{P.a}$ to a global list of *delivered messages* S_D; the list has the same structure as S_S.

Protocol states are denoted as $\mathcal{D}, S$, where $\mathcal{D}$ is a distributed protocol and $S = (S_S, S_D)$ is a pair of the (initially empty) lists of the sent and delivered messages. We define the *execution* (or *evaluation*) of a protocol $\mathcal{D}$ as a state transition relation $\longrightarrow$, which transforms a state $\mathcal{D}, S$ to $(\mathcal{D}, S)'$ as a result of a single action e, denoted $\xrightarrow{e}$; we sometimes omit the label e. The notation $(\mathcal{D}, S)'$ means $\mathcal{D}', S$ or $\mathcal{D}, S'$ or $\mathcal{D}', S'$, depending on the context. We also use $\Longrightarrow$ to denote a possibly empty sequence of small step transitions.

Communication and freedom

$$\frac{\begin{array}{c} a : (x, R) \\ m^{P.a} \notin set(S_S) \quad m^{P.a} \notin set(S_D) \\ m^{P.a} \in set(S'_S) \\ S''' = (S''_S, m^{P.a} :: S''_D) \\ a\,w \in P \quad w \in \{\updownarrow, \uparrow\} \quad P \in \mathcal{D}' \end{array}}{\mathcal{D}, (S_S, S_D) \xrightarrow{x(m)} \mathcal{D}, (S'_S, S_D) \Longrightarrow \mathcal{D}', (S''_S, S''_D) \xrightarrow{[m]P.a} \mathcal{D}', S'''} \;\text{(Comm)}$$

$$\frac{S = (S_S,\ S_D) \quad S_S|a = S_D|a}{(a, (\mathcal{D},\ S))\ \textsc{Free}} \qquad\text{(Freedom)}$$

Module bindings

$$\frac{a\,w \in P \quad w \neq w'}{a\,w' \notin P} \;\text{(Sanity-1)} \qquad\qquad \frac{\begin{array}{c} a : (x, R) \quad b : (x, R') \quad a \neq b \\ a \updownarrow \in P \quad b\,w \in P \end{array}}{w = \uparrow} \;\text{(Sanity-2)}$$

Fig. 2. The DPU model: Operational semantics.

Communication. We write $set(S_i)$ to denote a set of all elements in list S_i. The rule (Comm) in Fig. 2 says that each delivery action $[m]P.a$ in a stack P must be preceded in the execution trace by a corresponding call $x(m)$, where module a provides x (remember that our stacks are symmetric). There can be an arbitrary number of evaluation steps in-between since different protocol (or update) actions can be interleaved. The sets of sent, S_S, and delivered messages, S_D, are modified accordingly.

The details of message routing within a stack and between stacks are omitted here, as they are not useful in this paper. Example approaches can be found in [23], where we describe the semantics of module interaction and binding in Cactus and Appia – two example protocol frameworks that can be used to encode modular protocols in Java.

In network protocols, we can usually identify different levels of abstraction at which communication takes place. Consider delivery $[m]P.a$ of message m in stack P by module a, as the result of a service call $P'.x(m)$ in some other stack P'. The call may trigger several calls of services that x depends on (all that services are known from module type). In protocol frameworks, each of these calls gets as its argument a message m', that contains m and any additional data that are required in order to complete the call and to deliver the message using corresponding modules in stack P'.

Freedom. In this paper, we consider network protocols that execute in terminating rounds, where a *round* is a sequence of reduction steps that has commenced with a service call $P.x(m)$ for some stack P, where message m must be fresh. The round terminates with delivery of message m for the last time. Or, more precisely, a round spawned with a fresh message m *terminates* (or *com-*

pletes) in a state $\mathcal{D}$, (S_S, S_D) if $S_S|m = S_D|m$, where $S_i|m$ $(i = S, D)$ is a list that is constructed from S_i by removing from it all messages other than m.

There can be many rounds executed concurrently. A distributed protocol $\mathcal{D}$ does not *get stuck* if all its rounds eventually complete.

A module a of a protocol $\mathcal{D}$ is *free* in a state $\mathcal{D}$, S, denoted $(a, (\mathcal{D}, S))$ FREE, if there is currently no active round of the protocol that would deliver a message using either module a or any module (in any stack) that has the same type as a. We can define this property formally using sub-histories $S_i|a$ of messages that were sent $(i = S)$ and delivered $(i = D)$ by all modules of type of module a; see rule (Freedom) in Fig. 2 and the definition of $S_i|a$ in Fig. 1.

Bindings. We assume that modules can be added and removed from stacks at runtime. This means that modules can be *dynamically bound* and *rebound*. Consider a module a of type (x, R) for some x and R. We write $a \updownarrow$ to denote the module a which has been *bound*, i.e. calls of service x to deliver a fresh message can use a, and messages can be also delivered by a.

We write $a \uparrow$ to denote a module a which is *passive*, i.e. calls of a service x provided by a are not allowed, unless there is another module b in the same stack that provides service x, and b is bound. A passive module can however deliver messages. Therefore, any round of a protocol $\delta(a)$ can complete using passive modules in $\delta(a)$, assuming that any services that are required by $\delta(a)$ to complete the round in a given stack, have bound modules in the stack.

Each module in a stack is either bound or passive. We also assume that for a given service in each stack, there can be at most one bound module at a time providing the service; these sanity conditions are defined formally in the bottom of Fig. 2.

4   Dynamic Protocol Update

We define *dynamic protocol update (DPU)* as a dynamic change of a distributed protocol, i.e. replacement or addition of its modules. We require that the change must eventually occur in all protocol stacks within, say, a cluster of servers or a large LAN. Below we use our model to formalize this definition.

Replaceability. We can replace a module a by a module b in a protocol stack P only if b has the interface of a (or at least of a, if we had a notion of interface subtyping). This is motivated by requirements of real systems. If module b does not provide the service of a, then it means that the distributed protocol updated with b may get stuck since not all service calls can be effectuated, thus violating the (desirable) termination property of protocol rounds. We must also require that stack P provides all services that are required by b. These two requirements are expressed in Fig. 3 as a *replaceability property* $P\{b/a\}$, read "a replaceable by b in P". The property can be verified statically by checking module types.

Global update. A *global update* $GU(\mathcal{D}, a, b)$ in Fig. 3, updates all stacks of a distributed protocol $\mathcal{D}$ with a module b, yielding an updated protocol $\mathcal{D}'$. To update a stack locally, GU calls a local update function LU (explained below).

$$\frac{\begin{array}{c} a:(x,R) \quad a \in P \\ b:(x,R') \quad R' = \{y \mid \exists c:(y,..) \;\; c \in P\} \end{array}}{P\{b/a\}} \qquad \text{(Replaceable)}$$

$$\frac{P\{b/a\} \quad w \in \{\updownarrow, \uparrow\}}{LU:(P,a,b) \rightarrow (P \setminus \{a\;w\}) \cup \{a\uparrow\} \cup \{b\updownarrow\}} \qquad \text{(Local-Update)}$$

$$\frac{\mathcal{D} = \{P_1,...,P_n\} \quad \mathcal{D}' = \{LU(P_1,a,b),...,LU(P_n,a,b)\}}{GU:(\mathcal{D},a,b) \rightarrow \mathcal{D}'} \qquad \text{(Global-Update)}$$

Fig. 3. The DPU specifications.

For practical reasons, global update should be concurrent with the execution of system services whenever possible. Blocking the whole system during update is unrealistic for large systems, and also not acceptable for non-stop systems. Thus, the transition $\mathcal{D}, S \stackrel{GU(\mathcal{D},a,b)}{\Longrightarrow} \mathcal{D}', S'$ consists of many evaluation steps that may be interleaved (under control of GU) with actions of the protocol that gets updated. Moreover, several global updates can occur concurrently.

Local update. A *local update* function LU in Fig. 3 takes as arguments a stack P, an old module a, and a new module b, and yields a new stack in which the new module is bound and the old one is passive. This has the effect of replacing a by b in stack P in one atomic action. After a call of LU returns, any calls of the service provided by a and b will use the new implementation b instead of a. However, any pending rounds can still complete using the old module.

The definition of global update does not specify *when* a function LU is actually called. Updating some protocols at "wrong" moment may invalidate safety properties of these protocols. In Section 5, we identify two safety properties (strong and weak) that cover a broad range of distributed protocols. Then we describe in Section 6 two implementations of GU; the first one satisfies strong safety, while the second one satisfies weak safety (but not strong safety).

5   Dynamic Update Correctness

The static replaceability property is necessary but not sufficient for DPU correctness. In this section, we define some safety properties that formalize what we regard to be correct DPU.

Correctness. Intuitively, global update GU is correct if updating a distributed protocol does not interfere with the concurrent execution of the protocol, i.e. the update cannot be observed by any services of the protocol. In our model, the only observable actions of the distributed protocol are message outputs and deliveries (since they can modify state S). Obviously, correct global update must not cause the updateable protocol to loose nor duplicate messages. Some applications may also require that GU does not change the order of message delivery.

Judgments

$$x \vdash_h S \qquad S \text{ is a correct message history of service } x$$
$$\vdash_{dpu} GU \qquad GU \text{ is a correct DPU algorithm}$$

DPU correctness

$$\dfrac{S = (nil, nil)}{x \vdash_h S} \quad \text{(Null-History)}$$

$$\dfrac{\begin{array}{c} \mathcal{D}, S \overset{GU(\mathcal{D}, a, b)}{\Longrightarrow} \mathcal{D}', S' \\ a : (x, R) \\ \hline x \vdash_h S \quad x \vdash_h S' \end{array}}{\vdash_{dpu} GU} \quad \text{(Correct-Update)}$$

$$\dfrac{\begin{array}{c} x \vdash_h (S'_S, S'_D) \\ x \vdash_h (S''_S, S''_D) \\ S = (S'_S @ S''_S, \; S'_D @ S''_D) \end{array}}{x \vdash_h S} \quad \text{(Consistent-Cut)}$$

DPU properties

$$\dfrac{\begin{array}{c} \mathcal{D}, S \overset{GU(\mathcal{D}, a, b)}{\Longrightarrow} \mathcal{D}', (S'_S, S'_D) \\ \mathcal{D}, S \Longrightarrow \mathcal{D}, (S''_S, S''_D) \\ set(S'_S) = set(S''_S) \end{array}}{set(S'_D) = set(S''_D)} \text{(Weak-Update)}$$

$$\dfrac{\begin{array}{c} \mathcal{D}, S \overset{GU(\mathcal{D}, a, b)}{\Longrightarrow} \mathcal{D}', S' \\ \mathcal{D}, S \overset{[m]P.b}{\Longrightarrow\Longrightarrow} \mathcal{D}'', S'' \\ S'' = (S''_S, S''_D) \end{array}}{S'_S | a = S''_D | a} \text{(Strong-Update)}$$

Fig. 4. Judgments and DPU properties.

We define DPU correctness using two judgments, one for message histories, and one for the GU algorithm; the judgments and the rules for reasoning about the judgments are given in Fig. 4. The message history judgment has the form $x \vdash_h S$, read "S is a correct message history of service x". The algorithm correctness judgment has the form $\vdash_{dpu} GU$, read "GU is a correct DPU algorithm".

The rule (Correct-Update) says that global update of a service x with a DPU algorithm GU is *correct*, if given a distributed protocol $\mathcal{D}$ and a correct history of messages S, the algorithm would transform the system $\mathcal{D}$, S into system $\mathcal{D}'$, S' where S' describes a correct message history from the point of view of x.

The rule (Consistent-Cut) is a core rule for reasoning about message histories. It states that a message history constructed by appending two (possibly empty) histories that are themselves correct is also correct. The Lisp-like append operation $S_i @ S'_i$ returns a new list whose elements are the elements in the given lists S_i and S'_i, in the order that they appear in the argument lists.

Properties. We can identify at least two update safety properties: strong and weak; they specify some desirable guarantees on a message history. We can then say that global update GU is *correct for updating a service x*, if it satisfies safety properties that are required by the correct execution of x. It depends on the semantics of x which property the implementation of GU should hold. (Obviously, we assert that updateable services must be themselves correct.)

Below are the two safety properties defined informally; a precise semantics is given in the bottom half of Fig. 4.

Property 1 (Weak Update) *A global update GU of a distributed protocol $\mathcal{D}$ has the* weak update *property if: (i) GU eventually terminates, (ii) if $\mathcal{D}$ does* *not get stuck, then the updated $\mathcal{D}$ will deliver exactly the same set of messages as the non-updated $\mathcal{D}$ would.*

The DPU algorithms that only satisfy the weak safety property cannot be used to update services that order messages. Below we define a stronger property.

Property 2 (Strong Update) *A global update GU replacing old modules by new modules in a protocol $\mathcal{D}$ has the* strong update *property if: (i) GU eventually terminates, (ii) after a new module has been used to deliver a message in some stack, the old module will never be used to deliver messages in any stack.*

Theorem 1 (Strong Update Correctness). *Global update that ensures the strong update property is correct.*

Proof. Consider update $\mathcal{D}, S \stackrel{GU(\mathcal{D}, a, b)}{\Longrightarrow} \mathcal{D}', S'$, where a, b provide x and $x \vdash_h S$. Take any state $\mathcal{D}'', S''$ such that $\mathcal{D}, S \Longrightarrow .., X \stackrel{[m]P.b}{\longrightarrow} .., Y \Longrightarrow \mathcal{D}'', S''$ and b is used a first time. Then

1. $x \vdash_h X$ by $x \vdash_h S$ and premise that up to this state x can only use $\delta(a)$,
2. $x \vdash_h Y \setminus X$ [1] by premise that b can replace a,
3. $x \vdash_h S'' \setminus X$ by 2. and $S''_S | a = S''_D | a$ (from definition of (Strong-Update)),
4. $x \vdash_h S''$ by 1. and 3. and (Consistent-Cut),
5. $\vdash_{dpu} GU$ by premise $x \vdash_h S$ and 4. and (Correct-Update). $\square$

Below are two examples of services that can be updated with a DPU algorithm that has the strong update property.

Consider a bug-fix of a security protocol that is used by a distributed transactions service to encrypt transaction-related communication. After a local update action terminated in a stack, and the newly added change has been applied to the security protocol, the strong update property guarantees that no transaction (on any node) will commit using the old erroneous security protocol.

Consider services that must deliver messages in a certain order. The strong update property guarantees that the old module is used only until the new module is used (somewhere) for the first time. Up to this (global) time, all messages are delivered (with order) by the old protocol, after this time all messages will be delivered (also with order) using only the new protocol.

Theorem 2 says that weak update can be always replaced by strong update (the opposite is obviously not true); the proof is straightforward.

Theorem 2 (Strong Update Implies Weak Update). *Any implementation of global update satisfying strong update, also satisfies weak update.*

6   Dynamic Update Algorithms

Consider updating a distributed protocol $\mathcal{D} = \{P \mid P = \{a \updownarrow, b \updownarrow, ..\}\}$ with a new module b [2]. Below we describe two example DPU algorithms. They are defined

---

[1] We write $Y \setminus X$ to denote a prefix of list Y obtained by removing sublist X.

[2] Updating $\mathcal{D}$ with b may involve adding new modules to each stack, so that all services required by b are eventually provided; the algorithm is similar to L-DPU in Section 6.

Synchronized DPU

$$\frac{a\updownarrow \in P \quad P\{b/a\}}{P, S \xrightarrow{P.\mathrm{ABcast}(S1,a,b)} P, S} \quad (S1)$$

$$\frac{[S1, a, b]\, P.abcast \quad abcast : (\mathrm{ABcast}, ..)}{P' = (P \setminus \{a\updownarrow\}) \cup \{a\uparrow\} \cup \{b\uparrow\}}{P, S \longrightarrow P', S \xrightarrow{P.\mathrm{ABcast}(S2,a,b)} P', S} \quad (S2)$$

$$\frac{S = (S_S, \ S_D) \quad S_S|P.a = S_D|P.a}{(a, P\ S)\ \mathrm{IDLE}} \quad (\mathrm{Idle})$$

$$\frac{[S2, a, b]\, P.abcast \ \text{from all}\ P' \in \mathcal{D}}{(a, P\ S)\ \mathrm{IDLE}}{P, S \xrightarrow{P.\mathrm{ABcast}(S3,a,b,\mathrm{Idle})} P, S} \quad (S3)$$

$$\frac{[S3, a, b, \mathrm{Idle}]\, P.abcast \ \text{from all}\ P' \in \mathcal{D}}{P, S \longrightarrow (P \setminus \{a\uparrow\} \setminus \{b\uparrow\}) \cup \{b\updownarrow\}, S} \quad (S4)$$

Lazy DPU

$$\frac{\begin{array}{c}[m, b]\, P.c \ \text{for some}\ c \in P \\ b \notin P \quad a\updownarrow \in P \quad P\{b/a\} \\ P' = (P \setminus \{a\updownarrow\}) \cup \{a\uparrow\} \cup \{b\updownarrow\} \\ S = (S_S, \ S_D)\end{array}}{P, S \longrightarrow P', S \xrightarrow{[m]P.b} P', (S_S, \ m^{P.b} :: S_D)} \quad (L1) \qquad \frac{\begin{array}{c}[m, b]\, P.c \ \text{for some}\ c \in P \\ b \in P \\ S = (S_S, \ S_D)\end{array}}{P, S \xrightarrow{[m]P.b} P, (S_S, \ m^{P.b} :: S_D)} \quad (L2)$$

Fig. 5. Synchronized and lazy DPU algorithms.

using a set of transition rules, each rule describing a single or double (atomic) evaluation step. The rules are expressed using the syntax in Fig. 1, extended with polyadic messages, i.e. a message is a sequence of names. For readability, we give in each rule only part of the state, i.e. the name of a local protocol stack in which a given action occurs (instead of $\mathcal{D}$). The steps of the algorithms can be freely interleaved with the steps of the protocol $\mathcal{D}$ being updated.

Synchronized update. The *Synchronized Dynamic Protocol Update (S-DPU)* algorithm in the upper part of Fig. 5, updates a distributed protocol by replacing *old* modules by *new* ones. Firstly, it "passivate" bindings of the old and new modules in each stack so that the modules are passive. Then, the old module is removed and the new module is bound in every stack; this takes place locally only after it can be guaranteed that the old module is not needed anymore to complete any round of the distributed protocol.

To support concurrent global updates and termination under stack crashes, our algorithm communicates control messages using a *totally ordered broadcast* [7, 14] service ABcast. We assume *abcast* to be some implementation of ABcast.

Execution of ABcast(m), where m is a fresh message, broadcasts m to all stacks with a guarantee that the round of ABcast terminates and if some stack delivers m before another broadcast message m', then every stack delivers m before m'.

Formally, if we take any two stacks $P, P' \in \mathcal{D}$ and modules $a \in P$ and $a' \in P'$ of type (ABcast, R) for some R, then for any state $\mathcal{D}, S$ and $S = (S_S, S_D)$ such that $(a, (\mathcal{D}, S))$ FREE and $(a', (\mathcal{D}, S))$ FREE, we have $S_D | P.a = S_D | P'.a'$, where the FREE property is defined in Fig. 2.

Below are steps of the S-DPU algorithm. Note that the output and delivery of update-related control messages *do not modify message histories!*

S1. Broadcast a fresh message (S1, a, b) to all stacks, where module a is bound in the local stack P and replaceable in P by module b. (We assume that initially, i.e. when a message history is (nil, nil), all stacks are identical.)
S2. Upon receipt of (S1, a, b), passivate module a in the local stack P and extend P with passive module b. Then, broadcast a fresh message (S2, a, b).
S3. A module a of stack P is *idle*, denoted $(a, P\ S)$ IDLE where S is a message history, if all messages sent to a (by any stack) have been delivered by a [3]. Upon receipt of (S2, a, b) from all stacks, wait until module a is idle in the local stack P, then broadcast a fresh message (S3, a, b, Idle).
S4. Upon receipt of (S3, a, b, Idle) from all stacks, remove module a from the local stack P and bind module b.

Lemma 1 (Safe Rebinding) *If S-DPU algorithm binds a new module in some state, then a module being replaced with the new module is free in this state.*

Proof. Consider binding of some module a in step (S4) of S-DPU. Then

1. by premise of (S4) and ABcast, each stack $P \in \mathcal{D}$ has executed (S3)
2. by 1. and (S3) and definition of $(a, (P, S))$ IDLE, each stack $P \in \mathcal{D}$ has been in a state $\mathcal{D}, S$, such that $S_S | P.a = S_D | P.a$,
3. by premise of (S3) and ABcast, each stack has executed (S2),
4. by 3. and (S2), each stack has unbound a in (S3), so $S_S | P.a = S_D | P.a$ is true not only in (S3) but also in (S4),
5. by 4. and premise of (S4) and ABcast, $S_S | P.a = S_D | P.a$ for all stacks $P \in \mathcal{D}$,
6. by 5. and definition of $S_i | a$ ($i = S, D$) in Fig. 1, $S_S | a = S_D | a$,
7. by 6. and (Freedom), $(a, (\mathcal{D}, S))$ FREE. $\square$

We conclude that the S-DPU algorithm satisfies strong update.

Theorem 3 (S-DPU Strong Safety). *Updating a distributed protocol with the S-DPU algorithm satisfies strong update.*

Proof. By Lemma 1 and (S4), when a new module is bound in $\mathcal{D}, S$, the old module a is free. By (S2), a is unbound in $\mathcal{D}, S$, i.e. for any state $\mathcal{D}', S'$ following $\mathcal{D}, S$, we have $S'_S | a = S'_D | a$. By (Strong-Update) this completes the proof. $\square$

---

[3] We assume the existence of a *global snapshot* algorithm [11] to determine this predicate.

Lazy update. The *Lazy Dynamic Protocol Update (L-DPU)* algorithm in the bottom of Fig. 5, updates a distributed protocol lazily, by extending stacks with a new module whenever needed.

We associate messages with modules that are used to deliver the messages. If a module required to deliver a message is not in a local stack, then it is added to the stack, bound, and the binding of the old module providing the same service is "passivated", so that any new protocol round in this stack can use the new module. The algorithm allows however the old and new modules to coexist in the distributed protocol, i.e. they can deliver their messages concurrently.

The L-DPU algorithm does not require any distributed infrastructure, except the one used by protocol $\mathcal{D}$ to communicate messages via network. Thus, it scales to large networks. Below are actions of the L-DPU algorithm.

L1. Upon delivery of a message (m, b) by some module c in the local stack P, if module b is not in P, then take any module a in P that is bound and replaceable by b, passivate a and bind b. Finally, deliver m using b.

L2. Upon delivery of a message (m, b) by some module c, if module b is available locally, then deliver m using b.

To guarantee termination of the global update, we could require that stacks periodically broadcast and deliver an "update" message containing new modules.

According to Theorem 4, the Lazy DPU algorithm guarantees that all protocol messages are delivered but message ordering is not preserved.

Theorem 4 (L-DPU Weak Safety). *Updating a distributed protocol with the L-DPU algorithm satisfies weak update.*

Proof. Straightforward by (Weak-Update) and atomicity of rebinding in (L1). □

7   Practical Experiment

To facilitate experimentation, we have designed and implemented DPU support for Fortika [13, 14] – a group communication middleware that is developed within our project. We have encoded middleware components using the SAMOA library [24]. The most complex components that Fortika uses are two agreement services: *distributed consensus* and *totally ordered broadcast* (ABcast). We have proposed DPU algorithms that can switch between different implementations of these services dynamically, while preserving safety properties of each service. By exploring the semantics of consensus and ABcast, the DPU algorithms can be less synchronous than the S-DPU algorithm in Section 6. In effect, the service is available almost continuously while it is updated.

Consider update of the consensus service [5]. The service ensures that given a group of distributed processes, after a round of consensus, all processes would agree on the same value, which has been chosen from values proposed individually by each process. Our DPU algorithm uses the semantics of consensus for replacement of the consensus implementation; it has three steps. Firstly, an intend to replace a consensus protocol $\delta(a)$ by $\delta(b)$ is broadcast. Then, all processes must decide when b can be bound locally. For this, b could be piggybacked on any message that must be also processed by the consensus service. Finally, when the decision about b has been delivered (that means *all* stacks reached consensus about binding b), a is passivated and b is bound. The time between binding a new module and making the old one passive is therefore maximally reduced.

The results of our practical experiment demonstrate that dynamic replacement of network protocols in a group communication system can be done efficiently. Description of the DPU algorithms for agreement protocols and performance measurements are in our companion paper [16].

8   Related Work

In this section, we describe some of the work most closely related to ours.

There are quite a number of implementations that support dynamic updating of software components. For example, the Erlang programming language [1] allows software modules to be replaced at runtime, however with no safety guarantees. A Java HotSpot VM [20] allows a class instance to be replaced with the new instance in a running application through the debugger APIs.

There have been work on safe dynamic software updating by construction, ensuring that if an update is accepted by the system, then the resulting program will be type-correct. Dynamic ML [22] enables type-safe module replacement at runtime; changes can include the alternation of abstract types at update-time, and the addition (and possibly removal) of module definitions via garbage-collection. Dynamic Java classes [12] offer type safety preservation but compromise portability by modifying the Java Virtual Machine; also, class replacement is not synchronized with threads using old code.

Duggan [8] describes a type-safe approach that allows a new module to change the types exported by the original module; it however does not discuss the re-binding facility. Bierman *et al.* [3] study dynamic software updating with a small extension of a lambda calculus that supports an Erlang-like updating features. A preliminary discussion of safety properties is included, however without considering the use of concurrency and coordinated updates. Stoyle *et al.* [19] investigate type-safe dynamic updating in C-like languages. However, this work does not address the issues of global coordination of local updates.

Few systems offer support for coordinating local updates. For example, Van Renesse *et al.* [21] describe a switching protocol, which synchronizes dynamic replacement of protocols in the Ensemble protocol framework, however it does so only for whole stacks, thus blocking applications on top of the stack during update. Chen *et al.* [6] describe switching between network components within the Cactus protocol framework. A replacement manager on each host interacts explicitly with replaceable network components; it uses barrier synchronization for coordinating the beginning of the replacement across different hosts. A similar solution has been proposed in [18], but it uses a centralized manager, which limits its scope of applicability. However, in none of the above systems is there any well developed evidence as to what conditions are needed to guarantee the correctness of updating distributed protocols on-the-fly.

To date relatively little work has been carried out on formalization of dynamic protocol update. The previous work closest to our own is by Bickford *at al.* [2] on designing a generic switching protocol for Ensemble using the NUPR logical programming environment. They have formally defined several communication (not structural, though) meta properties on traces of send and deliver events, that should be preserved by updateable protocols. While we have identified space between lazy and synchronized updates, they only describe one example switching protocol. The algorithm is correct only for replacement of protocols that must exhibit all their (six) meta-properties; it cannot be applied for arbitrary protocols, contrary to the S-DPU algorithm presented in this paper.

Methods of distributed versioning, such as Sewell's [17] fine-grain versioning control of values of abstract types, could be used to support interoperation of old and new modules, and e.g. verify statically the replaceability property.

9   Conclusions and Future Work

In this paper we make several contributions. We have defined a simple but expressive model of dynamic protocol update (DPU). We use our model to define static and dynamic requirements that, we believe, should be considered by any valid dynamic protocol update support:

- The replaceability property specifies minimal structural, static requirements on module replacement;
- The strong and weak update safety properties specify that updating a distributed protocol must not cause message loss; the strong property additionally requires that message order is always preserved.

Based on the above requirements, we have constructed two DPU algorithms which are based on synchronized and lazy updating strategies. The former algorithm exhibits strong safety guarantees but requires a subtle distributed infrastructure (totally ordered broadcast) which does not scale to large networks. The latter algorithm scales well but the order of message delivery by updateable service is not respected that limits its applicability.

Our DPU algorithms work correctly also in the presence of stack crashes, in the sense that all non-crashed stacks are guaranteed to get eventually updated.

In the future work, it may be worthwhile to extend the model presented in this paper with system failures and message omissions; this would allow us to reason about such cases formally.

References

1. J. L. Armstrong and S. R. Virding. Erlang – An experimental telephony switching language. In *Proc. XIII International Switching Symposium*, May 27–June 1, 1990.
2. M. Bickford, C. Kreitz, R. van Renesse, and R. L. Constable. An experiment in formal design using meta-properties. In *Proc. DISCEX-II '01: The 2nd DARPA Information Survivability Conference and Exposition*. IEEE, June 2001.

3. G. Bierman, M. Hicks, P. Sewell, and G. Stoyle. Formalizing dynamic software updating. In *USE '03: Workshop on Unanticipated Software Evolution*, Apr. 2003.
4. T. Bloom and M. Day. Reconfiguration and module replacement in Argus: theory and practice. *Software Engineering Journal*, 8(2):102–108, 1993.
5. T. D. Chandra and S. Toueg. Unreliable failure detectors for reliable distributed systems. *Journal of the ACM*, 43(2):225–267, 1996.
6. W.-K. Chen, M. A. Hiltunen, and R. D. Schlichting. Constructing adaptive software in distributed systems. In *Proc. ICDCS '01*, Apr. 2001.
7. X. Défago, A. Schiper, and P. Urbán. Totally ordered broadcast and multicast algorithms: A comprehensive survey. Tech. Report DSC-2000-036, Communication Systems Department, EPFL, Sept. 2000.
8. D. Duggan. Type-based hot swapping of running modules. In *Proc. ICFP '01: The 6th ACM SIGPLAN Int'l Conference on Functional Programming*, Sept. 2001.
9. M. W. Hicks, J. T. Moore, and S. Nettles. Dynamic software updating. In *Proc. PLDI '01: The ACM SIGPLAN Conference on Programming Language Design and Implementation*, June 2001.
10. S. Liang and G. Bracha. Dynamic class loading in the Java virtual machine. In *Proc. OOPSLA '98*, Oct. 1998.
11. N. A. Lynch. *Distributed Algorithms*. Morgan Kaufmann, 1997.
12. S. Malabarba, R. Pandey, J. Gragg, E. Barr, and J. F. Barnes. Runtime support for type-safe dynamic Java classes. In *Proc. ECOOP 2000*, LNCS 1850, June 2000.
13. S. Mena, X. Cuvellier, C. Grégoire, and A. Schiper. Appia vs. Cactus: Comparing protocol composition frameworks. In *Proc. SRDS '03*. IEEE, Oct. 2003.
14. S. Mena, A. Schiper, and P. T. Wojciechowski. A step towards a new generation of group communication systems. In *Proc. Middleware '03*, LNCS 2672, 2003.
15. L. Moreau. A syntactic theory of dynamic binding. *Higher-Order and Symbolic Computation*, 11(3):233–279, Dec. 1998.
16. O. Rütti, P. T. Wojciechowski, and A. Schiper. Dynamic update of distributed agreement protocols. Tech. Report IC-2005-012, I&C, EPFL, Mar. 2005.
17. P. Sewell. Modules, abstract types, and distributed versioning. In *POPL '01*, 2001.
18. N. Sridhar, S. M. Pike, and B. W. Weide. Dynamic module replacement in distributed protocols. In *Proc. ICDCS '03*, May 2003.
19. G. Stoyle, M. Hicks, G. Bierman, P. Sewell, and I. Neamtiu. *Mutatis Mutandis*: Safe and predictable dynamic software updating. In *POPL '05*, Jan. 2005.
20. Sun Microsystems, Inc. *Java HotSpot*. http://java.sun.com/products/hotspot/.
21. R. van Renesse, K. Birman, M. Hayden, A. Vaysburd, and D. Karr. Building adaptive systems using Ensemble. *Software Practice & Experience*, 28(9), 1998.
22. C. Walton, D. Kirli, and S. Gilmore. An abstract machine model of dynamic module replacement. *Future Generation Computer Systems*, 16:793–808, May 2000.
23. P. T. Wojciechowski, S. Mena, and A. Schiper. Semantics of protocol modules composition and interaction. In *Proc. Coordination '02*, LNCS 2315, Apr. 2002.
24. P. T. Wojciechowski, O. Rütti, and A. Schiper. SAMOA: A framework for a synchronisation-augmented microprotocol approach. In *Proc. IPDPS '04: The 18th IEEE Int'l Parallel and Distributed Processing Symposium*, Apr. 2004.

Property-Driven Development
of a Coordination Model
for Distributed Simulations*

Rolf Hennicker and Matthias Ludwig

Institut für Informatik
Ludwig-Maximilians-Universität München
Oettingenstr. 67, D-80538 München, Germany

Abstract. The coordination of time-dependent simulation models is an important problem in environmental systems engineering. We propose a solution based on a rigorous formal modelling of the participating processes. Methodologically, our approach is driven by property processes which are used for the formal specification of the coordination problem. Property processes are supported by the CSP-like language FSP of Magee and Kramer which will be used throughout this paper for modelling the system requirements and the system design. The heart of our design model is a global time controller which coordinates distributed simulation models according to their local time scales. We will show with model checking techniques that all safety and liveness requirements are guaranteed by the timecontroller design.

The strong practical relevance of the approach is ensured by the fact that our strategy is used to produce a formally verified design for the kernel of the integrative simulation system DANUBIA developed within the GLOWA-Danube project.

1 Introduction

In the last decade environmental systems engineering became an important application area for information and software technology. Setting out from geographical information systems and GIS-based expert systems nowadays one is particularly interested in the development of integrative systems with a multi-lateral view of the world in order to understand better the mutual dependencies between environmental processes. Of particular importance are water-related processes which have an impact on the global change of the hydrological cycle with various consequences concerning water availability, water quality and water risks like water pollution, water deficiency and floods.

There are several projects dealing with methods, techniques and tools to support a sustainable water resource management, for instance within the European research activity EESD (Energy, Environment and Sustainable Development,

---

* This work is partially supported by the GLOWA-Danube project (07GWK04) sponsored by the German Federal Ministry of Education and Research.

M. Steffen and G. Zavattaro (Eds.): FMOODS 2005, LNCS 3535, pp. 290–305, 2005.

cf. [3]) or within the German initiative GLOWA (Global Change in the Hydrological Cycle; cf. [4]). Within the GLOWA framework the project GLOWA-Danube [8] deals with the Upper Danube watershed as a representative area for mountain-foreland regions. The principle objective of GLOWA-Danube is to identify, examine and develop new techniques of coupled distributed modelling for the integration of natural and socio-economic sciences. For this purpose the integrative simulation system DANUBIA is developed which supports the analysis of water-related global change scenarios. DANUBIA is designed as an open, distributed network integrating the simulation models of all socio-economic and natural science disciplines taking part in GLOWA-Danube. Actually seventeen simulation models are integrated in the DANUBIA system covering the disciplines of meteorology, hydrology, remote sensing, ground- and surface water research, glaciology, plant ecology, environmental psychology, environmental and agricultural economy, and tourism. As a result of coupled simulations transdisciplinary effects of mutually dependent processes can be analysed and evaluated.

An important characteristics of DANUBIA is the possibility to perform integrative simulations where the single simulation models run concurrently and exchange information at run time. Since any simulation models water-related processes over a specific period of time (usually some years) a global time control is necessary which coordinates the distributed models to work properly together. This is a non-trivial task since each simulation model has an individual time step in which computations are periodically executed ranging from hours, like in meteorology, to months, like in social sciences. To ensure that an integrative simulation provides reliable results it must be guaranteed that during the simulation run

- all values accessed through model interfaces are in a stable state (which corresponds to the usual read/write exclusion) and, moreover, that
- every simulation model is supplied with valid data, i.e. with data that fits to the local model time of the importing simulation model.

This informal description of the synchronization conditions provides only an intuitive idea of the coordination problem to be considered. For a full understanding it is necessary to clarify several issues, like the notion of time and the precise timing conditions for correct data exchange on the basis of the local time scales of the cooperating models. Taking into account that a distributed simulation is an open system where in principal arbitrarily many models (with different time scales) can participate it is obvious that the coordination problem soon becomes untractable without the use of formal specification techniques.

An example of a formalization of the coordination problem on a meta level using purely mathematical notations is given in [2]. Here we will use as a specification formalism the language FSP (Finite State Processes) of Magee and Kramer [9] which provides an appropriate basis for applying model checking techniques. Moreover, FSP allows us to follow a property-oriented approach where first the system requirements are specified by means of so-called property processes. The use of property processes has several advantages which are essential for our application. First, a requirements specification can be developed piecewise by collecting single property processes which focus on one aspect of the system at a time. This is particularly useful for the coordination problem where it is sufficient to consider the cooperating simulation models pairwise and under different roles, one model acting (only) as a provider and the other one acting (only) as a user of information. In this way the complexity of the problem can be drastically reduced. Also the exclusion condition for providing and retrieving data can be specified by a seperate property process. However, as usual, there is still a danger that the requirements are not adequately met by the single property processes. To deal with this issue FSP assigns to each property process a finite labelled transition system which can be animated with the LTSA tool (Labelled Transition System Analyzer; cf. [7]). Thus we can reveal the legal and illegal execution paths which is indeed helpful to analyse and validate whether the single property processes reflect correctly the desired time dependent coordination constraints. In addition to the property processes which represent safety conditions we also specify liveness conditions stating that each simulation model must repeatedly provide data during the whole simulation period according to its local time scale.

The requirements specification developed in this paper is a good example of a highly non-constructive formal specification in the sense that it cannot be directly transformed into an executable program. In the next step we will focus on the design of a constructive solution for the coordination problem. For this purpose we define a global timecontroller process which stores the current status of all simulation models in order to coordinate them appropriately. The design of the whole simulation system is then given by the parallel composition of the timecontroller and all concurrent simulation models. It is shown with model checking techniques that the design model indeed satisfies the desired safety and liveness properties. All processes occurring in the system design are also represented in terms of FSP notation and model checking is performed with the LTSA tool. The separation of property specifications from design is of great methodological value for our application. This approach is well supported by FSP but not e.g. by SPIN [6] or related model checkers where it is necessary to integrate the assertions into a given design model.

The proposed approach can be applied to all kinds of systems where concurrently executing components must be coordinated in accordance with some discrete order. Within the GLOWA-Danube project the approach is of high practical relevance for the development of the DANUBIA system because integrative simulations are the heart of all current and future features of DANUBIA and hence the reliability of the whole system depends on the correctness of the coordination implementation.

2   A Brief Introduction to FSP

The language FSP has been introduced by Magee and Kramer as a formalism for modelling concurrent processes. An elaborated description of the syntax and semantics of FSP can be found in [9]. Syntactically FSP resembles CSP [5]. Frequently used constructs for building FSP processes are

STOP	process termination
$(a \rightarrow P)$	action prefix
$(a \rightarrow P \mid$ when $(cond)$ $b \rightarrow Q)$	choice (involving a guarded action)
$P + \{a_1, \ldots, a_n\}$	alphabet extension
$(P \| Q)$	parallel composition
$P \setminus \{a_1, \ldots, a_n\}$	hiding
$P@\{a_1, \ldots, a_n\}$	interface definition

Each process P has an alphabet, denoted by αP, consisting of those actions in which the process can be engaged. If we build the parallel composition $(P \| Q)$ then actions that are shared by P and Q (i.e., belong to αP and αQ) must be performed simultaneously. For the non-shared actions interleaving semantics of parallel processes is used. The hiding operator allows to hide certain actions which are then invisible and represented by τ. The construction of an interface is the complement of hiding.

Processes can be defined by process declarations of the form $P = E$ or, in the case of parallel processes, by $\| P = (E \| F)$. A (non-parallel) process declaration can be recursive and can involve local, indexed processes of the form

$$P = Q[value],$$
$$Q[i : T] = E.$$

where T is a (finite) type and i is an index variable of type T.

Often we will use indexed actions of the form $a[i]$. A shorthand notation for a choice over a finite set of indexed actions is $(a[T] \rightarrow P)$, which is equivalent to $(a[x] \rightarrow P \mid \ldots \mid a[y] \rightarrow P)$, where range $T = x..y$. We will also use labelled actions of the form $[label].a$ and choice over a finite set of labelled actions $[T].a$ with T as above. To obtain several copies of a process P we use process labelling $[label] : P$ which denotes a process that behaves like P with all actions labelled by $[label]$.

The semantics of a process is given by a finite labelled transition system (LTS) which can be pictorially represented by a directed graph whose nodes are the process states and whose edges are the state transitions labelled with actions. Since FSP is restricted to a finite number of states one can automatically check safety and progress properties of processes. This will be essential for checking the correctness of our design model for distributed simulations. FSP is equipped with a model checking tool LTSA [7] which will be used for this purpose.

3 Simulation Models

Before we can specify the system requirements we have to analyse the problem domain. Let us first consider single simulation models and provide a formal description of their general behaviour. A simulation model simulates a physical or social process for a certain period of time which we call simulation time. The simulation time is finite which means that there is always a start and an end time. The whole simulation period is represented by a strictly ordered, discrete set of points in time (denoted by natural numbers), at which data is provided by a simulation model. Each model has an individual time step which determines the distance between two subsequent simulation points. For instance, a meteorological model provides the air temperature every hour, while a groundwater model provides the amount of groundwater withdrawal only once a day. We assume that the time step of a model remains fixed during the whole simulation.

A simulation model provides data for other models via export ports and gets data from other models (needed for its own computations) via import ports.

3.1   Lifecycle of a Simulation Model

After a simulation model has been started it provides first some initial data. Then it performs periodically the following steps until the end of the simulation is reached:

1. Get required data from other models (via the import ports).
2. Compute new data which are valid at the next simulation point.
3. Provide the newly computed data (via the export ports).

Since any simulation model has the same lifecycle we can model its general behaviour by the following (generic) FSP process which is parameterized w.r.t. the individual time step of a simulation model. Note that in the process defintion we have to provide a default time step (e.g. Step = 1) which is necessary according to the finite states assumption of FSP. For the same reason it is necessary to model the simulation start and the simulation end by some predefined constants.

```
const SimStart = 0
const SimEnd = 6
range Time = SimStart..SimEnd

MODEL(Step = 1) = (start -> INIT),
INIT = (prov[SimStart] -> M[SimStart]),
M[t:Time] =
     if (t+Step <= SimEnd)
     then (get[t] -> compute[t] -> prov[t+Step] -> M[t+Step])
     else STOP.
```

In the above process description the (indexed) actions prov[x] represent providing of export data which are valid at time x, the actions get[x] represent getting of import data which are valid at time x and the actions compute[x] represent the computation of new data based on import data which are valid at time x. Indeed the choice of the time dependent indices of the actions is crucial for the behaviour of the whole system to be developed. To explain our choice let us assume for the moment that the simulation time is a multiple of the model's time step. Then, according to the above process description, the last data that a model gets is valid at time $SimEnd - Step$ and the last data a model provides is valid at time $SimEnd$. For the whole simulation, this means that imported data is considered to be *last recently valid* for the computation of new export values to be valid at time t if the imported data is valid at time $t - Step$.

Of course, there are other choices for the definition of last recently valid data. For instance, the intuitively best choice would be to require that the imported values used for the computation of exported values to be valid at time t are also valid at time t (instead of being valid at time $t - Step$). But then the analysis of any attempt to construct a design model for the coordination problem will show that there is no deadlock-free solution (whenever there are, as usual, mutually dependent export and import data). Exactly for this kind of problem analysis, which is not further elaborated here, the use of formal models is indispensable.

To represent a particular instance of a simulation model we have to provide a model name (model identifier) and the particular time step of the model under consideration. For specifying model identifiers we use process labels (cf. Section 2) and the time step of a model is determined by an actual parameter. For instance, the FSP processes $[1] : MODEL(2)$ and $[2] : MODEL(3)$ represent two simulation models, one with number 1 and time step 2 and the other one with number 2 and time step 3, resp. The behaviour of model 2 is illustrated by the following LTS.

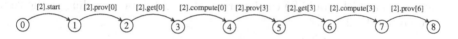

3.2 Integrative Simulations

In an integrative simulation various simulation models work together by mutually exchanging data via their import and export ports.

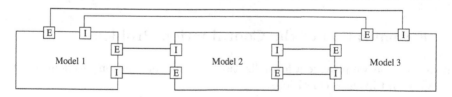

Each of the participating models performs a local simulation for the same overall time period (the global simulation time) but has usually a different local time step. It is crucial for integrative simulations that each model gets, whenever needed, the last recently valid data from partner models. A first attempt to model an integrative simulation could be to simply combine the processes which represent the single simulation models by parallel composition. For instance, for the two simulation models from above we would obtain the following composite process:

```
const NrModels = 2
range Models = 1..NrModels
```

||SYS = (([1]:MODEL(2)||[2]:MODEL(3))/{start/[Models].start}

The relabelling clause {start/[Models].start} ensures that the processes synchronize on the start action. Let us now consider some possible execution traces of the composite process which illustrate three characteristic problems that we have to take into account when we want to specify the desired safety properties for the system.

1. *Missing import data*

$$\text{start} \rightarrow [1].\text{prov}[0] \rightarrow [1].\text{get}[0] \rightarrow \dots$$

Model 1 gets data while model 2 has not yet provided data.

2. *Obsolete import data*

$$\begin{aligned} \text{start} &\rightarrow [2].\text{prov}[0] \rightarrow [1].\text{prov}[0] \rightarrow [1].\text{get}[0] \rightarrow [1].\text{compute}[0] \\ &\rightarrow [1].\text{prov}[2] \rightarrow [1].\text{get}[2] \rightarrow [1].\text{compute}[2] \rightarrow [1].\text{prov}[4] \\ &\rightarrow [1].\text{get}[4] \rightarrow \dots \end{aligned}$$

Model 1 gets data expected to be valid at time 4 while the last data provided by model 2 was valid at time 0 and model 2 has not yet provided data valid at time 3 (which would be the last recently valid data according to the time step of model 2).

3. *Overwritten import data*

$$\begin{aligned} \text{start} &\rightarrow [2].\text{prov}[0] \rightarrow [1].\text{prov}[0] \rightarrow [2].\text{get}[0] \rightarrow [2].\text{compute}[0] \\ &\rightarrow [2].\text{prov}[3] \rightarrow [1].\text{get}[0] \rightarrow \dots \end{aligned}$$

Model 1 gets data expected to be valid at time 0 while model 2 has already provided data that is valid at time 3.

4   Formalization of the Coordination Problem

In this section we provide a formalization of the coordination problem in terms of safety and liveness conditions.

4.1   Safety Properties

In Section 3 we have pointed out the essential difficulties concerning the validity of exchanged data when simulation models cooperate concurrently with different time scales. We start by formalizing the corresponding synchronization conditions by means of FSP property processes. The crucial idea is that the problem can be simplified if we consider only two simulation models at a time and, moreover, if we consider each of the two models only under one particular aspect, either as a provider or as a user of information. In the following let U denote a user model and let P denote a provider model. From the user's point of view we obtain the following condition (1), from the provider's point of view we obtain condition (2).

(1) U gets data expected to be valid at time t_U only if the following holds:
   P has last provided data valid at time $last_P$ with $last_P \leq t_U$ and the next data that P provides is valid at time t_P with $t_U < t_P$.
(2) P provides data valid at time t_P only if the following holds:
   The next data that U gets is expected to be valid at time t_U with $t_U \geq t_P$.

An execution trace w of an integrative simulation with an arbitrary number of simulation models [1] : MODEL($Step_1$),..., [n] : MODEL($Step_n$) is called *legal* w.r.t. a user U and a provider P, if w meets the above requirements (1) and (2). We model the legal execution traces by a generic FSP property process which is parameterized w.r.t. the model number and the time step of the user and the provider model respectively.

```
property VALIDDATA(User=1,StepUser=1,Prov=1,StepProv=1) =
  VD[SimStart][SimStart],

VD[nextGet:Time][nextProv:Time] =
  (when (nextProv-StepProv<=nextGet & nextGet<nextProv)
     [User].get[nextGet] -> VD[nextGet+StepUser][nextProv]
  |when (nextGet>=nextProv)
     [Prov].prov[nextProv] -> VD[nextGet][nextProv+StepProv]).
```

The first alternative of the property process formalizes condition (1) from above where the index variable `nextUser` corresponds to t_U, `nextProv` corresponds to t_P and hence `nextProv-StepProv` corresponds to $last_P$. The second alternative formalizes condition (2) from above. For the sake of simplicity we did not take into account the end of a simulation in the above process definition. For this purpose the process can be appropriately extended in order to avoid index overflow when the simulation end is reached and to ensure that the user and the provider have a clean termination.

All system requirements concerning the validity of data are now obtained by pairwise instantiations of the generic property process VALIDDATA. As an example let us consider model 1 with time step 2 as a user and model 2 with time step 3 as a provider. The corresponding safety property is then given by the property process VALIDDATA(1,2,2,3). The labelled transition system of this process is shown in Figure 1.

Labelled transition systems assigned to property processes have an error state, pictorially represented by -1, and are complete in the sense that for any action and any state (apart from the error state) there is always an outgoing transition. This transition leads to the error state if it is not properly defined in the property process definition. Thus the legal and illegal execution traces determined by a property process are revealed. For instance, the

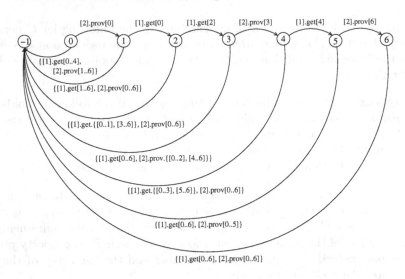

Fig. 1. LTS of the property process VALIDDATA(1,2,2,3)

three example traces considered in Section 3.2 are illegal w.r.t. the property process VALIDDATA(1,2,2,3), because their restrictions to the alphabet of VALID-DATA(1,2,2,3) lead to the error state.

Besides the requirements concerning the validity of exchanged data we have to cope also with data access. Since, in reality, getting and providing data are non-atomic actions we have to ensure that a model gets data only if no other model provides data at the same time and vice versa.

To formalize mutual exclusion we first enclose the critical regions, which in our case are represented by the `get` and `prov` actions, by corresponding `enter` and `exit` actions. For this purpose the process definition for simulation models of Section 3.1 is slightly adapted in the following way.

```
MODEL(Step=1) = (start -> INIT),
INIT = (enterProv[SimStart] -> prov[SimStart] ->
        exitProv[SimStart] -> M[SimStart]),
M[t:Time] =
  if (t+Step <= SimEnd)
  then (enterGet[t] -> get[t] -> exitGet[t] -> compute[t] ->
          enterProv[t+Step] -> prov[t+Step] ->
          exitProv[t+Step] -> M[t+Step])
  else  STOP + {Labels}.

    where

set GetProvs = {{get,prov}[Time]}
set EnterExits = {{enterGet,exitGet,enterProv,exitProv}[Time]}
set Labels = {GetProvs,EnterExits}
```

Note that the alphabet extension by `Labels` is necessary for technical reasons because the alphabet of property processes must be included in the alphabet of processes to be checked. By means of the `enter` and `exit` actions the desired exclusion conditions can now be expressed by a further property process, called EXCLUSION, which follows a standard scheme; cf. [9].

```
const NrModels = 2
range Models = 1..NrModels
range CountModels = 0..NrModels

property EXCLUSION =
  ([Models].enterGet[Time] -> GET[1]
  |[Models].enterProv[Time] -> PROV[1]),
GET[i:CountModels] =
  ([Models].enterGet[Time] -> GET[i+1]
  |when (i>1) [Models].exitGet[Time] -> GET[i-1]
  |when (i==1) [Models].exitGet[Time] -> EXCLUSION),
PROV[i:CountModels] =
  ([Models].enterProv[Time] -> PROV[i+1]
  |when (i>1) [Models].exitProv[Time] -> PROV[i-1]
  |when (i==1) [Models].exitProv[Time] -> EXCLUSION).
```

4.2 Liveness Properties

In contrast to the safety properties it is easy to identify the required liveness properties for integrative simulations. Obviously, we want that each simulation model provides data during the whole simulation period at any time that fits to its local time step. More formally, this means that for all execution traces w of an integrative simulation, for all models $m \in Models$ and for each time $t \in Time$ with $t\%Step_m = 0$ we have $[m].prov[t] \in w$.

5   Design Model for Integrative Simulations

5.1   Design of the Timecontroller

The specification of the system requirements of the last section is highly non-constructive. In this section we focus on a solution of the coordination problem which can be easily transformed into an executable program. The basic idea is to introduce a global timecontroller that coordinates appropriately all simulation models participating in an integrative simulation. More precisely, we want to design an FSP process, called TIMECONTROLLER, such that for n simulation models the composite process

$$||SYS = ([1]:MODEL(Step_1)||\ldots||[n]:MODEL(Step_n)||$$
$$TIMECONTROLLER(Step_1,\ldots,Step_n))/\{start/[Models].start\}$$

restricts the execution traces of the uncontrolled simulation models to the legal ones. The composite process SYS is then considered as the design model for the system. The (static) structure of SYS is represented by the diagram in Figure 2 which indicates the required communication links.

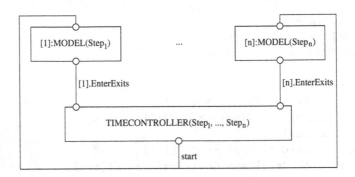

Fig. 2. Structure diagram of the design model

The communication links show that each simulation model m communicates with the timecontroller via the shared **enter** and **exit** actions in the (labelled) set **[m].EnterExits** (see Section 4.1 for the definition of **EnterExits**). This means that the simulation models synchronize with the timecontroller on actions of the form **[m].enterGet[t]** etc., where $m \in$ Models and $t \in$ Time. It is then the task of the timecontroller to guarantee that synchronization can only occur if the constraints determined by *all* property processes (given in Section 4) are satisfied. For this purpose the **enter** actions of the timecontroller are guarded by appropriate conditions which monitor the validity of the safety properties. To express the necessary conditions the timecontroller is equipped with a local state (modelled by index variables) which records the execution status of all simulation models to be coordinated. More precisely, the timecontroller stores for each model the time for which it gets the next import data (represented by the index **nextGet**) and the time for which the model will provide the next export data (represented by the index **nextProv**).

The following time controller definition is formulated for the case of two simulation models where the time steps of the two models are given by parameters. It is obvious that this description provides a general pattern which can be easily applied to an arbitrary number of simulation models. For a timecontroller definition which is generic w.r.t. the number of simulation models one would need array types which are not available in FSP (but would be available in SPIN [6]). Let us still remark that the guards of the **enter** actions are inferred from the requirements specification by building the conjunction of the guards occuring in the property processes for the validity of data. Moreover, note that model checking shows that the exclusion property for **get** and **prov** is already guaranteed by these conditions and therefore does not need a special treatment.

```
TIMECONTROLLER(Step1=1,Step2=1) =
  (start -> TC[SimStart][SimStart][SimStart][SimStart]),

TC[nextGet1:Time][nextProv1:Time][nextGet2:Time][nextProv2:Time] =
  (dummy[t:Time] ->
    //enterGet
    (when (nextProv1-Step1<=t & t<nextProv1 &
           nextProv2-Step2<=t & t<nextProv2)
           [Models].enterGet[t] ->
              TC[nextGet1][nextProv1][nextGet2][nextProv2]
    //exitGet
    |[1].exitGet[t] -> TC[t+Step1][nextProv1][nextGet2][nextProv2]
    |[2].exitGet[t] -> TC[nextGet1][nextProv1][t+Step2][nextProv2]
    //enterProv
    |when (nextGet1>=t & nextGet2>=t)
          [Models].enterProv[t] ->
              TC[nextGet1][nextProv1][nextGet2][nextProv2]
    //exitProv
    |[1].exitProv[t] ->
          if (t+Step1<=SimEnd)
          then TC[nextGet1][t+Step1][nextGet2][nextProv2]
          else TC[SimStart][SimStart][SimStart][SimStart]
    |[2].exitProv[t] ->
          if (t+Step2<=SimEnd)
          then TC[nextGet1][nextProv1][nextGet2][t+Step2]
          else TC[SimStart][SimStart][SimStart][SimStart]
    |dummy[t] -> TC[nextGet1][nextProv1][nextGet2][nextProv2])
  )\{dummy[Time]}.
```

Let us still comment the role of the actions dummy[t:Time] in the above process description. In fact, we would not need these actions if we could write

```
TC[nextGet1:Time][nextProv1:Time][nextGet2:Time][nextProv2:Time] =
  //enterGet
  (when (nextProv1-Step1<=t & t<nextProv1 &
         nextProv2-Step2<=t & t<nextProv2)
         [Models].enterGet[t:Time] ->
            TC[nextGet1][nextProv1][nextGet2][nextProv2]
  ...
```

This would make perfect sense expressing that for any $m \in$ Models *and* for any $t \in$ Time the action [m].enterGet[t] can only happen if the guard is satisfied for t. Unfortunately FSP does not support this possibility since the index variable t is considered to be undefined in the guard. However, if we first introduce the (non-sense) actions dummy[t:Time] then the index variable t is known where necessary. The dummy actions are made invisible by applying the hiding operator.

As an example, the design model of a distributed simulation with two simulation models having time steps 2 and 3 resp. is given by the following composite process.

```
const StepModel1 = 2
const StepModel2 = 3
||SYS =
    ([1]:MODEL(StepModel1)||[2]:MODEL(StepModel2)||
    TIMECONTROLLER(StepModel1,StepModel2))/{start/[Models].start}.
```

We cannot visualize the labelled transition system of the process SYS because it has too many states and transitions. However, for an analysis of the behaviour of the design model we can consider different views on the system which can be formally defined by means of the interface operator. For instance, if we want to focus only on the get and prov actions executed by the system we can build the process SYS@{[Models].GetProvs} where the set GetProvs has been defined in Section 4.1. The corresponding LTS, after minimalization w.r.t. invisible actions, is shown in the following diagram.

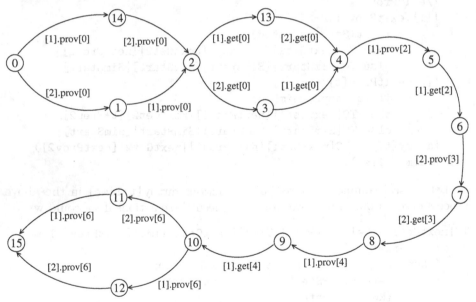

5.2   Checking the Safety Properties

In order to check that the design model indeed satisfies the required safety properties we apply standard model checking techniques. For this purpose we construct for each property process the parallel composition with the design model. If in the resulting LTS the error state is not reachable then the safety property is fulfiled, otherwise it is violated. For instance, if the two simulation models from above are involved in an integrative simulation we construct the following processes.

```
||CHECK_VALIDDATA_USER1_PROV2 =
    (SYS||VALIDDATA(1,StepModel1,2,StepModel2)).
||CHECK_VALIDDATA_USER2_PROV1 =
    (SYS||VALIDDATA(2,StepModel2,1,StepModel1)).
||CHECK_EXCLUSION = (SYS||EXCLUSION).
```

The analysis with the LTSA tool shows that no errors occur, i.e. the design model satisfies the coordination requirements for the validity of data and for get/provide exclusion. For more complex configurations more efficient model checkers like SPIN [6] should be used. Several runs with SPIN have shown that the efficiency of model checking the design of the timecontroller depends strongly on the distribution of the individual model steps whereby it is beneficial if their greatest common divisor is as small as possible. Otherwise one may run out of memory and therefore appropriate abstraction techniques have still to be investigated.

5.3 Checking the Liveness Properties

In section 4 we have stated a liveness property which requires that each simulation model provides data during the whole simulation period at any time that fits to its local time step. To check this condition with LTSA we can define a collection of progress properties of the form

```
progress PROV_Modelm_t = {[m].prov[t]}
```

for each $m \in Models$ and $t \in Time$ with $t\%Step_m = 0$. With this approach, however, two difficulties arise. First, we obtain quite a lot of progress properties to be considered and, more seriously, none of the properties will be fulfilled because simulations are finite but progress properties assume infinite execution traces.

The first difficulty can be easily solved by using indexed progress properties. In our case we define for each model a family of progress properties indexed by the time for which the model should provide data. This means that for each $m \in Models$ we obtain an (indexed) progress property of the following form:

```
progress PROV_Modelm[i:0..(SimEnd-SimStart)/StepModelm] =
    {[m].prov[SimStart + i * StepModelm]}
```

To overcome the second problem the idea is to introduce artificial cycles such that after a simulation is finished it is automatically restarted. We will not further detail here the necessary, straightforward modifications of the processes occurring in the design model. It should be obvious that for checking the required liveness property for integrative simulations it is now (necessary and) sufficient to check that the modified design model satisfies all progress properties from above. Indeed a progress analysis with LTSA shows that no progress property is violated. Thus, in summary, we have shown that the timecontroller-based design model is a correct solution of the coordination problem.

6   Conclusion

We have demonstrated the usefulness of a rigorous formal modelling approach for the development of a solution for a non-trivial coordination problem occurring, for instance, in environmental systems engineering. The general strategy of this approach which is driven by property processes can, however, be applied in all situations where single components run concurrently with local time scales but must cooperate according to some predefined global order. We believe that the incremental specification of system requirements by using property processes is methodologically very useful. This method is supported by the language FSP [9] but not by SPIN [6] or related model checking approaches. On the other hand we have seen that FSP has also some technical deficiencies (concerning array types and guarded indexed actions) which is not the case for SPIN. Also for checking complex models the performance of the SPIN tool is much better than the one of the FSP tool LTSA. To check complex configurations, however, we still need appropriate abstraction techniques to overcome the problem of state explosion.

For lack of space we have not shown in this paper how to construct an implementation of the timecontroller-based design model. Indeed for this purpose we can apply a general translation scheme which transforms the design model into a Java implementation realizing the single simulation models by concurrently executing threads and the timecontroller by a monitor object with appropriate synchronized methods which implement the enter and exit actions of the timecontroller.

Acknowledgement

We are grateful to Alexander Knapp for carefully reading a draft of this paper and for valuable suggestions. Many thanks also to Michael Barth for in-depth discussions on the coordination problem and for a timecontroller implementation and its integration in the DANUBIA system.

References

1. Barth M., Hennicker R., Kraus A., Ludwig M.: DANUBIA: An Integrative Simulation System for Global Research in the Upper Danube Basin. Cybernetics and Systems, Vol. 35, Nr. 7–8, pages 639–666, 2004.
2. Barth M., Knapp A.: A Coordination Architecture for Time-Dependent Components. Proc. 22nd Int. Multi-Conf. Applied Informatics. Software Engineering (IASTED SE'04), pages 6–11, 2004.
3. EESD, http://www.cordis.lu/eesd (last visited 2005/03/17)
4. GLOWA, http://www.glowa.org (last visited 2005/03/17)
5. Hoare, C. A. R.: Communicating Sequential Processes, Prentice-Hall, 1985.
6. Holzmann, G., The SPIN Model Checker – Primer and Reference Manual, Addison-Wesley, 2004.
7. LTSA, http://www-dse.doc.ic.ac.uk/concurrency/ (last visited 2005/03/17)

8. Ludwig R., Mauser W., Niemeyer S., Colgan A., Stolz, R., Escher-Vetter H., Kuhn M., Reichstein M., Tenhunen J., Kraus A., Ludwig M., Barth M., Hennicker R.: Web-based Modeling of Water, Energy and Matter Fluxes to Support Decision Making in Mesoscale Catchments - the Integrative Perspective of GLOWA-Danube. Physics and Chemistry of the Earth, Vol. 28, pages 621–634, 2003.
9. Magee J., Kramer J.: Concurrency – State Models and Java Programs, John Wiley & Sons, 1999.

A Timing Analysis of AODV

Sibusisiwe Chiyangwa and Marta Kwiatkowska

School of Computer Science
The University of Birmingham
Edgbaston, Birmingham, B15 2TT, UK
{syc,mzk}@cs.bham.ac.uk

Abstract. Mobile ad hoc networks (MANETs) are wireless networks formed spontaneously. Communication in such networks typically involves multi-hop relays, and is subjected to dynamic topology changes and frequent link failures. This complex scenario demands robust routing protocol standards that ensure correct and timely delivery of messages. Recently, formal verification has been successful in detecting ambiguities in protocol standards. We consider the Ad hoc On Demand Distance Vector (AODV) protocol, a reactive protocol currently undergoing standardisation at the IETF (RFC3561). AODV performs route discovery whenever a route to the destination is needed, and retains routing information for a period of time specified by the standard. We apply the real-time model checker UPPAAL to consider the effect of the protocol parameters on the timing behaviour of AODV, thus complementing the earlier untimed verification effort. Our study of the recent versions of the standard (RFC3561-bis-01) has highlighted a dependency of the lifetime of routes on network size, which can be alleviated by allowing the route timeouts to adapt to network growth.

1 Introduction

Mobile ad hoc networks (MANETs) are networks of mobile devices that communicate without the need for a central authority and infrastructure, formed without a-priori knowledge or planning. Ad hoc networks can be set up anywhere and anytime, are dynamic and often exhibit frequent topology changes due to loss of contact and movement. Three basic approaches to routing are taken: proactive protocols, which continuously exchange routing information between the nodes (e.g. OLSR); reactive, which build routes on demand (e.g. AODV); and hybrid combinations of the two (e.g. ZRP).

The Ad hoc On Demand Distance Vector (AODV) protocol [6] is a reactive routing protocol currently in the process of being standardized at the IETF (RFC3561) and implemented [12, 19]. To transmit data over such a network, the AODV protocol enables dynamic, multihop routing between devices. AODV is an *on demand* algorithm, meaning that a route discovery mechanism is invoked only when the sender wishes to transmit data. These routes are maintained as long as they are needed by the senders, and are deleted after a certain amount of time has passed so as not to overload the routing tables. AODV is designed

M. Steffen and G. Zavattaro (Eds.): FMOODS 2005, LNCS 3535, pp. 306–321, 2005.

for ad hoc networks of a wide range of sizes, from the very small to networks of tens to thousands of mobile, Internet enabled, nodes. Simulation experiments for 1000 nodes have been reported, and first implementations are available [19].

The dynamic aspects of mobile ad hoc networks mean that both the topology of such networks and their size varies over time, giving rise to an unbounded execution tree and *infinitely many* states. This scenario is much more complex than for existing network protocols, and consequently designing protocols that achieve correct and timely delivery of messages is inherently more difficult. Much valuable effort is therefore being directed towards the formulation of routing protocol *standards* for MANETs, of which AODV RFC3561 is one example, to serve as a *specification* to which a protocol *implementation* must conform. The implementations are then developed according to the guidelines set by the standard. Unfortunately, the resulting protocol complexity sometimes results in unintentional ambiguities introduced into the standard, which, if undetected, can be transferred to the implementation. An analysis of the proposed standards is therefore desirable, and it results in subsequent revisions.

Recently, formal verification has been successfully employed as an aid to detect ambiguities in the proposed AODV standards and implementations [9, 15], resulting in the discovery of routing loop errors in early protocol versions (version 4) that have been addressed in later revisions of the draft standard. Both these approaches do not model real-time, and instead replace the real-valued timer events with non-deterministic time-outs. This can result in false positives, i.e. error traces that do not correspond to realistically timed scenarios, and is undesirable since the AODV protocol uses real-valued timers in an essential way, for example to determine the lifetime of routes. It is important that routing is handled in a timely manner, i.e. route discovery and message delivery happen without unnecessary time delays. The timing values are determined by formulas dependent on protocol parameters (constants) specified by the standard. Clearly, the choice of the constants and the route lifetimes will affect the timeliness of protocol actions, especially as the network size and topology change dynamically over time.

In this paper, we complement the existing analyses of the AODV protocol by model checking its timing aspects. Working from the most recent draft standard documents, we build a timed automata model for AODV using the UPPAAL [22, 24] model checker. We consider the effect of the default protocol parameters on the timing behaviour of AODV, and investigate properties such as timely route discovery and the ability to deliver messages within a specified time period. Our study of the AODV draft standard has highlighted a dependency of the lifetime of routes on network size, which may lead to failure to discover the route if it exists or failure to deliver the data to destination. The observation pertains to the latest version (RFC3561-bis-01 [6]) and, in a simpler form, to earlier versions (13 and RFC3561-bis-00) of the draft standard. Having inspected a recent implementation of AODV [19], we confirm our observation also for this implementation with the help of an ns-2 simulation experiment. We propose a modification to the standard that alleviates the problem by allowing the route timeouts to adapt to network growth.

2   The AODV Protocol

The Ad Hoc On-Demand Distance Vector (AODV) Protocol is an IP routing protocol that allows users to find and maintain routes to other users in the network. AODV is *on-demand*, or *reactive*, in the sense that routes are established only when needed. The routing decisions are made using distance vectors, i.e. distances measured in hops to all available routers. The protocol supports unicast, broadcast, and multicast. The version of AODV we describe below is based on the RFC draft standard [6].

Each nodes maintains a *sequence number*, which saves a time stamp, and a *routing table*, which contains routes to destinations. Sequence numbers are used to determine the freshness of routes (the higher the number, the fresher the route, and the older one can be discarded). Each table entry contains the address of the next hop (next node to destination), a hop count (number of hops to the destination) and a destination sequence number. Since this is an on-demand distance vector scheme, routers maintain distances of those destinations only that they need to contact or relay information to. Each active route is associated with a lifetime stored in the table; after this time has passed route timeout is triggered, and the route is marked as invalid and later on removed. AODV uses two main procedures, *route discovery* and *route maintenance*, which are described below.

Route Discovery. If a sender (source node) needs a route to destination, it broadcasts a *ROUTE REQUEST* (RREQ) message. Every node also maintains a *broadcast_id* which, when taken together with the originator's IP address, uniquely identifies a RREQ. Every time a sender issues a RREQ, it increments its broadcast_id and sequence number by one. The sender buffers this RREQ for *PATH_DISCOVERY_TIME* (PDT) so that it does not reprocess it when its neighbours send it back. The sender then waits for *NET_TRAVERSAL_TIME* (NETT) for a *ROUTE REPLY* (RREP). If a RREP is not received within this time, the sender will rebroadcast another RREQ up to *RREQ_TRIES* times. With each additional attempt, the waiting time (NETT) is doubled.

When a node receives a RREQ message it has not seen before, it sets up a reverse route back to the node where the RREQ came from. This reverse route has a lifetime value of *ACTIVE_ROUTE_TIMEOUT* (ART). The reverse route entry is stored along with the information about the requested destination address. If the node that receives this message does not have a route to the destination, it rebroadcasts the RREQ. Each node keeps track of the number of hops the message has made, as well as which node has sent it the broadcast RREQ. If nodes receive a RREQ, which they have already processed, they discard the RREQ and do not forward it.

If a node has a route to the destination, it then replies by unicasting a RREP back to the node it received the request from. The reply is sent back to the sender via the reverse route set by the RREQ. As the RREP propagates back to the source, nodes set up forward pointers to the destination. Once the source node receives the RREP, the route has been established and data packets may be forwarded to the destination.

Route Maintenance. The role of route maintenance is to provide feedback to the sender in case a router or link has gone down, to allow the route to be modified or re-discovered. A route can stop working simply because one of the mobile nodes has moved. If a source node moves, then it must rediscover a new route. If an intermediate node moves, it must inform all its neighbours that needed this hop. This message is forwarded to all the other hops and the old route is deleted. The source node must then re-discover a new route.

One proposed way for a node to keep track of its neighbours is by using *HELLO* messages. These are periodically sent to detect link failures. Upon receiving notification of a broken link, the source node can restart the rediscovery process. If there is a link breakage, a *ROUTE ERROR* (RERR) message can be broadcast on the net. Any host that receives the RERR invalidates the route and rebroadcasts the error messages with the unreachable destination information to all nodes in the network.

3   Correctness Requirements for Routing Protocols

Reactive routing protocols for mobile ad hoc networks are complex schemes for the following reasons. Firstly, the scheme must allow for an unbounded number of nodes acting in parallel, with each node acting as a router, destination and relay node. Secondly, the topology can change dynamically, and hence the protocol must be able to recover from link failures. Finally, real-time clocks play a key role in the protocol, both in setting the lifetimes of routes and triggering timeouts. Achieving efficient and correct routing in such scenarios is a non-trivial undertaking for standardisation efforts. The main correctness requirements for a routing protocol, first stated in [27], are:

I. If a path exists between two nodes, then a route between them will eventually be discovered.
II. When a route has been discovered and it is valid, packets are eventually delivered from source to destination.

Property II implies that a so-called routing loop is prevented. A routing loop is a situation in which, during the route discovery process, a flawed route is formed in which nodes point to each other in a forwarding circle. Thus, packets are not delivered to the destination. Such a situation can arise if a link breaks during route discovery and a node is not notified that its route became invalid.

The conventional approach to analysing network protocols is via testing and simulation. Neither is able to rule out logical flaws in the protocols because of partial coverage of executions: simulation or test runs can often miss certain conditions dependent on timing, so called 'corner cases', thus bypassing a possible erroneous execution that may be exhibited by an implementation in future. On the other hand, subjecting the protocol to *formal verification*, for example via *model checking*, enables detailed and exhaustive analysis of network protocols. A model of the protocol together with the required properties, usually expressed in temporal logic, is submitted to a software tool called a model checker. The process of model checking can definitively establish that the property holds, or that it is violated, in which case a trace leading to error is produced. The limitation of model checking is that only finite-state models/configurations can be handled, and thus infinite-state systems can be verified only if they have property preserving finite-state abstractions. Thus, these tools are particularly useful to demonstrate violations of properties that can serve as important feedback for the standardisation effort. A more powerful approach is that of *theorem proving*; it enables correctness proofs for all possible parameter values, but at a substantial manpower effort.

The use of formal verification methods to analyse Internet standards has been advocated in [10, 15]. A model of the protocol can be built from the standard specification and subjected to verification. In [10], a routing loop error detected in AODV version 2 with the SPIN model checker and verification of routing loop freedom was performed with the help of HOL theorem prover. However, newer versions of AODV, version 5 onwards, crucially depend on timing. The standard sets certain parameters (constants), and those are then used to assign route lifetimes and define event timeouts. There are then two issues that one needs to consider about the protocol. Firstly, properties I and II should be established with the additional proviso of "in a timely manner". More importantly, the particular combination of timing constants may have an effect on the correctness of the protocol: for example, routes may time out too early. With the exception of a small-scale study in [29], this issue has not been investigated; the models built were untimed, derived by replacing a delay with a non-deterministic timeout event. This may miss timing errors. Therefore, as already suggested in [10] [page 566], AODV from version 5 onwards necessitates a real-time verification. We address this in this paper by analysing most recent versions of AODV [6] using a state-of-the-art real-time model checker UPPAAL [24], with emphasis on how the parameters as set by the standard affect the *correctness* of routing and message delivery (properties I and II) of the protocol.

4   Modelling AODV Using Timed Automata

Since we are interested in analysing timing aspects of AODV, we model the protocol with timed automata as opposed to a C-like program in previous works [10, 15]. UPPAAL [24] is an established and widely used model checker which provides an easy to use environment for constructing timed automata models and verifying them against timed temporal logic specifications. The UPPAAL model-checking engine works on-the-fly and takes advantage of some advanced techniques to overcome the state space explosion. Experimental results show that, thanks to these techniques, UPPAAL is significantly faster than other real-time verification tools [23] and also able to verify more complex systems [7]. Some of the industrial case studies include: the *Bounded Retransmission Protocol* whose correctness was shown [16] to be dependent on correctly choosing timeout values; the *Bang & Olufsen Audio/Video Protocol*, known to be faulty, for which an error trace was uncovered [20] and a corrected model automatically verified; and the *Collision Avoidance Protocol*, which was shown to be collision free [1].

This paper concerns the latest version RFC3561-bis-01 of the standard. Every node in an AODV network acts as a sender, router (intermediate node) or destination depending on the situation. Therefore, all nodes in an ADOV network have identical functions. We first model this behaviour as a *generic* AODV node. Since an AODV network is symmetric, we can use a template of UPPAAL to simplify the model.

We define node parameters as set by the draft standard [6]. As we investigate the effect of the timing values that are suggested in the draft standard on the correctness of the protocol, we can abstract the actual control packets from the model since they are of no interest in this particular case. For simplicity, we also abstract the use of RERRs and HELLO messages since we only analyse the *route discovery* process and not the *route maintenance* process. If a node receives a data packet, and the intended destination's route is expired or does not exist, we halt the verification. The model of the generic node can be found in [14]. An *n-node* AODV network is then modelled using *n* instances of the generic node.

Since we have worked from the draft standard [6], the model that we have derived can serve as standard *timed specification*. We have performed an analysis of thus derived specification, and were able to confirm a routing loop error of [10] for an appropriately adapted version of the model. However, the state-space explosion means that the maximum size of the network that we could consider by direct verification is 5. For larger network sizes the verification becomes infeasible. We note, however, that the routing loop error has been exhibited in [15] with 4 nodes and in [10] with 3 nodes. We therefore seek ways to reduce the size of the model while preserving the properties of interest. For a protocol model S (*specification*) and its refinement R (*implementation*), denoted by $R \leq S$, we say R preserves S's properties of interest if $R \models \varphi$ implies $S \models \varphi$.

AODV Specification vs Implementation. Observe that, for the properties we are interested in analysing, it suffices to consider one specific sender and one destination. This can be achieved by refining the generic node into nodes that perform the specific functions, while preserving key behaviour. The generic node is thus refined separately into three main functions, the sender, destination and intermediate node, as follows:

- *sender*: this node will only generate and send RREQs, receive RREPs and send data packets,
- *intermediate node*: this node will only receive RREQs, RREPs and data packets and forward them,
- *destination*: this node will only receive RREQs and data packets, and generate and send RREPs.

Since we only consider the route discovery process, only the destination node will increment its own destination sequence number. The individual nodes in the model, see [14] for the timed automata, behave as follows:

The Sender Node. The *sender* will increment its *sequence number* and *broadcast_id* by one, then sends a RREQ and moves to state *wait_for_reply* to wait for a RREP. If a RREP is not received within *NET_TRAVERSAL_TIME* time

(NETT), the sender times out and sends another RREQ. The NETT is doubled and the *broadcast_id* incremented by one every time a RREQ is resent. The sender will resend RREQs up to *RETRIES* times. If a RREP corresponding to a RREQ that has timed out is received, it is ignored. When the anticipated RREP is received, the sender establishes the route to the destination node and starts sending data packets. When the sender has tried *RETRIES* times for a route and still times out after the $RETRIES^{th}$ time, the sender node concludes that a route to the desired destination does not exist.

The Intermediate Node. The intermediate node will accept a RREQ, RREP or data packets from its neighbouring nodes, update its own routing table, broadcast the RREQ or forward the RREP/data packets to the next node along the route to the destination node for the data packets and the source node for the RREPs, according to its (intermediate node) routing table only if the route is still active. If the route has expired, the intermediate node does not forward the RREPs or data packets. If intermediate nodes are allowed to reply to RREQs, an intermediate node will generate a RREP to a RREQ if it knows the route to the destination sought. Every RREQ has a flag that is set to enable, or unset to disable, intermediate nodes to reply to RREQs.

The Destination Node. The destination node will accept RREQs from its neighbouring nodes, then updates its routing table, increments its *sequence number* (destination sequence number) by one, and generates a RREP. The destination node will also accept data packets. We model the destination to receive just the first data packet, and, once the first data packet gets to the destination node, we restart the route discovery process.

Establishing Refinement Between AODV Specification and Implementation Models. When deriving the specialised nodes from the generic node model, we must ensure that the properties of interest are preserved through this derivation, i.e. $R \leq S$ and $R \models \varphi$ implies $S \models \varphi$. In our case, S is a parallel composition of individual components, for example $S = S_1 \| S_2$, where each component has a corresponding implementation (refinement) R_1, R_2 respectively. The principle of compositionality allows us to tackle the state space explosion in the following way.

We first need to establish that R_i are true implementations (refinements) of S_i, i.e. $R_i \leq S_i$. A number of relations are possible as refinement in the context of timed automata. Since we have used timed automata with committed locations (no delay is allowed to occur in a committed state), urgent channels (in a state where two components may synchronize on an urgent channel, no further delay is allowed) and shared variables (global variables), we work with *timed ready simulation* [21] as refinement; it relates states of one timed automaton A to states of another timed automaton B in such away that the actions and their timings in admissible timed executions correspond (as in timed simulation) in the presence of shared variables, urgent channels and committed states. Unlike timed simulation, timed ready simulation $\leq$ is a pre-congruence for the parallel operator, that is, $R \leq S$ implies $R \| A \leq S \| A$. Let $\leq$ preserve a chosen class of properties, i.e. $R_i \leq S_i$ and $R_i \models \varphi$ implies $S_i \models \varphi$. In UPPAAL, the verification of $A \leq B$ can be reduced to the following reachability problem:

$$A \leq B \text{ iff } A \| T_B \text{ does not reach } error$$

where T_B is the test automaton derived from B [28]. Next, assuming we have established that $R_i \leq S_i$ holds for $i = 1, 2$, by compositionality based on the result of [2, 21] we have:

$$\frac{R_1 \leq S_1 \qquad R_2 \leq S_2}{R_1 \| R_2 \ \leq \ S_1 \| S_2}$$

We represent the AODV protocol *specification* as a network of generic AODV nodes, i.e. a composition of the form:

$$AODV_{spec} \equiv generic_1 \| \ldots \| generic_{n-1} \| generic_n$$

and, as *implementation*, we can consider a network, where we have one sender node requesting a route, several intermediate nodes to forward packets, and one destination node, namely:

$$AODV_{impl} \equiv sender \| inter_1 \| \ldots \| inter_n \| dest$$

Thus, application of the technique of [28] to the AODV node models, that is, a manual derivation of the test automaton in each case and execution of a reachability check confirming that *error* is not reached, allows us to conclude by compositionality:

$$AODV_{impl} \leq AODV_{spec}$$

In the test automaton, *error* is a designated error-location entered whenever the behaviour of $AODV_{impl}$ is outside the behaviour specified by $AODV_{spec}$. With this approach, we reduce the size of the models that have to be analysed, in a manner preserving chosen properties. We focus on *existential* properties, which are preserved under refinement, i.e. $R \leq S$ and $R \models \varphi$ implies $S \models \varphi$, where φ is of the form E<> ψ (eventually ψ) and may refer to real-time deadlines.

The model $AODV_{impl}$ is a refinement of the original specification model $AODV_{spec}$ built from generic nodes, which is nevertheless sufficiently detailed to exhibit a timing flaw in the specification, described in the next sections.

5   The Verification Approach

We consider the effect of default timing constants on the properties of eventual route formation and eventual delivery of packets. It suffices, in our case, to assume absence of data loss. In this paper, we focus on route discovery and management and consider active routes.

A route is deemed active as long as there are data packets periodically travelling from the source to the destination along that path. Once the source stops sending data packets, the links will time out and eventually be deleted from the intermediate node routing tables. We focus on specific verification scenarios with finite static topologies and look for property violations. Since we have established refinement, it follows that any existential properties true of the implementation also hold for the specification. The model of the protocol can be investigated under different topology scenarios; the analysis we report here pertains to the (static) linear topology.

The Linear Topology Scenario. We arrange nodes of an *n-node* network into a chain, with one sender and one destination, as follows. IP addresses are selected using integers from 0 to $n-1$. Node 0 will be our originating node (sender), node $n-1$ will be the destination node, and the rest are intermediate nodes with IP addresses allocated consecutively. Thus, node 0 has node 1 as its neighbour and the destination node has $n-2$ as its neighbour.

The AODV draft standard [6] suggests that a sender tries three times to discover a route before concluding that a node cannot be reached. To allow easy instantiation of the model for different numbers n of the intermediate nodes, we have formulated an *n_nodes* node which combines n nodes linearly into one multiple node.

Thus, the obtained *n_node* has fewer states, which ensures feasibility of the verification. The correctness of the construction is confirmed by checking refinement as before. Now, we model the linear topology scenario with one sender, one destination and three identical sets of intermediate nodes, one for each RREQ attempt. In other words, we have three copies of each intermediate node running in parallel, as illustrated in Figure 1.

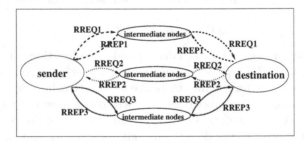

Fig. 1. The AODV linear topology model

For the remainder of the paper we consider the simplified model for $AODV_{impl}$ which employs the *n_node*. We successfully proved that twelve intermediate nodes simulate a *12_node* multiple node. The automata models can be found in [14].

6   A Timing Analysis of AODV

In this paper we consider some of the default constants suggested in the latest version of AODV draft standard [6]. We are particularly interested in the *NET_DIAMETER* (ND) value. This value is a measure of the network size, defined as the maximum possible number of hops between two nodes in the network, and is used to determine route lifetime and time-out values. The protocol suggests that the value of ND be a constant, but does not mention how this value should be adjusted to suit the dynamic changes in network size. The following are some of the default constants suggested in [6]:

$NODE\_TRAVERSAL\_TIME$ = $10ms$. This is the time taken by a node on average to process a packet.

$NET\_DIAMETER$ = 20. We use 2 for model reduction.

$NET\_TRAVERSAL\_TIME$ = $2 * NODE\_TRAVERSAL\_TIME *$ $NET\_DIAMETER$ ms. Time a sender waits for a RREP.

$ACTIVE\_ROUTE\_TIMEOUT$= $max(3000, PATH\_DISCOVERY\_TIME)$
(abbrev. ART) where $PATH\_DISCOVERY\_TIME =$ $2* 2 * NET\_TRAVERSAL\_TIME$. This is lifetime of a valid route. If maximum is 3000ms then we have the situation described version 13, else version 00.

$RETRIES$ = 3.

Though we work with average message delivery times, it is also possible to rerun the analysis for an interval of values. We separately consider two cases set out in the standard:

1. when intermediate nodes are allowed to respond to RREQs, and
2. when intermediate nodes are **not** allowed to respond to RREQs, with only the destination node allowed to respond.

Below we describe the outcome of our analysis when intermediate nodes are allowed to reply to a RREQ; the other case is omitted for reasons of space. Assume we have a linear topology with fourteen nodes in the network, one sender (number 0), one destination (number 13) and twelve intermediate nodes (numbered 1 to 12). We also assume that we have no message loss and no delays in the network. The sender (node 0) sends a message to node 13, and is allowed to try three times for a route to a destination. We refer to each route discovery attempt as the *Route Request Process* (RRP). We ensure that the sender issues five RRPs, each with three attempts, before it can conclude that a route does not exists. In real life a sender might try one RRP and conclude that a route does not exist. At a later stage the same node may try again to find a route to the same destination, maybe for a different set of data packets, and the topology might have changed.

We first investigate the correctness property I, i.e. eventual route discovery, assuming the route exists, in negated form.

I. Can a sender fail to find a route to a destination when the route exists? Using UPPPAL we verify the property 'eventually the sender reaches a state with no route found':

$$E<> sender.no\_route$$

where the *no_route* state is a state in which the sender learns that no route exists, for a situation in which the route is known to exist.

Because the topology remains static, the number of RREQs the sender issues does not affect the outcome. This undesirable property is satisfied and the following trace is produced, where we use 'ip[n]=m' to denote that the node with the IP address n is sending to node with address m, and similarly for destination IP address 'dip[n]=m':

$$
\begin{array}{ll}
\textbf{RREQ trace} : & ip[0] = 13 \quad ip[1] = 11 \quad ip[2] = 7 \\
\textbf{RREP trace} : & dip[0] = 1 \quad dip[1] = 2 \quad dip[2] = 3
\end{array}
$$

This trace (see detailed illustration in Figures 2 and 3) means that the first RREQ (RREQ1) gets to the destination node (node 13). The first RREP (RREP1) is generated and sent back to the sender. When RREQ1 is at node 4, the sender's RREQ timer times out and the second RREQ (RREQ2) is sent. RREQ2 gets to node 11 and finds a route (set by RREP1). RREP2 is generated by node 11. The sender's RREQ timer times out again and another RREQ (RREQ3) is sent. RREQ3 gets to node 7 and finds that node 7 has a route to the destination (set by RREP1). RREP3 is generated by node 7. When RREP1 gets to node 1, the route to the sender has timed out and is not forwarded. When RREP2 and RREP3 get to node 1, they are both not forwarded as well, as the route to the sender node has since expired. Thus, eventually the sender times out, failing after 3 attempts to find a route to the destination when, in fact, the route existed.

Note that, in Figures 2 and 3, we show route timers for the intermediate nodes only, i.e. nodes 1 to node 12. After 70ms, RREQ1 is at the destination and RREQ2 is at node 8. In the first step, after 40ms in Figure 2, the sender times out as the RREQ timer is initially set to 40ms. A second RREQ is sent, and the sender's RREQ timer is set to 80ms (2*40ms).

In step 3, in Figure 2, RREP1 has been generated by the destination and has been propagated to node 10. RREQ2 is at node 11. Node 11 has a route to the destination set by RREP1 and because intermediate nodes are allowed to reply

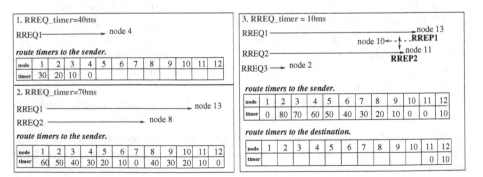

Fig. 2. RREQ1, RREQ2, RREP1 and RREP2 generations

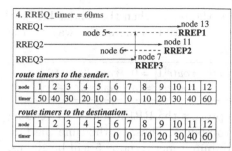

Fig. 3. RREP3 generations

to RREQs, RREP2 is generated by node 11. RREQ2 has been updating the life of the route to the sender on its way to the destination. RREQ3 is at node 2.

After 60ms, see Figure 3, RREP1 is at node 5, RREP2 at node 6 and RREQ3 at node 7. Node 7 has a route to the destination set by RREP1, and hence can reply to RREQ3. RREP3 is generated. RREQ3 has been updating the route to the sender. After 100ms, as shown in Figure 3 (since RREQ3 was sent), RREP1 is at node 1, and RREP2 and RREP3 are at nodes 2 and 3 respectively. The route lifetime at node 1 is 90ms (which is greater than ART=80ms), and hence RREP1 will not be forwarded to the sender. RREP2 and RREP3 will be forwarded to node 1 where the route has expired and will not be forwarded to the sender either. The sender will eventually time out and conclude that the route does not exist.

Next we consider property II, again in negated form.

II. Can a route expire before a data packet is transmitted? We assume that the sender starts sending data packets as soon as the route is found. We consider the first data packet along the way from the sender to the destination and test to see if any of the intermediate node's routes to the destination will time out before they have actually forwarded the first data packet. The property, 'eventually the intermediate node times out', is as follows:

$$E<> (\text{inter.data\_route\_timeout})$$

Assume we have 7 nodes in the network, one sender, one destination and five intermediate nodes. When the first data packet gets to node 5, the route to the destination at that node would have timed out, and this property is satisfied. Below is the trace that is obtained:

RREQ trace	: $ip[0] = 6$ $ip[1] = 6$ $ip[2] = 0$
RREP trace	: $dip[0] = 0$ $dip[1] = 0$ $dip[2] = 0$
Route Lifetime	: $route[0] = [170, inf]$ $route[1] = 30$ $route[2] = 20$
	$route[3] = 10$ $route[4] = 0$ $route[5] = 100$
Data trace	: $dataip = 5$

To explain this outcome, let us consider the point when the sender has just received RREP2. Below are the values of route timers along the way to the destination:

Route Lifetime : $route[0] = [170, inf]$ $route[1] = 0$ $route[2] = 10$	
$route[3] = 20$ $route[4] = 30$ $route[5] = 50$	

The sender will take another 10ms to process the RREP and start sending data packets, then another 40 ms to get to node 5. Thus, by the time the first data packet gets to node 5, after 50ms the route timer at node 5 will be 100ms, which is greater than ART=80ms.

In summary, we have established that, in a network with (constant) default parameters set by the standard, the correctness requirements I and II are not satisfied. We have exhibited this property in the refined implementation model, assuming absence of message loss and delays; since it is existential, it follows that it is also exhibited by the specification, and in a realistic scenario with message loss and delays.

How to Define NET_DIAMETER. The AODV draft standard may be improved by allowing the value of $NET\_DIAMETER$ to grow with the network size. Initially, we can set it to be e.g. the constant suggested by the standard, and then let individual nodes modify it. If a node receives a RREQ, RREP, or RERR packet that has a hop count that is greater than the node's $NET\_DIAMETER$, then the node should adjust its $NET\_DIAMETER$ to the value of this hop count. This allows the nodes to learn and adapt to the new network size.

We have modified the model accordingly and re-verified the corrected model for the variant where intermediate nodes are allowed to reply to RREQs. The automata for this model can again be found in [14]. We observe that the properties I and II are now satisfied; in particular, the validity of routes is prolonged. Note that this does not amount to a full verification of correctness, which would have required a theorem prover, but is automatic.

For a decrease in network size, we propose to leave the $NET\_DIAMETER$ unchanged. This ensures that, if a route exists, the requesting node will eventually find it. However, if the route does not exist, then the requesting node has to wait longer before it can conclude that this is so.

7   Related Work

Model checking has been successfully used to analyse various distributed protocols, but few papers have applied model checking in the context of mobile ad hoc network routing. We mention the discovery of a routing loop error found in early versions of AODV with the SPIN model checker [8] and Murphi [15]. Engler et al [18] have analysed three AODV implementations using CMC (a model checker for the C programming language), reporting several errors of which one can be attributed to the standard specification on RERR handling. In their earlier work [15], they explain how reordering of RERR messages by the link layer could lead to a routing loop. Other errors reported include mishandling of memory allocation, missed essential checks of packets and routing loops. Their handling of time to ensure a compact model can miss timing errors. A predicate abstraction approach (requiring human intervention) was used in [17] to verify the absence of routing loops. In [9], an automated proof of routing loop freedom is given under certain conditions, using the model checker SPIN and theorem prover HOL. Real-valued time-outs are represented as non-deterministic time-out events, which does not faithfully model real-time passage.

None of the verification studies that we are aware of considered the timing aspects of AODV, with the exception of [29] which used DTSpin [11], an extension of SPIN with discrete time, but was not as extensive as our study. They reported that their DTSpin version was too unstable and abandoned their automatic verification attempt using DTSpin in favour of a manual proof. All the above AODV studies concern earlier, less complex versions of the standard. Some aspects of timing properties have been analysed for the LUNAR protocol [27], using the UPPAAL model checker, but for very small models only.

The *NET_DIAMETER* issue has been raised briefly on the MANET mailing list [25, 26], but not followed up since. Preliminary reports of this work appeared as [13, 14].

8   Conclusion

We have modelled the AODV protocol with timed automata and analysed certain configurations using a number of techniques developed for the UPPAAL model checker to obtain model reductions. We observe that the protocol as specified may unnecessarily result in failure to discover the route or deliver the message. The problem occurs because nodes wait for a fixed time for RREPs that, in a dynamically growing network, may take much longer to reach the requesting node. We propose a modification to the AODV routing algorithm by allowing the nodes to amend the value of *NET_DIAMETER* through learning about the size of the network from the incoming packets. To our knowledge, this is the first solution to this problem.

In contrast with previous work, we have analysed the latest draft specification [6], as well as earlier versions 00 [4] and 13 [5]. All three exhibit this problem, albeit in slightly different form. As a sanity check, we ran ns-2 experiments for the AODV-UU implementation code [30] that complies with version 13, confirming our observations for this implementation also by obtaining identical traces to those exhibited by the model. We have notified the AODV authors about our findings and they have accepted our suggestions [3].

References

1. L. Aceto, P. Bouyer, A. Burgueño, and K. G. Larsen. The Power of Reachability Testing for Timed Automata. In *Proceedings of the 18th Conference on Foundations of Software Technology and Theoretical Computer Science, Chennai, India, December 1998*, volume 1530, pages 245–256. Springer, December 1998.
2. L. Aceto, A. Burgnueno, and K. G. Larsen. Model Checking via Reachability Testing for Timed Automata. Technical Report RS-97-29, BRICS, November 1997.

3. E. M. Belding-Royer and I. D. Chakeres. Private e-mail communication.
4. E. M. Belding-Royer, I. D. Chakeres, and C. E. Perkins. Ad hoc On-Demand Distance Vector (AODV) Routing: *Work in progress*, September 2003. http://www.ietf.org/internet-drafts/draft-perkins-manet-aodvbis-00.txt.
5. E. M. Belding-Royer, I. D. Chakeres, and C. E. Perkins. Ad hoc On-Demand Distance Vector (AODV) Routing: *Work in progress*, February 2003. http://moment.cs.ucsb.edu/AODV/ID/draft-ietf-manet-aodv-13.txt.
6. E. M. Belding-Royer, I. D. Chakeres, and C. E. Perkins. Ad hoc On-Demand Distance Vector (AODV) Routing: *Work in progress*, July 2004. Internet Draft, RFC 3561bis-01, http://moment.cs.ucsb.edu/pub/draft-perkins-manet-aodvbis-02.txt.
7. J. Bengtsson, K. G. Larsen, F. Larsson, P. Pettersson, and W. Yi. UPPAAL - A Tool Suite for Symbolic and Compositional Verification of Real-Time Systems. In *Proceedings of the First Workshop on Tools and Algorithms for the Construction and Analysis of Systems*, volume 1019 of *Lecture Notes in Computer Science*. Springer–Verlag, May 1995.
8. K. Bhargavan, C. A. Gunter, M. Kim, I. Lee, D. Obradovic, O. Sokolsky, and M. Viswanathan. Verism: Formal Analysis of Network Simulations. In *Proceedings of the 2000 ACM SIGSOFT International Symposium on Software Testing and Analysis (ISSTA 2000)*, pages 2–13, Department of Computer Science, Stanford University, Stanford, CA 94305, U.S.A, August 2000.
9. K. Bhargavan, C. A. Gunter, I. Lee, O. Sokolsky, M. Kim, D. Obradovic, and M. Viswanathan. Verisim: Formal Analysis of Network Simulations. *IEEE Transactions on Software Engineering (TSE)*, 28(2):129–145, 2002.
10. K. Bhargavan, C. A. Gunter, and D. Obradovic. Formal Verification of Standards for Distance Vector Routing Protocols. *Jounal of the ACM*, 49(4):538–576, July 2002.
11. D. Bosnacki and D. Dams. Discrete Time Promela and SPIN. Dept. of Computing Science, Eindhoven University of Technology ,Eindhoven, The Netherlands. DTSpin web site: http://www.win.tue.nl/ dragan/DTSpin/.
12. I. D. Chakeres and E. M. Belding-Royer. AODV routing protocol implementation design. In *Proceedings of the International Workshop on Wireless Ad hoc Networking (WWAN)*, pages 698–703, Tokyo, Japan, March 2004.
13. S. Chiyangwa and M. Z. Kwiatkowska. Modelling Ad hoc On-Demand Distance Vector (AODV) Protocol with Timed Automata. In *Proceedings of the Third Workshop on Automated Verification of Critical Systems (AVoCS'03)*, Southampton, UK, April 2003.
14. S. Chiyangwa and M. Z. Kwiatkowska. Analysing Timed Properties of AODV using UPPAAL. Technical Report CSR-04-4, School Of Computer Science, The University of Birmingham, UK, March 2004.
15. A. Chou, D. L. Dill, D. R. Engler, M. Musuvathi, and D. Park. CMC: A Pragmatic Approach to Model Checking Real Code. In *Proceedings of the Fifth Symposium on Operating Systems Design and Implementation*, December 2002.
16. P. R. D'Argenio, T. C. R. Joost-Pieter Katoen, and G. J. Tretmans. The Bounded Retransmission Protocol Must Be on Time! Technical Report CTIT 97-03, Faculty of Computer Science, University of Twente, The Netherlands and Lehrstuhl fur Informatik VII. University of Erlangen, Germany, 1997.
17. S. Das and D. L. Dill. Counter-Example Based Predicate Discovery in Predicate Abstraction. In *Proceedings of the Fourth International Conference on Formal Methods in Computer-Aided Design (FMCAD) 2002*, volume 2517 of *Lecture Notes in Computer Science*, pages 19–32, Portland, Oregon, USA, November 2002. Springer-Verlag.

18. D. R. Engler and M. Musuvathi. Static Analysis versus Software Model Checking for Bug Finding. In *Proceedings of the Fifth International Conference on Verification, Model Checking and Abstract Interpretation (VMCAI '04)*. Springer-Verlag, 2004.

19. E. N. et al. AODV-UU: Ad-hoc On-demand Distance Vector Routing. http://user.it.uu.se/~henrikl/aodv/.

20. K. Havelund, K. G. Larsen, K. Lund, and A. Skou. Formal Modelling and Analysis of an Audio/Video Protocol: An Industrial Case Study Using UPPAAL . In *Proceedings of the 18th IEEE Real-Time Systems Symposium*, pages 2–13, San Francisco, California, December 1997. BRICS RS-97-31.

21. H. E. Jensen, K. G. Larsen, and A. Skou. Scaling up UPPAAL - Automatic Verification of Real-Time Systems using Compositionality and Abstraction. In *Proceedings of the Sixth International School and Symposium on Formal Techniques and Fault Tolerant Systems (FTRTFT00)*, volume 1926 of *Lecture Notes in Computer Science*, pages 19–30, Pune, India, 2000. Springer-Verlag.

22. K. G. Larsen and P. Pettersson. Uppaal2k. *Bulletin of the European Association for Theoretical Computer Science*, 70:40–44, February 2000. http://www.uppaal.com.

23. K. G. Larsen, P. Pettersson, and W. Yi. Compositional and Symbolic Model-checking of Real-time Systems. In *RTSS '95: Proceedings of the 16th IEEE Real-Time Systems Symposium (RTSS '95)*, page 76. IEEE Computer Society, 1995. ISBN 0-8186-7337-0.

24. K. G. Larsen, P. Pettersson, and W. Yi. UPPAAL in a Nutshell. *International Journal on Software Tools for Technology Transfer*, 1(1-2):134–152, 1997.

25. J. Macker. Re; [manet] 400 nodes in NS. MANET mailing list, 26 July 2002. Message ID: 5.1.1.5.2.20030313133000.01565e78@pop.itd.nrl.navy.mil.

26. P. Neumiller. OSPF to AODV bridging. MANET mailing list, 13 March 2003. Message ID: 01a701c234a390027b470ab0110ac@meshnetworks.com.

27. J. Parrow, A. Pears, and O. Wibling. Automatized Verification of Ad Hoc Routing Protocols . In *Proceedings of the Formal Techniques for Networked and Distributed Systems (FORTE), FORTE'2004*, volume 3235 of *Lecture Notes in Computer Science*. Springer-Verlag, 2004.

28. D. P. L. Simons and M. Stoelinga. Mechanical Verification of the IEEE 1394a Root Contention Protocol using Uppaal2k . *International Journal on Software Tools for Technology Transfer*, 3(4):469–485, 2001.

29. R. Talreja. Formal Verification of AODV. Master's thesis, Department of Computer Science and Information Science, University of Pennsylvania, April 2002. Advised by Carl Gunter and Karthikeyan Bhargavan.

30. B. Wiberg. Porting AODV-UU Implementation to ns-2 and Enabling Trace-based Simulation. Master's thesis, Department of Computer Science, Uppsala University, Sweden, December 2002.

Author Index

Acciai, Lucia   47
Agha, Gul   211

Barragáns-Martínez, Belén   147
Bidinger, Philippe   31
Boreale, Michele   47
Bradley, Margarita   227
Broch Johnsen, Einar   15
Busi, Nadia   259

Chiyangwa, Sibusisiwe   306
Corin, Ricardo   131

De Nicola, Rocco   1
Di Caprio, Gaetano   131
Díaz-Redondo, Rebeca P.   147
Duchien, Laurence   163

Etalle, Sandro   131

Fernández-Vilas, Ana   147

García-Duque, Jorge   147
Gil-Solla, Alberto   147
Gnesi, Stefania   131
Gorla, Daniele   1

Hennicker, Rolf   290

Kwiatkowska, Marta   306
Kyas, Marcel   83

Lenzini, Gabriele   131
Llana, Luis   227
López-Nores, Martín   147
Ludwig, Matthias   290

Martí-Oliet, Narciso   227
Martinelli, Fabio   115
Moiso, Corrado   131
Mota, Alexandre   99

Owe, Olaf   15

Padovani, Luca   259
Pawlak, Renaud   163
Pazos-Arias, José J.   147
Pugliese, Rosario   1

Ramos, Rodrigo   99
Ramos-Cabrer, Manuel   147
Rasch, Holger   67
Reisig, Wolfgang   243
Robles, Tomás   227
Roth, Andreas   195
Roşu, Grigore   211
Rütti, Olivier   275

Salvachúa, Joaquín   227
Sampaio, Augusto   99
Schmitt, Alan   31
Seinturier, Lionel   163
Sen, Koushik   211
Simplot-Ryl, Isabelle   15
Stefani, Jean-Bernard   31

Truong, Hoang   179

Verdejo, Alberto   227

Wehrheim, Heike   67
Wojciechowski, Paweł T.   275

Lecture Notes in Computer Science

For information about Vols. 1–3424

please contact your bookseller or Springer

Vol. 3535: M. Steffen, G. Zavattaro (Eds.), Formal Methods for Open Object-Based Distributed Systems. X, 323 pages. 2005.

Vol. 3532: A. Gómez-Pérez, J. Euzenat (Eds.), The Semantic Web: Research and Applications. XV, 728 pages. 2005.

Vol. 3526: S.B. Cooper, B. Löwe, L. Torenvliet (Eds.), New Computational Paradigms. XVII, 574 pages. 2005.

Vol. 3525: A.E. Abdallah, C.B. Jones, J.W. Sanders (Eds.), Communicating Sequential Processes. XIV, 321 pages. 2005.

Vol. 3524: R. Barták, M. Milano (Eds.), Integration of AI and OR Techniques in Constraint Programming for Combinatorial Problems. XI, 320 pages. 2005.

Vol. 3523: J.S. Marques, N.P. de la Blanca, P. Pina (Eds.), Pattern Recognition and Image Analysis, Part II. XXVI, 733 pages. 2005.

Vol. 3522: J.S. Marques, N.P. de la Blanca, P. Pina (Eds.), Pattern Recognition and Image Analysis, Part I. XXVI, 703 pages. 2005.

Vol. 3520: O. Pastor, J. Falcão e Cunha (Eds.), Advanced Information Systems Engineering. XVI, 584 pages. 2005.

Vol. 3518: T.B. Ho, D. Cheung, H. Li (Eds.), Advances in Knowledge Discovery and Data Mining. XXI, 864 pages. 2005. (Subseries LNAI).

Vol. 3517: H.S. Baird, D.P. Lopresti (Eds.), Human Interactive Proofs. IX, 143 pages. 2005.

Vol. 3516: V.S. Sunderam, G.D. van Albada, P.M.A. Sloot, J.J. Dongarra (Eds.), Computational Science – ICCS 2005, Part III. LXIII, 1143 pages. 2005.

Vol. 3515: V.S. Sunderam, G.D. van Albada, P.M.A. Sloot, J.J. Dongarra (Eds.), Computational Science – ICCS 2005, Part II. LXIII, 1101 pages. 2005.

Vol. 3514: V.S. Sunderam, G.D. van Albada, P.M.A. Sloot, J.J. Dongarra (Eds.), Computational Science – ICCS 2005, Part I. LXIII, 1089 pages. 2005.

Vol. 3513: A. Montoyo, R. Mu\'noz, E. Métais (Eds.), Natural Language Processing and Information Systems. XII, 408 pages. 2005.

Vol. 3510: T. Braun, G. Carle, Y. Koucheryavy, V. Tsaoussidis (Eds.), Wired/Wireless Internet Communications. XIV, 366 pages. 2005.

Vol. 3509: M. Jünger, V. Kaibel (Eds.), Integer Programming and Combinatorial Optimization. XI, 484 pages. 2005.

Vol. 3508: P. Bresciani, P. Giorgini, B. Henderson-Sellers, G. Low, M. Winikoff (Eds.), Agent-Oriented Information Systems II. X, 227 pages. 2005. (Subseries LNAI).

Vol. 3507: F. Crestani, I. Ruthven (Eds.), Information Context: Nature, Impact, and Role. XIII, 253 pages. 2005.

Vol. 3505: V. Gorodetsky, J. Liu, V. A. Skormin (Eds.), Autonomous Intelligent Systems: Agents and Data Mining. XIII, 303 pages. 2005. (Subseries LNAI).

Vol. 3503: S.E. Nikoletseas (Ed.), Experimental and Efficient Algorithms. XV, 624 pages. 2005.

Vol. 3502: F. Khendek, R. Dssouli (Eds.), Testing of Communicating Systems. X, 381 pages. 2005.

Vol. 3501: B. Kégl, G. Lapalme (Eds.), Advances in Artificial Intelligence. XV, 458 pages. 2005. (Subseries LNAI).

Vol. 3500: S. Miyano, J. Mesirov, S. Kasif, S. Istrail, P. Pevzner, M. Waterman (Eds.), Research in Computational Molecular Biology. XVII, 632 pages. 2005. (Subseries LNBI).

Vol. 3499: A. Pelc, M. Raynal (Eds.), Structural Information and Communication Complexity. X, 323 pages. 2005.

Vol. 3498: J. Wang, X. Liao, Z. Yi (Eds.), Advances in Neural Networks – ISNN 2005, Part III. L, 1077 pages. 2005.

Vol. 3497: J. Wang, X. Liao, Z. Yi (Eds.), Advances in Neural Networks – ISNN 2005, Part II. L, 947 pages. 2005.

Vol. 3496: J. Wang, X. Liao, Z. Yi (Eds.), Advances in Neural Networks – ISNN 2005, Part II. L, 1055 pages. 2005.

Vol. 3495: P. Kantor, G. Muresan, F. Roberts, D.D. Zeng, F.-Y. Wang, H. Chen, R.C. Merkle (Eds.), Intelligence and Security Informatics. XVIII, 674 pages. 2005.

Vol. 3494: R. Cramer (Ed.), Advances in Cryptology – EUROCRYPT 2005. XIV, 576 pages. 2005.

Vol. 3493: N. Fuhr, M. Lalmas, S. Malik, Z. Szlávik (Eds.), Advances in XML Information Retrieval. XI, 438 pages. 2005.

Vol. 3492: P. Blache, E. Stabler, J. Busquets, R. Moot (Eds.), Logical Aspects of Computational Linguistics. X, 363 pages. 2005. (Subseries LNAI).

Vol. 3489: G.T. Heineman, I. Crnkovic, H.W. Schmidt, J.A. Stafford, C. Szyperski, K. Wallnau (Eds.), Component-Based Software Engineering. XI, 358 pages. 2005.

Vol. 3488: M.-S. Hacid, N.V. Murray, Z.W. Raś, S. Tsumoto (Eds.), Foundations of Intelligent Systems. XIII, 700 pages. 2005. (Subseries LNAI).

Vol. 3486: T. Helleseth, D. Sarwate, H.-Y. Song, K. Yang (Eds.), Sequences and Their Applications - SETA 2004. XII, 451 pages. 2005.

Vol. 3483: O. Gervasi, M.L. Gavrilova, V. Kumar, A. Laganà, H.P. Lee, Y. Mun, D. Taniar, C.J.K. Tan (Eds.), Computational Science and Its Applications – ICCSA 2005, Part IV. XXVII, 1362 pages. 2005.

Vol. 3482: O. Gervasi, M.L. Gavrilova, V. Kumar, A. Laganà, H.P. Lee, Y. Mun, D. Taniar, C.J.K. Tan (Eds.), Computational Science and Its Applications – ICCSA 2005, Part III. LXVI, 1340 pages. 2005.

Vol. 3481: O. Gervasi, M.L. Gavrilova, V. Kumar, A. Laganà, H.P. Lee, Y. Mun, D. Taniar, C.J.K. Tan (Eds.), Computational Science and Its Applications – ICCSA 2005, Part II. LXIV, 1316 pages. 2005.

Vol. 3480: O. Gervasi, M.L. Gavrilova, V. Kumar, A. Laganà, H.P. Lee, Y. Mun, D. Taniar, C.J.K. Tan (Eds.), Computational Science and Its Applications – ICCSA 2005, Part I. LXV, 1234 pages. 2005.

Vol. 3479: T. Strang, C. Linnhoff-Popien (Eds.), Location- and Context-Awareness. XII, 378 pages. 2005.

Vol. 3478: C. Jermann, A. Neumaier, D. Sam (Eds.), Global Optimization and Constraint Satisfaction. XIII, 193 pages. 2005.

Vol. 3477: P. Herrmann, V. Issarny, S. Shiu (Eds.), Trust Management. XII, 426 pages. 2005.

Vol. 3475: N. Guelfi (Ed.), Rapid Integration of Software Engineering Techniques. X, 145 pages. 2005.

Vol. 3468: H.W. Gellersen, R. Want, A. Schmidt (Eds.), Pervasive Computing. XIII, 347 pages. 2005.

Vol. 3467: J. Giesl (Ed.), Term Rewriting and Applications. XIII, 517 pages. 2005.

Vol. 3465: M. Bernardo, A. Bogliolo (Eds.), Formal Methods for Mobile Computing. VII, 271 pages. 2005.

Vol. 3464: S.A. Brueckner, G.D.M. Serugendo, A. Karageorgos, R. Nagpal (Eds.), Engineering Self-Organising Systems. XIII, 299 pages. 2005. (Subseries LNAI).

Vol. 3463: M. Dal Cin, M. Kaâniche, A. Pataricza (Eds.), Dependable Computing - EDCC 2005. XVI, 472 pages. 2005.

Vol. 3462: R. Boutaba, K.C. Almeroth, R. Puigjaner, S. Shen, J.P. Black (Eds.), NETWORKING 2005. XXX, 1483 pages. 2005.

Vol. 3461: P. Urzyczyn (Ed.), Typed Lambda Calculi and Applications. XI, 433 pages. 2005.

Vol. 3460: Ö. Babaoglu, M. Jelasity, A. Montresor, C. Fetzer, S. Leonardi, A. van Moorsel, M. van Steen (Eds.), Self-star Properties in Complex Information Systems. IX, 447 pages. 2005.

Vol. 3459: R. Kimmel, N.A. Sochen, J. Weickert (Eds.), Scale Space and PDE Methods in Computer Vision. XI, 634 pages. 2005.

Vol. 3458: P. Herrero, M.S. Pérez, V. Robles (Eds.), Scientific Applications of Grid Computing. X, 208 pages. 2005.

Vol. 3456: H. Rust, Operational Semantics for Timed Systems. XII, 223 pages. 2005.

Vol. 3455: H. Treharne, S. King, M. Henson, S. Schneider (Eds.), ZB 2005: Formal Specification and Development in Z and B. XV, 493 pages. 2005.

Vol. 3454: J.-M. Jacquet, G.P. Picco (Eds.), Coordination Models and Languages. X, 299 pages. 2005.

Vol. 3453: L. Zhou, B.C. Ooi, X. Meng (Eds.), Database Systems for Advanced Applications. XXVII, 929 pages. 2005.

Vol. 3452: F. Baader, A. Voronkov (Eds.), Logic for Programming, Artificial Intelligence, and Reasoning. XI, 562 pages. 2005. (Subseries LNAI).

Vol. 3450: D. Hutter, M. Ullmann (Eds.), Security in Pervasive Computing. XI, 239 pages. 2005.

Vol. 3449: F. Rothlauf, J. Branke, S. Cagnoni, D.W. Corne, R. Drechsler, Y. Jin, P. Machado, E. Marchiori, J. Romero, G.D. Smith, G. Squillero (Eds.), Applications of Evolutionary Computing. XX, 631 pages. 2005.

Vol. 3448: G.R. Raidl, J. Gottlieb (Eds.), Evolutionary Computation in Combinatorial Optimization. XI, 271 pages. 2005.

Vol. 3447: M. Keijzer, A. Tettamanzi, P. Collet, J.v. Hemert, M. Tomassini (Eds.), Genetic Programming. XIII, 382 pages. 2005.

Vol. 3444: M. Sagiv (Ed.), Programming Languages and Systems. XIII, 439 pages. 2005.

Vol. 3443: R. Bodik (Ed.), Compiler Construction. XI, 305 pages. 2005.

Vol. 3442: M. Cerioli (Ed.), Fundamental Approaches to Software Engineering. XIII, 373 pages. 2005.

Vol. 3441: V. Sassone (Ed.), Foundations of Software Science and Computational Structures. XVIII, 521 pages. 2005.

Vol. 3440: N. Halbwachs, L.D. Zuck (Eds.), Tools and Algorithms for the Construction and Analysis of Systems. XVII, 588 pages. 2005.

Vol. 3439: R.H. Deng, F. Bao, H. Pang, J. Zhou (Eds.), Information Security Practice and Experience. XII, 424 pages. 2005.

Vol. 3438: H. Christiansen, P.R. Skadhauge, J. Villadsen (Eds.), Constraint Solving and Language Processing. VIII, 205 pages. 2005. (Subseries LNAI).

Vol. 3437: T. Gschwind, C. Mascolo (Eds.), Software Engineering and Middleware. X, 245 pages. 2005.

Vol. 3436: B. Bouyssounouse, J. Sifakis (Eds.), Embedded Systems Design. XV, 492 pages. 2005.

Vol. 3434: L. Brun, M. Vento (Eds.), Graph-Based Representations in Pattern Recognition. XII, 384 pages. 2005.

Vol. 3433: S. Bhalla (Ed.), Databases in Networked Information Systems. VII, 319 pages. 2005.

Vol. 3432: M. Beigl, P. Lukowicz (Eds.), Systems Aspects in Organic and Pervasive Computing - ARCS 2005. X, 265 pages. 2005.

Vol. 3431: C. Dovrolis (Ed.), Passive and Active Network Measurement. XII, 374 pages. 2005.

Vol. 3430: S. Tsumoto, T. Yamaguchi, M. Numao, H. Motoda (Eds.), Active Mining. XII, 349 pages. 2005. (Subseries LNAI).

Vol. 3429: E. Andres, G. Damiand, P. Lienhardt (Eds.), Discrete Geometry for Computer Imagery. X, 428 pages. 2005.

Vol. 3428: Y.-J. Kwon, A. Bouju, C. Claramunt (Eds.), Web and Wireless Geographical Information Systems. XII, 255 pages. 2005.

Vol. 3427: G. Kotsis, O. Spaniol (Eds.), Wireless Systems and Mobility in Next Generation Internet. VIII, 249 pages. 2005.